LAND
OF
CROSSES

By the same author:

Opium of the People:
    the Christian religion in the Soviet
    Union

Religious Ferment in Russia:
    Protestant opposition to Soviet
    religious policy

Patriarch and Prophets:
    the persecution of the Russian
    Orthodox today

Faith on Trial in Russia

Aida of Leningrad
    (with Xenia Howard-Johnson)

All the above are available from Keston College

LAND OF CROSSES

The struggle for religious freedom in Lithuania, 1939-78

by

Michael Bourdeaux, M.A., B.D.

with a Foreword by

CARDINAL FRANZ KÖNIG

ARCHBISHOP OF VIENNA

DEVON, MCMLXXIX

© KESTON COLLEGE, 1979

ISBN 0 85172 730 1

Land of Crosses — *Keston Book No. 12*

Photoset by Aycliffe Press Ltd, Barnstaple,
in 10 on 11pt Times,
printed and bound by The Pitman Press, Bath,
and published October 1979 by
AUGUSTINE PUBLISHING COMPANY · CHULMLEIGH · DEVON
EX18 7HL, UK

DEDICATION

To my friends John, Peter and Leonard,
as a small token of thanks for support
over many years

CONTENTS

CHAPTER I

The Soviet Invasion in June 1940 – The hierarchy and church
administration – The persecution of the clergy – The abolition of
seminaries and monasteries – The closure of churches – The
attack on shrines and feast days – Mass deportation – The
secularisation of education

CHAPTER II

The Basic Aims of German and Soviet Policy   23

The German occupation – Nazi record as bad as the Soviet –
The renewal of Soviet violence, 1945-53 – Lithuania after Stalin,
1953-7 – The Khrushchev campaign against religion, 1957-64 –
1965 . . . a year of uncertainty – Mounting tension, 1966-75

Document

CHAPTER III

Kremlin or Vatican Rule?   51

The destruction of the hierarchy, 1944-53 – New bishops
ordained in 1955, then exiled– Change of Soviet policy –Doubts
about some of the bishops ordained in the 1960s.

Document

CHAPTER IV

The Central Issues   81

Stalin and the Lithuanian clergy – Heroes of the faith – The
failure of Khrushchev's virulent anti-clerical campaign – Continuing Soviet restrictions on the clergy – State interference in
parish life – The clergy unite in protest – Over 50% of the clergy
have signed petitions calling for religious liberty – The clergy in
court again – Father Juozas Zdebskis.

CHAPTER V

The Central Conflict   115

The Memorandum of the 17,000 – Retribution – The Explosion
– Sowing discord, anonymous letters – Relations with the
Vatican

CHAPTER VI

The Theological Seminary of Kaunas   143

Historical perspectives – Resistance brings improvement –
Modes of State interference – The training programme – Secret
ordination – The Riga seminary – The fate of monasteries and
convents – Underground convents.

CHAPTER VII

The Churches   166

Statistics – Closures of churches – Typical difficulties
confronting the faithful – The profanation of churches –
Church robberies condoned – Church-yards – State
interference in parish administration – Church repairs – The
fate of the new church at Klaipeda

CHAPTER VIII

The Faith of the People   190

The Attempt to Abolish the Christian Calendar – The *rites de passage* – The strong demand for the Sacraments – Personal piety – The vast crowds on pilgrimages.

Document

CHAPTER IX

The Battle for the Minds of the Young   215

Document

CHAPTER X

Christian Publications   247

Historical survey – Religious printing under Soviet rule – A new underground literature – religious books printed and confiscated–the *Chronicle of the Lithuanian Catholic Church.*

Document

CHAPTER XI

Case 345: The KGB's Pursuit of the Chronicle of the Lithuanian Catholic Church   264

Police methods – Sakharov's initiative – The trial of the five, December 1974 – Further developments – The trial of Juozas Gražys, March 1975 – The trial of Nijole Sadunaite, June 1975 – The trial of Sergei Kovalyov, December 1975 – The trial of Vladas Lapienis, Jonas Matulionis and Ona Pranckunaite, July 1977 – A new dawn.

Document

CHAPTER XII

Religion, Nationalism and Human Rights 294

Divergent views – Examples of nationalist "crimes" and their punishment – the Church and the nation – Those who fight the Church dig the grave of their nation – The Church and human rights – The growing link with Moscow-based human rights groups – Support for the Eastern-rite Catholics of Ukraine – Foreign radio, a link with abroad – The achievement of the *Chronicle of the Lithuanian Catholic Church*.

CHAPTER XIII

Conclusion 323

ILLUSTRATIONS

(between pages 214–215)

Plate

FOREWORD

Dear Father Bourdeaux,

Some time ago I received the news that you are writing a new book about Lithuania.

Lithuania has been in the news prominently because of its struggle for human rights and its attempt to deepen religious faith. As I am informed by reliable sources, the people of Lithuania deserve the recognition of Christians everywhere for their regilious faith and loyalty. I know that your book does not stress negative factors, but that you attempt to describe conditions as they are and to let facts speak for themselves. The Russian nation itself, which has a religious soul and which in its totality refuses to accept atheism, has certainly a deep sympathy for the people of Lithuania. It is an insight of our time that religion cannot be eliminated by a change in social and economic conditions; indeed, the persecution of religion achieves just the opposite. The courageous people of Lithuania must suffer for their religious loyalty, but, as a Russian told me one time, whoever wants to experience real Christianity should visit Lithuania.

I hope that you and your book will spread knowledge about Lithuania and its people to East and West and in this way give moral help for these brave men and women.

✝ FRANZ CARDINAL KÖNIG
ARCHBISHOP OF VIENNA
Vienna, 4 August 1978

PREFACE

My first acknowledgment must be to the Lithuanian people, whose outstanding qualities – loyalty to their heritage, and dedication to their beliefs, despite the most systematic persecution over decades – inspired me in the first place to tell the story of their faith. In a more technical sense, they made the book possible by their determination to speak out for themselves to the world, hoping that all those who care for religious liberty would listen and act.

One of the main aims of this book, as so often with the work of Keston College in general, is to give oppressed people the chance to present their case in their own words. Every chapter, therefore, contains an appendix, integral to the work as a whole, where essential documents are presented. Chapter IX consists of documents alone, because it seemed that they spoke so eloquently on the subject of young people and their faith that any words of mine would have been superfluous.

Keston College does, of course, have many other aims also. It is the only institution in the English-speaking world which seeks, however inadequately, to study and document all aspects of religious life (both Christian and non-Christian) in those countries which are governed by Communist or Marxist regimes.

Although of recent origin (it was founded in 1969, building on the work I had been doing during the previous decade as a private individual) Keston College has been increasingly helped by donations from private individuals and parishes. There is no central subsidy. The most significant grant received by Keston College to date was from the Ford Foundation of New York, the aim of which was to enable us to carry out a study of the relations between the Kremlin and the Vatican. The first part became this book, *Land of Crosses*. Professor Bohdan Bociurkiw, of Carleton University, Ottawa, is engaged on a parallel study of the Eastern-rite Catholics in Ukraine, while Professor Dennis Dunn's account of Kremlin-Vatican relations since Stalin is nearing completion.

At an earlier stage, before the Ford Foundation grant, I was encouraged to begin assembling the materials for this series of studies by support from Aid to the Church in Need, a Catholic relief organization now based in Königstein, West Germany, and by the Royal Institute of International Affairs (Chatham House), London.

For two years I was on the staff of the latter. The support from both not only made this book possible, but without them we might never have launched Keston College itself.

My staff at Keston College have offered magnificent help, especially Marite Sapiets, who acted as my research assistant throughout the project, tirelessly organizing and collating translations from the originals. Without the help in this of the Lithuanian community in London I would have been much more limited in the range of materials from which I could select my text. Mavis Perris and Sandy Oestreich typed the text.

The Ford Foundation grant further enabled me to call together a small panel of scholars in July 1976, when we went over the whole first draft. At this stage the advice from Professors Dennis Dunn (Southwest Texas State University, San Marcos) and Bohdan Bociurkiw and from Father Juozas Vaišnora (Rome) was invaluable. The shortcomings are my own and only with great diffidence do I, as a non-Catholic, sign my name to a book about a Catholic nation which I have come to love so dearly.

Since the election of Pope John Paul II from Poland, the importance of the Lithuanian stand will be much more readily appreciated.

Michael Bourdeaux
Keston College,
Keston, Kent BR2 6BA, England

November 1978.

ABBREVIATIONS

CCE   *Chronicle of Current Events,* the *samizdat* journal of the Soviet human rights movement, based in Moscow. Page references are to the Russian version, published by Khronika Press, New York.

CLCC   *Chronicle of the Lithuanian Catholic Church.* This, the vital source for the present book, has appeared regularly in *samizdat* since 1972. The literal translation of its title would read "Chronicle of the Catholic Church of Lithuania", but we have chosen the former title for the sake of euphony. There should be no confusion with the "Lithuanian National Catholic Church" which the Soviet authorities at one time wanted to establish. In the text, it is usually referred to as the *Lithuanian Chronicle.*

    References to the *Chronicle of the Lithuanian Catholic Church* are detailed in the notes located at the end of each chapter, and are made as follows:

    Chronicles 1-3 and 15-20 have page references to the Lithuanian version only, to be found in Radio Liberty *Arkhiv Samizdata,* Munich 1976; *Chronicles* 4-14 have references to both English (E) and Lithuanian (L) versions, the Lithuanian being published in Radio Liberty *Arkhiv Samizdata,* the English version in separate booklets by the Lithuanian Roman Catholic Priests League of America, New York 1972-6. Where translations have, with permission, been used from this source, amendments have been made in style. *Chronicles* 21 and 22 have page references to the Lithuanian version published in book form in the United States: *Lietuvos Kataliku Baznyčios Kronika,* Vol. 3, Chicago, USA, 1976. *Chronicles* 23 and 24 were available only in typescript, from Radio Liberty, when this book went to press and page references are to this version. The references to subsequent issues are to the original *samizdat* text. The dates of the *Chronicles* are: 1972, 1-5; 1973, 6-8; 1974, 9-13; 1975, 14-20; 1976, 21-25; 1977, 26-29.

CPSU   Communist Party of the Soviet Union.

GPU   Another term for the NKVD.

KGB   Committee of State Security (secret police).

LSSR   Lithuanian Soviet Socialist Republic. Sometimes it is shown as Lithuanian SSR.

NKVD   People's Commissariat of the Interior (secret police).

RCL   *Religion in Communist Lands,* the journal of Keston College, Keston, Kent. Published since 1973, each volume covers a calendar year.

RUSSIAN TERMS

Kolkhoz	collective farm.
Komsomol	Communist Youth League.
Kulaks	Russian peasant proprietors.
Pioneers	Communist organisation for school children.
Samizdat	literally "self-publication", this term is commonly used for any literature – political, religious, satirical, historical – which is not allowed past the censor, but which the author circulates privately, using any means of reproduction to hand. Though such activity is not in itself illegal, much of it is by its very nature clandestine (see Chapter X for an account of its genesis).
Soviet	policy-making and administrative council under the Communist Party.
Sovkhoz	state farm.

NOTES ON TEXTUAL LAYOUT

. . .	indicate passages omitted by the original author.
. . . .	indicate passages omitted by the present author.

All diacritical marks in Lithuanian names have been omitted except for ˇ over c and s.

Square brackets in Document texts indicate editorial explanations or summaries of omitted passages.

The titles of all Documents are editorial, except where otherwise stated. Original titles, where appropriate, are sometimes given beneath these. For consistency and readability, it has been essential to make stylistic changes to most of the sources, where already printed in English. These are too numerous to designate individually, but we have obtained permission, where it was possible.

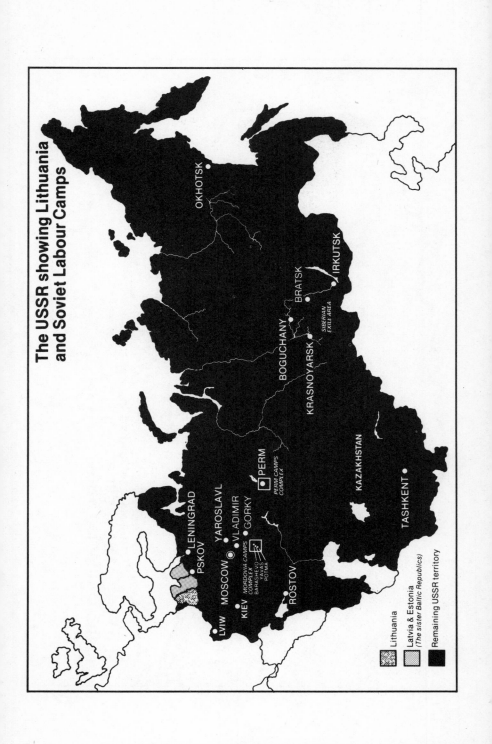

The USSR showing Lithuania and Soviet Labour Camps

OKHOTSK

IRKUTSK

BRATSK

BOGUCHANY

SIBERIAN
EXILE AREA

KRASNOYARSK

PERM
PERM CAMPS
COMPLEX

KAZAKHSTAN

TASHKENT

LENINGRAD

PSKOV

YAROSLAVL

MOSCOW

VLADIMIR

GORKY

MORDOVIA CAMPS
COMPLEX

KIEV

BARASHEVO
YAVAS
POTMA

LVIW

ROSTOV

Lithuania

Latvia & Estonia
(The sister Baltic Republics)

Remaining USSR territory

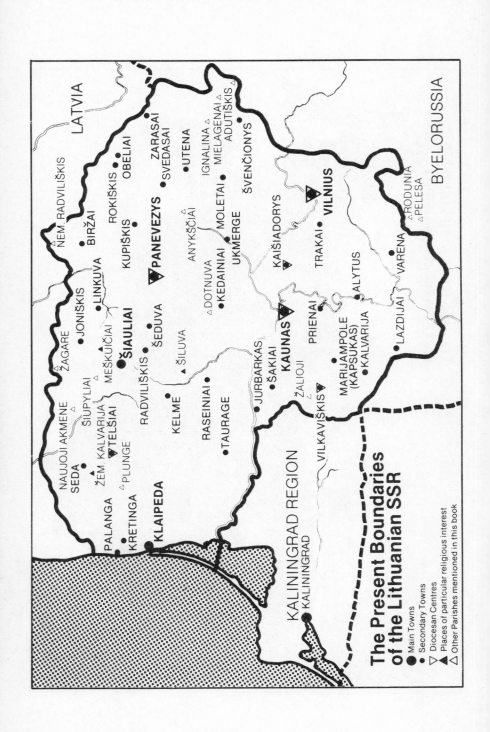

The Present Boundaries
of the Lithuanian SSR

● Main Towns
• Secondary Towns
▽ Diocesan Centres
● Places of particular religious interest
△ Other Parishes mentioned in this book

I

THE FIRST SOVIET INVASION:
A FORETASTE OF PERSECUTION

ON 14 May 1972 a young worker walked into a large city park, poured petrol over himself and set it alight, in protest at the oppression of the people in his country. Some hours later he died in hospital. His funeral was marked by demonstrations of people demanding national and religious freedom; these lasted for two days, during which hundreds of young people were arrested. Perhaps many people in the West would be sure they remembered this incident, until they look at the date. No, this was not in Czechoslovakia in 1969, nor was the young man's name Jan Palach. His name was Romas Kalanta, the city was Kaunas and his action did put his country, Lithuania, briefly into the headlines of the world's press.[1] Many people, however, must have asked, "Where is Lithuania?"

The united Kingdom of Lithuania-Poland once stretched from the Baltic to the Black Sea. In 1427 the Grand Duchy of Moscow was ruled by a son-in-law of the Lithuanian King, Vytautas the Great. In later centuries this situation was reversed: Lithuania and most of Poland came under the autocratic rule of the Russian Tsar and remained Russian imperial possessions until 1917. Yet they retained their Catholic religion, in spite of attempts to convert them to the Orthodox Church of Russia. In 1939 over 85 per cent of the Lithuanian population were Roman Catholics.[2]

The Russian Revolution gave both Lithuania and Poland the opportunity to regain their national independence. In 1943 the Anglican Bishop of Gloucester, Arthur Headlam, well acquainted with Lithuania, recalled the enthusiasm shown by its people in building a new national state:

> The Baltic States are all alike in having suffered centuries of foreign domination. For many hundred years they lost their freedom. Yet through all those dark days, they preserved their nationality, their languages and their traditions. Then after the Great War there came to them the greatest of all gifts – national freedom. They seized on the gift with eagerness, with enthusiasm and with wisdom, and began to build up their national life . . . . In 1938 . . . . I could see everywhere signs of a reconstituted society, of a careful agriculture . . . . I met them in the services of their church and their universities, and learnt something of their invigorated intellectual life.[3]

1

Not even the bishop, perhaps understandably for that time, mentioned that the remarkable recovery of the Baltic States in the 1920's had been shattered, not by the Germans, but by the Soviet Union, which was then Britain's ally. On 15 June 1940 a massive invasion of 300,000 Soviet troops engulfed Lithuania, bringing to an end two decades of precarious independence, during which all Lithuanians had come to hope that the accident of geography, sandwiching their small nation between the might of the Soviet Union and of Germany, would not lead to its erasure from the map of Europe.[4] The Molotov-Ribbentrop Pact, awarding the Baltic States and part of Poland to the Soviet Union in return for German possession of the rest of Poland and a free hand in Western Europe, crushed that hope.

The diplomatic exchanges of the summer of 1940 made it clear that the Kremlin did not acknowledge that small nations on the Soviet doorstep had any right to independent existence. Lithuania offered no armed resistance to the invasion, but the reward for this was merely that it became easier for the Communist authorities to claim a month later that 95.1 per cent of the population had gone to the polls and cast their votes almost unanimously for the Soviet list of candidates. As a London newspaper, quoting a Soviet news-agency, published the results twenty-four hours before the polls were closed, the Soviet claims are somewhat suspect.[5] The story behind this is revealing.

The so-called People's Parliament of 1940-1 was elected on a single list of candidates, which consisted of thirty Communist Party members and forty-one non-party members of the Union of Lithuanian Working People. These non-party candidates actually belonged to the Komsomol (Communist Youth League) or to trade unions, co-operative and cultural societies affiliated to the Communist Party. All other political parties or organizations had been banned, despite the fact that in 1935 there had been only 1790 members of the Communist Party of Lithuania (0.07 per cent of the population).[6] An identical list was nominated in every electoral district in Lithuania by the "organizations of the working people," who had the sole right to nominate candidates. (These organizations were, of course, the same as those represented in the Union of Lithuanian Working People.) Voting was compulsory; the daily newspaper, *Vilniaus Balsas,* emphasized the duty of all citizens to vote:

> People who do not vote, who do not take part in elections, are not concerned with the future of the people. They are the enemies of the people. There is no longer any place for such persons in working Lithuania.[7]

Voting took place in the presence of a Russian soldier who could observe whether the individual approved the electoral list or not; officials stamped citizens' identity cards after they had voted. In spite of such pressure, the turn-out on 14 July was so low that the authorities extended the voting time by twenty-four hours to enable the police to organize transport to the polls and further warn the population of its duty to vote.[8]

Immediately, and in their only session, those who had been "elected" voted to apply for the incorporation of Lithuania into the Soviet Union, although this had never been mentioned as part of the electoral platform of the Union of Lithuanian Working People. The Supreme Soviet granted the request on 3 August 1940.

The fact that Lithuania "joined" the Soviet Union twenty-three years after the Revolution meant that, if was going to be Sovietized, the process had to be an accelerated one. V. G. Dekanozov, the official trusted with the Sovietization of the country, told Bishop Vincentas Brizgys that what the Soviet authorities had achieved in Russia in twenty years they would carry out in two years in Lithuania.[9] But, as if to remove any possible remaining ambiguity, in Lithuania the Soviet authorities had to initiate the process of Sovietization twice. The first occupation lasted barely a year (June 1940 to June 1941). The latter date was the month of the Nazi invasion of the Soviet Union, when the Lithuanians immediately and spontaneously revolted against their Soviet overlords and established a Provisional Goverment for six weeks before it was suppressed by the Nazis.[10] Then, after their "liberation" of Lithuania in 1944, the Soviet authorities had to begin the process all over again.

Apart from the constitutional changes incorporating Lithuania into the Soviet Union and establishing the Communist Party as the only one legally permitted, all aspects of Lithuanian society had to be adapted to the Soviet model – education, industry, the press were all now subordinated to the "leading role of the party." The areas of greatest conflict in this programme of Sovietization were, as they had been in Russia in the 1920s, those of agriculture and religion. Agricultural reforms carried out in Lithuania in 1922 had redistributed land formerly belonging to Polish and Russian nobility to 43,000 farm workers. Individual peasant ownership of land did not quite fit in with the Soviet view of their exploitation by capitalists and landlords: to the Soviet authorities, Lithuania was a land of *kulaks*. These smallholders were the core of Lithuanian opposition to the collectivization of the land, and they were among the first to suffer deportation to remote areas of the Soviet Union.

Soviet policy towards religion has always been dictated by Marxist-Leninist ideology which maintains that religion is an unscientific and untrue view of the world, deliberately used by the exploiting classes to keep the workers in a state of subjection and ignorance. As an ideological error, it cannot be tolerated; as a weapon of the class enemy, it must be actively fought and its influence among the workers must be eradicated.

Although during the first Soviet occupation the persecution of the Church could not be carried through to its logical conclusion and had to be resumed in 1944-5, these twelve months give us a guide to Stalin's policy towards religion in the Soviet Union in the 1940's – and with but a few exceptions it still applies to Soviet policies over all the vast territories of the USSR today.

A formal constitutional principle of Soviet religious policy has always been the so-called "separation of Church and State", – ever since Lenin passed his first decree to this effect in January 1918, just after the Revolution.[11] The Lithuanian experience demonstrates clearly that "separation" in the somewhat inexact Soviet terminological usage means abolition of the power of the Church, so that it can be controlled by the State. If religion is to be tolerated for an interim period, then at least the State must have the monopoly of it – this would be a summary of the Soviet attitude. The authority of the Lithuanian Church was transmitted from Rome, so the Soviet regime decided that an essential prerequisite to the reduction of that authority would be to sever diplomatic links with the Vatican. Accordingly, as early as 25 June 1940, even before the elections for an assembly and a mere ten days after the invasion, the decree on the separation of Church and State was promulgated; five days later the Soviets ordered the expulsion from the country of Luigi Centoz, the Papal Nuncio.[12] On 3 July the new government abrogated the existing agreement with Rome in the following statement:

> The Lithuanian Government has decided to break the Concordat of 17 September 1927. The Lithuanian Government considers itself no longer bound by its provisions.[13]

The central church administration immediately received a crippling financial blow, because not only were all state subsidies cut off, as might have been expected, from the curia, the seminaries and from pensions, but the Soviet regime also confiscated all church property, leaving each parish with a mere three hectares (seven and a half acres), which was to include the land occupied by the church buildings and the cemetery, while private land-owners were permitted to retain thirty hectares (seventy-five acres) each.[14] The regime went even further in infringing the liberty of the individual when it confiscated the savings of the clergy, as well as the bank accounts of parishes and all religious organizations.[15]

Although some form of central administration was allowed to continue (as it had not been with the Russian Orthodox Church in the 1920s and 30s), the State attempted not only to inconvenience the Church, but to expose it to ridicule – as when it moved the administration of the Diocese of Vilkaviškis to the premises of a mental hospital. The Bishop of Panevežys found himself reduced to living in one room.[16]

Much more than the Orthodox Church, the Catholic Church has always emphasized a wealth of activities, charitable, educational, recreational, outside the confines of worship. Soviet law had always proclaimed that the whole of religious practice was to be no more than what occurred in the context of worship within the four walls of a registered church building.[17] Therefore the annihilation of all Catholic societies and organizations, with the confiscation of all their assets, was a body-blow to the many-faceted influence of the Church.[18]

The aspect of Soviet religious policy which proves most clearly that that policy is synonymous with persecution lies in what is beyond law: in secret instructions, in attempts to subvert the Church from within. In the 1960s and 70s this has finally come out into the open and been documented,[19] but the first Lithuanian experience had already demonstrated it thirty years earlier. The Soviet Deputy Commissar of the NKVD (Secret Police), Gladkov, instructed all district chiefs of the NKVD on 2 October 1940 that they must execute a catena of measures designed to subvert the power of the Church. They must keep the closest watch on all bishops and clergy. There must be an enrolment campaign to enlist priests and suitable laymen as spies, so that dossiers could be built up detailing all the continuing activities and contacts of the faithful. The agents must even recruit school-children to establish these continuing contacts from the other side. Gladkov, not the first Soviet official to hinder his own task by attempting to reduce religion to an economic formula, estimated that the recent measures which ensured the poverty of the clergy would also hasten their submission. He informed his underlings that they had no longer than eight days to put this programme into operation (Document 1).

Three months later, on 21 January 1941, Alexander Guzevičius, Commissar for Internal Affairs, ordered the secret police to submit to him a list of clergy of all denominations, together with an estimate of their influence on the populace and on the political life of the community (Document 2). Again, a mere week was deemed the maximum time limit for the task, so pressing was it. It is now believed that this was only a preliminary step to the planned total elimination of the clergy, but public reaction was such that this was to be delayed until the mass deportations were under way.[20] The execution of the plan was interrupted by the Nazi invasion of the Soviet Union, but the Soviets would return to it, with intensified zeal, upon their reoccupation of the country.

There were many other restrictions, apart from the all-embracing plans for the future outlined above, which pared away the varied work of the clergy.

All specialized activities became illegal. This spelled the end for the religious orders, with their traditions of different types of service within the Church, as Guzevičius proclaimed in his decree of 28 November 1940.[21] This was also the end of all the chaplaincy work in the army, prisons, schools, hospitals and old people's homes, which had been such an active feature of Lithuanian church life between the wars. The new regulations curtailed pastoral work of this type even by ordinary parish priests. The simple visiting of the sick, even taking the Sacrament of Extreme Unction to the dying, became a bureaucratic problem for the clergy. The sick themselves had to initiate the visit by submitting a request to the authorities in writing[22] – which was sometimes possible, and sometimes, obviously, not. The more the person needed the ministration, the less likely his ability to complete the formalities. But, given the system, there was no guarantee that even the most meticulous compliance with these requirements would lead to the request being correctly processed by the bureaucracy. The possibilities for delay or inaction were boundless.

Even worse than these physical limitations on the activity of the clergy was the imposition of the obligation to be loyal to the Soviet State. Loyalty to independent Lithuania was one thing, but loyalty to a State which proclaimed, practised and imposed atheism was something quite different, setting a problem which has been with the Protestant and Orthodox Churches in the USSR for more than half a century without their finding a truly satisfactory solution. The subject of loyalty was one of the main themes in the conversation between Bishop Brizgys and the state official, to which we referred above,* and the bishop was left in no doubt but that the demand was for active, not passive loyalty.[23]

This demand was reinforced by the declaration of loyalty which priests were compelled to sign.[24] Many refused, but a full trial of strength did not ensue, as the Nazi invasion of the Soviet Union occurred before events could evolve to this point.

However, the developments thus far left no doubts whatsoever that the Soviets intended to carry out their threats by physical force if necessary. Already they had attempted to soften and prepare public opinion by printing harangues against the clergy in the press.[25]

Then the persecution began in earnest. Dispossessed monks and nuns found themselves thrown on the streets, their homes and livelihoods gone.[26] The clergy, already impoverished, had to pay triple the rent of the laity after the seizure of their presbyteries.[27] The Soviets marked their very last days in Lithuania before withdrawing by arresting, deporting, torturing and – in the last hours – murdering priests whom they could locate. Forty-four of the 1,450 in the country suffered severely: sixteen were murdered, twelve were deported, never to be heard of again, and sixteen were imprisoned but liberated after the Soviet withdrawal in 1941. Thirty-two priests and nineteen theology students managed to escape westwards.

Even more harmful in effect than the physical persecution was the attempt, repeated so often before and since in the Soviet Union, to undermine the clergy morally, either by infiltrating traitors among them or by pressurizing and blackmailing ordained men in good standing. Such a campaign, to stand any chance of success, clearly needs

*Cf. page 3.

time to prepare and a developed system of observing and informing. It is surprising (as we see in Document 2) that the Soviet authorities not only tried it in the short time available to them, but in their hurried departure even left documentary evidence behind of their intentions, betokening the immense self-confidence which must have been generated by success already achieved in such tactics over the previous twenty-three years in the Soviet Union.

We have already mentioned the confiscation of monastic and seminary land, but the Soviets did not confine themselves merely to economic persecution of the most elevated aspect of the educational and communal activities of the Church. The seventy-three monasteries and eighty-five convents were totally abolished.[28] The same fate befell the faculty of philosophy, social science and Catholic theology at Kaunas University, not to mention the Protestant theological faculty in the same university.[29]

The Church lost the buildings of its four theological seminaries (at Vilnius, Kaunas, Vilkaviškis and Telšiai) at the same time, but managed to win the concession of keeping just one going, though in new premises – that at Kaunas.[30] There was no doubt, however, that the State intended this as a temporary concession only. Dekanozov claimed to Bishop Brizgys that a seminary was not really needed, in spite of the fact that in 1939 there were 417 seminary students, and that it was deceitful of the Church to entice young men into the seminaries when there would be no future for them in the Church.[31]

While the Soviet regime clearly intended to close down most, if not all, the churches in Lithuania in the long term (the process was already well advanced in the Soviet Union), it did not dare to do this all at once, for fear of exacerbating the feelings of believers to such an extent that there would be a popular revolt.[32]

The first to suffer, probably as a trial to test public reaction, were institutional chapels in prisons and hospitals and garrison churches. These uniformly suffered confiscation and they were quickly reabsorbed into the general purposes of the rest of the building, often as store rooms. The authorities organized auctions for the sale of their contents.[33]

The ubiquitous wayside crosses and shrines, such a feature of Christian Lithuania, were an affront to the Soviet regime which it could not support, so they were desecrated and demolished.[34] Crosses had been visible everywhere – on the walls of hospitals and schools and in private gardens. The Soviets made a systematic effort to remove them, replacing them by red stars and other symbols and slogans of Soviet power.[35]

The continuation of religious holidays was also intolerable to the new regime, though its leaders tried to mask the *diktat* with which they abolished them by the sham of calling workers' meetings and forcing a vote on the issue. Silence was taken to indicate approval.[36]

However, even this policy was not carried out consistently, and before the end of 1940 the Soviets promulgated decrees which must have seemed to the faithful as if they were proclaiming their power over the spirits themselves, for they introduced the strictest controls over All Saints Day and All Souls Day, abolishing them as public holidays, and they followed this immediately by doing the same for Christmas itself (Document 3). Thus Lithuania came forcibly into line with the Soviet Union, where these days had long since lost their status as public holidays. As in the Soviet Union, the intention was to propagate new atheist holidays for the new Soviet man,[37] but this would have demanded lengthy indoctrination and the occupiers had withdrawn before they could do much in this direction. In conjunction with this, all street processions, such as those which enlivened the Feast of Corpus Christi, were banned.[38]

Many Sundays, too, became working days. Not even Communist workers could have been very pleased when one of their own new holidays merely replaced a Sunday, which became a working day in the week when the new holiday fell.[39]

There were punishments in store for those who failed to report for work on these secularized holy days, but intimidation of ordinary believers went much further than this. For example, NKVD agents photographed the faithful who, completely within their rights, attended church at times other than during working hours, leading innocent people to think they were preparing secret dossiers for use in some future campaign.[40] Intimidation of priests led to some becoming agents of the NKVD, but the mass of believers and clergy stood firm in their loyalty to the Church (Document 4).

The atheist authorities did not launch any major campaign against the practice of baptism and the rituals of church marriage and funerals at that time, but they punished those who broke the new laws.

It became increasingly obvious that the Soviet regime was planning something much more devastating than the imposition of new restrictions and penalties for resisting genocide. The continued existence of the Lithuanian nation itself was at stake. To recount the whole story of this plan would take us far beyond the confines of our present work,[41] but we must mention the relevance of all this to the Church. There was to be a mass deportation of huge sections of the population out of Lithuania altogether; they would be transported to whatever fate awaited them in Siberia. The first aim, obviously, was to decapitate the nation, to remove the whole flower of two generations – not only those who had reached positions of leadership in the varied facets of national life, but also those who showed potential for replacing them – so that only an intimidated, leaderless mass would be left, who could be moulded and indoctrinated by new Soviet taskmasters into the docile conformity necessary to qualify for the family of nations designated by the phrase "Union of Soviet Socialist Republics".

Before the process reached its culmination, it was interrupted by the Nazi invasion. However, enough had already happened to demonstrate that the Soviet threats were not idle. Arrests began immediately after the Soviet invasion and 2,000 leaders lost their freedom on the night of 11 July 1940 alone. But the pace of the campaign was too slow to suit its Moscow masterminds. On 28 November Guzevičius issued an order for the registration of fourteen categories of people supposed to be hostile to the new regime, including not only political parties, but the clergy of all denominations, members of some religious societies, philatelists and students of Esperanto.[42] This was in preparation for their liquidation.

The swoop came during 13-15 June 1941, when 34,260 people were arrested, packed into cattle trucks and dispatched on a fearful journey eastwards. It was a prelude to a bigger planned deportation, which was interrupted by the war but recommenced after 1944. On this first occasion people were deported according to categories, together with their families. There were many sick, elderly people and children among the victims. Men were often separated from their families (Document 5); those who lost their provisions by such separation often died of starvation before reaching their destination, which could have been Siberia, Kazakhstan or Central Asia. Some died of suffocation even before leaving the confines of Lithuania.

One of the intentions of this action was obviously to intimidate the religious life of the faithful into complete inactivity, not merely to remove the most distinguished leaders of the Church. As stated above, there were only twelve members of the clergy among this first huge group of deportees, but many more were designated to follow. Those who did reach their destinations in Central Asia or Siberia exhibited a will to survive and much is now known about them,[43] though there is no space to tell their story here.

Even these terrors were not sufficient, according to official Soviet thinking, to guarantee the future atheism of Lithuania. The regime devoted much attention to planning education so as to ensure that religion should be eradicated from the minds of the people.

The Soviet Constitution proclaimed the "separation of the school from the Church". In practice, this meant a total ban on all forms of religious education for any below the age of eighteen, and its restriction above that age to a handful of people who managed to enter the theological seminary.

The massive involvement of the Catholic Church in Lithuanian education at all levels was therefore doomed, from university teaching right down to the kindergarten. The State took over every church school in the land. Assembly prayers and religious instruction were banned in state schools (Document 6). Sanctions were imposed against teachers who attempted to compensate for this enactment by teaching religion under other guises or who even legally expressed their own religious adherence to the extent of going to church.[44] For example, a headmaster, Povilonis, was dismissed from a Vilnius secondary school for refusing to forbid prayers before and after lessons.[45]

Even in the general atmosphere of intimidation, parents petitioned for the reinstatement of some form of religious education. This was ignored by the Government, but the clergy responded by organizing informal classes as and when they could – in churches, in their own homes or in the homes of the children's parents.[46]

On 2 April 1941 the regime began circulating a declaration among the clergy for their signature, in which they were forced to promise that they would dissociate themselves totally from any form of teaching and even from contact with the young which would involve the discussion of religious questions (Document 7). Many refused and they would have undoubtedly suffered the consequences of their resistance if Soviet plans had not been interrupted by the Nazi invasion.[47]

The other main vehicle of education was the printed word. Religious publishing houses were naturally in the direct line of fire and when the regime took them over and nationalized their assets this meant the end of all religious newspapers, journals and books.[48] The State even seized existing stocks of books and the efforts of the hierarchy to save a small proportion of them came to nothing (Document 8). Whole editions were pulped.

Even this was not enough. Libraries, schools, monasteries and archives had to surrender their sacred books. They were burned in pyres.[49] Not only were secular newspapers compelled to discontinue any discussion of religious themes, but they also had to replace them with crude anti-religious articles of the type which the Soviet anti-God movement, so prominent in the 1930s, had long been foisting on an unwilling Russian public.[50] Added to this was the promotion of anti-religious lectures, often held to coincide with church services.[51]

The situation in Lithuania in 1940-41 presents us with a microcosm of Soviet policy towards religion. The Soviet persecution of the Catholic Church in Lithuania, which corresponds to its persecution of the Church in the USSR as a whole, continues to the present day, as described in the outline above. This anti-religious policy may be analyzed under the following headings, which also represent several chapters of this book:

a) The subversion of the hierarchy and the abolition of normal church administration (Chapter III);
b) The restriction of the multifarious activities of the clergy to merely officiating at worship (Chapter IV);
c) The closure of monasteries and seminaries (Chapter VI);

d) The closures of churches (Chapter VII);

e) The destruction of the roots of the popular faith and of the religious element in family life (Chapter VIII);

f) The abolition of religious education in schools and the demand that young people should become atheists (Chapter IX);

g) The virtual prohibition of religious literature and its replacement by anti-religious literature (Chapter X).

At the end of the sixth decade of Soviet power there is still not a church or denomination in the country which does not suffer from the above forms of persecution, and the sum total of Soviet concessions, while not wholly insignificant in one or two defined areas, is nevertheless minimal when compared with the persisting massive needs of believers everywhere. For it to apply to any individual church, the above list has only to be adapted to the particular traditions of the church in question.

The chapters that follow tell how the Roman Catholic Church of Lithuania, though three times crushed by two of this century's superpowers within a span of five years and to this day totally barred from any independent action by Soviet might, nevertheless has within the last decade led a nation to rediscover its unity, its sense of purpose and its idealism.

DOCUMENTS

1. SECRET POLICE INSTRUCTIONS

Strictly confidential

To all chairmen of the local branches of the NKVD*
[secret police]

From material gathered by the NKVD it is evident that the Lithuanian priests and the leaders of the former Catholic parties and organizations and their active members have initiated their hostile activities by proceeding along three principal lines:

1. By propagating nationalist and chauvinistic ideas, both covertly and often even openly during services for believers in churches and by endeavouring to influence them against the Soviet Government.

*NKGB in the original text.

2. By establishing relations with schoolchildren and students at all levels. According to available information, upon the instruction of Bishop Brizgys special priests were appointed in almost every parish to engage in illegal activity among young people, by educating them in a nationalist and chauvinistic spirit and by provoking in them a hatred against the Bolshevik order. The clergy have extended this campaign all over Lithuania, especially on Sundays in the churches, during special services arranged for young people, as well as in their homes where young people gather in groups of a dozen or so. They have also influenced parents to implant Catholic ideas in their children.

3. They carry on anti-Communist work among the population through illegal Catholic religious orders [monasteries] and clerical groups (such as the Apostolic Community of Men, the Apostolate of Prayer Society, the Association of the Third Order of St. Francis) which are political instruments in the hands of the clergy.

In order to organize the fight against the hostile activities of the clergy I hereby order you to:

1. Place all clergy in your district under formal control.
2. Find out about all the leading personalities of the Catholic organizations and communities and place them under formal control.
3. Obtain information immediately through agents on all the members of the deanery and the church offices of your area.
4. Enlist as soon as possible the services of clergy and employees in the churches (organists, sacristans) who have close connections with the leading personalities of the Catholic parties, groups and communities as a means of obtaining information concerning the activity of above-mentioned parties. From among these simultaneously enlist agents and informers and order them to split the Catholic organizations from the inside.
5. Find out which clergy as well as which leaders of communities within your area are in close touch with the inhabitants, ascertain the character of these relations and submit this information.
6. Place all monks under control in areas where there are monasteries. Put their abbots under formal control. Recruit a network of agents and informers among the monks.
7. Ascertain where the priests meet schoolchildren in order to carry out their hostile activities. Students in the upper forms must be recruited to prepare for and execute the inside work of dividing the Church.
8. Find out which priests and active members of the communities are now organizing the collection of signatures among the people for the submission of an appeal to the Government to obtain permission for religious instruction in schools, and place them under control.
9. Avoid mistakes in recruiting agents. Candidates must be carefully prepared and information about them shoud be obtained by other agents. Remember that some priests have no material provision and therefore waver in their idealistic opinions.

10. Document all cases of anti-Soviet, anti-revolutionary tendencies among the clergy which you have discovered and forward the material to the NKVD of Lithuania.

11. Submit by 10 October 1940 a detailed report on the hostile activities of the clergy within your area.

12. Deliver a memorandum by 15 October 1940 to the Second State Security Department of the NKVD on the actions taken against the clergy, at the same time indicating the material to hand, how it was obtained and the steps you intend to take in the future.

(signed) Gladkov,
Major of State Security,
Acting People's Commissar for the
2 October 1940. Internal Affairs of the LSSR.[52]

2. SECRET POLICE PLANS DEVELOP AGAINST PRACTISING CHRISTIANS

Strictly confidential

The State Security Division of the People's Commissariat for Internal Affairs in the USSR has drawn up a plan of operations concerning practising Christians in the new Soviet republics.

Acting thereunder, I order you to take the following action:

1. Draw up a list of all Roman Catholic, Orthodox and Protestant sectarian societies and organizations which were legally or illegally active within your respective area under the old regime.

2. Describe the influence of each of these organizations upon the masses and on public political life (give the approximate number of practising Christians in the organizations and their position in the public or political life of the country).

3. Prepare a list of all churches and chapels in your area.

4. Submit a list of all pastors, parish priests and leaders of sects in your area, indicating the influence of individual religious authorities upon the masses and on the public and political life of the country.

5. Specify in considerable detail any interior dissensions within the religious organizations, why these have occurred and between which clergy relations are strained.

6. Suggest how these dissensions could be used for recruiting agents and for undermining these organizations within your area.

7. Send me a detailed report on the activities of agencies formed within your area to investigate Roman Catholic and Orthodox clergy and Protestant sectarians; also submit your plans for further operations.

8. Describe and characterize any agents you may be able to recruit among the clergy and the sectarians.

9. Send me an exhaustive report on all these questions by 30 January.

Use the services of the clergy within the network of agent-informers to obtain this information.

(signed) Guzevičius,
Major of State Security,
People's Commissar for the
Internal Affairs of the LSSR.[53]

Kaunas,
21 January 1941.

3.   STRICT CONTROLS OVER ALL SAINTS AND CHRISTMAS DAY

Strictly confidential

The Commissariat for Internal Affairs of the LSSR, 27 October 1940.

To the leaders of the local branches of the NKVD:

All faithful Catholics celebrate the so-called All Saints' Day on Friday, 1 November and All Souls' Day on 2 November.

They will hold special services during the holy days in all the churches and processions with candles to the cemeteries will take place on the night of 1 November.

No doubt the clergy will increase their anti-revolutionary activity on this occasion and will take advantage of the feast to agitate, incite outrages and spread anti-revolutionary appeals.

The NKVD has moreover learned that nationalist students have planned to hold anti-Soviet demonstrations in cemeteries at the graves of soldiers on All Souls' Day.

In order to prevent possible anti-revolutionary outrages, the spreading of anti-Soviet appeals and so on, I command you to:

1. Send operative personnel to the meeting places of believers and to cemeteries on holy days; also assign plain-clothes men for this duty.
2. Inform the agents to this effect: order them to advise the NKVD immediately of all anti-Soviet outrages observed, such as the spreading of anti-revolutionary appeals and the delivering of anti-Soviet speeches.
3. Arrest those who are prominent for their anti-Soviet activity, but at the same time avoid arousing popular indignation.

(signed) B. Baranauskas
Acting People's Commissar for the
Internal Affairs of the LSSR.

Strictly confidential

To the Commander of the Division of the City of Vilnius; The Chief of the NKVD for the LSSR; To the leaders of the local branches and subdivisions of the NKVD of the LSSR.

On 25 and 26 December Catholics celebrate so-called Christmas. On these days (beginning with the evening of 24 December) there will be services in the churches with sermons. Believers consider both days as very holy days and thus do not work on them. This year the nationalist anti-revolutionary elements, and especially the clergy, will endeavour to exploit Christmas for their hostile activity, mainly by the following means:

a) By attempting to prevent work in the factories and teaching in the schools.

b) By agitating from the pulpit against participation in the elections – this will be more or less camouflaged in the form of religious sermons. The clergy will exert influence upon believers, individually or in groups, in churches, vestries and assembly halls.

c) By circulating anti-revolutionary literature – some of which will be religious.

d) By attempting to lead the believers out on the streets to demonstrate or to provoke excesses.

In order to prevent such happenings in advance you must:

1. Study again the directives of Order No. 1919 of 27 November 1940; adhere to them most carefully.

2. Instruct the whole network of agents and informers to bring the preparations of the anti-Soviet clergy and the sects closely connected with them (*Ateitininkai* [a Catholic youth movement] and others) before the public; summon the agents between 20-29 December, according to the enlarged plan of operations.

3. Together with the police organizations, guarantee the maintenance of public order during the festival days, but avoid police concentration in front of the churches.

4. Take measures to guarantee normal work in factories and offices and normal teaching in schools.

5. Arrange for controls and patrols in the towns during the nights 23-25 December. In consultation with the secretary of the Executive Committee, summon party members and the Komsomol for active service for this purpose.

6. Write down and report to me immediately any instances of anti-Soviet outrages.

(signed) Guzevičius,
People's Commissar for
Internal Affairs of the LSSR.[54]

12 December 1940.

4. BISHOP BRIZGYS REPORTS TO THE VATICAN

Kaunas, October 1940.

I feel it to be my duty to inform the Holy See . . . . of the latest events in the ecclesiastical life of Lithuania.
. . . .

For their part, the clergy do not give vent to their feelings through action. We have to be very cautious not to say or do anything incompatible with loyalty or with prudence. Up to now the clergy have not taken any imprudent steps. A missionary, Father Bružikas, S.J., who continued his missions in various parishes, has been arrested. So far about 10,000 people have signed an appeal to liberate him.

Although there are some individuals among the clergy who have no connection with the curia and do not celebrate Holy Mass, there have been no public acts of apostasy, and up to the present no one has wished to take advantage of civil marriage. A few lukewarm ones have become warmer.

. . . . A few more priests have been gaoled, so that there are about twenty priests in prison altogether. Four or five of them were taken without any pretext, the others on trumped-up charges for a few words or deeds of minimal significance. The attempted arrests of a Jesuit and a parish priest did not succeed because the believers prevented them . . . .   I know that four of five priests have signed a promise to the GPU [NKVD – the secret police] to inform this agency, within the limits of "conscience", about things which might interest the Government. They have not hidden the step that they have taken from their superiors, which provides some mitigation. For a business like this the GPU always uses priests who life is slack and who are poorly esteemed by the faithful. After repeated threats some yield.

The behaviour of the Catholic laity is consoling: religious practices, church attendance and participation in catechism hours are becoming more numerous all the time. Outstanding among the whole population for courage in professing their faith are the universities, the young people of the grammar schools and the Lithuanian soldiers. We can also be proud, for the most part, of the teachers. This renaissance of a sort is also beginning among the workers, where Communism has lost all sympathy.

A few thousand unfortunates among teachers, office workers, soldiers, students, workers and grammar school pupils are already among those exiled to Russia. Nothing more is known of them, nor of those who have been arrested in general. This number of unfortunates grows every night. A few good people have been imprisoned for interceding with the government for the release of the missionary, P. Bružikas, S.J.

The Russian political agents are fanatically opposed to religion and attempt to spread atheist propaganda among the Lithianians, too, but without notable results so far. The Russian soldiers are not hostile to religion; on the contrary, in conversations without witnesses they show concern and sympathy for religion every time. It seems that, when freedom comes, there is hope, through religious propaganda, that missionaries will not find unfeeling hearts in Russia. Our desire must be to play a part in that sacred undertaking of the future. This idea is being propagated among our clergy, who are preparing it as far as possible. However, my desire would be to send selected young priests to the Russicum* in Rome. For my own part, I ask Your Excellency to transmit my desire to the Holy See or to the Russicum to obtain permission from the Italian Government for a certain number of young priests to go to Rome to study, and we, after selecting the best, will send them to prepare themselves for missionary work among the Russians.

A month ago the Archbishop of Kaunas, his auxiliary bishop and the curia were forced to abandon the archbishop's palace. Until recently the palace remained empty, but now Russian soldiers are occupying it.

In these days the Eastern-rite Catholic Russian priest X has had to leave Kaunas for Rome. He was also imprisoned just over a month ago. Why the Russians are sending him to Rome is a mystery. According to general opinion, it would be very prudent to be very cautious and careful with him. By his behaviour here in Kaunas he left quite a bad reputation and it may be averred that he is not suitable for any kind of pastoral work. It is not improbable that he will inform the Embassy of the USSR in Rome what is going on among the Catholics in Rome, especially at the Russicum.[55]

5.   THE FIRST DEPORTATION

Thoughts on Victory Day

[original title]

Thirty years have gone by since the fires of war went out. We must rejoice over that, but Lithuanians also have much to mourn. The land of the Nemunas River, like a dried pea on the highway, has been thrown to and fro between East and West. Those from the West shouted about the "thousand-year Reich" which has now passed into infamy for ever. The brown "liberators" planned to resettle the "unworthy Lithuanians" near the Urals, while the red "liberators" planned to go further still – by scattering the Lithuanians throughout

*The College in Rome originally founded with the aim of preparing missionaries for Russia. In recent years it has changed its focus more to one of establishing ecumenical relations with the Russian Orthodox Church.

all Siberia. In our nation it is hard to find a family without a close relative who "voluntarily" went on a journey to take a look at the polar bears . . .

In 1941 exiled families were torn apart – the men were separated from the others. The slave-exploiters of the twentieth century picked out from among the exiles those capable of work or employment, giving them 400 grammes of bread a day, while the rest received 200 grammes. Children die not only in Africa, as victims of drought, but also in the land of Communist humanism, where certain categories of human beings have been turned into slaves. Lithuanian exiles often heard the words, "You've been brought here to die!" This was no empty phrase – children born of Lithuanian mothers left their bones scattered from the Urals to Magadan, from icy Arkhangelsk, Vorkuta and Norilsk to the scorched lands of Kazakhstan.

There was a plan to create a "Lithuania without Lithuanians", while the people were supposed to become like other small nations, such as the Kalmyks and Tartars, who have been scattered and dissolved in the melting-pot of "brotherly nations". It is fortunate that this "historical process" was halted by Stalin's death, which brought some relaxation of pressure. The crude method of physical genocide was renounced, giving way to spiritual genocide.

. . . . Even by official statistics, in spite of the influx of colonizers, 40,000 less people live in Lithuania now than in 1897, according to the census of that year.[56]

6. THE FIRST ATHEIST ATTACK AGAINST THE SCHOOL

When Lithuania was occupied in 1940, the Soviet Government gave its first priority to the schools, in an effort to make them atheist.

Immediately they banned prayers before and after lessons and removed crucifixes from the class-rooms. In one secondary school at Panevežys the headmaster gave orders that, without letting the pupils know, crucifixes should be collected from class-rooms and destroyed. The pupils, however, blocked the school keeper's path.

"We won't allow the cruxifix to be profaned!" the pupils shouted.

"I'm only carrying out the head's orders," the keeper explained. The pupils seized the basket in which he was collecting the crucifixes and divided them up to take home.

At a vocational school in Panevežys a teacher ordered the girls to take down the crucifixes, but not one obeyed.

"Well, you certainly are cowards!" fumed the teacher. "Suveizyte,* you're a member of the Komsomol. Show everyone a good example. Take down the crucifixes in all the rooms."

*Female surnames in Lithuanian have two forms: names ending in -iene or -aine, for example, Kalačuviene, show that the woman is married; names ending in -aite or -yte denote unmarried status.

The girl turned pale and began to weep. "Miss", she pleaded, "my conscience won't let me do that."

That day no one touched the crucifixes. The next day Russian soldiers took them down from the walls and threw them out of the windows into the street. People wept and picked them up from the pavement, kissing them respectfully.[57]

7. RELIGIOUS EDUCATION BANNED

LSSR
The District Executive Committee of Kaunas,
25 April 1941.

To all chairmen of Village Executive Committees within the jurisdiction of Kaunas district and the town of Jonava.

I hereby order you, immediately upon receipt of this letter, to summon all the clergy (parish priests, curates) domiciled within your jurisdiction and to inform them that they are strictly forbidden to give children any religious instruction and to demand that each sign the attached form. The priest must enter his first name and surname, as well as his address on the form before he signs it.

You must call in each priest individually or visit him at his home.

This letter must not be shown to the clergy.

The signed forms must be forwarded to me in a letter marked "confidential, personal" by 10 May 1941. This letter and the unused forms must also be returned to me.

Since this matter is strictly confidential, I order you to keep it completely secret and not to discuss it or show it to anyone. This letter must not be recorded in the book of incoming mail and therefore should not be shown to your secretary.

(signed) Bilis,
Chairman of the Executive Committee.

I, the undersigned priest . . . residing in . . . region, . . . district, . . . village, sign the attached as evidence that I was informed on . . . April 1941 that I am strictly enjoined not to give religious instruction to primary or secondary school children, either in churches, or in the homes of the children, or in my own home or elsewhere. Thus I have no right whatsoever to talk to them about religious matters.

I was clearly told that I should be held responsible for any non-observance of this warning signed by me.

Signature . . . [58]

8. BISHOP BRIZGYS APPEALS FOR RELIGIOUS LITERATURE

We have just learned that, by order of the People's Commissariat for Education, the stock of the little prayer book, *Our Father*, has been confiscated at the former firm of Spindulys printers because it was a book of religious instruction. I hereby respectfully request the Council of the People's Commissars of the LSSR to consider the following:

1. This booklet explains the fundamental principles of the Catholic faith and the first Sacraments of devotion – Confession and Communion. The Stalin Constitution of the LSSR clearly allows freedom of faith and of worship. Therefore these booklets explaining their faith to believers are absolutely necessary. Since all religious instruction has been eliminated from school curricula, we ask the People's Commissariat of Education not to ban these booklets which describe the personal aspects of religious faith, especially as they do not contain any anti-Communist propaganda.

2. The Church put the print order in hand some time ago and the printing was begun; while the book was in the process of printing the publishing house became the property of the State, but no difficulties appeared at first. When its author called upon the director of the Department of the Press and Associations on 26 September 1940, he was definitely assured that no difficulties would arise in releasing this booklet.

3. Considering its importance to the faithful and because we did not foresee any difficulties, the office of the Archbishop of Kaunas has already paid all the printing bills. I therefore ask you, on behalf of myself and of all bishops and the faithful in the LSSR, to release the booklet, *Our Father,* from the printers.

(signed) Dr. V. Brizgys,
Kaunas, 9 October 1940.   Auxiliary Bishop of Kaunas.[59]

NOTES TO CHAPTER I

1. For the whole story of Kalanta, partly as told by an eyewitness, see *The Violations of Human Rights in Soviet Occupied Lithuania, A Report for 1972,* Delran, N.J., 1973, pp. 17-24.
2. V. Stanley Vardys, *Lithuania Under the Soviets: Portrait of a Nation,* New York, 1965, p. 22; J. Savasis, *The War Against God in Lithuania,* New York , 1966, p. 13.
3. *The Lithuanian Bulletin,* New York, Vol. I, No. 7, 25 September 1943, pp. 5-6.

4. For an account of Lithuania's inter-war revival, after nearly four centuries of Russian domination, or the threat of it, see Vardys, *op. cit.,* pp. 21-46.
5. *The Lithuanian Bulletin,* Vol. III, No. 1, January-February 1945, pp. 1-4.
6. *Mažoji Lietuviškoji Tarybine Enciklopedija* (Concise Lithuanian Soviet Encyclopaedia), Vilnius, 1968, Vol. 2, p. 380.
7. *Vilniaus Balsas,* Vilnius, 9 July 1940.
8. *USA House of Representatives Select Committee to Investigate Communist Aggression: Hearings on the Baltic States,* Washington, DC, 1953-5, pp. 354-5.
9. Vardys, *op. cit.,* p. 218.
10. For an account of these events, see *ibid.,* pp. 66-72.
11. Text in William B. Stroyen, *Communist Russia and the Russian Orthodox Church, 1943-62,* Washington, DC, 1967, pp. 117-8.
12. Vardys, *op. cit.,* p. 216.
13. *Documents de Saint-Siège,* Vatican 1967-70, Vol. III, p. 270.
14. Vardys, *op. cit.,* pp. 216-7.
15. J. Savasis, *The War Against God in Lithuania,* New York, 1966, p. 17.
16. A. Trakiškis, *The Situation of the Church and Religious Practices in Occupied Lithuania, Part I, 1940-1,* New York, 1944, p. 28. This is an especially valuable source, because it was written before the second Soviet occupation of Lithuania and is therefore uncoloured by subsequent events.
17. For a study of the Soviet laws on religion, see Michael Bourdeaux, Hans Hebly and Eugen Voss (eds.), *Religious Liberty in the Soviet Union,* Keston College, Keston, Kent, 1976, pp. 25-53. There is a shorter account in Michael Bourdeaux (ed.), *Religious Minorities in the Soviet Union,* London, 1973, pp. 6-11 (revised edition).
18. Trakiškis, *op. cit.,* pp. 16-17.
19. See, for example, *RCL* 1, 1973, pp. 30-3; 2, 1976, pp. 32-4; 4, 1976, pp. 24-34; *Zakonodatelstvo o religioznykh kultakh,* ed. G. R. Golst and D. M. Nochvin, Yuridicheskaya Literatura, Moscow 1971 (marked "for official use only"); *Washington Post,* Washington, DC, 12 January 1977.
20. Vardys, *op. cit.,* p. 219.
21. Trakiškis, *op. cit.,* p. 19.
22. *Ibid,* p. 14.
23. Savasis, *op. cit.,* p. 19.
24. Trakiškis, *op. cit.,* p. 13.
25. *Ibid.,* p. 28.
26. *Loc. cit.*
27. Vardys, *op. cit.,* p. 217.
28. Savasis, *op. cit.,* p. 13.
29. Trakiškis, *op. cit.,* p. 9.
30. *Loc. cit.*
31. Vardys, *op. cit.,* p. 218.
32. Trakiškis, *op. cit.,* p. 33.
33. *Ibid.,* pp. 14-15.
34. *Ibid.,* p. 32.
35. *Ibid.,* p. 14.
36. *Ibid.,* p. 23.
37. Savasis, *op. cit.,* p. 75.
38. Savasis, *op. cit.,* p. 18.
39. *Loc. cit.*
40. Trakiškis, *op. cit.,* p. 32.
41. For an account of this, see K. Pelekis, *Genocide: Lithuania's Threefold*

    Tragedy, "Venta", West Germany, 1949. Pp. 35-93 deal with the first occupation.
42. Savasis, *op. cit.*, p. 21.
43. Not only through scattered references in Solzhenitsyn's *Gulag Archipelago* (e.g. Vol. 2, London 1975, pp. 249, 259, 438, 599, 621) and other prison-camp literature, but more especially in a remarkable booklet published in Italian without designated authorship, *Siberia: Cimitero del Popolo Lituano*, Urbania, 1975, with an introduction by Teresa Carloni.
44. Savasis, *op. cit.*, p. 18.
45. *CLCC* 11, p. 6 (E), p. 3 (L).
46. Trakiškis, *op. cit.*, pp. 11-12.
47. *Ibid.*, p. 13.
48. *Ibid.*, pp. 19-20.
49. *Ibid.*, pp. 21-2; see also M. Gelžinis, *Christenverfolgung in Litauen*, n.d., Königstein/Taunus, p. 22.
50. Trakiškis, *op. cit.*, pp. 8-9.
51. *Ibid.*, p. 31.
52. *Ibid.*, pp. 29-30.
53. *Ibid.*, pp. 18-19.
54. *Ibid.*, pp. 24-5.
55. *Documents de Saint-Siège*, Vatican 1965-70, pp. 312-5.
56. *CLCC* 17, pp. 21-2.
57. *CLCC* 11, p. 5 (E), p. 2 (L).
58. Trakiškis, *op. cit.*, pp. 12-13.
59. *Ibid.*, pp. 20-1.

II

THE BASIC AIMS OF GERMAN AND SOVIET POLICY

AFTER the invasion of 1941 and the fall of the Lithuanian Provisional Government six weeks later, the German occupying forces continued some of the Soviet policies towards the Roman Catholic Church to a surprising degree: her land was not returned; and although religious education was permitted, religious organizations continued to be banned, as were Catholic publications. On the surface, this might seem surprising. Why did the Nazis not take advantage of the good will, almost theirs for the taking, latent in Lithuania as a result of the extreme hostility the Soviet Government had shown towards anything Lithuanian? A closer acquaintance with the history of the period demonstrates that the ultimate aim of Nazi policy for small nations situated as inconveniently as Lithuania was not so far removed from that of Soviet policy: the suppression of national characteristics as a prelude to incorporation into the impersonal larger unit of power.[1] Nazi racial ideology marked Lithuanians low in the scale of "Aryan" nations, as they were "strongly subject to Jewish and Russian influences". There were plans to exile the "racially inferior" Lithuanian population in "considerable numbers".[2] The Catholic Church stood unambiguously for national independence, as well as for the allegiance of the individual to ideals higher than those of any political system.

The underground press, which continued under Nazi occupation as it had begun under Soviet, made this categorically clear:

> The Lithuanian people have never staked their destiny on the victory of either of the occupying powers – German or Russian . . . Lithuania is resolved . . . to regain a free and independent life and to carry on her creative work for her people and for the peace and happiness of mankind.[3]

The underground press consistently opposed the Nazis; it had its effect, for example, in building up awareness of what the Nazi plan of deportation to Germany for forced labour meant, thus inspiring determined resistance to it. There were almost thirty such underground publications which appeared more or less regularly during the German occupation.[4]

This already makes nonsense of the later Soviet claim that the Lithuanians were "collaborators" with the Germans and that the

Nazis inspired the widespread resistance to renewed Soviet rule from the autumn of 1944.[5] This accusation becomes even more absurd when it is claimed that church leaders inspired such collaboration. As subsequent propaganda has shown,[6] the Soviet authorities have trotted out this charge ever since, whenever it suits them. If the facts do not fit the case the Soviets want to bring against the Church, they simply rewrite them in any way they please.

As regards the charge of collaboration, decisive evidence exists which demonstrates the record of the church leaders under Nazi occupation. In 1943, at the height of the Nazi terror, the Lithuanian bishops addressed a memorandum to the occupying powers and saw that this document found its way abroad, to be published in New York in July 1943 (Document 9). The memorandum proves that the situation was little better than it had been under the Soviets. Although the Germans reopened two theological seminaries besides that at Kaunas, they closed the seminary at Vilnius and deported fifty of the students to Germany.[7] Not a single one of the main problems bequeathed by the Soviets had been resolved and the Nazis had failed to grant repeated requests from the hierarchy to help in working out difficulties.

The bishops set forth the situation under seven headings:

1. The property which the Bolsheviks had confiscated had still not been returned.
2. The Germans were breaking many promises of safeguards concerning the deportation of Lithuanian nationals to Germany – such as that they would be permitted chaplains of their own nationality.
3. Young people of both sexes were among those deported, the girls being subjected to grave moral risks.
4. Secular interference in theological education was continuing.
5. Religious organizations in schools were still banned.
6. The church press still could not function.
7. Finally, a general increase in religious freedom was demanded, together with freedom of action for the Church in its own sphere.

Far from granting these requests, the Nazis continued their brutality. On numerous occasions the invaders violated the performance of the liturgy, driving people out of church and sometimes rounding up victims for deportation while they were gathered for worship.[8]

As in every country invaded by the Nazis, some national groups were found willing to assist the German SD forces [security police] in organizing the extermination of local Jews, as in the infamous Kaunas pogrom of 25 June 1941 and at the Ponary extermination pits, where 25,000 Vilnius Jews were shot. However, Lithuanian participation in such atrocities was strongly condemned by the underground press:

More than 80 per cent of Lithuanian Jews have been murdered. The shooting orgies were commanded by Germans only. They were executed by Germans and renegades in Lithuanian uniforms, criminals who were filled with alcohol by the Germans and allowed to rob the victims. Lithuanian people kept away from these wholesale murders . . . The veteran Lithuanian statesman Dr. Grinius, Father Krupavičius and Professor Aleksa, in a memorandum for which they were sent to Germany, have protested to the General Kommissar against the murdering of Jews.[9]

It is significant that although SS legions were organized from the local population in the other Baltic States, the Germans failed to establish a Lithuanian SS Legion, in spite of four attempts to do so. Instead, Lithuania was made to provide 40,000 slave workers for German industry.

Lithuania had no breathing space between the retreat of the Germans and the reoccupation of their land by the Red Army. During the years 1944-53 over 200,000 Lithuanians were deported to various "islands" of the Gulag Archipelago.[10] The populace realized that a time of renewed terror awaited them, rather than any fruits of peace, though for some years after the German retreat in the autumn of 1944 many naively hoped that the western allies were preparing to liberate those in Eastern Europe who remained oppressed. This hope found practical expression, as in Ukraine, in a prolonged guerilla campaign, supported by an underground press, which the Soviets did not finally eradicate until 1952, after eight years of effort. Various underground newspapers continued to appear even as late as 1951, mostly proclaiming Christian and democratic principles. The last trials of partisans in Lithuania were still taking place in 1961-3. It was only the strength of the guerilla organization in many country districts and the physical fear experienced by the NKVD in carrying out their operation of terror there which prevented the Church from suffering even worse calamities – and sooner – than she did.

At this time the Soviet regime renewed its determined campaign to reduce the Catholic Church in Lithuania to the kind of position the Russian Orthodox Church had been forced to assume since the 1920's: a state of inactivity and passivity in every area of life other than religious ritual and theology. Although the Orthodox Church improved its position after the Second World War,[11] largely because of its public patriotic support for the Soviet Government, the favours it received were confined to the right to perform the ritual and to theological education. Despite the naked terror of the new wave of deportations to Siberia,[12] the situation of the Catholic Church as an organization in the parishes never quite deteriorated to what it was in those areas which had been under Soviet rule since 1917. In Lithuania, as as Western Ukraine, a far higher proportion of churches was open than elsewhere, even taking into account the reopening of many Russian churches during or just after the war. It is probable that this was a concession to the strength of Catholic feeling in these areas, combined with the continuing struggle against the partisans.

Accounts filtering out of Lithuania just after the war show clearly how the Soviets were determined to stick to their policy of 1940-1:

> Clergy are being continually shadowed and watched by NKVD agents. The priests are 'top priority' suspects, suspected of dealing with guerillas. A number of priests were arrested and taken to unknown destinations on suspicion of contacts with the underground liberation movements. In a certain region of Sudavia (Suvalkija), affected by guerilla operations, the rectories were repeatedly searched – ostensibly for radio transmitters. A number of young priests were arrested and several churches were shut down.[13]

In Vilnius, however, the Church held her own, with most of the buildings open for daily worship and crowds openly showing their devotion.[14]

The Soviets soon came to know of the close affinity between the Church and the guerillas – a relationship of substance and quite unlike the fabrications alleging support for the Nazi cause. V. Stanley Vardys best sums this up:

> The groups were united into conspiratorial military formations under religious and nationalist symbols, which were helpful in maintaining both secrecy and disciplined standards of behaviour. Partisan groups usually held prayer meetings and frequented the sacraments of the Roman Catholic Church, to which the majority of the partisans belonged. The oath for new members was a semi-religious ceremony.[15]

As the NKVD gradually tightened its stranglehold on Lithuania, so the situation in the Church became more tense, as a result of placing so much hope in the West, which in spiritual matters meant support from the Vatican. The deteriorating situation is well documented, especially in a letter to the Pope of 20 September 1948, which the partisans somehow sent out of the country. Because it has remained so little known we quote a substantial portion of it (Document 10), a declaration unique for its time, which remains in so many of its essentials as relevant now as it was when it was written.

Both internal armed opposition and appeals for intervention from outside failed. Geography had defeated Lithuania once again. When confronted by the colonialism and utter ruthlessness of Moscow, the new Soviet republic (together with the other Baltic States of Latvia and Estonia) had to face integration into a system which was hostile to almost every strand of Lithuanian history, tradition and culture. The Roman Catholic Church stood then, as she does today, right at the pressure point of the struggle. In terms of physical confrontation, the Lithuanian nation was doomed. In terms of the allegiance of men's minds, the contest continues unabated, though there have been changes in Soviet tactics over the years.

No sooner had the Soviets eliminated the last pockets of physical resistance in 1952 than the mastermind of the terror himself died (March 1953). For a few years after Stalin there was a moratorium on

physical methods of repression. The *Gulag* prison camp network con-
tracted, though it never yielded up the key men taken in the struggle
for national independence. Twenty-five years later these unknown
prisoners, unsupported by anyone outside the narrowest and most
isolated groups in the West, are still expiating crimes which, in other
circumstances, would have made them international heroes.

Some of those deported who had not been active partisans could
now return home. A few years after Stalin's death about 35,000
people, a mere tenth of those who had originally been deported,[16]
began to arrive home. As there were church leaders in this number,
this naturally encouraged the faithful in Lithuania, though in common
with most of the others who returned they remained barred from the
full exercise of their civil rights and could not resume the positions
they had been forced to vacate or to which their suffering now entitled
them (see Chapter III).

Two bishops, Petras Maželis and Julijonas Steponavičius, were consecrated with government permission on 11 November 1955; they
were appointed to the Telšiai and Panevežys dioceses. This was in
itself a considerable concession to the religious feelings of the people.

The faithful in this period gained further encouragement from what
looked like becoming a full-scale public debate on the nature of Soviet
policy towards religion. Khrushchev himself, soon to emerge as the
dynamic leader of the Kremlin, initiated this policy with his decree on
10 November 1954 to the Central Committee of the Communist
Party, in which he claimed that the physical nature of the war against
religion had not furthered the cause of atheism and that the educational quality of the campaign had been so low as to be valueless.[17]

This was ironic in view of the fact that, a few years later, he himself
was to conduct just such a violently hostile campaign against religion.
The official voice of the Lithuanian Communist Party took up the
debate in cautious but conciliatory tones (Document 11).

The section of Lithuanian Communism responsible for atheist
policies clearly did not know how to react in the wake of such a
changed line from Moscow. By the summer of 1956 a Lithuanian
newspaper was able to print the nearest to a public defence of religion
ever presented to Soviet readers, in an article by L. Drotvinas, a
researcher at the Lithuanian Academy of Science:

> We always had clergy who appeared on the scene as leaders of the masses
> in their battle for freedom. Thus the positive significance of religion today
> is that many of our older generation have been brought up under certain
> religious precepts forbidding stealing, lying and so on . . . . Religion is no
> obstacle to an educated man . . . . Religion does not repress a worker's
> or a farmer's intitiative [18] [fuller text in Document 12].

As the debate was flowering its root began to wither. Already the
autumn of 1956 demonstrated categorically that post-Stalin relaxation in no way implied a loosening of the Soviet Union's political grip

on its colonies, whether "internal" like Lithuania or "external" like Hungary. Lithuanians had demonstrated in the streets of Vilnius and Kaunas at the time of the Hungarian Revolution, but the Soviet tanks on the streets of Budapest in November 1956 brought up short any Lithuanians in whom ideas of help from the West either lingered on or had developed as a result of the freer atmosphere. Only changes in the Kremlin itself could now bring about a political change in Lithuania. However, the role of the Church, as the only viable non-Communist organization in the country, in keeping the flame alive in the hearts of people was now of greater importance than ever. The Church was challenged truly to live up to her calling of humility and service in circumstances very different from those when armed guerillas were still at large in the countryside. However, the suppression of the latter meant that the regime was now able to concentrate much more intensely on the control and the intended elimination of the Church.

More than a decade after his fall, Khrushchev is still not generally seen in focus. He is regarded too simply as a "liberalizer" of the Soviet system, the man who dethroned the memory of Stalin and physically eliminated him from his place of honour in the mausoleum on Red Square. Most of his more liberal statements – including his condemnation of physical violence in combatting religion (1954) mentioned above – date, however, from the time when he was still disputing supreme leadership with his rivals.

The most repressive aspect of his domestic policy was his treatment of religion. It is not an exaggeration to say that the period of his rule plunged the churches into physical persecution reminiscent, at its worst, of Stalin's purges of the 1930's. The atheist agencies did not carry their campaign to its intended conclusion of the physical annihilation of the Church as an institution, because the fall of Khrushchev in 1964 called a peremptory halt to its more violent aspects. This purge hit all denominations (though some suffered more than others) with mass closure of churches, public character assassination of the clergy without right of reply, closure of more than half of the theological seminaries of the Russian Orthodox Church, the arbitrary seizure of monasteries, widely publicized trials and the imprisonment of any laity or clergy who resisted the campaign. There is now extensive documentation available detailing what occurred and the shock which it administered to the faithful, who were accustoming themselves to a partial religious freedom which had not been known earlier in the Soviet period[19] (Document 13). The precise origins of this campaign and the real reason for it are still obscure, like so many other aspects of Soviet policy, despite the detailed information available concerning its practical effects on the life of the Church. The date of the beginning of this wave of persecution is usually given as 1959-60, but there are definite signs that it was beginning before this. Vittorio Vignieri, the pseudonym of a leading Lithuanian expert on religion, writing even before the fall of Khrushchev, clearly dates the emergence of the new persecution as early as 1957.[20] The explanation is that, in the vast bureaucracy of the Soviet Union, the new policy took time to gather its forces and reveal its brutality.

The Lithuanian Catholic Church was one of the objects of this campaign, although it was less violent in Lithuania than in other parts of the Soviet Union. This may have been due partly to a fear of reviving active resistance to Sovietization by an all-out attack on the mass allegiance of Lithuanians to the Catholic Church.

The vigour of religious commitment in Lithuania was still remarkable, resulting from the deep penetration of the Church into all strata of the country's life. While the new campaign was partly a physical one, the atheists showed more clearly than ever that they were prepared to fight a battle for the mind.

For the first time, a museum of atheism was established in Lithuania by the regime, housed in the former church of St. Casimir in Vilnius.[21] One of the aims was to penetrate the countryside with travelling exhibits. The media and educational programmes began to take on a much sharper tone again in the struggle to secure the allegiance of the younger generation.[22]

One the regime's most formidable weapons became the exploitation of renegade clergy, who were deployed to mock, cajole or threaten the faithful through the media and in personal appearances.[23] The most prominent of these was Jonas Ragauskas, from whom flowed a stream of atheist propaganda,[24] and whose role is closely parallel to that of Alexander Osipov, formerly of the Russian Orthodox Church, and active in Russia at the same time.[25]

Only the fall of Khrushchev gave the faithful in Lithuania, as elsewhere in the Soviet Union, a short breathing space. Political uncertainty inevitably engulfs the country upon the fall or death of a Soviet leader, because there are no democratic safeguards or assurances of continuity. In the inevitable jostling for leadership (as after the death of Stalin) immediate ideological control of the population was not as important as winning its acceptance of the new leaders.

The moratorium on religious persecution of 1965 was not a policy uniformly imposed. In some places the juggernaut moved forward under its own impetus. Local party officials had been too used to unchecked expression of violence towards believers to be able to curb it because of a change in policy. The main effect generally in the Soviet Union was to halt a rapidly deteriorating situation, not to restore to it the benefits of the pre-1957 period which no one in Lithuania had experienced anyway.

Almost without exception, the thousands of churches which Khrushchev had closed throughout the USSR remained so,[26] but some of the prisoners received an amnesty.[27] The State was prepared to allow one or two modest concessions, such as the printing of a new edition of the Bible, which appeared in 1968, but which must, of course, have been prepared earlier.[28]

For Lithuania the concessions were perhaps slightly more substantial than the average elsewhere. The State countenanced the consecration of a new bishop, Juozas Matulaitis-Labukas. Although this occurred in Rome, where he had gone to attend the Vatican Council, he was able to fulfil his new office on return to Lithuania.[29] The Lithuanian Church received permission to print a tiny edition (without a print number, like all ecclesiastical publications, but unlike secular books) of a prayer book[30] and of the decisions taken by the Second Vatican Council.[31] Kaunas Seminary, the only one open in Lithuania, succeeded in raising its complement by five to thirty students in all.

The atheist organs published articles, both in Lithuania and in the rest of the Soviet Union, in which the tone was less hostile to the Church than what had been appearing in the previous six or seven years. For example, *Nauka i religia* ("science and religion" – the chief atheist journal) published an extensive article on Lithuania in April/May 1966, but undoubtedly based on materials prepared in 1965, where the author, V. Pomerantsev, portrays Lithuanian priests he met in a manner not wholly unsympathetic (Document 14).

For the last decade Soviet atheist agencies have clearly been grappling intensively with the problem of the persistence of religion in Lithuania. Probably the mood has been one of increasing frustration, as it becomes more and more clear that religion, far from dying out, is retaining its hold, perhaps even strengthening it in recent years as the mood of civil rights activists has gradually become more determined in the Soviet Union. It is difficult to tell whether the Lithuanians have become more vocal in response to increasing pressure or whether the State has resorted to stronger measures in the face of increased church activity.

The main agency for controlling religious activity is the Lithuanian branch of the government body, the Council for Religious Affairs. Until December, 1965, there were two bodies in Moscow, the Council for Russian Orthodox Church Affairs and the Council for the Affairs of Religious Cults, the latter being responsible for all denominations and religions other than the Orthodox, including the Roman Catholic Church in Lithuania. Then the Government united the two bodies,[32] which may have been an administrative convenience or the decision may have been in some way connected with the general tightening of anti-religious policy at the time. Until 1975 this body possessed only the most shadowy existence under Soviet law, since there was no public statute defining its position.

The new codified legislation on religion of July 1975 gave it public status for the first time.[33] However, Soviet legislation on religion, including secret instructions and the Council's statutes, can be found in full in a classified book, *Soviet Laws on Religious Cults,* which was recently brought out to the West. It is marked "For official use only."

The Lithuanian branch of the Council for Religious Affairs is clearly an agency for carrying out Moscow's policies on religion and is closely allied with the KGB (secret police). Recent information from Lithuanian Catholics has also begun to give us a clear indication of the way in which the Council for Religious Affairs works in the republic. Its general functions are informally assessed in Document 15, which designates it as an organ for "terrorizing priests and interfering with their work". Like its Russian equivalent, it has relied extensively on verbal instructions to those whom it seeks to control, so that incriminating evidence should be kept to a minimum.[34]

Nevertheless, just such evidence has surfaced in Document 16, which shows, as do few other pieces of evidence in the history of the Soviet campaign against religion, just how extensively Soviet agents are instructed to penetrate into the activities of the Church. The local government agencies must monitor every aspect of the life of the Church. The sermon comes at the top of the list for attention, with precise details as to how it should be recorded. This testifies to the power which the authorities feel the clergy are still wielding through the spoken word. From this, the atheist infiltrators must build up the characteristics of the individual priest, paying especial attention to his relations with children and their parents and with the local intelligentsia. This then broadens into a required study of the "demographic" make-up of the individual congregation and the activities of its members in other contexts.

From 1972 the Lithuanian Catholic community began to be much more organized in expressing its opposition to the new wave of Soviet repression. The nationwide organization of petitions and appeals found both inspiration and reflection in a new clandestine journal, the *Chronicle of the Lithuanian Catholic Church,* closely resembling in character the Moscow human rights journal, the *Chronicle of Current Events.*[35] It rapidly became obvious to the KGB that the regular appearance of this journal was a major obstacle both to the propagation of the atheist programme and to the control of Lithuanian nationalism. Its suppression became a prime concern of security agencies in the country (see Chapter XI). But the tension found other forms of expression too.

There was a series of clashes, some of them public and physically violent, between the security agencies and the people, culminating in the suicide of Romas Kalanta in May, 1972.[36]

As with the Orthodox and Baptist reformers elsewhere in the Soviet Union, the State's policy seems to have become more and more an attempt to isolate the ringleaders both from the people and from the state-approved church leadership (see Chapter III), and to cut away their popular support by offering certain limited concessions[37] as a prelude to a brutal campaign against a relatively limited number of prominent individuals. The imprisonment of the Baptist leader, Georgi Vins (1966),[38] and of the Orthodox priest, Vasyl Romanyuk (1975),[39] parallels the measures taken against those who have been associated with the *Chronicle of the Lithuanian Catholic Church* (Chapter XI).

The concessions offered by the State included the consecration of two new bishops in December 1969 and a limited number of articles in the Soviet press in 1972 warning against the danger of insulting believers by the "wrong methods of combatting religion" which lead to the "intensification of religious fanaticism, hidden forms of service and rites, cause discontent and distrust among the believers and aggravate them".[40] Permission was even given for the publication of 10,000 Lithuanian New Testaments.[41]

In this context, the dismissal of Justas Rugienis, head of the Lithuanian branch of the Council on Religious Affairs and one of the most hated and ruthless men in the republic, appeared at first as a conciliatory gesture on the part of the State, but the *Lithuanian Chronicle* was quick to point out that the "more tactful" approach of his successor, Kazimieras Tumenas, offered no hope for an improvement (Document 17). The author's worst fears were justified. At the time of writing no solution to the problem of Church and State in Lithuania is even in prospect. The only long-term hope would seem to be a change in the basic policies of the Kremlin, but even this would seem to be a distant one, despite the willingness of the present regime to make some concessions to other minorities, as in the case of the emigration of the Jews. However, the Lithuanians have a homeland, they have no wish to emigrate *en masse* and they refuse to adapt to the Soviet model, either on religion or on national identity.

DOCUMENTS

9. THE BISHOPS PROTEST AGAINST GERMAN OPPRESSION

The following is a summary of a memorandum handed to the Commissar-General in Kaunas by the Lithuanian Catholic bishops on 13 October 1942. It gives the best evidence of the relations at that time between the Church and the German authorities in Lithuania.

This document states that at their annual conference the bishops had discussed questions concerning the situation of Catholics in Lithuania and decided to inform Dr. von Renteln of their opinion of the present conditions, asking him to cancel all measures that put restraint on religious freedom and the education of Lithuanian youth.

Their claims were summarized in the following seven points:

1. Regarding the Church's property, the bishops pointed out that the German authorities had on several occasions declared their intention of restoring property rights in Lithuania in the near future. This question is important to all Lithuanian people and to the Catholic Church, because nearly the whole of the Church's property and that of the Catholic organizations has been nationalized. The bishops, as it was indicated in the memorandum, had several times declared that Catholics could not recognize such expropriation as legal. Respect for property rights was always considered by them as the mark of Christian civilization. All European peoples respected property rights; they were respected in the Reich also. The Roman Catholic Church, it was further said, considered property not only as a purely economic question; it was a postulate of natural and Christian morality, confirmed by the positive Divine Law . . .

   Then the bishops compared the situation of property rights under the Bolshevik and present regimes. They explained that the Lithuanian people condemned Bolshevism and its consequences, and among them all confiscation of private property.

   It had come to the knowledge of the bishops, they went on, that the German civil administration had considered the problem of a reform of ecclesiastical land properties in Lithuania. In the opinion of the bishops, the time was ripe for such a reform; however, it should be introduced only by agreement with the Holy See.

   They then stated that the Bolsheviks had taken away from the dioceses and parishes various documents, church registers and archives which were indispensable to the ecclesiastical authorities. The conference of bishops therefore requested the return of this property to the dioceses and parishes without further delay.

   The bishops further pointed out that, owing to the transfer of property from its rightful owners and the report that further evictions were to take place, these parish and ecclesiastical documents were of urgent importance.

2. The second point of the memorandum concerned the situation of the Lithuanian workers deported to work in German industry in the Reich. The bishops observed that most of the workers were Catholics. When exhorted to go to Germany, they had been promised that Lithuanian priests would be appointed to care for their religious needs. The conference of bishops stated, to their great sorrow, that these promises, although repeated many times, had not been kept; the priests appointed for this purpose had not received permission to perform their duties. Thus the bishops by virtue of their position called the attention of the

Commissar-General to this fact and asked him to take the necessary measures to keep the Germans to their promise.

3. The third point dealt with the German order to enlist the graduates of Lithuanian higher schools for labour service abroad. Their parents would not be able to care for them there and they would be without religious and moral support. Still more dangerous, according to the bishops' opinion, was the intention of sending young girls to labour service in Germany. This would damage their health and corrupt their morals to a still higher degree than those of the young men. The despatch of the younger generation to foreign countries would be regarded by the Lithuanian people as an infringement of the rights of parents.

In making such a statement, the bishops declared that they were expressing not only their own anxiety and concern but also that of the parents. Lithuanian parents, it was said, could not forget the measures taken to encourage the enlistment of young men to labour service by means of alcohol and tobacco. The Lithuanian people and all the bishops were certain that the young men and girls would do their labour service to the best purpose in their own country.

4. In the fourth point the bishops attacked the German authorities for the obstacles placed in the way of theological education in Lithuania. They pointed out that during the 1941-2 academic year normal studies at the theological faculty had been disturbed. In spite of the oft-repeated promises to give the Lithuanian people full freedom in the domain of education, the faculty, the bishops observed, had met with difficulties that had not been overcome. Further, it was stated that the position of the theological faculty at the University of Kaunas had been secured by a Concordat and Lithuanian law from the very foundation of this university. Therefore the bishops declared that in accordance with this legal basis and with the needs of Catholics, the bishops were unable either to change the legal status of the theological faculty or to renounce the right to it.

The memorandum touched on the present situation of the Lithuanian universities in Kaunas and Vilnius and explained that both of them were great cultural achievements of the free Lithuanian people. Therefore there were no groups nor any individuals in Lithuania who were not interested in the existence of these universities.

5. The fifth point of the memorandum was devoted to the activity of religious societies in Lithuanian schools. The bishops emphasized that, in spite of the fact that scientific societies were being permitted in Lithuanian schools, religious societies were forbidden. Thus pupils were not allowed to increase their knowledge in religious and moral matters. Parents and all Catholics regarded such an unequal treatment of the school societies as religious persecution.

6. In the following section the bishops expressed their point of view on the difficulties of the Catholic press in Lithuania under the German regime. This press had ceased to exist, although many requests to recommence publishing Catholic newspapers, so numerous before the war, had been handed to the German authorities. The Lithuanian Catholic population noticed with astonishment that while luxury papers, read only by a

small group of the population, were published in Lithuania, the Catholics, though in a great majority, were not allowed to publish a simple paper. The bishops therefore impressed upon the Commissar-General the necessity for one weekly popular magazine and one monthly review for the clergy and educated classes.

According to the declaration of the bishops, this matter was of great importance. The Catholics had their own printing offices acquired by donations and loans which imposed certain obligations. The present managers of the nationalized printing offices were unable to meet these obligations. The printing offices should be returned to their legal owners at once.

7. Finally, the memorandum demanded general religious freedom and freedom of action for the Church in its special sphere. Even if there were no Concordat with the Holy See, the bishops emphasized, the Church would still have the right to establish the Catholic organizations so necessary for religious action.

The memorandum closed with an expression of hope that the Commissar-General would take the necessary measures to solve all the above-mentioned questions in the near future.[42]

10. APPEAL TO THE POPE, 1949 (p. 26)

Holy Father, Shepherd of Catholics!

By the commission of our Lord Jesus Christ, you are the leader and shepherd of all Catholics. Therefore we, Roman Catholic Christians of the Republic of Lithuania, appeal to Your Holiness for help . . . .

[The writers describe the difficult history of Lithuania up to that point, including the terror under the Soviet occupation.]

85 per cent of Lithuanians are Roman Catholics. The influence of religion upon our people has been and today still is very strong. Our nation has a particularly deep reverence for the Virgin Mary. Pius XI called Lithuania the Land of Mary. Religious images and crosses used to stand on all the streets and roads of our land, like symbols of the suffering of our nation. The Bolsheviks are well aware that our people will be able to resist as long as the influence of religion remains intact. That is why our Catholic faith has to bear the heaviest blows of the occupation . . . .

[The Bolsheviks have subjugated all religion. At the present time they exploit the Russian Orthodox Church, but assiduously spread atheism.]

In Lithuania, too, religious services are partially permitted. But the Catholic clergy are supposed to act as informers. After severing them from Rome, the Government aims to make them in every respect its accomplices and submissive tools. When the Lithuanian Catholics resisted this, the campaign of terror and annihilation began . . . .

Ever since 1944 the authorities have been trying to establish a "national church" in Lithuania, as in that part of Ukraine which was taken from Poland . . . . At the same time the government press depicts the Pope as a traitor: Rome is described as a refuge for the scum of all the earth, including murderers. The Pope, they say, has constantly betrayed the Lithuanian people and is an arch-enemy of the freedom of all small nations – and of Lithuania in particular. Believers are forced to listen to all this, but it does not penetrate to their souls, for the Bolsheviks have not found any accomplices among the priests.

From the very first days of the occupation Bolshevik agents have been constantly gathering material on the "crimes" of the priests, whether political or moral. Their concept of crime is extremely one-sided. If someone within a priest's family circle has aroused the authorities' displeasure, this makes the priest himself a criminal. If someone belonged to Catholic Action ten years ago, that is sufficient for his arrest. Armed with this kind of "material", the Bolshevik hang-men go to the priests. They begin with promises, then they confront the victim with his supposed "crimes" and resort to terror and force. For months they try to break the victim's will-power with such tortures. Priests who stand firm often disappear without trace during the night. Dossiers are soon drawn up on honest clergymen with the help of torture and false witnesses. At the same time the press is full of accusations. The finest priest is branded as a thief, a debauchee, a bandit and murderer, whom the court then sentences – exercising leniency on account of his clerical standing – to a mere fifteen years forced labour in Siberia. If they cannot find anything to pin on a man, he is liquidated by means of provocation, even the abuse of the most sacred things. It sometimes happens that a priest is called to a dying man, who is in fact a police informer. The priest is then accused of having rendered his services to a member of the secret resistance movement, and sentenced to fifteen years forced labour . . . .

Despite all this, the clergy are extremely steadfast, although hundreds of them have already been deported to forced labour. They enjoy the unreserved trust of the people. The lesser servants of the Church are equally harassed and persecuted with very similar provocations. Every priest is kept under surveillance by several agents. Watch is kept from neighbouring houses to see who visits him, with whom he has contact . . . . If a priest even addresses someone on the street, it arouses the suspicion of the police . . . .

[Priests are subject to excessive taxation and other disabilities. The churches also have to pay exorbitant taxes on their own buildings.]

Despite many efforts, there is no longer any religious press. Even the printing of the smallest prayerbook is forbidden. There is only a government press which never prints anything about religion but disparaging criticisms and defamation. Woe to the man who attempts to reply to these attacks from the pulpit! . . . .

[Art and education are totally dominated by the Soviet atheist outlook.]

In 1944 there were three theological seminaries in Lithuania. Two were closed in 1946 – allegedly because the rooms were needed for military purposes, although they have remained unused to the present day. The students were allowed to move to the seminary at Kaunas. In the same year a decree was passed to the effect that the total number of students could not exceed 150: none of the rest, about 200 of them, could continue to follow their vocation. Meanwhile the number of students has been further reduced to sixty. In future there will only be eight new priests each year for the whole of Lithuania, while every year 25 to 30 clergymen die – apart from the arrests and deportations. Already there are many congregations where three or four priests have been arrested one after the other. Meanwhile one priest has to look after two or more congregations. Priests who are old or sick have to resume their ministry. The seminaries are maintained exclusively out of gifts from believers.

During the war, about a hundred churches were destroyed or severely damaged in Lithuania. There is no chance of their restoration. The authorities will not give any building materials for this purpose and they refuse building permission for the restoration of the churches. What is done here and there happens in secret. In many places believers pray secretly in barns.

The Government aims to abolish the old system of church elders in the congregations and to replace them by state church councils, on the Orthodox pattern. Church affairs in Lithuania are under the representative for religious affairs of the Council of Ministers Gailevičius, party member and former secret policeman. Councils of twenty* are supposed to be formed under each district official and in every church. Some of the members of the council are to be named by the Government, the others require government approval. The Government has given no guidelines or directives concerning the activity, duties and rights of these councils. Up to now it is only known that when the council is formed and has been approved by the Government, it is supposed to conclude a contract with the responsible government body for the leasing of the church. The council also has the right to close a church and to reject or remove a priest. It is most important that the members of the council can easily be enlisted by the secret police. The Catholic Church is resisting the formation of such councils. There has been a severe struggle over this matter for several years now . . . .

*The *dvadtsatka*, the statutory group necessary to found any religious congregation and apply for its registration.

[The writers describe Bolshevik methods of subjugation, by which people are terrorised into compliance and deceit. Conditions of detention are shocking. Party members enjoy no respect from the people.]

Foreign visitors are even shown secret policemen kneeling in the churches, pretending to be devout worshippers – this is all part of the propaganda.

The four-year-long struggle which the Lithuanian people have waged for religious and national freedom has had frightful consequences. The whole land is full of violence, fear, blood and torment. More than 100,000 believers have been murdered after torture, starved or frozen to death in Siberia. Every day claims fresh victims. There is not a single house where tears have not been shed. A high percentage of the clergy is either in Siberia or in hiding or with part of the underground movement in the forests. There is only one bishop left in the whole of Lithuania. Two are dead (Karevičius and Karosas), four have been imprisoned (Borisevičius, Matulionis, Ramanauskas and Reinys). The activity of the Curia has been severely restricted, the seminary is barely still functioning, the monks have been liquidated or exiled. No one knows when the secret police will knock at his door. Everything is going on very quietly, inconspicuously, in order to keep the outside world in ignorance . . . .

[Lithuanians will continue their struggle for freedom, despite the terrible sacrifices involved.]

Holy Father! We know how many cares lie heavy upon Your Holiness today. But in the name of the torments we have already undergone and are still suffering, we nevertheless venture to ask you, as the head of all Catholics, for your help. We have no more neighbours to whom we can entrust our destiny and the destiny of our people. We, the Catholic inhabitants of Lithuania, are – under your leadership – the only Catholics in north-east Europe, a little island in the sea of other confessions. We cannot survive this pressure much longer, we are on the point of perishing. Our faith, our customs, our traditions, even our language – everything will be destroyed. We often think of the Turkish invasion in the Middle Ages, of the Arab hordes, of the time when the great men of Rome arose: Urban II, Innocent III. The hordes from the east today fear neither speeches nor diplomatic protests. We often ask ourselves: where are the people of the civilised world? Where are the hundred million Christians? Are there no more fighters for truth, no great men in the world any more? Do they not know how their Christian brothers and sisters are being destroyed? Are the Christians of the world caught in a deceptive slumber, believing themselves secure, do they think that the hordes from the east will call a halt after they have destroyed us? No! . . . . Bolshevism is getting ready to destroy the civilisation, the culture and the Christianity of the world . . . .

Holy Father! We ask you to proclaim for all believers of the world a Lithuanian day, as Benedict XV of pious memory did in 1917. Let the world learn of the torments, persecutions and distress of the Lithuanian Catholics, caused by twentieth-century godlessness.

We ask Your Holiness to direct a word of public comfort and encouragement to the Lithuanian people. Holy Father, speak a word of encouragement, as the first Pope, St. Peter, once did in Rome. What we are suffering for our Mother, the Catholic Church, is just as great.

We ask you to pass our complaints on to the United Nations, so that the rulers of the nations may put an end to our torments.

We ask for more frequent and longer Lithuanian broadcasts. Do we not deserve this on account of the sacrifices we are making for our holy faith? . . . .

We are dying, but in our death we wish to hear your word of comfort, and the assurance of the Catholic world that our children will not have to bear the yoke of slavery any more. We are convinced that your mighty word will shake the leaders of the freedom-loving peoples awake.

Holy Father, this letter is not written as we would have wished. We are writing underground, by flickering lamplight, every moment expecting the arrival of the secret police. We deliberately avoid giving the exact name of this place and our own names, so as not to divulge any information to the secret police.

When this letter reaches Your Holiness, we may no longer be alive. By the time it reaches its goal, some of those who carried it on them may have been felled by the bullets of the secret police.

Holy Father, give us, those who are dying for the freedom of the faith and of your people, your blessing!

Praise be to Jesus Christ, Lord of the living and the dead!

Vilnius, in occupied Lithuania, 20 September, 1948
                    Roman Catholic Christians of the Republic of Lithuania[43]

11. TWO OFFICIAL SOVIET DOCUMENTS: A MILDER ATTITUDE (1955-6)

There are many collective farmers and workers in our republic who, while engaged in productive work and conscientiously performing their duties of citizenship, are still influenced by religious beliefs. Our party teaches us to be more considerate in our dealings with these people. It would be foolish and harmful to treat them with suspicion solely because of their religious beliefs, which are merely a residue of the past. Our struggle with religious superstitions must now be viewed as a struggle of the ideological, scientific, materialistic concept against the unscientific and religious point of view.[44]

Religion does not make people bad collective farmers, bad workers or in general bad citizens of our socialist fatherland. Each of us is probably acquainted with some believers who are industrious, conscientious and efficient in the performance of their duties. These people would undoubtedly achieve even better results, greater victories, if they did not poison their minds with religious superstitions.[45]

12.   THE SOVIET PRESS COMMENDS RELIGION (1956)

We must not forget that in the course of history religion has played a double role: art – painting, music, architecture – owes much to religion; at the same time religion has helped to exploit people and to repress their initiative in the struggle for freedom, though in this respect we must recall that we always had clergy who appeared on the scene as leaders of the masses in their battle for freedom. Thus the positive significance of religion today is that many of our older generation have been brought up under certain religious precepts forbidding stealing, lying, and so on. On the other hand, we have many who, though irreligious, are not necessarily immoral.

Religion is no obstacle to an educated man. Present day religion is so modernized and makes so many allowances that one cannot say that it hinders the development of science, engineering or art. The technical and scientific progress of mankind can be clearly seen, even in countries where religion has a certain legal status, where scientists are religious men. Conversely, art – especially painting – when we compare it to that of previous centuries, has sunk to a much lower level, even though the twentieth century is noticeably more godless.

Religion does not repress a worker's or a farmer's initiative, for it does not urge him to work badly or not to work at all. Holy days and religious services, with their music, hymns, ceremony and glitter, are a pleasant habit, especially for the older generation, and have not been replaced – nor can they be replaced – by cinema or other cultural entertainment, of which there is too little and which is not always cultural.

In the olden days, the few atheists in Lithuania led exemplary lives and merely contended with their state-protected clerical adversaries.

Among present-day atheists we find many unsavoury, loose-living individuals. So it is impossible to say who is better: the person who goes to church or the one who frequents the bar. This question is far too complex to be solved easily . . . But the religious bigot and antireligious fanatic are both comically stupid: one believes in superstitions while the other attacks them. It is not clear what the one believes or why; neither is it clear what the other is attacking, nor why he becomes so excited about religion, if God and the rest are all a fiction.[46]

13.   THE ATHEIST EDUCATION CAMPAIGN, 1964

Measures to strengthen the atheist education of the population
[original title]

The Ideological Commission of the Central Committee of the CPSU has worked out its programme, "Measures to Strengthen the Atheist Education of the Population . . ."

Scientific solution of the problems of atheism and the preparation of anti-religious specialists

The decision has been taken to create an Institute of Scientific Atheism in the Academy of Social Sciences under the Central Committee of the CPSU. The task of the Institute will be to lead and co-ordinate all scientific work in the field of atheism which is being conducted by the institutes of the USSR Academy of Sciences, the higher educational establishments and the institutions of the USSR Ministry of Culture. It will also prepare personnel with advanced qualifications, solve complex vital problems of scientific atheism and organize all-union scientific conferences and theoretical seminars. On the academic council of the Institute of Scientific Atheism there will be representatives of the Ideological Department of the Central Committee of the CPSU, the central scientific and ideological foundations and social organizations . . . .

Atheist courses for personnel

From the 1964-65 academic year there will be a compulsory course (with examination) in "The Fundamentals of Scientific Atheism" at universities and in the medical, agricultural and pedagogical institutes of the higher educational system. In other higher educational establishments an elective course will be taught . . . . Syllabuses and text-books are being prepared which take into account the special needs of the students. A compulsory course of seminar studies is envisaged in teaching plans and programmes, as well as the preparation of extended essays and taking examinations in practical atheism. The atheist content of courses in the natural sciences and the humanities will be strengthened . . . .

The introduction of seminars on questions of atheist education is recommended. These will be for party, soviet and trade union workers and activists, for teachers, doctors, Pioneer [pre-Komsomol] leaders and assistants in pre-school establishments . . . .

Using all means of ideological coercion in atheist education

Together with the Central Committee of the Komsomol, the Trades Union Council and the USSR Ministry of Culture, the All-Union *Znanie* ["knowledge"] Society will hold a consultation on questions of improving the organization and content of scientific atheist propaganda in lectures . . . .

The government committee for cinematography of the USSR Council of Ministers envisages an annual output of films on atheist themes: artistic, popular-scientific, documentary and cartoons. It is intended to show atheist films on television and free of charge in institutes of cultural education and in schools . . . .

It is intended to improve the methods of publishing atheist literature, to broaden its thematic content, to use various literary genres and to elevate its ideological, political and publicistic level. The government committee on the press of the USSR Council of Ministers is entrusted with the task of formulating an outline plan for the future publication of atheist literature, including an increased quantity in the languages of the nationalities and also special works for children and adolescents . . . .

The All-Union Trades Union Council, the USSR Ministry of Culture and the *Znanie* Society are recommended to strengthen the material and technical basis of the atheist campaign in lectures and in the programme of cultural education. They should also activate the atheist campaign in museums, especially those devoted to historical and regional studies, in planetaria, mobile exhibitions and motor clubs, and they should increase the production of filmstrips, and so on.

. . . .

In order to inculcate non-religious festivals and rituals more deeply upon the life of Soviet people, it is intended to hold a meeting of party, soviet, Komsomol and trades union officials, together with ethnographers, propagandists and ZAGS [marriage-registry] representatives.

The atheist education of children and adolescents

The anti-religious emphasis of school curricula is to be strengthened, especially in social studies. Methodological text-books on anti-religious education in schools will be issued for teachers. It is suggested that various forms of extra-curricular and after-school activity (atheists' clubs and corners, lectures, talks, parties, excursions, and cultural expeditions to the cinema and theatre) should be widely used for the atheist education of schoolchildren . . . .

Controlling the observation of Soviet legislation on religion

So as to prevent illegal activity among the clergy, religious groups and individual believers, there is to be an increase in the control over safeguarding children and adolescents from their influence and from parental compulsion to carry out religious rites . . . .

The commissions controlling the observation of the laws on religion under the district or town executive committees of the soviets of Workers' Deputies are to be more active in their work.

The organization of the atheist campaign

Local party organizations are obliged to appoint Communists who will be responsible for the organization of the atheist campaign and to unite round them groups of public-spirited people concerned with propaganda and the organization of active atheism in factories, on building sites, in *kolkhozy* and *sovkhozy,* in institutions, schools, Pioneer organizations, and so on . . . .[47]

14. A PRIEST'S CRITICISMS OF THE STATE'S ATTITUDE TO THE CHURCH, 1966

[This is a unique example of the Church's criticisms of society being published in a Soviet source]

My meeting was with a priest. He was just under sixty years old, but had hardly any wrinkles on his face; a thin, healthy-looking, unsmiling man, in civilian clothes.

"I don't understand what you would like to hear from a servant of a church which you don't belong to . . . You should have gone to the diocesan authorities instead . . . Am I afraid to speak without their permission? No, indeed. We receive instructions from them only on doctrinal questions. But I can merely express a personal opinion except, of course, on matters over which servants of the Church can hardly disagree. What are these matters? All right, I'll tell you. Neither I nor other priests hide our attitude to these things . . .

"Our church, as you know well, is in step with the times. This is evident in all the sessions of the Vatican Council, its appeal to the community of Christian churches, its tolerance towards all other religions, its condemnation of rich people's selfishness, of racial prejudice, the Pope's condemnation of the atomic bomb . . . And the Communists of Europe admit, value and respect the efforts of the Catholic Church to make the world more just than it is at present. European Communists try to find a common language with Catholics; they don't make religious faith an object of attack, but call on priests to work together with them. But here? . . . I am deprived of the right to teach children the word of God . . . I cannot engage in charitable works, either, for now welfare grants and pensions have been established and there is no need for philanthropic organizations. I am the spiritual leader of my parishioners, but outside the church, when these parishioners are transformed into citizens, they have no right to elect me as their representative in any official capacity. I know the thoughts and problems of the local inhabitants as no one else does, because it is to me that they confess their sins, but when the authorities make decisions concerning their lives, they do not ask for the opinion of one who knows them . . . I am an outcast . . . I go out on the street in civilian clothes, to avoid the insults of rude young men. And what is the result of all this? The result is alcoholism, which was formerly almost unknown in Lithuania, hooliganism, which the police are unable to deal with, theft on such a scale that the law is helpless, although it is much more severe than it used to be, and divorces, which never used to happen here . . ."

He said the same thing as an old man I met in a village near Vilnius. Obviously, the opinions of people left behind by the new life are almost alike. And he spoke with feeling, although he had begun in a very cool manner. Forgetting his office, forgetting to be polite, he almost prevented me from expressing a contradictory opinion. I could not answer that I also value the Vatican Council, but that it is not a benevolent organization – it is necessary to the Catholic Church; that, even if western Communists were trying to unite their activities with those of Catholics, the Church forbids such united action; that, in his annoyance at atheist power, which has removed the clergy from secular affairs, he himself was being intolerant, as he compared atheists to a lower breed of animals in all his sermons – so I was told. I could, in short, have said many truthful things, but he did not want to hear them and I felt that the problem was not one of proofs. After all, his arguments were based wholly on the fact that his pride was hurt. . . .

He himself admitted this and betrayed his feelings when, at the end of our conversation, he commented agitatedly:

"The clergy are more educated than the majority of Communists; there are many Latinists, linguists, gifted and well-spoken people among us . . . A priest is a man, and he cannot be contented when his intellectual powers are wasted, when he finds the road closed to wider activity on behalf of the people."[48]

15. THE FAITHFUL'S VIEW OF THE GOVERNMENT'S WAR AGAINST RELIGION, 1974

The atheist government is not satisfied with propaganda, but also takes advantage of well-planned administrative measures. Under the Council of Ministers of the USSR there is a Council for Religious Affairs, which officially sees that the laws governing religious cults are observed. In reality, this agency uses administrative means to fight against religion throughout the Soviet Union.

In Lithuania there is an office of the executive for Religious Affairs, which wages a war on religion adapted to local circumstances. Councils for the co-ordination of atheist action function in the capitals of the republics. Their affiliates are the district atheist councils*, presided over by the vice-chairman of the district Executive Committee.

Within the boundaries of the district these officials have almost unlimited authority to terrorize priests, interfering with their work. Usually these interventions are made verbally, with the official crushing in his hand some secret instruction taken out of the safe. The atheists have no desire to leave their shameful documents for history.

Every section of the country has its atheist council, whose task is to organize atheist action, to spy on the priests' work and on believers.

The KGB assiduously watches the religious situation in Lithuania, since any more open expression of religion is considered a threat to the Soviet Government.

The present situation of the Catholic Church is causing deep concern both in the Central Committee of the Communist Party and in the KGB. Believers are going to church in great numbers, receiving the sacraments and even daring to defend their rights.

Moscow demands that the atheists in Lithuania, in their war on the Church, make use of the means tested in Russia after the October Revolution. In Lithuania however, the desired results are more difficult to achieve, since the headquarters of Catholics are not in Moscow, but Rome.[49]

*Official title: Commission for the Supervision of Implementation of Laws on Religious Cults by the Executive Committees of Soviets of Workers' Deputies [author's note].

16. DOCUMENTARY PROOF OF ILLEGAL GOVERNMENT CONTROL

[This document is undated, but the final paragraph clearly refers to Vatican II and therefore puts it post-1965.]

Government Instruction to Soviet Agencies
(Official)

"Catholicism in Lithuania and the present"

Method of Collecting

Material on the above-mentioned theme should be gathered for scientific purposes, in order to understand more deeply the dynamics of contemporary Catholicism and of other faiths. Material is to be gathered in all its aspects: preaching activities and other forms of pastoral work, the role of the active church element in the community of believers and in the activities of ministers of religion; the material base of religious propaganda (such as churches, cultic objects, choirs) and the modernization of worship should be watched.

Preaching Activities

Those chosen to monitor sermons should be active atheists with sufficient education. Without participating actively in religious practices, but behaving politely, the atheist attentively listens to sermons and later reconstructs their content, adding nothing of his own. The report of the sermon should contain the following information:

(a) The place (region, church), time (date, hour), the preacher's name and where he is from.

(b) The contents of the sermon should be reconstructed as fully and correctly as possible, in strict keeping with the principle of objectivity.

In no way is one allowed to incorporate one's own comments or deductions into the contents of the sermon. Personal remarks, comments, and conclusions may be submitted under the heading "Remarks", after the description of the sermon's contents.

(c) Form of the sermon: whether the speaker read from notes, used an outline, spoke without notes or outline; shortcomings of the sermon; other means used by the preacher to influence the believers.

In the remarks one should indicate how many believers took part in the devotions (split into men, women, young people, school children). State who served at the devotions (adults or children). Describe the religious services, their solemnity and emotionalism (organ, choir, orchestra, soloists); the participation of the faithful (whether they sang, prayed from books, made responses); who took up the collection (the priest or a representative of the active parish element).

Other Pastoral Work of the Priest

(a) The priest and the faithful.
   Is the priest active in pastoral work? If so, how can this be seen? Does
   he adapt his work to different groups of the faithful (men, women,
   young people, children)? Does he observe Soviet law concerning
   religious cults? If he does not, then note concrete instances of his
   breaking the law. What peculiarities are there in the pastoral work of
   this priest? (The opinion of the faithful about the priest.)

(b) The priest and children.
   Does the priest try to increase parental responsibility for the religious
   education of children? If so, by what means? How are the children of
   believing parents prepared for catechization and for the Sacrament of
   Confirmation?

(c) The situation of the priest, his personal life.
   Relationship of the priest to local intelligentsia. Cultural life of the
   priest (television, radio, telephone, newspaper subscriptions, books
   read, visits to the theatre, concerts).

Active Elements of the Parish

It is necessary to indicate the basic demographics of the active
element of the church: its executive committee, board of trustees and
church choir:-

   i) sex: men, women;
   ii) age: 18-25, 26-30, etc.;
   iii) education: elementary (completed or otherwise); intermediate (completed or otherwise); higher education (graduated or otherwise), and
   so on;
   iv) social status: worker, member of collective farm; white-collar worker;
   pensioner or housewife;
   v) occupation: indicate duties of working members of the active element
   of parish in manufacturing collectives:
   vi) participation of parish council members in community life: indicate
   members of the parish council actively engaged in social life, in art co-
   operatives, political groups and so on.

Go on to describe the relationship of the active church element
with the parish priest and other clergy. Do the executive committee of
the religious community and its board of trustees make use of their
rights, as provided in the Soviet law pertaining to religious cults, or has
the parish priest usurped these? The role of the unorganized active
church element in the parish (devout women and any monks and nuns
that may remain) should also be described.

The Material Base of the Religious Community

(a) Facilities for Worship.
   The condition of the exterior and surroundings of the chapel should be
   described, whether it has been renovated or not, whether the church

yard is clean or otherwise; and whether there are gardens or rockeries. Describe the interior of the chapel, whether it is painted, decorated, wired for electricity, or has a public address system. Are there any signs of modernism in the arrangement of the interior and the decorations?

(b) Bells and their use.

The liturgical vestments and their condition, whether they are in good order, clean, worn or neglected; the quality of objects used in church processions, the baldachino, chalices, shrines, banners: all these should be itemised and described.

The Attitude of the Faithful Toward the Modernizing of Cult

How do the believers regard the introduction of the vernacular into worship? What do they think of the reduction of the fast before communion to one hour? What do they think of the other liturgical innovations?[50]

17. A CATHOLIC VIEW OF THE ATHEIST ADMINISTRATION, 1973

In February 1973 Justas Rugienis, head of the Lithuanian Council for Religious Affairs, was succeeded by Kazimieras Tumenas.

Rugienis, a veteran of the KGB, often behaved like a Chekist [member of Stalin's secret police] in the course of performing his duties – chiding, scolding and threatening priests. Tumenas is a party worker and has a degree in history. In 1964 he graduated from the Academy of Social Sciences in Moscow and afterwards worked as a leader of the lecturers' group in the Central Committee of the Communist Party of Lithuania.

The change bodes no good for the church in Lithuania. Tumenas, it appears, will be more tactful, but like Rugienis he will carry on the job of wrecking the Church.[51]

NOTES TO CHAPTER II

1. Vardys, *Lithuania under the Soviets*, pp. 66-84.
2. A. Dallin, *German Rule in Russia*, London and New York, 1957, p. 185.
3. *Nepriklausoma Lietuva* ("Free Lithuania"), 15 June 1943, quoted in K. V. Tauras, *Guerilla Warfare on the Amber Coast*, New York, 1962, p. 30.
4. They are listed in Pelekis, *Genocide: Lithuania's Threefold Tragedy*, p. 167.
5. Pelekis, *op. cit.*, pp. 135-8.
6. J. Aničas, *The Establishment of Socialism in Lithuania and the Catholic Church* [in English], Vilnius, 1975, pp. 30-57.
7. Savasis, *The War Against God in Lithuania*, p. 23.
8. Pelekis, *op. cit.*, p. 126.
9. *I Laisve* (underground partizan publication), 25 May 1943.
10. Vardys, *op. cit.*, pp. 240-1.
11. Nikita Struve, *Christians in Contemporary Russia*, London, 1967, pp. 76-7.
12. K. Pakštas, *Lithuania and World War II*, Chicago, 1947, p. 43.
13. *Lithuanian Bulletin*, Vol. IV, No. 1, January 1946, p. 14.
14. *Ibid.*, Vol. IV, No. 4, November 1946, p. 5.
15. Vardys, *op. cit.*, p. 96.
16. *Ibid.*, pp. 223-4.
17. *Pravda*, Moscow, 11 November 1954.
18. *Tiesa*, Vilnius, 11 December 1956.
19. See, for example, D. A. Lowrie and William C. Fletcher, "Khrushchev's Religious Policy 1959-64" in ed. R. Marshall, *Aspects of Religion in the Soviet Union, 1917-67*, Chicago, 1971; Michael Bourdeaux, *Religious Ferment in Russia: Protestant Opposition to Soviet Religious Policy*, London 1968; Michael Bourdeaux, *Patriarch and Prophets: Persecution of the Russian Orthodox Church Today*, London, 1970.
20. Vardys, *op. cit.*, p. 224.
21. *Ibid.*, p. 229.
22. Savasis, *op. cit.*, pp. 52-67.
23. *Ibid.*, pp. 40-1.
24. See, for example, *Ite, Missa Est*, Vilnius, 1960.
25. Michael Bourdeaux, *Opium of the People*, London 1965, pp. 109-122.
26. Bourdeaux, *Patriarch and Prophets*, pp. 32-3.
27. Bourdeaux, *Religious Ferment in Russia*, pp. 33-4.
28. *RCL* 6, 1975, p. 9.
29. J. Rimaitis, *Religion in Lithuania*, Vilnius, 1971, p. 21 (published in English and other western languages, apparently as a propaganda exercise).
30. Rimaitis, *op. cit.*, p. 19.
31. *Loc. cit.*
32. *RCL* 4, 1976, p. 27; *Izvestia*, 30 August 1966.
33. *Vedomosti Verkhovnogo Soveta RSFSR*, Moscow, 3 July 1975, pp. 487-91.
34. Bourdeaux, *Patriarch and Prophets*, p. 193.
35. For an analysis of the contents of the early issues, see Peter Reddaway, *Uncensored Russia*, London, 1972.
36. For fuller details, see "Self-Immolation as National Protest" in the report by the Lithuanian American Community, *The Violations of Human Rights in Soviet Occupied Lithuania. A Report for 1972*, Delran, NJ, 1973, pp. 17-24; *Chronicle of Current Events*, 26, 1972, pp. 22-5, and 27, 1972, pp. 17-20.

37. Bohdan R. Bociurkiw, "Religious Dissent in the USSR: Lithuanian Catholics", pp. 18-19. Now published in *Marxism and Religion in Eastern Europe,* ed. R. T. de George and J. P. Scanlon, papers presented at the Banff International Slavic Conference, 4-17 September 1974; Sovietica, Vol. 36, Dordrecht, Holland 1976, pp. 147-75. All footnote references are to the manuscript article as the published work appeared only when *Land of Crosses* was at proof stage.
38. Georgi Vins, *Three Generations of Suffering,* London, 1976.
39. *RCL* 1, 1976, p. 48.
40. *Sovetskaya Litva,* Vilnius, 12 August 1972.
41. *CLCC* 6, 1973, p. 10 (E), p. 5 (L).
42. *Lithuanian Bulletin,* Vol. 1, No. 5, July 1943, pp. 5-7. The war conditions of the time make it impossible to check the provenance of this document, nor have we traced the original, of which this is a summary.
43. Gelžinis, *Christenverfolgung in Litauen,* pp. 39-53.
44. *Tiesa,* 10 August 1955.
45. *Ibid.,* 21 October 1956.
46. *Ibid.,* 11 December 1956.
47. *Sovetskoe gosudarstvo i pravo* ("The Soviet State and Law"), Moscow 1 January 1965, pp. 42-5. Translation taken from Bourdeaux, *Patriarch and Prophets,* pp. 39-43.
48. *Nauka i religia,* Moscow, April 1966, p. 38.
49. *CLCC* 10, pp. 9-10 (E), pp. 3-4 (L).
50. *CLCC* 6, pp. 17-20 (E), pp. 7-9 (L).
51. *Ibid.,* p. 24 (E), p. 10 (L).

III

KREMLIN OR VATICAN RULE?

OF ALL the provisions of the Soviet Constitution, the "separation of the Church from the State" is one of the furthest removed in practice from the theory. Indeed, certain stipulations of the law, such as that requiring religious associations to register, the right of the State to refuse such an application and to exclude individuals from membership of a congregation's executive body,[1] directly contradict the constitutional provisions, even though individual laws are supposed to clarify and uphold the "supreme law" of the Constitution.

The total disregard of the Soviet regime for its own Constitution was as evident in the destruction of the leadership of the Lithuanian Catholic Church immediately after the second occupation as it was during Stalin's comparable treatment of the Russian Orthodox hierarchy after 1927. The new Soviet rulers either destroyed or severely weakened every aspect of organized religious activity. Catholic societies, publications and educational work, already devastated during the first Soviet occupation, had not been able to recover during the period of Nazi rule. Diocesan administration has never at any time been abolished, but the Soviet aim was to paralyse it by the arrest and deportation, even the death, of the bishops. The regime did not mount show trials of religious leaders, but by the time the stage was set for such trials in Poland and Hungary, the Lithuanian hierarchy had already been devastated. Before the end of 1947 three of the four diocesan bishops and one auxiliary had disappeared at the orders of the Soviet authorities. Archbishop J. Skvireckas and two other auxiliary bishops had already fled to the West in 1944.

The Archbishop of Vilnius, Mečislovas Reinys, was arrested and deported in 1947, after being forced to sign a statement proclaiming that the Catholic Church enjoyed full freedom and prosperity under the Soviet regime. He received a sentence of eight years and was sent to the notorious prison in the old Russian town of Vladimir, where he died in 1953.[2]

The Bishop of Telšiai, Vincentas Borisevičius, was shot in 1947 after a secret trial in Vilnius the previous October. Several Jewish witnesses whose lives the bishop had saved under the Nazis came to his defence, but he was condemned as a "bourgeois nationalist leader". He is reported to have said on being sentenced, "Your hour of victory is brief. The future is mine. Christ will be victorious just as my Lithuania will be victorious."[3]

Their example, like that of other Lithuanian martyrs, has inspired the faithful ever since and made them even more determined to resist the inroads of atheism into the life of the Church:

> We remember the death in the camps of Bishops Reinys and Borisevičius and of a number of priests. We honour the holy martyrs who have adorned the history of the Church. We should bow our heads before their resolution, bravery and sacrifice; we should learn from this and imitate it. We bow our heads, too, before the brave ones of our own time.[4]

The later life of Bishop Teofilius Matulionis of Kaišiadorys was a story of repeated sufferings, yet heroically he survived them to die a natural death in 1962 at the age of 89. He was serving in Russia at the time of the Revolution and appeared with Bishop Cieplak in the first Soviet show-trial against religion in March, 1923. There were fifteen other defendants in this notorious case, one of whom, Father Constantin Budkiewicz, was subsequently executed. The sentence passed on Matulionis was three years, but his release was followed, a few years later, by a further arrest and a sequence of camps. In 1929 he was secretly consecrated a bishop in Leningrad; this was followed by a sentence of ten years and transfer to the Solovki prison in the White Sea. Finally, in 1933 as a Lithuanian subject he had the good fortune to be exchanged by the Soviet Government, together with twelve other priests, for twenty-six Communists imprisoned in Lithuania. Directly after his return to Lithuania in 1933, Bishop Matulionis said:

> I am thankful to God that I could suffer for Christ. And if I could suffer more for Him I would do that with pleasure.[5]

He was indeed destined to suffer more for Christ. Through all the ordeals of the triple occupation of Lithuania Bishop Matulionis stayed faithfully with his suffering people. He became Bishop of Kaišiadorys in 1943 and he stood out against Soviet interference in the internal affairs of the Church after the war.[6] Although now well into his seventies, he had to face another decade of prison from 1946. Then, after the death of Stalin, the prison camps began to empty. Many people, long since thought dead, began to re-appear in the towns and villages, their former homes. The return of Bishop Matulionis, his face bearing the suffering of the cross, was like a miracle to the faithful. Although he was refused the right to resume the administration of his diocese, he could say Mass at Birštonas, his place of residence, a fact which the Soviet propaganda machine exploited to illustrate the "freedom" of religion in the USSR.[7] He even secretly consecrated Vincentas Sladkevičius as an auxiliary bishop, and for this he was sent to Šeduva. He never regained his health, but remained alive until 1962, a potent spiritual influence and sign of hope to his people to the end.

The Auxiliary Bishop of Telšiai, Pranas Ramanauskas, was also among those who returned in the 1950's. In 1947 he had been forced to give written evidence against himself, enumerating his crimes and those of the Catholic Church against the Soviet Government. Part of his 'confession' reads as follows:

> I am guilty of many things with regard to Soviet society . . . While I have been in prison, I have had the opportunity to think seriously and realise that life continues on the path of progress, that those who do not march in step with life are brushed aside.[8]

His health broken by ten years in Siberian camps, he died on 17 October 1959, only three years after his return to Lithuania.

Bishop Kazimieras Paltarokas of Panevežys did not meet the same immediate fate as the other three diocesan bishops. Some say this was because of his old age (he was 70 in 1945), but he was younger than Bishop Matulionis and lived on until 1958. Possibly he was spared because he was the only bishop who agreed to appeal to the partisans to lay down their arms. Most likely too the regime needed one bishop at liberty for propaganda purposes. However, he did not really compromise with the atheists, as becomes apparent from a recent document of the highest importance, published in the unofficial *Chronicle of the Lithuanian Catholic Church* (Document 18). This is a letter written by Fr. Pranas Račiunas on 20 March 1974, replying to an attack against him earlier that month in *Kauno Tiesa* ("Kaunas Truth"). The letter demonstrates the total failure of the regime to achieve its aim of cutting off contact between the leadership of the Lithuanian Catholic Church and the Vatican. In 1947 Fr. Račiunas managed to go to Moscow and contact Fr. Laberge, then chaplain at the American Embassy, "to request him to obtain the Pope's permission to consecrate new bishops for Lithuania". He went "at the request of his spiritual superiors", because Bishop Paltarokas "could not consecrate new bishops without the permission of the Vatican". This act earned Fr. Račiunas a sentence of twenty-five years, of which he served sixteen without even being brought to trial.

Soviet concessions on religion are relative. After the almost total purge of the Church leadership under Stalin there came a brief respite. On 11 November 1955 Bishop Paltarokas consecrated Julijonas Steponavičius as Bishop of Panevežys and Petras Maželis as Bishop of Telšiai.[9] The Pope had authorized this step and it seems that the Soviet authorities also countenanced it.

Of these two, only Bishop Maželis was able to exercise his office for long. He was then 61, but he was ill and based at Telšiai, at some distance from the main problems of the administration of the Lithuanian Church.[10] Bishop Steponavičius (born 1911), who was consecrated on the same day, fell victim to Khrushchev's anti-religious purge six years later, in 1961, and was exiled to the village of Žagare. At the end of 1971 a group of 134 priests from his diocese of

Panevežys claimed that the reason for his removal was that he had "carried out his pastoral duties as a shepherd without compromise".[11] In April 1972 he sent a letter to the Soviet Government demanding the right to resume his duties, but Rugienis turned down the request.[12] On 20 July that year a parish priest, Fr. B. Laurinavičius, sent a long letter to Rugienis in which he took up the case of Bishop Steponavičius, declaring that he was totally innocent of any crime and stating that, as he had been accused of none, the law was being broken in this denial of a Soviet citizen's legal rights. He should be restored to his proper duties "because the Archdiocese of Vilnius needs a ruler in the real sense of the word".[13] No one has ever even given an official explanation for the bishop's exile, though there is no doubt that the real reason was the total lack of compromise with which Bishop Steponavičius undertook his duties (Document 19). An atheist lecturer, Jonas Aničas, came close to admitting this when he spoke at the Vilnius Institute of Zoology on 12 September 1974:

> Some priests were teaching children and involving them in active participation in church services. When it was necessary to approach Bishop Steponavičius for him to restrain such priests, he refused point-blank. Therefore, he was invited to move to Žagare.[14]

Bishop Steponavičius himself has stated (Document 19) that his exile was due to his refusal to comply with certain official atheist policies: he would not forbid priests to hold confirmation or first communion classes for children or to permit children to serve at the altar; he would not agree to ban from ecclesiastical activity priests who had no government registration; he opposed government-inspired expulsions of students from the seminary. The bishop based his refusal to comply with these policies on Soviet law and the Constitution of the USSR.

The faithful, far from forgetting Bishop Steponavičius, hold him up as their "pride" and inspiration, perhaps even more so recently, now that the State seems determined to make his position worse rather than better.[15] In 1970, sixty-one priests of Vilnius Archdiocese wrote a petition to Brezhnev and Kosygin, asking for the reinstatement of Bishop Steponavičius as acting administrator of his diocese (Document 20). Despite his exile, he has just occasionally been able to make an appearance, such as on 7 March 1974, when he was one of 3 bishops and 180 priests present at the funeral of Canon Petras Rauda at Svedasai in his own diocese.[16]

The Lithuanian faithful often mention the other banned bishop, Vincentas Sladkevičius of Kaišiadorys, in the same breath and with the same reverence as Bishop Steponavičius. His time in active office was even shorter. The authorities barred him from exercising his duties eighteen months after his secret consecration on 25 December 1957 at the age of 37 by Bishop Matulionis.[17] The Soviet authorities are using his consecration "without the knowledge of the Lithuanian Government" as an excuse for banning him from office.[18] Lithuanian believers are making a spirited attempt to win back the right of Bishop Sladkevičius to officiate in his diocese, as the conversation which Canon Jonas Pilka had with Tumenas, the successor of Rugienis, reveals (Document 21).

Although believers have expressed concern for his health,[19] he leads an active life, while confined in the village of Nemunelio Radviliškis. He was reported in 1973 as being especially concerned with teaching religion to children and in confirming them (Document 22). When the fifteenth anniversary of his exile fell on 17 March 1974 he received "stacks of greetings".[20] Here there is a resemblance to the case of Bishop Afanasi of the Russian Orthodox Church who, after thirty-three years as a bishop – during which he was able to spend only one-twelfth of his time officiating in his diocese – nevertheless received over 200 gift parcels from the faithful in the last year of his exile in 1954.[21]

In July 1974, forty-five priests from the diocese of Bishop Slad-kevičius appealed to the Soviet Government in vain for permission for him to resume his episcopal duties.[22]. So, although he is impeded (impeditus) from carrying out his duties, in Vatican sources available in Lithuania at the time he was listed merely as sedi datus (assigned to his see), which angered many Lithuanians because it did not represent the full truth.[23]

However, it is perhaps a sign of the times that on 27 January 1977, at a service in Kapsukas (formerly Marijampole) commemorating the fiftieth anniversary of the death of the Lithuanian Archbishop Matulevičius, one of the two bishops celebrating the jubilee Mass turned out to be Sladkevicius. The latter also preached the sermon to a crowded congregation, urging those present to follow the path of sacrifice. His appearance was a complete surprise to most of those present, but had obviously been permitted by the Soviet authorities as a calculated concession to Roman Catholic feeling in Lithuania. This point was emphasized by the *Lithuanian Chronicle* in its report on the anniversary service. The editors state that even six years ago in 1971, on the hundredth anniversary of the birth of Archbishop Matu-levičius, no one would have dared to mention Bishop Sladkevicius publicly and it would have been quite unthinkable for him to celebrate Mass or deliver a sermon in Marijampole. "This change of mood clearly proves that the sacrifices made in the fight for the Church's freedom have not been in vain."[24]

Neither the "soft line" of the mid-1950's nor the later, much toughter, atheist policy of Khrushchev won the gains against the Lithuanian Church for which the Soviets had hoped. Of all republics in the Soviet Union, Lithuania remained the most united in its religious loyalties. The Council for Religious Affairs gained no allegiance for Communism by acting against the bishops. Perhaps, then, new church leaders could be found who would act in the interests of the Council, while appearing to use their own authority and that of the Church? This, after all, is precisely what the Soviet authorities had had some success in achieving with the Moscow leadership of both the Baptists and the Orthodox in the early 1960's.[25] The policy henceforth would be to divide and rule, to elevate a pliant leadership, to isolate and remove those who objected. The recurrence of the pattern in Lithuania is of great significance in assessing the real nature of current Soviet atheist policies, while the failure of the Soviets to achieve anything like the same degree of success in Lithuania highlights this. The unity among Lithuanian Catholics is the clear reason for the lack of success. In other parts of the Soviet Union, manipulation of the Church and its leaders has led to serious schisms.

The clearest exposé of current Soviet policies is contained in what is in fact an open letter to the Vatican, though not designated as such, included as the introductory article to No. 10 of the *Lithuanian Chronicle* (Document 23). The dominant theme of this anonymous but authoritative essay is: "Do not make a single move to recognize the attempt of the State to appoint untrustworthy men to key positions".

Bishop Juozapas Pletkus, who became vicar capitular of the Diocese of Telšiai in 1966 at the age of 71, after the death of Bishop Maželis, does not seem to have attracted much attention from the atheists and his name only infrequently features in the voluminous information coming from the faithful in Lithuania. The Vatican nominated him apostolic administrator in 1967 and in February 1968 he was consecrated bishop. He died on 21 September 1975 and was replaced by an administrator, Mgr. Antanas Valančius.

It is the three other new bishops consecrated in the 1960's (Matulaitis-Labukas, Povilonis and Krikščiunas) whose activities come under intense scrunity. Though between them they have had a great deal to say for western consumption which compromises their integrity, criticism of them as people is more cautious than that which has frequently been expressed by Soviet Baptists and Orthodox about some of their leaders.

The most stringent criticism so far of the alleged compromise made by these leaders came in 1972, when part of the editorial of No. 4 of the *Lithuanian Chronicle* carried the heading: "Church leaders are co-opted to serve the purpose of the atheists" (Document 24). The criticism singled out the words of the bishops as the first target, but went on to illustrate how they are obliged to manipulate their clergy and place them at the whim of the atheist authorities.

The evidence on the Bishop of Kaunas, Juozapas Matulaitis-Labukas, clearly shows a man struggling to do what he can to maintain his ministry in conditions of extreme difficulty. His consecration took place in Rome in December 1965 during the last session of the

Second Vatican Council, which he had received permission to attend.[26] Every April he has ordained the handful of seminarians ready for the priesthood,[27] even though he was criticised in 1974 for holding the service during working hours on 9 April (a Tuesday), which the faithful believed to be a compromise.

Matulaitis-Labukas has kept his compromising rhetoric to the basic minimum – or perhaps even below it – for he has resolutely refused to denounce the *Lithuanian Chronicle:*

> It is no secret that KGB officials came to Bishop Matulaitis-Labukas, Apostolic Administrator of the Dioceses of Kaunas and Vilkaviškis, with a demand that he should condemn the *Chronicle of the Lithuanian Catholic Church* in a pastoral letter. The bishop refused to satisfy their demands, stating that such a step would compromise the clergy in the eyes of the faithful, as had already occurred with the attempt to condemn the memorandum with 17,000 signatures.

> At the beginning of September, Bishop Labukas and other diocesan bishops received an anonymous letter in the name of a 'group of priests of the Diocese of Vilkaviškis', in which the 'reactionary' clergy of the diocese are criticized. It further contained the demand that when Bishop Labukas was next in Rome he should go on Vatican Radio to censure those who were trying to 'turn back the wheel of history'. The priests of Lithuania do not exclude the possibility that the KGB might force Bishop Labukas to take this letter to the Vatican as evidence of what 'real' priests think about the present position of the Lithuanian Catholic Church.[28]

Whether or not he was forced to take the letter, the bishop did not carry out the threat when he visited the Vatican in 1974. One can see the kind of pressure he has been under from the way Rugienis tried to force his hand over the posting of a priest, Fr. Vytautas Pesliakas, from one parish to another where his duties would be less. The State used the latter's absence from his parish on sick leave as the occasion for removing him. He refused to go, claiming that this was the doing of the State, not the ecclesiastical authority. Bishop Labukas suspended him, but eventually "the suspension was lifted by Bishop Labukas and Fr. Pesliakas went on a second medical leave," after which he had to go to the new place to which he was assigned, but not on active duty.[29] Fr. Pesliakas made his position clear to other bishops and he received one reply which gives a deeply-felt commentary on the tortured situation (Document 25).

In December 1972 Bishop Labukas took steps to protect the churches of his diocese against what the *Lithuanian Chronicle* calls the "marked increase in the incidence of burglaries and desecration of churches."[30]

However, Bishop Labukas was 84 years old in 1978; as he is also partially blind, he is rumoured to have recently submitted his resignation. [He has since died on 28 May 1979.]

In looking at the two new episcopal consecrations of 21 December 1969,[31] one can deduce that not all the concessions came from the

Church. While the *Lithuanian Chronicle* has had criticisms to make of Bishop Krikščiunas, Auxiliary Bishop of Kaunas and Vilkaviškis, the consecration of Liudas Povilonis as Auxiliary Bishop of Telšiai on the same day was quite clearly a major gain for the faithful. He has been one of the heroic figures of the Lithuanian Church over the past two decades.

He was formerly a parish priest at the port of Klaipeda, on the Baltic Sea. In the "thaw" of 1954 he received permission to build a new church, but when it was finished seven years later the authorities seized the church in January 1961 and turned it into a concert hall. They accused Povilonis of illegally acquiring the building materials, and imprisoned him.* His sentence was eight years, but he received an amnesty after serving four of them. He then became assistant of the Vilnius parish of Maria Immaculata, Auxiliary Bishop of Telšiai in December 1961 and auxiliary to Bishop Matulaitis-Labukas at Kaunas in July 1973.[32]

Popular enthusiasm has swept Bishop Povilonis along on a tide which the atheists, despite strenuous efforts, have not had much success in stemming. The *Lithuanian Chronicle* paints a picture of multitudes of people thronging to hear him − 10,000 on one occasion in July 1973 in one town, with the police having to set up roadblocks to keep away people who were trying to come in hired buses from the neighbouring republic of Belorussia (Document 26). The bishop confirmed 2,600 people on that occasion.

Two months later the atheists again acted in strength, but with only partial success, to keep children away from another church where the bishop was dedicating five altars.[33]

As regards Bishop Romualdas Krikščiunas, consecrated on the same day as Bishop Povilonis in 1969, the criticisms of the faithful are sometimes severe. Nevertheless, these criticisms are not one-sided; the picture that emerges of him is one of energetic pastoral activity under conditions of severe restraint. He was only forty when he was consecrated as Auxiliary Bishop of Kaunas and Vilkaviškis, having spent four years as priest of the parish of the Resurrection in Kaunas, followed by four years in Rome, where the Soviet Government allowed him to go and study, after which he became Chancellor and later Vicar-General under Bishop Labukas.[34]

Bishop Krikščiunas has an almost established position as an international figure at Christian "peace conferences" and similar occasions; he has been criticised by the *Lithuanian Chronicle* for making statements to the foreign press exaggerating the availability of religious literature in Lithuania.[35] Nevertheless, the Soviet authorities do not seem to regard him as "their man", as an incident reported in a 1976 issue of the *Lithuanian Chronicle* demonstrates: on his return from an official visit to Rome, Bishop Krikščiunas, together with Bishop Povilonis, was subjected to a humiliating search by customs

*See pp. 174-5, 184-8.

officials in Moscow. Female customs employees acted towards them in an insulting manner, taking the bishops' rosaries and hanging them round their necks, laughing.[36] Opinion in Lithuania is divided on the reason for such behaviour on the part of the Soviet authorities: some thought the bishops had failed to fulfil tasks assigned to them by the Government, while others felt it might be a cunning move to raise the bishops' standing in the eyes of the Vatican.

In 1973 Bishop Krikščiunas even called off his confirmations at Obeliai, Alunta and Joniškelis at the behest of the atheist authorities "so as not to compromise himself"[37], yet he made up for this the next year by confirming no less than 2,860 children and young people at Obeliai, immediately after there had been a major confrontation at Kriaunos over the preparation of the local children for confirmation.[38]

In 1974 Bishop Krikščiunas ordained two priests at Panevežys Cathedral – the first ordination to have been held there since 1945. There was a big turn-out, even though the authorities ensured that the ceremony took place during working hours.[39]

Mgr. Česlovas Krivaitis, Administrator of the Archdiocese of Vilnius, addresses the foreign press more frequently and goes further in his claims on religious liberty than does Bishop Krikščiunas. For this he was criticized in 1972,[40] while the next year he gave an interview to an Italian journalist, who reported:

This senior clergyman gave me an objective account of Roman Catholic Church activities in Lithuania and of the situation of the clergy and faithful. The concrete facts he presented convinced me that the Catholic Church in Soviet Lithuania is functioning normally.[41]

Early in 1975 Mgr. Krivaitis was a member of a varied and numerous Soviet church delegation to the United States of America and his remarks there, reported back to Lithuania, caused a "storm of disapproval" (Document 27).

In the context of such criticism, it is not surprising to find the name of Mgr. Krivaitis listed (even before the visit to the USA) as one of the clergy "lacking credibility" among the faithful and therefore unsuitable for elevation to a bishopric. The authors of the *Chronicle* have done their utmost to make their views known to the Vatican (see Document 23).

One of the most pressing issues for both hierarchy and laity at the moment is the consecration of new bishops. Bishop Matulaitis is old and weak and wishes to retire, and Bishops Sladkevičius and Steponavičius are in exile, so that Lithuania now has only two active Bishops – Krikščiunas and Povilonis. In the present situation it will be hard to find candidates who would be acceptable both to the Soviet authorities and to the Lithuanian believers as a whole.

Although the degree of compromise into which the Lithuanian hierarchy has been forced seems to stop well short of that among Baptist and Orthodox leaders, the reaction to it among the clergy has been outspoken and highly organized, as we shall see.

DOCUMENTS

18. CONTACT BETWEEN LITHUANIA AND THE VATICAN

Open letter to A. Augas,
Honourable Senior Lecturer at the Kapsukas State University of Vilnius.

You wrote an article, "Behold the Cassocked Friends of the People", in issue No. 31, 1 March 1974, of *Kauno Tiesa* in which you stated:

> At the beginning of 1945 Bishop Bučys, urged by the Vatican Secretary of State, Cardinal Montini (the present Pope Paul VI) assigned the priest Pranas Račiunas to gather intelligence data about the Red Army.

> Račiunas was supposed to hand on the information to the Vatican spy Laberge, then in Moscow, he to the Vatican and the Vatican to U.S. Intelligence. Račiunas, firmly believing that the Americans would liberate Lithuania, eagerly served them.

In your article you do not mention that I was imprisoned for twenty-five years without a trial. You do not indicate the true reason for my confinement. Here it is.

By 1947 in Lithuania, the Bishop of Telšiai, Vincentas Borisevičius, his auxiliary, Bishop Pranciškus Ramanauskas, and the Bishop of Kaišiadorys, Teofilius Matulionis, were arrested. The danger loomed that the dioceses of Lithuania would be left without bishops. According to canon law, the Bishop of Panevėžys, Kazimieras Paltarokas, could not consecrate new bishops without the permission of the Vatican, but the bishop had no direct way of making contact. For this reason, upon orders from my spiritual superiors I went to Moscow to visit Fr. Laberge, chaplain at the U.S. Embassy, to request him to obtain the Pope's permission to consecrate new bishops for Lithuania. On my arrival in Moscow I obtained written permission from the local police to live temporarily in Fr. Laberge's quarters. This request was the basic reason for my imprisonment.

You accuse me of rushing "to serve them"; that is, to gather and transmit information about the Red Army. I ask you to show specifically when, where and what kind of information I gathered, and when, where and to whom I handed it on, or even tried to do so.

It seems that you have never read, or do not wish to relate accurately, the records of my interrogation, not even the account of one of the most important sessions, supervised by Lt. Col. Chistyakov, head of the interrogation section of Vilnius security police. The question of espionage against the Red Army does not figure at all, either in the records of my interrogation in 1949, or in the decision in the review of my case by the Military Tribunal of the Moscow Military Region.

I served sixteen years without seeing a judge, hearing the accusations of the prosecutor, or the testimony of witnesses, or hearing the reasoned judgment of a court, even though I demanded such a trial many times in writing, even though the Soviet Constitution guarantees every citizen of the Soviet Union the right to defend his innocence in court. The method of punishing *in absentia,* such as was used in my case, was condemned by the Soviet Communist Party Congress in 1956.

Living with professional thieves and robbers in the labour camps, I had occasion to hear that their ethic forbids the beating of a man who is bound. Among them breaking that rule is punishable by death. It is a cheap trick for you today to write articles libelling priests when it is practically impossible for the latter to refute them in the press, on radio or television.

If I, for example, were to call you, even in a private letter, a spy for the Chinese or English, you, as an innocent party, could take me to court and I should be punished for libel. But when you libel me, even publicly in the press, I cannot defend myself in that same press, even though the law provides for no exclusion of priests or believers.

Does your atheist conscience consider it honourable to abuse the situation which has developed? Should not your self-respect as a university teacher be greater than that of the criminals mentioned above? . . . .

[The author cites legal authority for the right of defence against libel.]

On what basis do you affirm that in 1945 Bishop Bučys assigned me to spy on the Red Army? Bishop Bučys left for Rome before 15 June 1941 and from the time when the Soviet Army marched into Lithuania in 1944 I had no contact with him. Read about this in the records of my interrogation.

You state categorically that Fr. Laberge was a Vatican spy. Look at the decision of the Moscow Military Tribunal in its review of my case in 1965.

There it is clearly stated: "It is not proven that Laberge was an agent of foreign intelligence." Who is to be believed? Your libellous article or the document of the Military Tribunal?

. . . .

Finally, can you submit evidence that the present Pope Paul VI (Montini) ever urged Bishop Bučys to spy on the Red Army? Can you specifically show where, under what circumstances, Pope Paul VI gave such instructions? On what documents do you base your statements? Show which records of my interrogation speak of this.

I do not know what urged you to write such untruths and to mislead the Soviet reader, libelling Pope Paul VI, the late Bishop Bučys,

Fr. Laberge and me. I do not know whether you concocted such an article, or whether someone else wrote it and you simply signed it.

Perhaps you wished in this way to serve atheist propaganda in Lithuania. However, even atheists are obliged to keep to the norm of ethics. Do you not, by such an uncritical article, lower the prestige of the honourable title of Senior Lecturer of the University of Vilnius? I do not know your moral standards. I do not know whether you, as a representative of learning, who had the nerve to write falsehood without ascertaining the facts, will have the will to apologise. An honourable person of strong character who makes an error will always do so. But after having the effrontery to defame several people, even the Pope, will you have the courage and self-respect to recant, or at least to see that *Kauno Tiesa* prints the text of my open letter?

Your article appeared in the press just a few days after the visit of the Soviet Foreign Minister, Andrei Gromyko, to Pope Paul VI. Do you think that your article, accusing a Pope of organising espionage against the Red Army, is the beginning of a new campaign against the present Pope, fitting in with the present course of Soviet foreign policy?

On the basis of Paragraph 7 of the Civil Code of the Lithuanian SSR, I demand that you legally prove the truth of the accusations you have made against me. If you cannot, you are obligated to retract these accusations. Otherwise, I retain the right to take you to court.

The Rev. Pranas Račiunas

Paluobiai, 20 March 1974.[42]

19. APPEAL BY BISHOP STEPONAVIČIUS TO THE SOVIET AUTHORITIES

It is now over fourteen years since I was dismissed from my proper duties and compelled to take up residence in a place assigned to me by the local authorities: the town of Žagare in the Joniškis district. In removing me from my post no accusation was made against me. I still do not know for what reason and for how long I am to be banished from my diocese. It is true that the then Executive for Religious Affairs, J. Rugienis, told me that I was being removed as the result of a resolution of the Council of Ministers of the Lithuanian SSR. However, the request which I made – that I be informed about the resolution, be given a copy or that it at least be read to me – was denied me by Rugienis. Wishing to remove me as soon as possible, he resorted to force and called in the help of administrative organs who compelled me to leave Vilnius and the confines of the Vilnius Diocese. It is still not clear to me, therefore, whether my removal from my current duties was effected by a resolution of the Council of Ministers of the Lithuanian SSR or by the arbitrary actions of Rugienis.

While I was at my post, I conscientiously attempted to fulfil my duties as bishop and shepherd of my flock, being concerned with the spiritual welfare of the priests and the faithful. I do not feel that I have ever infringed Soviet laws. Nowhere, never, have I done or said anything against the Soviet Union or the Soviet system.

At the suggestion of the Soviet Government I went to Hungary, and after my return I made a report on the radio. I was invited to take part in peace conferences and did so. I tried to calm down priests and believers when they had been provoked by administrative interference of government officials in the life of the Church. I also had to defend my own juridical rights when the Executive for Religious Affairs sought to limit them by administrative interference. Here is the evidence of such administrative interference.

In January 1958, when I took up my duties as apostolic administrator of the Vilnius Diocese with the rights of a resident bishop, the Executive for Religious Affairs declared that I was to inform the priests that they neither teach those preparing for first confession and Holy Communion nor carry out group examinations – that only individual examination was allowed. When I claimed that Bishop Paltarokas had gone to Moscow and reached clarification and agreement with the Council for Religious Affairs that priests could prepare children for first confession and Holy Communion in small groups and had announced the terms of this agreement in a circular after his return, the official called the agreement a fantasy of Bishop Paltarokas. When I said that I could not announce to the priests a regulation forbidding them to prepare children for first confession and Holy Communion and allowing them only to examine children individually, since this was contrary to a bishop's conscience, to canon law and the resolutions of the Synod of Bishops, the official said that if the regulation was not carried out both the priests and the bishop would experience unpleasant consequences. This was indeed the case: there were summonses against priests who did not comply with the official's ruling on the catechization of children and the bishop was constantly reprimanded.

The appointment of priests and their transfer is the prerogative of the diocesan administrator. The Executive for Religious Affairs issues a registration certificate to priests appointed to another parish. It is necessary for the priest to register in his new place of work. Exploiting his right to issue a registration certificate, the official began to interfere in the appointment of priests. The appointment of every priest has to be co-ordinated with the official. In addition the latter began to persecute some priests by taking away their registration certificates and requiring the diocesan administrator to appoint another priest in place of the one being persecuted. The priest would then be

left without either parish or pastoral work. The priests were mostly persecuted for purely ecclesiastical activity – for example, for conducting retreats for priests and the faithful. I used to defend the priests who had been wronged. I would not agree to leave them without pastoral work. I would move them to another parish and would not appoint another priest in their place until the official had issued a registration certificate to the persecuted priest who had been assigned a new parish. When I defended the wronged priests, threats were heard from the official that the diocese might be left without a bishop
. . . .

Neither was the sphere of purely spiritual matters overlooked. In 1960 the Executive for Religious Affairs informed me that children were forbidden to take part in religious rites: boys were banned from serving at Mass, girls from taking part in processions. Also forbidden were retreats for the faithful, invitations without government permission to other priests to help in annual local festivals, visits by priests to their parishioners, and the collection of alms by means of visits. Priests were not to gather in significant numbers for group retreats. The official demanded that I inform the priests of all these prohibitions in writing and remind them that those who did not comply with the restrictions would be punished. I myself was merely informed verbally of these restrictions.

After listening to these unjust and inconsistent demands, I pointed out that I could not announce them to the priests because, as a bishop of the Catholic Church:

a) I am obliged to elevate the religious and spiritual life of priests and believers and not to impede and destroy it. Canon law and the rulings of the Synod of Bishops require that priests themselves participate in retreats and that they conduct them for believers;

b) I must urge my entire flock, with no age discrimination, to take part in religious services and make zealous use of the means of salvation – prayer and the Sacraments;

c) I know of no Soviet law which forbids children to go to church and take part in liturgical services. If the laws of the State do not forbid children to accept the Sacraments of Baptism, Penance, Communion and Confirmation, then on what basis is it required that they be forbidden to take part in liturgical services, which are of less significance than the acceptance of Sacraments?

Finally, the Soviet Constitution, in common with the obligations accepted under the signature of the Soviet Government, acknowledges freedom of conscience and the practice of religious rituals without any age discrimination.

I refused to meet these demands and was removed soon after . . . .

I trust that the case of my exile will be reviewed and that I will be allowed to pursue my duties as bishop and shepherd of the Archdiocese of Vilnius.

Žagare, 15 September 1975

Apostolic Administrator of
the Archdiocese of Vilnius
Bishop Julijonas Steponavičius.[43]

20. APPEAL OF 61 VILNIUS PRIESTS IN 1970

In January 1961, for unknown reasons and without any court hearing, the Apostolic Administrator of the Archdiocese of Vilnius and of the Diocese of Panevėžys, Bishop Julijonas Steponavičius, was relieved of his duties and exiled far beyond the diocesan boundaries.

There have been cases where registration has been taken away from some priests and they were temporarily forbidden to carry out priestly duties. However, when the period of prohibition had passed, they were again allowed to work in the church. There have also been cases where a priest sentenced to imprisonment returned to his work, on the completion of his sentence, and was even promoted in his duties by the State.

We therefore ask the Soviet Government to turn its attention to this fact and to reinstate Julijonas Steponavičius in his duties as Administrator of the Archdiocese of Vilnius and Bishop of the Diocese of Panevėžys.

Signed by 61 priests, including
B. Laurinavičius.[44]

8 September 1970

21. APPEAL FOR REINSTATEMENT OF BISHOP SLADKEVIČIUS

Declaration

To the Executive of the Council for Religious Affairs in the Lithuanian SSR

We, the undersigned priests of the Diocese of Kaišiadorys, ask that the Bishop of Kaišiadorys, Vincentas Sladkevičius, now living in Nemunelio-Radviliškis, Biržai district, should be allowed to carry out his episcopal duties in the Diocese of Kaišiadorys.

30 July 1974

Sender: Canon Jonas Dzekunskas, resident of Žiežmariai, Kaišiadorys district.

Forty-five priests of Kaišiadorys Diocese signed this declaration [the names follow].

On 5 August 1974 K. Tumenas, Executive of the Council for Religious Affairs, summoned Canon Jonas Pilka, the rector of Dangai parish.

"Why are you dissatisfied with the present Administrator of Kaišiadorys?" asked the official. "I have a declaration here which you, among others, have signed. We know that you weren't the least among those who initiated this document."

"The document isn't directed against the Administrator", stated Canon Pilka. "We have a bishop, Sladkevičius, who is not being allowed to perform his duties, so while the diocese is ruled by an administrator, an abnormal situation exists."

"Yes," agreed Tumenas, "the situation is indeed abnormal, but by your declaration you've created a great deal of unpleasantness for the administrator of the Diocese of Kaišiadorys."

Tumenas went on to state that Bishop Sladkevičius had been consecrated without the consent of the authorities and therefore could not carry out the functions of a bishop in the Diocese of Kaišiadorys.

"Did Bishop Sladkevičius ask the priests to request the authorities to allow him to carry out his duties?" asked Tumenas.

"No, he didn't."

"Perhaps he himself doesn't wish to carry out episcopal duties and you've acted in this way without consulting him."

"If a man agrees to accept the rank of bishop, he thereby shows he's willing to fulfil the functions appropriate to the office."

"When did you decide to write this declaration?"

"At the funeral of Canon Bakšys."

"Why is there no evidence in this declaration as to why you want Bishop Sladkevičius to carry out his episcopal duties?"

"What kind of evidence do you need?" exclaimed Canon Pilka. "He is the Bishop of Kaišiadorys and we priests are asking the authorities to allow him to exercise his office."

"The Vatican has made a mistake", Tumenas explained, "and should correct it".

"Bishop Sladkevičius was made a bishop with the consent of the authorities, but he is not being allowed to carry out his duties."

"He didn't observe Soviet laws."

Tumenas asked who had organized the declaration, drawn up the text and collected the signatures, but Canon Pilka refused to give information about this.

At the end of their conversation, Tumenas stated that there would be no written reply to the declaration and ordered Pilka to sign a statement that he had been informed why Bishop Sladkevičius was not allowed to carry out his episcopal duties.

"You've created a great deal of unpleasantness for your administrator with this declaration and have harmed your bishop; such declarations to the state authorities are not desirable."[45]

22. BISHOP SLADKEVIČIUS REMAINS ACTIVE

On 27 March 1973 Kalkys, the chairman of the Auksine Varpa *kolkhoz*, summoned the chairman of the parish council, Petras Šimukenas, and ordered him to take two more members of the parish council to call on His Excellency, Bishop Sladkevičius, who is at present living in exile in Nemunelio Radviliškis, and to accuse him of preaching against the Government, sending information abroad, catechizing children and conferring the Sacrament of Confirmation. The chairman of the *kolkhoz* further warned Šimukenas that if he did not obey these orders he would be denied pasture for his animals.[46]

23. APPEAL TO THE VATICAN: "STAND FIRM" (1973)

In 1956-7 hundreds of priests returned from the concentration camps to resume their apostolic labours. The atheist government began to realize that the Catholic Church of Lithuania would not be broken by repressions. Those who had died in the concentration camps were considered martyrs and some of them are even the subjects of religious devotion, as is Fr. T. B. Andruška, S.J.

Nikita Khrushchev's "gallant" Chekists in 1957-8 again arrested a considerable number of priests: Canon Stanislovas Kiškis, Frs. Petras Rauda, T. A. Markaitis, S.J., Algirdas Mocius, Jonas Balčiunas, Antanas Jurgaitis, Antanas Bunkus, A. Svarinskas, Pranas Adomaitis, M.I.C. (who had worked among German Catholics in Siberia) and Petras Jakulevičius.

Except for Frs. Jurgaitis and Bunkus, all were imprisoned for the second time – Fr. Markaitis for the third.

Such violence brought no results this time either: those arrested continued their apostolic endeavours in the concentration camps and upon their return to Lithuania resumed pastoral work.

The atheist Government especially tried to wreck the Catholic Church from within – at the hands of the clergy and faithful themselves. The Executive of the Council for Religious Affairs promoted priests who were either inactive or subservient to the atheists. The most seriously affected was the urban ministry.

Moreover, the atheists tried to make the Vatican, which was poorly informed, promote certain undeserving clergy.

"Why does the Holy See hold such priests in esteem and why does it propose them as an example to the others?" asked the priests of Lithuania.

Not one priest was recognized for good pastoral work, with the possible exception of Canon Kazys Žitkus. Those trying to mislead the Vatican wanted to disarm zealous priests psychologically and to embarrass the Roman Curia.

In the chanceries of Lithuanian dioceses a very bad habit has developed – that of concealing everything from priests and people. The curtain of silence enveloping them has been pierced by disturbing rumours that the atheists are determined once and for all to liquidate the bishops of Lithuania – the pride of the faithful – their Excellencies Julius Steponavičius and Vincentas Sladkevičius. The atheists would then be able to administer this blow to the church in Lithuania through the hands of the Vatican, if the latter appointed new candidates handpicked by the atheists themselves to the sees of the exiled bishops.

Among candidates mentioned for the episcopacy are: Mgr. Bronius Barauskas, Mgr. Česlovas Krivaitis, Canon Andriukonis, the Rev. Dr. Viktoras Butkus, Fr. Bernardas Baliukonis, Fr. Antanas Vaičius and others.

The faithful of Lithuania have no doubt that it is not out of love that the atheists want to push through candidates for bishoprics who lack credibility among the believing public or among priests. The wishes of the faithful of Lithuania are best expressed in the words of Fr. Stasys Yla: "We want to see as bishop not a puppet in bishop's robes, but a human being, a father and a teacher."

This is borne out by the stacks of greetings sent to His Excellency, Bishop Sladkevičius, on the fifteenth anniversary of his enforced exile (17 March 1974).

There is no doubt that the bishops in exile have been no less deserving than the bishops who are at their posts. It would be an irreparable blow to the prestige of the Catholic Church in Lithuania and to the Vatican if the bishops esteemed by the faithful were to be shuffled aside.

Lithuania today needs priests rather than new bishops.

The atheist Government has left bishops the right to consecrate the oils, to ordain four to eight priests annually and to preside at priests' funerals. Even the administration of the Sacrament of Confirmation and the appointment of priests to parishes is strictly controlled by the Government.

Moreoever, it is the wish of the atheists today to arrange the life of the Church in Lithuania in such a way that priests would become responsible not to the bishops, but to parish councils. This being the case, Lithuania has enough bishops for the present and does not want any more. If the atheist Government wishes to show its good faith, it should allow the bishops in exile to return to their posts.

The priests and Catholic faithful of Lithuania pray that as much objective information as possible may reach the Holy See concerning the plight of the Catholic Church in Lithuania; then the Holy Father will adequately take care of her needs, they feel.

The atheists seek to destroy the faith and want to become the absolute arbiters of people's spiritual life, unobstructed in the attainment of their ends by the popular belief in God or by religious ethics. Atheistic Marxism seeks to make all people think, speak and act only in accord with the Communist Party programme.

In their war against religion in Lithuania, the atheists are trying to break the spirit of the Lithuanian nation, to deprive it of its spiritual values, to lower Lithuanian self-esteem and assimilate the believing public. Once the Lithuanians have become atheists, and have begun to contract mixed marriages and deprecate their Christian culture, conditions will be ripe for them to merge into a homogeneous mass of people, all speaking the language of Lenin.

The people, however, are thoroughly disenchanted with Marxist Communism. Students and intellectuals only study Marxism under compulsion. The atheist Government is forced to grasp at every ideological and administrative measure to control the spirit of the people.

In Lithuania atheism has become the state religion, so to speak, it is served by the press, radio, television and propagated by all possible means. Not only teachers and educators are forced to spread atheism, but so is the entire intelligentisia. While libraries are full of atheist literature, Catholics have practically none of their own – and what they have is confiscated by the KGB.

Siberian forced labour faces the book smugglers of today, like those of the Tsarist era.* During the Tsarist prohibition of the press things were easier, since the Tsar did not have so many spies or traitors among the people.

. . . .

The atheists tear a page out of the Tsar's book and endeavour to exploit the role of ecclesiastical leadership in their war against the Catholic Church. They try to place bishops or priests who are submissive to the Government in responsible positions – men who would carry out directives detrimental to the Church, misinform the faithful world-wide about the alleged freedom of the Church, and promulgate the regulations of the atheist Government among the priests in

*See pp. 247-8.

order to restrict their pastoral work, such as catechizing children and the canonical visitation of parishes.

When they visit Rome our clergy submit to the Government. In Moscow they are instructed what they are to say, what they are to keep secret, with whom to associate and whom to avoid. Returning from the Vatican, they must make a "general confession" to the appropriate agencies.

Among Lithuanian clergy there are now widespread rumours that the Vatican might nominate new bishops proposed not by the faithful of Lithuania, but by the Council for Religious Affairs via clergy currying favour with the regime. If new bishops subservient to the Government were to be appointed, the atheists would have attained the following goals:

1. The authority of the Holy Father, which has been very strong among the faithful and priests of Lithuania up to now, would be wrecked. Even under the most difficult conditions, the priests of Lithuania have shown their loyalty to the Holy See. The atheists failed in their attempts to create a national Catholic Church in Lithuania* outside the jurisdiction of the Pope. One priest sentenced to 25 years was offered his freedom, the pastorate of the Church of St. John in Vilnius and a bribe of 100,000 roubles.

   The Church of Silence will never understand a diplomacy which enables the atheists to rejoice at the spectacle of the Vatican in disagreement with those priests and laity who are struggling and suffering for the faith. In return for diplomatic concessions, the atheist Government can promise much and sign the most admirable treaties, but these will remain a dead letter, like the Declaration of Human Rights, to which the atheist Government is a signatory.
   . . . .

2. The bishops of Lithuania, like Archbishops Matulaitis, Matulionis, Reinys and others, have won a high respect for episcopal authority in the estimation of the faithful. If the Holy See were to name unsuitable candidates as bishops, their authority would be destroyed and great damage would be done to the Catholic Church in Lithuania.

3. The faithful of Lithuania await support from their spiritual leaders. Meanwhile, clergy chosen by the Government proclaim that our Church is not persecuted. How disappointed the faithful of Lithuania would be if the Vatican were to increase the number of such priests!

4. The appointment of new bishops subservient to the Government would be a mortal blow to the bishops who are so highly respected by the people: the banished Bishops, Julius Steponavičius and Vincentas Sladkevičius. If this were to happen, their sacrifice would be rendered useless, their very loyalty to the Holy Father and to the Church would be condemned and it would be quite impossible for them to return to their duties.

5. When the atheist Government takes every possible advantage of the ecclesiastical authorities and forces them to publish regulations detrimental to pastoral work, it is easier for the priests of Lithuania to keep their bearings if the directives are signed not by a bishop, but simply by the administrator of the diocese.

*See p. 36.

The priests and faithful of Lithuania therefore humbly beseech the Holy Father and the Roman Curia:

(a) Not to appoint new bishops subservient to the atheists.

(b) In appointing bishops, to ascertain the worth of a candidate by checking with the bishops in exile, or with priests duly authorized by them. This would be possible if the Vatican announced the names of candidates no less than six months prior to their nomination.

(c) To make no diplomatic concessions to the atheists based on trust in their good faith. No concessions can be expected from the atheists through bargaining – the Catholics of Lithuania will have just as much freedom as they win for themselves. This fact is borne out by more than one recent victory. The Catholics of Lithuania will be able to accomplish something only when they receive broad support from world public opinion and the upper échelons of the Catholic hierarchy.

The Catholics of Lithuania are grateful to those responsible for the broadcasts of Radio Vatican, to the Lithuanian press abroad and to the Catholic and non-Catholic press world-wide for publicizing the wrongs perpetrated by the atheists in Lithuania, and to all who pray or take action that the Catholics of Lithuania might have more religious freedom. It is regrettable that the Voice of America pays no heed to this matter. It is therefore not surprising that its broadcasts are listened to very little. It is difficult to get a Lithuanian interested in economic crises or political affairs when he is suffering for his faith.

The faithful of Lithuania, who suffer the fury of the security organs, when one after another of the best sons of the nation and of the Church find themselves in prison, are surprised that till now the Catholics of the world have not come to the defence of those in prison. The atheist Government hopes that if the world remains silent it can more easily "take care" of them.[47]

24 CHURCH LEADERS CO-OPTED TO SERVE THE ATHEISTS, 1974

[original title]

The Soviet leadership, wishing to hide from the world its treatment of the Catholic Church in Lithuania and nurturing hopes of deceiving the Vatican in order to extract concessions from the latter, has more than once forced some Lithuanian bishops and administrators of dioceses to disseminate false information abroad. Examples are the interview of Bishop Labukas with *L'Humanité*; the interview of Mgr. Krivaitis, Chancellor of the Archdiocese of Vilnius, with the editor Jokubkas, and his 1972 interview with *Elta* [the official Communist news agency, not the organ of the same name in Rome]; and Bishop Pletkus' radio broadcasts to Lithuanians abroad. In these interviews it has been stated that the condition of the Catholic Church in Lithuania is normal and that the faithful are not persecuted by the Government. It is unclear whether these individuals really spoke thus, since it is known that on a number of occasions reports of interviews have been intentionally distorted.

Knowing that the priests and faithful of Lithuania have no way to inform the world about the true state of the Church, a most pitiful situation has developed over the years. When the Vatican conferred the title of monsignor on certain priests "loyal" to the Soviet system, thus to all appearances approving their behaviour, and when it nominated as bishops the hand-picked candidates of the Government but remained silent about the painful situation of the faithful in Lithuania, voices were heard to say, "The Vatican is deceived! The Chekists have infiltrated the Roman Curia! We are betrayed!"

At such a difficult time, the only recourse left to Catholics of Lithuania is to trust in Divine Providence and to seek ways by which the true message might reach the Vatican and the rest of the world that the worst dread for the Catholic Church in Lithuania is not persecution, but the noose being tied by some of our own people.

In an effort to undermine the influence of the priests with the faithful, the Government has more than once forced bishops to curtail priests' faculties. In 1968 under pressure from Rugienis, for several months His Excellency Bishop Labukas forbade Fr. S. Tamkevičius to preach. In July 1970 the bishop took away the faculties of the Diocese of Vilkaviškis and of the Archdiocese of Kaunas from the parish priest of Alksnine, Canon Bronius Antanaitis, former chancellor of the diocese of Panevežys, exiled in 1960 to the Diocese of Vilkaviškis. A circular letter of 30 March 1971 limited the faculties of priests to hear confessions and to preach. Priests from an outside diocese were not allowed to preach or hear confessions without permission from the local chancery. (This is the normal situation in any diocese, but in extraordinary circumstances such formalties would be abolished.) This restriction evoked protests from priests. Such a restriction is the customary diocesan rule in normal circumstances, but in time of persecution the faculties of priests should be expanded, not curtailed. The bishops had to enforce all those restrictions on priests in their own name, while the chief perpetrator, the Soviet Executive for Religious Affairs, Rugienis, remained in the shadows.

Bishops can appoint only certain priests to parishes; Rugienis often directs which priests to transfer, the bishop is only permitted to rubber-stamp the appointments. It is not by accident that the most zealous priests are scattered in small, out-of-the-way parishes, while lax or physically incapacitated men, or those who have compromised themselves in the eyes of the faithful, often occupy the most important ecclesiastical posts. Rugienis himself tells the bishop which priests are in favour with the regime and which ones out of grace – a form of guidance on the bishop's parish appointments. The bishop may not transfer any priest without Rugienis' approval, not even in cases of emergency.

In September 1972, for example, under pressure from Rugienis, Bishop Labukas forced the rector of Juodaičiai, Fr. Pesliakas, who was under threat of suspension, to take over the duties of assistant priest in the parish of Vidukle. If a zealous priest raises the spiritual level of a parish, if he comes to know the people and the situation, Rugienis takes steps to have him transferred and lets the bishop appoint a lax or renegade priest, so that everything may fall apart once more.

Rugienis forbids the bishop to mention that he controls the appointments of many priests. Thus the priests know absolutely nothing in advance about their appointments. They are knocked around like billiard balls, according to the tune Rugienis calls. If the people ask why a priest is being transferred, Rugienis refers them to the bishop, who gives them to understand that he is powerless to do anything. Priests realise that the bishops are subjected to this form of pressure by government officials and sometimes they try appealing to canon law, saying: "This transfer is uncanonical; please don't transfer me." On 19 November 1970, under direct or indirect pressure, Bishop Labukas obtained a dispensation from the Holy See from canons regulating the assignment of priests. This dispensation, in the opinion of the priests, subjected the bishop still more to Rugienis' manipulations. Previously, the bishop could always object to Rugienis, "I cannot transfer a good priest to a small parish, because canon law does not allow me to do so." Now, however, the representative of the Government can reply to the bishop's objections, "You have the Pope's dispensation, so transfer this priest from his parish."

The bishops were forced to conceal Rugienis' calculated interference in clergy appointments in a circular letter dated 30 March 1971, in which they wrote:

> The bishops, desiring to improve the quality of their ministry to the spiritual needs of the faithful, have decided to change the procedure of assigning priests to parishes. It has been decided in the future to assign young, zealous and suitable priests to parishes where there is much work, and to send older priests, unable to cope, to smaller parishes, where it will be easier for them to serve as pastors.

Reading the letter, one would think that bishops in Lithuania act with complete freedom, assigning priests as they see fit. However, the practice has been – and remains – quite the contrary. Immediately after publication of the circular letter, the young and energetic P. Dumbliauskas was transferred from Garliava to the little parish of Šunskai, while the pastor of Šunskai, Fr. I. Pilypaitis, born in 1903, was assigned to the parish of Aleksotas, in the Archdiocese of Kaunas.

. . . .

Bishops are likewise forced to keep in check congregations of religious sisters working underground, lest they "step out of line" and attract the attention of the Government. It is no wonder, then, that some of the latter have contented themselves with prayer and have not done their full share for the religious life of the people, even though meanwhile the raging storm of atheism has been destroying the life of the Church.

In September and October 1970 the priests of Lithuania, in an attempt to prevent the subjugation of the leadership of the Catholic Church to the ends of the regime, addressed to the bishops and administrators of their diocese an appeal in which they spelled out the kinds of appeasement which are intolerable. The appeal was signed by fifty-nine priests of the Diocese of Vilkaviškis and fifty from the Archdiocese of Vilnius.[48]

25. A BISHOP SUPPORTS HIS PRIESTS

Dear Father,

I received a copy of your letter to Bishop Labukas on 10 October. I am convinced that you, as an exemplary priest and loyal son of the Church, do not seek in this communication to accuse your bishop or to show him any disrespect, but simply try to describe the painful predicament confronting our bishops, administrators, priests and faithful as a result of interference in the life and administration of the Church in our country by government authorities – specifically on the part of Rugienis, of the Council for Religious Affairs.

In his articles and declarations marked for foreign consumption Rugienis tries to portray himself as an innocent lamb, as though the Church authorities were responsible for priests' appointments and he had no hand in the matter.

Your case is one more proof that all his declarations in this vein are merely propaganda, lies and hypocrisy.

Dear Fr. Vytautas, one can argue whether or not you should have written your declaration, but I believe that it serves the Church – at least in that it demonstrates the unjustifiable interference of government authorities in the internal life of the Church. These matters are painful to all of us, but especially to you, whom they affect personally. But let us not be dismayed, let us hope that the time will come when they will realize that they are hurting themselves by this policy; then they will decide to normalize their relationships with the Church, as has been done in Poland, Hungary and other socialist countries.

I am praying for you. I wish you spiritual perseverance, fortitude and every blessing from the Lord.

[Unsigned]   2 November 1972.[49]

26. A BISHOP'S PASTORAL MINISTRY

Statement of the Rev. Albinas Deltuva, Rector of the Parish of Veisiejai, to the Chancery of the Diocese of Vilkaviškis

On the occasion of the administration of the Sacrament of Confirmation on 28-29 July 1973 by His Excellency, Bishop L. Povilonis, a number of incidents occurred, causing scandal among the faithful.

With the rye harvest as an excuse, the authorities proclaimed the Sunday chosen for confirmation in the region to be a working day. The *kolkhozes* and *sovkhozes* [two types of collective farm] received orders not to issue any vehicles to the people. On Sunday it rained. The rye harvest was interrupted. Nevertheless, those manning roadblocks on the approaches to Veisiejai allowed only buses and private vehicles to pass. All other cars and wagons carrying passengers were turned back.

Hence only eleven people wishing to be confirmed reached Veisiejai from the parishes in neighbouring Belorussia.

On 28 July about 4 p.m., just before the bishop's arrival, I was summoned by the municipal Executive Committee. Vaikšnoras, chairman of the Council of Workers' and Peasants' Deputies, with three other KGB men, demanded that I forbid the sale of religious objects outside the church.

. . . .

About 10 o'clock, during the service, the policemen Savonis and Giedraitis, who were in uniform, led away a blind man, cruelly twisting his arms; they had observed rosaries and crosses on chains in his possession. Simultaneously, Vitas Karaliunas and some other man seized two bags from a woman and carried them off.

Immediately upon the bishop's departure, the policemen Savonis and Giedraitis summoned to their assistance a teacher from the technical school and tried to seize devotional objects from some man in the churchyard; but the angry crowd attacked the two policemen and ejected them from the churchyard. The policemen sent for help, but by the time it arrived the people had had time to disperse.

Such occurrences are of no benefit to anybody, nor do they bring honour. Perhaps the chancery could take the necessary steps with the appropriate agencies, so that they will not be repeated.

[Lithuanian Chronicle] Editor's note:

On 28-29 July approximately 2,600 of the faithful received the Sacrament of Confirmation. About 10,000 were present and 3,500 received Communion.[50]

27. CHURCH LEADER CRITICIZED FOR REMARKS ABROAD

On 20 February 1975 *Tiesa* [the official Vilnius newspaper] reported that a delegation of clergy from the USSR had visited America. One of the participants was Mgr. Krivaitis, Administrator of the Archdiocese of Vilnius. *Tiesa* reported him as saying at a press conference in New York:

> "The believers of Soviet Lithuania have every opportunity of fulfilling their religious needs. Neither they nor their children are persecuted because of their beliefs. As priests, we have every opportunity of carrying out our work."

This remark has raised a storm of protest among believers in Lithuania. They have no prayer-books or catechisms, schoolchildren are persecuted for their faith, crosses are destroyed, religious literature is confiscated, the work of priests is hindered, while abroad a priest is telling people about freedom of religion. Some people even doubt that the diocesan administrator said this. After all, Soviet journalists are capable of exaggerating and even of writing outright lies.

The Soviet clergy delegation was organized by the KGB. Their aim is to sway public opinion abroad, alleging that no one in the USSR is persecuted for his faith.[51]

APPENDIX

Bishops and Administrators* in Lithuanian dioceses from 1940 to the present day

Archdiocese of Kaunas

1. Archbishop Juozapas Skvireckas (1873-1959).
   Administered the diocese from 1926-1944. In 1944 he went into exile; in 1959 he died in Austria.
   From 1944 to 1965, the diocese was administered by capitular vicars:
   1944-46: Stanislovas Jokubauskis.
   1947-65: Juozapas Stankevičius.

2. Bishop Juozapas Matulaitis-Labukas (1894-).
   Consecrated in Rome on 5 December 1965. According to current rumours he might resign because of partial blindness.

*There are three types of administrators:
1) Apostolic administrators (bishops);
2) Ordinary administrators of dioceses, usually monsignors, appointed by the Vatican;
3) Vicars (deputies), appointed by a bishop.

Bishop Liudvikas Povilonis has been auxiliary bishop in this diocese since 7 July 1973.

Diocese of Telšiai

1. Bishop Justinas Staugaitis (1866-1943).
2. Bishop Vincentas Borisevičius (1887-1946).
   Administered the Diocese from 1944 to 1946. Ordained 1910; Rector of Telšiai Seminary until 1940, when he became a bishop. Condemned to death and shot in 1946.
3. Bishop Pranciškus Ramanauskas (1893-1959).
   Became apostolic administrator of the diocese in 1946, but in December of that year he was arrested and deported to Siberia. In 1956 he was amnestied and returned to Lithuania; he administered his diocese without official permission until his death on 15 October 1959.
4. Bishop Petras Maželis (1894-1966).
   Consecrated bishop in 1955; administered the diocese from 1959 to 1966.
5. Bishop Juozapas Pletkus (1895-1975).
   Made capitular vicar in 1966; consecrated bishop in 1968; administered the diocese from 1966 to his death on 29 September 1975.
   In 1969 Liudvikas Povilonis was consecrated auxiliary bishop in this diocese, but in 1973 he was transferred to Kaunas Diocese. The capitular vicar of this diocese is now Antanas Vaičius (born 1926), who has been administering it since 7 October 1975.

Diocese of Panevežys

1. Bishop Kazimieras Paltarokas (1875-1958).
   First bishop of this diocese, which he administered from 1926 until his death on 3 January 1958.
2. Bishop Julijonas Steponavičius (born 1911).
   Consecrated bishop in 1955; administered the diocese from 1958 to 1961, when he was exiled to the village of Žagare, in Kaunas Diocese. The Vatican appointed an administrator to the diocese in 1961, Paulus Šidlauskas, but later that year Šidlauskas was removed by the authorities and sent to Varena.
   From 1961-73 the capitular vicar was Paulius Bakšys.
3. Bishop Romualdas Krikščiunas (born 1930).
   Consecrated 21 December 1969, as auxiliary bishop of Kaunas. Transferred to Panevežys diocese on 7 July 1973.

Diocese of Vilkaviškis

1. Bishop Antanas Karosas (1856-1947).
   Administered the diocese as bishop from 1926 to his death in 1947.
   Capitular vicars: 1947-49 Vincentas Vizgirda, deported to Siberia 1949.
   1949-65 Juozapas Stankevičius.
   Since 1965 the Apostolic Administrator of this diocese has been Bishop J. Matulaitis-Labukas of Kaunas.

Diocese of Kaišiadorys

1. Bishop Juozapas Kukta (1873-1942).
   First bishop of this diocese, which he administered from 1926-42.
2. Bishop Teofilius Matulionis (1873-1962).
   Became Bishop of Kaišiadorys in 1943. Ordained 1900; served as pastor in Latvia and Petrograd. First arrested 1922, spent three years in prison in Russia. Consecrated a bishop in Leningrad 1929. Second term of imprisonment: 1929-33 (in camps at Solovki). Returned to Lithuania 1933. In 1946 he was exiled to Siberia. From 1946-56 the diocese was administered by capitular vicars – first by Bernardas Suziedelis (1946-49), after which he was sent to Telšiai Diocese, and then by Juozapas Stankevičius (1949-56).

   In 1956 Bishop Matulionis returned from Siberia, but he was not permitted to administer his diocese, and was sent to Birštonas. On 25 December 1957 he secretly consecrated Vincentas Sladkevičius as auxiliary bishop. He was then sent to Šeduva in Panevežys Diocese, where he died on 20 August 1962.

   Bishop Sladkevičius was exiled to Nemunelio Radviliškis in Panevežys Diocese in 1959 and is still banned from exercising his office.
   Capitular vicars since 1962:
   1962   : Juozapas Meidus (exiled from the diocese);
   1962-73: Paulius Bakšys;
   1973-   : Juozapas Andrikonis.

Archdiocese of Vilnius

1. Archbishop Romualdas Jalbrzykowski (1876-1955): 1926-1942.
2. Archbishop Mečislovas Reinys (1884-1953): 1942-4.
3. Archbishop R. Jalbryzykowski: from 1944-6.
4. Archbishop Mečislovas Reinys: administered the diocese from 1945-6, when he was deported from Lithuania and sent to Vladimir Prison, where he died on 8 November 1953.

Capitular vicars and apostolic administrators since 1946:

1946-49: Edmundas Basys;
1949 : Juozapas Vaičiunas;
1949-58: Bishop Kazimieras Paltarokas of Panevežys;
1958-61: Bishop Julijonas Steponavičius;
1961- : Česlovas Krivaitis.

N.B.: Under Soviet law every citizen must have a residence permit naming the place in which the bearer must legally live. The Soviet authorities exploit this to interfere in church administration – moving popular clergy from areas where they are doing good work and in some cases confining them to backwaters (a kind of exile).

NOTES TO CHAPTER III

1. Struve, *Christians in Contemporary Russia,* pp. 380-1. Appendix II gives the full text of the 1929 Law on Religious Associations, which was modified in July 1975 (*Vedomosti Verkhovnogo Soveta RSFSR,* 3 July 1975, pp. 487-91); see *Religion in Communist Lands,* No. 2, 1976, pp. 4-10.
2. *CLCC* 10, p. 6 (E), p. 2 (L), gives 25 years but we have corrected this from a private source of information.
3. Savasis, *The War against God in Lithuania,* p. 26.
4. *CLCC* 14, p. 35 (E), p. 29 (L); cf. *CLCC* 10, p. 13 (E), p. 6 (L).
5. Walter Kolarz, *Religion in the Soviet Union,* London, 1961, p. 207.
6. *CLCC* 10, p. 11 (E), p. 5 (L).
7. Kolarz, *op. cit.,* p. 208.
8. *Katolitsizm v SSSR i sovremennost* ["Catholicism in the USSR and the Modern World"], Vilnius, 1971, pp. 75-6.
9. Savasis, *op. cit.,* p. 31.
10. *La Chiesa in Lithuania: Situazione attuale,* Union of Lithuanian Priests in Italy, Rome, Second edition, 1970, p. 28.
11. *CLCC* 1, p.21.
12. *CLCC* 5, p. 4 (E), p. 5 (L).
13. *CLCC* 4, p. 19 (E), p. 10 (L).
14. *CLCC* 14, p. 20 (E), p. 16 (L).
15. *CLCC* 10, pp. 7 and 13 (E), pp. 2 and 6 (L).
16. *Ibid.,* p. 31 (E), p. 17 (L).
17. *CLCC* 14, p. 20 (E), p. 16 (L).
18. Rimaitis, *Religion in Lithuania,* p. 22.
19. *CLCC* 5, p. 4 (E), p. 5 (L).
20. *CLCC* 10, p. 8 (E), p. 3 (L).
21. Bourdeaux, *Patriarch and Prophets,* pp. 65-9.
22. *CLCC* 14, p. 5 (E), p. 2 (L).
23. *CLCC* 1, p. 12.
24. *CLCC* 26, pp. 17-18.

25. The case for this is made out in Bourdeaux, *Religious Ferment in Russia* (on the Baptists) and *Patriarch and Prophets* (on the Orthodox).
26. *La Chiesa in Lituania,* p. 28; Rimaitis, *op. cit.,* p. 21.
27. *CLCC* 2, p. 20; *CLCC* 6, p. 34 (E), p. 14 (L); *CLCC* 10, pp. 27-8 (E), p. 15 (L).
28. *CLCC* 12, p. 5 (E), p. 2 (L).
29. *CLCC* 5, pp. 44-6 (E), pp. 17-18 (L).
30. *Ibid.,* p. 44 (E), p. 17 (L).
31. *Tiesa,* 21 December 1969; Rimaitis, *op. cit.,* p. 8.
32. *La Chiesa in Lituania,* p. 27.
33. *CLCC* 8, p. 48 (E), p. 27 (L).
34. *La Chiesa in Lituania,* p. 27; Rimaitis, *op. cit.,* p. 21.
35. *Gimtasis Kraštas* ("Native Land", published for émigrés), 1 March 1973, quoted by *CLCC* 6, p. 10 (E), p. 5 (L); see also *CLCC* 6, pp. 23-24 (E), pp. 9-10 (L).
36. *CLCC* 24, p. 17.
37. *CLCC* 14, p. 42 (E), p. 35 (L).
38. *CLCC* 12, pp. 22-23 (E), pp. 19-20 (L).
39. *CLCC* 10, p. 28 (E), p. 15 (L).
40. *CLCC* 4, pp. 4-6 (E), pp. 4-5 (L).
41. *CLCC* 8, p. 5 (E), p. 2 (L).
42. *CLCC* 10, pp. 36-40 (E), pp. 20-23 (L).
43. *CLCC* 20, pp. 8-12.
44. *Arkhiv samizdata,* Radio Liberty, Munich, Vol. 17, AC No. 632.
45. *CLCC* 14, pp. 5-7 (E), pp. 2-3 (L).
46. *CLCC* 6, p. 43 (E), p. 17 (L).
47. *CLCC* 10, pp. 6-14 (E), pp. 2-7 (L).
48. *CLCC* 4, pp. 5-9 (E), pp. 4-6 (L).
49. *CLCC* 6, pp. 39-41 (E), pp. 16-17 (L).
50. *CLCC* 7, pp. 54-57 (E), , pp. 21-22 (L).
51. *CLCC* 15, p. 11.

IV

THE CENTRAL ISSUES

IN all the years of Soviet anti-religious persecution, probably the most solid and well-organized opposition has come from the Lithuanian Catholic clergy. If the body of the Church has Christ as its head, then its spinal chord in Lithuania is the relationship between the priests and their people. The atheists have tried every means to break that relationship – physical constraint, attempts to discredit the clergy, reducing their ranks by controlling the number of new ordinations from the theological seminaries – but all so far without success.

In the years between the second Soviet invasion of Lithuania and the death of Stalin the main aim of Soviet policy was to terrorize the clergy into submission. If they could be forced to go beyond a mere breaking of their relationship with Rome and be made to display hostility to the Vatican, this would also rupture the respect in which their parishioners held them. If such a display of hostility to the Vatican could be combined with a declaration of support for the Communist Party, the clergy would lose their special place in the people's affections as guardians of the Lithuanian national heritage.

If they were banned from all specialized activities*, the clergy would become atrophied. The atheist hope would then be to remodel the docile priesthood by raising up some sort of pro-Communist "peace-priest" movement, like that created in Czechoslovakia.[1] There was a completely unsuccessful attempt to do just that after the war, by founding a so-called "National Catholic Church"[2] of Lithuania.

It was to the same end that Lithuanian priests were made to sign a letter condemning the Pope (Document 28). This declaration illustrates the pressure put on the clergy in the late 1940s, but it also demonstrates the total lack of subtlety and sensitivity shown by those who led the atheist campaign. At this time senior Russian Orthodox clergy were prepared – or forced – to sign even more grossly political documents than the criticism of Pope Pius XII's condemnation of Communism quoted here.[3] The document that the Lithuanian Catholic priests were supposed to sign was of the same sort, but the opposition to it was stronger. Predictably, many priests refused to be intimidated. Imprisonment or exile awaited them. Thirty years later the authors of the *Lithuanian Chronicle* hold up their integrity and fearlessness as an example for the faithful today.

*See p. 5-6, 84.

Approximately 330 priests were imprisoned or exiled in the period 1945-53.[4] This is no less than thirty per cent of the total number of clergy in the country at the time. In 1974 an atheist writer, Pranas Mišutis, sought to justify this persecution by claiming that only those who took up arms against the Soviet Union suffered in this way.[5] The *Lithuanian Chronicle* replies:

> An interesting question is whether Mišutis himself believes what he writes. Between 1944 and 1962 in the smallest diocese in Lithuania, Kaišiadorys, forty-one priests (out of ninety in that diocese) were given prison sentences. A majority of them never had a firearm in their hands; yet they were given ten-year sentences, and some indeed were imprisoned for twenty-five years.[6]

Nothing is more inspiring in the recent history of the Lithuanian Catholic Church than the heroism of some of those who refused to yield to Stalin's threats. By their example they not only kept the faith alive, but inspired others to turn to God.

One man could be said to represent many others. When Canon Petras Rauda died in March 1974, his funeral was the occasion of one of the most impressive religious demonstrations that the Soviet Union can have witnessed. No fewer than 3 bishops and 180 priests took part (one-fifth of all the clergy in Lithuania). Forty cars processed past the huge mass of people who had assembled under the eyes of the atheists watching them in impotence – an astonishing number in a country where there are hardly any private vehicles. In post-war years, Canon Rauda had brought men to Christ while serving his prison sentence under Stalin. During his second term of imprisonment (1957-62), he befriended Archbishop (now Cardinal) Slipyj, the head of the suppressed Ukrainian Eastern-rite Catholic (Uniat) Church. Even though blind and broken in health, he continued his pastoral work after his second release. He undoubtedly inspired and influenced the young Nijole Sadunaite,[7] who herself was to follow his path of suffering.* The short account of Canon Rauda's life and death forms one of the most impressive passages in the *Lithuanian Chronicle* (Document 29). His heroism represents that of hundreds of other priests of his generation, who had been arrested under Stalin or Khrushchev or both.

From 1968 the Lithuanian clergy – an absolute majority of all priests in the country – have been involved in a campaign to win religious freedom from the Soviet Government. In doing so, they have assembled and released a large part of the information contained in this book. To understand the build-up of pressure which led to this, one must look back, firstly, to the slight relaxation enjoyed during the breathing space of 1953-6,† and secondly, to the termination of that period under Khrushchev's hegemony. The years 1959-64 must be studied with special reference to the Catholic clergy.[8]

*See pp. 271-3, 282-291. †See pp. 41-2.

The main aim of Khrushchev's new and virulent anti-religious campaign, which applied even more to the Russian Orthodox clergy,[9] was to undermine the credibility of the priests with their own faithful, as a prelude to eliminating them from society altogether. This aim failed, partly because the local resistance was once again greater than the atheists had anticipated, and partly because Khrushchev fell and the application of the policy changed before it could be carried through. Document 30 gives some idea of how the campaign appeared in the Soviet press during this period. Here are some of the main accusations: priests are engaged in a variety of criminal activity (Documents 30 and 31); they engage in illicit sex, they are persistently drunk,[10] and they go as far as becoming accomplices in murder.[11]

Even where no one stands up to accuse individuals of such crimes, the press designates them as "parasites" – a criminal offence covering the refusal of able-bodied people to work. The atheist campaigners on some occasions even made the relatives of clergy denounce them as being useless and dishonest. It is reported that one mother went insane after the publication of such a letter against her son.[12] One of the strangest accusations was against a priest who was said to be guilty of damage to public property (his nationalized cemetery) when he cut down some trees (obviously a measure to keep up the graveyard).[13]

Financial crimes are among the most common in the list of indictments. The clergy allegedly "force" people into giving donations – which is against the law[14] – and they have their hands constantly in the parish moneybags.[15] They profiteer in the selling of religious objects.[16] We should note in this context that the clergy and church are barred from any official participation in charitable or relief work, so there must be the constant temptation to remove money from the direct giving of the faithful for this purpose. Further, there are no proper provisions for the religious objects Catholics require, so individuals have to provide them by some sort of private enterprise.

An even more serious accusation – in Soviet terms – is that the clergy cultivate nationalism.[17] The standard formulation for making this "crime" appear much worse is to accuse individual clergy of giving aid to the "nationalist bandits"[18] (partisans), which, in Soviet inverted reasoning, is equated with co-operating with the Nazis.[19]

Another serious accusation, which makes sense only if one realises that such activities are serious crimes under Soviet law, is that the clergy "violate freedom of conscience" by refusing to teach the new Soviet morality, and by using every means at their disposal to come into contact with the young with the aim of committing the offence of teaching them religion.[20]

Although so frequently criticized for wanting to put the clock back and reverse the trend towards a new, "progressive" Communist society, the priests do not escape by being open to new ideas, as for example by looking for ways of reconciling science with religion, for they may be criticized for this too.[21]

A key figure in the Soviet state's offensive against religion in Lithuania has been the former priest, Jonas Ragauskas, who became one of the most active atheists in Lithuania after leaving the priesthood and marrying. He wrote over twenty-five books, of which the most important was *Ite, Missa Est,* an autobiographical novel describing how he broke with religion. Most of his writing is derisive and sarcastic, not serious criticism of religious philosophy. It is said that he wanted to return to the Church when he was dying, but that no priest was willing to come, as he had written a testament proclaiming that any stories of his deathbed recantation would be priestly fabrications. Nineteen other priests have broken with religion since 1945, but these mostly made a public statement on leaving the priesthood and then led a quiet life.

Although some "priests" have been insinuated into the Church by the authorities as active spies and collaborators with the regime, their identities are usually well known to believers and they are thereby discredited and rendered useless (Document 32).

Against all the slander and calumny listed above the clergy have no right whatsoever of redress in practice, though theoretically they do in law.[22] Their role is restricted at every point (Document 33). Annual pastoral visitations which the clergy make to the faithful are banned.[23] Other works of mercy, such as hospital visiting, are virtually reduced to nil.[24] The ban on preparing children for the Sacrament of Confirmation and the hindrances placed in the way of its administration are some of the hardest restrictions for the Church to bear.[25] There is a ban on the dispensation of charity[26] and on the priest's participation in any associations and activities outside the strict limit of his own liturgical function.[27] One unexpected line of attack is against the clergy's wish to keep records of parishioners, communions and baptisms[28] (Russian Orthodox priests have sometimes complained at having to keep various registers which could be useful to the KGB).[29] When priests are overloaded with work on major local saints' days (Document 34) they are not allowed to call in help from neighbouring parishes – indeed, they can never officiate in any parish except the one in which they are registered[30] without the permission of the official of the Council for Religious Affairs.

Priests who are not registered by the Government have no legal right to perform any priestly functions. There is evidence, however, that such unregistered clergy exist in Lithuania, doing their duty as priests while working at an ordinary job. In a situation where entrance to the seminary is restricted, it seems that some older priests train "disciples", who are then secretly ordained. However, it is probable that most of the unregistered priests in Lithuania are from Ukraine, where the Eastern-rite Catholic (Uniat) Church has been completely banned. There are said to be about thirty Uniat priests in Lithuania. For example, Fr. Vladimir Prokopiv, a Ukrainian Uniat priest, was working as a labourer in Lithuania while keeping in touch with his homeland. In 1973 he took a petition to Moscow from 1,200 Catholics in Lviw, asking for permission to open a Catholic Church there. Meanwhile the police searched his flat in Vilnius, he was arrested and sent to Kiev Mental Hospital.[31] It has been known for Lithuanian priests who cannot register in Lithuania to go to Ukraine and register there, as western Catholics. There are obviously still strong links between Catholics in both republics.

The 1929 "Law on Religious Associations" (amended in July 1975, but with a confirmation of this provision[32]), permits the atheist authorities to remove any member of the three-man parish council it does not like – one of the most grotesque infractions of the Soviet Constitution, which guarantees the separation of Church and State. Not all local *soviets* (councils) are actively anti-religious, of course; some have an ambivalent attitude and hardly ever interfere in church affairs.

With regard to the Russian Orthodox Church, a change took place in the ecclesiastical law affecting parish administration in 1961 without the authorization of the Sobor (a national meeting of the Church's representatives, the only authority entitled to make such a change). Since then the constitution of the parish council has always been a subject of dispute. The change was made by a "Synod of Bishops", which had no legal status, but it was eventually confirmed by the Sobor nine years later in 1971. Since 1961 the parish priest has had no right to be a member of his own parish council, being merely "hired" by it to perform the liturgy.[33] Every attempt is made to insinuate atheists on to parish councils.

Document 35 demonstrates clearly that atheist attempts to do something similar in Lithuania have met with much more limited success, doubtless due to the united opposition. The more hierarchical tradition of the Catholic Church has less place for parish councils, so even though they technically exist the loyalty of the faithful is such that they are at worst either inactive and do not interfere in the work of the priest, or at best assist him in his ministry. Both priests and laity refuse to accept the Soviet concept of the parish council as an administrative body "employing" the priest.

The person who has experienced freedom and lost it is much more likely to speak out than than someone who has never known it. The memory of independence and the taste of the comparative relaxation in the period 1953-7 were some of the stimuli which led the Lithuanian Catholic clergy to raise their voices in 1968, following the renewed persecution of the Khrushchev era. But there were undoubtedly other factors, such as Vatican foreign policy, which also provided the stimulus for action. The Baptists had been organizing protests against restrictions on religious liberty since 1960.[34] The "Democratic Movement" was now underway in Moscow, already leading to some specific instances of common action among writers and political activists (see Chapter XII), especially over the 1968 "Trial of the Four" (Galanskov, Ginzberg, Lashkova and Dobrolyubov) in Moscow, which led to the greatest wave of protests Moscow has ever seen. Then after the Six-Day War in 1967 the Jewish community became one of the most outspoken of all groups, but with the added advantage of being the first to gain a truly international hearing. 1968 saw the most serious upheaval in Eastern Europe since the Soviet invasion of Hungary twelve years earlier. Six months of ferment in Czechoslovakia, growing less and less restrained, resulted in the Soviet invasion in August. Through the medium of radio broadcasts from Western Europe, the Lithuanians were able to follow both the bid for freedom and its suppression. One might have expected the events in Czechoslovakia to dampen down the flame of growing protest, but in fact the opposite happened. The positive answer in Russia to these events was the founding of the *Chronicle of Current Events* in *samizdat*.

These bold steps unquestionably influenced the progress of events in Lithuania. Early in 1968 there was a completely new development in the demand for religious liberty in the Soviet Union. From the outset, the Lithuanian Catholic protest was to be as insistent as that of the Baptist movement since 1960 and even more unified than theirs, though it is harder to define the precise reasons why it began when it did than with the Baptists, who were reacting to a set of regulations controlling church life which had the appearance of coming from the Moscow Baptist leadership, but which in fact were rapidly seen as the work of Soviet atheist authorities.[35] The upsurge of protests in Lithuania in 1968-9 may have been stimulated in part by the passing of a decree in 1968, obliging local authorities to reply to letters from citizens within a month.

On 8 January 1969 no less than sixty-three Lithuanian priests protested to Mr. Kosygin, the Soviet Prime Minister, against the web of restrictions enveloping the training of the clergy in Lithuania and preventing the church from replenishing their ranks as the older men died.*

There was ample precedent for this form of "open letter" to the Soviet leaders, as it had been used not only by the Baptists since the early 1960's, but also by the Russian Orthodox Church and extensively by the human rights activists. At first the tendency in all these movements was to seek justice by emphasizing the Soviet authorities' infraction of their own laws, but gradually figures appeared in each who were prepared to challenge some of the legal formulations themselves. The hope was that such a campaign would

*See pp. 143-7.

mobilize support, both at home and abroad – and, in the case of Lithuania, from world Catholic opinion in general and the Vatican in particular.

At this time the activists must have established the groundwork for some sort of clandestine organization which would collect and verify the facts, as the Council of Prisoners' Relatives began to do for the Baptists from 1963,[36] under the authority of the Council of Evangelical Christian and Baptist Churches, which the State refused to recognize. No names of any comparable organizations have come to light in Lithuania, though abundant evidence exists of similar activity.

It rapidly became evident that there was a co-ordinated movement. Between 1968 and 1972 the Lithuanian clergy addressed at least fifteen known protest documents to the Soviet authorities, though it is probable that those published in the West form only a small proportion of the whole.[37]

The extent of the religious protest movement among the Lithuanian clergy is openly demonstrated in the pages of the *Lithuanian Chronicle:* issues 1-22 of the *Chronicle* mention 262 Lithuanian priests by name, over a third of the entire Lithuanian Catholic clergy, often providing details of restrictions suffered by them in their parishes. Only five to ten priests are mentioned unfavourably as collaborators with the authorities. The number of priests who have signed petitions calling for religious liberty is even higher: 56 priests from Telšiai diocese (1969), 134 from Panevežys diocese (1971), 72 from Vilkaviškis diocese (1970), 45 from Kaišiadorys diocese (1974) and 66 from Vilnius archdiocese (1976) – 373 out of 715 priests in Lithuania (over 50%), an amazingly large proportion in Soviet circumstances. Some priests have signed only one petition; others, like Fr.Bronislavas Laurinavičius, complain in writing to both local and central authorities whenever they find the law being infringed by those authorities, and are willing to sign all petitions calling for true freedom of conscience.

When the State began yet another round of judicial proceedings against the clergy in 1970, this time the latter were prepared to react in a highly organized way, for they had already spent two years protesting against the restrictions on the intake at the theological seminary (see Chapter VI) and similar issues.

Now the conflict focused on the denial of the right of the clergy to instruct young people in the faith – or even to have contact with them. In 1970-1 there were three trials of priests in close succession for this "offence", and though the sentences were relatively light (one year in each instance) they brought forth a storm of protest, the shock-waves of which produced a far more stubborn and prolonged reaction than the authorities had probably anticipated.

The first to suffer was Fr. Antanas Šeškevičius, parish priest of Dubingai, Moletai District. Fr. Šeškevičius is a Jesuit, born in 1914 and ordained in 1943. In 1946 he was deported to Siberia. Ten years later, in 1956, he was allowed to return to Lithuania, but after a short period at home he decided to go back to Siberia voluntarily, to serve as a priest to the Catholics there. He was then "exiled" back from Siberia to Lithuania by the authorities. He sent some devotional objects, including rosaries, to friends in Siberia; for this he was sentenced in 1967 to one year in a labour camp near Perm in the Urals, for "speculation". In 1968 he returned to Lithuania and was assigned the parish of Dubingai.[38] On 9 September 1970 the Moletai District People's Court sentenced him to one year of imprisonment (strict regime) for teaching religion to children, even though this was at their parents' request.[39] He was released three days before his full year's sentence had ended[40] and he immediately applied to his own diocese of Kaišiadorys for reinstatement in a parish.[41] The local representative of the Council for Religious Affairs stepped in and refused him registration for having broken the Soviet law, so he applied to the Lithuanian Council of Ministers. He wrote:

> Even if I have broken Soviet law, I have still served my sentence with a credit for good conduct. Further, I was released with no deprivation of rights. Why, then, am I being punished without trial for the rest of my life? . . . . Is there any other country in the world where the authorities behave like this to their subjects? How can this be reconciled with the Declaration on Human Rights which has been signed by the Soviet Union? Preventing me from fulfilling my duty as a priest forces me into a new crime, since I am still a priest and must perform at least some priestly duties; but the State will consider this illegal, so prison will again await me.[42]

Fr. Šeškevičius received no reply, so he appealed to other official bodies and, finally, to the Committee for the Defence of Human Rights, which the prominent Soviet scientist, Andrei Sakharov, had recently established in Moscow (see Chapter XII).

Whether this action, his general persistence, or the support of others prompted a positive response we cannot tell, but after a six months' campaign, he received an appointment in the diocese of Telšiai.[43] Before this happened, he was already supporting other priests in their efforts to win religious liberty and signed an appeal of forty-seven Vilnius priests dated 24 December 1971.[44]

The authorities did not allow Fr. Šeškevičius to take charge of a parish of his own, but he became an assistant priest at Šilale. His registration was only a temporary one for three months, as is the case with other priests who fall foul of the Soviet authorities.[45] Discrimination against him continued, however, and he was restricted by a sort of "parish arrest", during which neither he nor the parish priest could say the daily office in his church.[46]

Fr. Šeškevičius continued to appeal to the authorities for the reinstatement of his full rights and in January 1974 he complained at being prevented from assisting the chairman of the parish committee while he was collecting offerings. He wrote to the Council for Religious Affairs on 8 January:

> I was told that a priest may participate in making the collection, but in no case must he carry the plate. It is useless for a priest to 'assist' in taking a collection if he has no useful function, but only observes the action as a steward. That merely irritates the faithful. How do such prohibitions conform to Article 96 of the Constitution of the Lithuanian SSR, which provides for the separation of Church and State? In this case the State is telling the Church how to conduct collections. Do not such actions mystify a thinking man of the twentieth century?[47]

Petty acts of discrimination continued and on 13 March 1974 a Communist official, Jankus, summoned him and threatened him with prison yet again. He said he was ready to die in a Communist prison and took the initiative against the threats.[48] When he was further criticized for obtaining publicity in the foreign press, a group of priests from the diocese of Vilkaviškis defended him and said that this had happened for the sole reason that he had remained faithful to his duty in teaching the catechism.[49]

There are several other priests who also feature prominently in the *Lithuanian Chronicle* at this time, without actually being imprisoned for their activities. Among them are Fr. Algimantas Keina (ordained 1962) who received a fine of fifty roubles in September 1970 for teaching religion to children. He claimed that the authorities falsified several details of the case.[50] In August 1973 an atheist official burst in on him with a photographer while he was testing two girls on their catechism[51] and later that year (20 November) he was one of several people singled out for an intensive house-search. This lasted eighteen hours, followed by an overnight interrogation.[52]

The atheist authorities had evicted Fr. V. Merkys from the Kaunas Seminary in 1959, after which he received a secret ordination. The State would not register him as a priest and he had to work in Vilnius as a gardener. In April 1972 Rugienis called him in and offered him a parish if he revealed the details of his ordination.[53]

The authorities turned their attention to Fr. P. Masilionis of Krikliniai for the double reason that he applied for permission to visit his relatives in the United States in 1971 and because his sermons were too "practical"(which obviously meant that he was giving a Christian answer to the attempts by the Communists to impose their own beliefs and practices).[54] In this he annoyed the authorities for the same reason as Fr. Dmitri Dudko in Moscow, whose informal sermons led to his expulsion from two parishes successively in 1974 and 1975.[55]

The most extraordinary case of persecution in the post-Khrushchev period so far, both in its effect and in the detail in which we have been able to follow it, is that of Fr. Juozas Zdebskis, (born 1929, ordained 1952) who was imprisoned a year after Fr. Šeškevičius

(1971), also for teaching religion to children. Because his case provides many of the most vivid pages of the *Lithuanian Chronicle,* we will let the evidence speak entirely for itself in recounting it (Document 36). However, it should be noted that Fr. Zdebskis was already active in the 1960s in initiating appeals to increase the size of the seminary and the numbers of priests.*

A third case, very similar to that of Fr. Zdebskis, was the trial of Fr. P. Bubnys, pastor of Girkalnis, which took place at the same time as that of Fr. Zdebskis. Fr. Bubnys was also sentenced to one year in prison.[56]

DOCUMENTS

28. MANY PRIESTS REFUSE TO CONDEMN THE POPE (1949)

From the archives of the Chronicle of the Lithuanian Catholic Church

In the post-war years the authorities tried to make the priests of Lithuania sign the following document composed by the Communists:

We thoroughly condemn and protest against this!

Pope Pius XII issued a decree on 13 July 1949 through the so-called 'Holy Office', excommunicating all Catholic Communists and their supporters from the Catholic Church. The decree forbids Catholics to join the Communist Party or to support it; it forbids them to publish, distribute and read Communist books, newspapers and journals, and also to write for them. The decree calls for Catholics suspected of the above activities to be turned away from communion and other sacraments. The appearance of this decree, reminiscent of the Middle Ages, which is now being condemned by a wide section of Catholics, shows that the Catholic Church is disturbed by the rejection by millions of Catholics of the reactionary course so passionately promulgated by the Vatican. They have rejected the reactionary politics of the Vatican, an accessory to to the plans of aggressive imperialism.

Catholics workers throughout the world are raising their voices ever more loudly in support of peace and against war; this also explains their attraction to and support for progressive organizations which stand for peace and happiness between nations, especially in the case of workers' Communist Parties, marching in the forefront of the battle for peace and democracy.

The Vatican hopes to strengthen its waning influence on the believing masses by means of threats and repressive measures.

*See pp. 154-5.

Pope Pius XII, by his decree, has denounced about a third of mankind. In accordance with the legal sense of the Vatican decree, the Catholic Church should excommunicate 70 million trade unionists and about 600 million people represented by delegates to the World Peace Congress in which they participated together with Communists. In addition, the Pope holds a curse over the head of every citizen of any country which includes Communists in its government, if they carry out laws passed by that government.

. . . .

The Vatican's decree is a coarse insult to the religious feelings of believers. The decision of the Vatican is directed at those who, in the name of freedom and independence, have taken on their shoulders the whole weight of the great struggle against the Hitlerite barbarians.

Furthermore, everyone knows that in its attitude to Fascism and Hitlerism, which have committed the most bloodthirsty crimes in the history of humanity, the Vatican has shown full approval and tolerance, basically giving open and full support to their policies. That is why this decree has aroused such deep disapproval among believers.

. . . .

We, the priests of the Lithuanian SSR, thoroughly condemn the Vatican policy of igniting a new world war, its policy of smashing the united front of the struggle for peace, a policy directed against the working class, with the aim of helping imperialism and large monopolies.

We, the priests of the Lithuanian SSR, also energetically protest against the decree of Pope Pius XII, by means of which he has done untold harm to the Catholic Church and has for ever put himself in the position of passionately encouraging a new world war. The demon of war, which once somehow entered the youthful soul of Pius XII, will not let him rest even now in his old age.

We, the priests of the Lithuanian SSR, call on all workers – Catholics and non-Catholics, believers and non-believers, without regard to nationality or race – to form even stronger ranks against war and in the fight for peace.

Long live the unity of all workers in the fight against imperialists and exploiters!

The following reaction is typical of that of the majority of priests, when required by force to condemn the Pope unjustly:

Fr. Jonas Skardinskas, parish priest of Rudiškes who had been summoned to Trakai by the Chairman of the Executive Committee and had been shown the above document, said to the officials present:

You are young and don't know the basic truths of the catechism. The Pope is the Head of the Church, the representative of Christ on earth. And you ask me, an aged priest, to sign a libellous document directed against him. Young men, that is in very bad taste. Don't do it any more!

When Fr. Pranas Beliauskas, parish priest of Valkininkai, was summoned by the chairman of the Executive Committee and realised why, he asked the chairman to read the document he was being asked to sign. When he had done so, Fr. Beliauskas asked him to explain the meaning of the statement: "The demon of war, which once somehow entered the youthful soul of Pius XII, will not let him rest even now in his old age."

The chairman became confused and stated that he could not explain its meaning. Then Fr. Beliauskas said, "Chairman, we are both intelligent educated people. If we do something, we do it after thinking about it and fully understanding it. This document contains things which we do not understand. Tell me, can an intelligent person sign a document which he does not fully understand? That is why I will not sign it."

Mgr. Jonas Ušila, who was once rector of the Vilnius Theological Seminary until 1940 when he was deported by the Germans, was summoned together with Fr. J. Elert, by B. Pušinis, the senior executive of the Council for Religious Affairs, in order to sign the document against Pope Pius XII. The priest rose to his feet and said:

Sir, in spite of your elevated position, you are behaving dishonourably. You have dared to ask us to sign this rudely composed document against the Pope. What do you take us for? We are representatives of the Catholic Church, ageing priests. All my life I have taught candidates for the priesthood and believers to respect the Holy Father and to obey him. You want me, at the end of my life (the priest was in his eightieth year – Ed. of *CLCC*) to despise what I have held most dear, what I have believed, loved and taught. We protest most strongly against this insult to the Pope, the Head of the Church, to the Church herself and her priests. You persecute the Church, you have desecrated our beautiful and precious shrines and closed many of them down, you have turned monuments of art and beauty into warehouses, you have destroyed the Church's property – organs, liturgical vessels and vestments – unbelievably you have turned valuable theological works in the libraries of the theological seminaries and the universities into pulp. You don't allow the Seminary to function in Vilnius, you have closed the monasteries and confiscated them and their property, you have driven away the monks and nuns and forced them to write declarations denouncing monasteries, you have left them without shelter, without work or a crust of bread; you make priests and believers spy for you and act against their consciences. You are trying to destroy the Church from within, trying to find traitors among priests and believers. Such people exist and will be found – there is no lack of them even among you. You slander those who hold fast to Catholic principles, imprison them and hound them into camps. You should know that you will not tear faith out of our hearts by such terrorist actions. A reed sways and bends, but oak trees stand firm and produce new oaks, even stronger and more long-lived. The Church has lived through many persecutions. She has emerged purer and stronger from each of them. She will firmly endure even the present waves of terror. In persecuting the Church, you will achieve contradictory results: new heroes will be born – martyrs, who with their blood and suffering will wash away the blots caused by the weak-willed and careerists and will beautify the Church with their crowns of martyrdom, self-sacrifice and love. We shall have no lack of such people. If you torture some to death, others will arise in their place. Not only in the first centuries has Christian blood been the seed of new generations, but this has happened over and over again and will continue to happen in future. Whatever terrible and shameful method you use, you will not destroy faith, for faith is not of man, but of God. As God is eternal, so faith is eternal. You are to be pitied if you try to fight against God. I have finished. Now you can take me away.

After saying this, Mgr. Ušila and Canon Elert went out, leaving the official holding the shameful document in his hand.

It must be admitted that a few priests were found who signed the document. They were called progressive priests "who understand the spirit of the times well".

If Soviet officials could force Lithuanian priests to sign this document against the Pope, we should not be surprised if, nowadays, they make priests travel to peace conferences or the USA for propaganda purposes, alleging that the church in Lithuania is not persecuted. Praise be to those who have not bowed the knee to force![57]

29. THE FUNERAL OF CANON RAUDA

At 11 a.m. on 7 March 1974, Canon Petras Rauda died at Svedasai. He was born in 1894 in Radviliškis of a father who had been a book smuggler during the Tsarist interdict against the [printing of the] Lithuanian language and he himself had occasion to "take tutoring" [the clandestine study of Lithuanian].

Becoming a priest in 1917, he performed his duties faithfully all his life. As an assistant priest in Joniškis he contributed much to the birth of the Republic of Lithuania. For many years he served as a parish priest at various places in Lithuania. In Utena he saved the lives of several citizens of Jewish nationality. In 1944 Bishop Kazimieras Paltarokas elevated him to the position of Honorary Canon.

. . . .

During the post-war years he was harassed by security organs and sentenced to eight years in prison, because he had known of the memorandum directed abroad which had been prepared by P. Klimas, Mrs. Lastiene and others, but had not informed the security agencies.

Canon Rauda was imprisoned in camps at Turinsk, Okunev and Molotovsk. In Kaunas security prison Canon Rauda happened to be confined with Toliušis, a lawyer and leader of the Populist Party, and with "Vanagas" ("the Hawk"), leader of a partisan unit. The intelligence and placidity of the Canon, together with the heroic suffering and death of "Vanagas", led Toliušis to God and the Church. Upon his return from the camp, Toliušis used to say: "Seeing the church steeples, one wants to weep – Lithuania still lives!"

In 1957 Canon Rauda was arrested again, for keeping a diary in which he described the interrogations during his first imprisonment and life in the camps. He was sentenced to ten years' imprisonment. Confined in the camps of Mordovia, Canon Rauda made the acquaintance of the Primate of the Ukrainian Catholic Church, Metropolitan Slipyj (now a Cardinal and a member of the Sacred College) and became firm friends with him.

After five years, broken in health, Canon Rauda returned to Lithuania. In 1965, now completely blind, he still continued his pastoral ministry in Svedasai. During his final illness he said that he was offering his final sufferings for the Diocese of Panevežys. In response to one priest who asked him what he would like to say to the clergy he replied:

"All priests should be as dutiful as Canon Bronius Antanaitis."*

Canon Rauda knew foreign languages. In his homeland and in the camp he was surrounded by young people and the intelligentsia. Throughout his life he rejoiced over priests who performed their duties faithfully and prayed for those who betrayed the Church.

Canon Rauda prepared Professor Jurgutis for death and the author Vienuolis-Žukauskas went to him to confession on two occasions. The nation has lost a noble Lithuanian, and the Church a loyal defender and a man of sacrifice. A great light has gone out – a light which kindled hundreds of smaller lights.

The inhabitants of Svedasai came in great numbers to the church to pray for the soul of the beloved Canon. Preachers gave a good account of the life, work and suffering of the deceased.

It had been planned to bury him on Sunday, but the Executive Committee of Utena District would not allow it, for fear of a massive religious demonstration which might "negatively" influence school children. The local *soviet* of Utena would not allow participants in the funeral to prepare lunch in the dining room. Anykščiai and Utena would not allow taxis to take people from Svedasai to Utena. The collective farms of the Anykščiai, Kupiškis, Rokiškis and Utena Districts were forbidden to release lorries for the funeral.

Anykščiai permitted the hire of a car only to transport the coffin. What surprising solicitude on the part of the atheists, not to forget a deceased priest!

A car to carry the flowers was obtained from the seminary. Forty private cars accompanied the remains of Canon Rauda from Svedasai

---

Editorial Note
Born in 1925, Antanaitis was ordained as a priest in 1948; he was chaplain to Bishop Paltarokas until 1956, when he was appointed as parish priest in Zarasai. He was known as a zealous priest; as a result, he was forced by the authorities to leave Zarasai in 1962 and his next parish of Bartininkai some time later. He was then sent to the parish of Avilia in the Diocese of Panevežys.

to Utena. The streets were lined with people everywhere. Government officials who assiduously observed the funeral procession were able to see how the people of Lithuania can honour their spiritual leaders. Bishops Romualdas Krikščiunas, Julijonas Steponavičius and Liudvikas Povilonis assisted at the funeral, as well as 180 priests.[58]

30.   THE ECCLESIASTICAL WARRIOR
[original title, from a Soviet press article]

The sky was overcast. It was a slushy Saturday afternoon.

The priest of the Zarenai-Latveliai church, Petras Venckus, sat sadly at a table. It was not the overcast sky which put him in a bad mood: he was disturbed by the deterioration of spiritual matters. As darkness dies away and disappears before morning, so had the ranks of the lambs which he tended. Ever fewer were the squeaking boots to be heard in the church. Ever less roubles were to finish up in his ample pockets.

The spiritual shepherd, Venckus, annointed his tongue with a few goblets of vicarage brandy so that the voice of God would sound more sweetly from his lips and decided to herd some lambs.

He began to herd them or, to put it more accurately, to chase them.

Hurrying out, the little priest rolled up his sleeves, opened the door of the Zarenai dispensary and forced his way in.

Seeing Komsomol member, R. Ružauskaite, the intoxicated priest gesticulated, as though making the sign of the cross in the air, and struck the girl in the face as he shouted: "You so and so! Get out of here!"

Seized with fear of the stampeding spiritual shepherd, the girl ran out.

The next victim of a surprise attack by the parish priest was the nurse, Miss A. Lalaite, who was dealing with a patient's bandage. Without saying a word, the spiritual shepherd struck her in the face with his fist, accompanied with a stream of curses. "You will burn in hell, you lost sheep! . . . . This is for you!"

Knocked out by the blow, Miss Lalaite fell to the ground.

E. Jonušas, a young man who had brought his father to the dispensary, leaped forward and helped her up from the floor. When the battered and tearful nurse ran out, the priest shouted after her: "Oh, you anti-Christ!" The enraged cleric also hurled himself on Jonušas. "What sort of person are you? The scourge of God will also descend on you!"

As he wanted to strengthen his spiritual authority amongst the non-believers, the priest kicked Jonušas a few times, cursing vilely as he did so.

In the heat of the crusader's struggle Jonušas seized the enraged priest by his arms, subdued the spiritual shepherd and pushed him out through the door. The name of God and the aid of the devil for which Venckus cried out in his attempts to re-enter having failed him, he kicked the door a few times and then made off.

A blessed silence descended. Jonušas went home with his father. Fr. Venckus calmed down and dwelt upon his unsuccessful mission to return people to the ranks of the believers, drowning his sorrows in brandy, which he drank from a bottle as he stood in his garden.

When he became sober again, the priest realised that he had not brought any straying lambs to the path of righteousness and, sensing that he would have to account for his hooliganism under the law, he sent his housekeeper to Nurse Lalaite to ask her forgiveness.

"The father has asked you to forgive him . . . Let Almighty God be his judge . . ."

However, Fr. Venckus is an old acquaintance of earthly punishment. In the first years of the Soviet system in Lithuania he crossed the state frontier illegally and fled to Hitlerite Germany. During the occupation the holy man clattered back to Lithuania with the Hitlerite murderers. He honoured and blessed the brown killers who destroyed the peaceful Soviet people. In the post-war years Venckus became a close friend of the armed bandits, hiding these murderers beneath the wide skirts of his soutane. He himself also had to hide – he lived with falsified documents. After running amok, Venckus would now like to wriggle out under the pretext of "God's judgment". His efforts are useless. To keep hooligans in order, no matter which clothes they flaunt, we have the People's Court.[59]

Akmene district.   A. Tarka

31. WHEN THE BELLS ARE SILENCED
[original title, from a Soviet press article]

The church bells ring and again they fall silent. The festival is at its height. The church servants scurry around nimbly. Like the embodiment of goodness, the parish priest of Ylakiai, Skirmontas, rises from among them into the pulpit. One looks at him and wonders: how beautifully he walks on this sinful earth, his eyes are always cast down, his lips pressed together to form a tiny heart, lost in deep meditation.

And when Skirmontas gives voice, then all sinful thoughts flee and one's conscience can find no respite.

What, asks the priest, is the value of life in this vale of tears?

What use has a pure and God-fearing Catholic for all those earthly fortunes and riches? What wordly avarice or pagan pleasure can vie with the kingdom of heaven?

It was as if a prophet was speaking through the lips of the parish priest. "How pure he is, how good and selfless," the parishioners of Ylakiai think, as they throw their savings into the pastor's silver plate. As the saying goes, one could give even one's last shirt to such a priest, purely for the greater glory of God. It is doubtful, however, that the believers of Ylakiai parish know where their savings go when given to "the greater glory of God." It transpires that without any miracle their money finds its way to Palanga where, at No. 11 Draugystes Gatve [Friendship Street], they have become . . . not a church, but a truly splendid house. From the mere fact that the very elite of the priesthood deigns to stay at Skirmontas's cottage, it can be seen that the parishioners' money has not been thrown away on some dog's kennel or other, but used for something substantial.

Perhaps Skirmontas, as a God-fearing Catholic, had no thought of using that little castle with evil intent, perhaps he erected it with the believers' money for their use? Perhaps the old ladies who pray at Ylakiai can find shelter with their priest when they travel to Palanga? Let them try, but for time being he takes one and a half roubles a day for a bed.[60]

32.   KGB ATTEMPTS TO RECRUIT PRIESTS

The KGB tries to recruit priests through its network to serve as agents. To draw them into their sinister work of ruining the Church, security officials cajole and threaten the clergy, promising in exchange to let them work in a good parish, to be made parish priests, to advance even higher, to study in Rome, to travel in the United States – at times they even offer them a monthly wage outright.

KGB agents blackmail morally weak priests: "If you don't sign up and co-operate, all your sins will be dragged out into the open." KGB agents have been successful in enlisting various problem priests, forcing them to carry out assignments for the Soviet Government. Such co-opted priests never work seriously for the police; rather, feeling an internal conflict, they finally succumb psychologically and have an emotional breakdown, or take to drink. Such priests try to justify their actions, claiming that they are not wrecking the Church, but merely seeking "dialogue" with the Soviet Government.

*The Vatican, it seems, does not understand what such "dialogue" means. It is utter capitulation, the complete betrayal of the Church's cause.** This is borne out by the experience of priests since the Second World War. Foreigners consider that priests who have been recruited by the security apparatus are able to adapt to conditions under persecution. This shows utter ignorance of the situation in our country.

*Italics in the original.

Bishops are forced by the Government to assign more active priests "on probation" to timid parish priests, or to those recruited by the KGB. The latter convince such priests that they must answer for all their assistants' "intemperate actions". They order them to see that they do not travel too much, and so on . . . . Nowadays many of the more zealous priests suffer more from their own than from government functionaries. In this manner the Government polarizes the clergy, pitting priest against chancery and chancery against priest.

Priests working for the security organs call their conscientious colleagues hotheads, extremists and revolutionaries, saying that they are banging their heads against the wall. They consider themselves, on the contrary, as wise and able calmly to "keep up the good work", even though their church is left meanwhile with just a few old people.

. . . .

The special task of recruited priests is to "straighten out" the thinking of tourists from abroad, and especially that of priests. They describe the situation of the Church falsely, as if religion were not harassed, as if all who wished could pray, as though the seminary provided enough priests for parish work, and making out that some priests are just hotheads. "If it weren't for them, the bishops could obtain more privileges from the Government", they claim.

In an effort to prove how good the Soviet Government is to priests, visitors from abroad might be shown the villa of Mgr. Krivaitis on the Neris River, or the home of Fr. S. Lydžius, parish priest of the Immaculate Conception in Vilnius. The foreigner cannot reach the backwaters and see how priests sometimes lack the bare necessities of life. For example, the parish priest of Valakbudis, Fr. A. Lukošaitis, spent the summer of 1972 in a tent pitched in the churchyard, because the Government would not let him purchase a house, even though a building confiscated from the parish was standing practically empty.

To know the real truth, to feel the disguised ill-will of the Soviet officials, their hypocrisy and deceit, one must spend a longer time in Lithuania. So it is not surprising that even the Vatican has long been deceived.

From the viewpoint of us who live in Lithuania, there have been decisions not in the best interests of the Catholic Church here. Even now the priests and the faithful of Lithuania are disturbed that the Holy See, while defending victims of discrimination all over the world, barely mentions the "Church of Silence and Suffering", and does not point out or condemn the secret or open persecution of the faithful in the Soviet Union.

In Lithuania no one believes that dialogue with the Soviet Government is possible. It is needed by the atheist government only so that, after gaining our confidence, they might more easily wreck the Church from within. In Lithuania it is plain to all that the Church will not be destroyed if priests are imprisoned, if school children are forced to speak and to act against their own convictions, if there is no press, no officially published prayer book or catechism. However, the Catholic Church in Lithuania will lose the people if it loses credibility by licking the boots of the Soviet regime. This is what has happened to the Orthodox Church in Russia.[61]

33. A PRIEST DESCRIBES HIS MINISTRY

In the Soviet Union there is separation of Church and State and yet there is probably no other State in the world which is so inclined to interfere in the life of the Church.

. . . .

Everyone knows that in the Soviet Union specialists treat patients, teach medical students and generally train other specialists. However, the Soviet Government has entrusted the instruction of priests to incompetent individuals, fanatical atheists. Atheists tell priests how they must carry out religious rites.

When I was working in Švenčioneliai, V. Bukielskis, chairman of the local Executive Committee, told me: "If you want to accompany the deceased to the cemetery, take off your vestments and walk at the rear of the column. You may only walk behind." When I asked on what procedure he based this order, he replied pompously, "It's a government regulation!" What would the faithful think if I accompanied the deceased to the cemetery and there recited only the final requiem, as I was instructed to do by the chairman of the Executive Committee of Švenčioniai on 2 October 1972?

I cannot perform religious rites in any way other than that indicated by the Roman Catholic Ritual for Lithuanian Dioceses, which is edited by the Liturgical Commission of the Bishops of Lithuania, passed by the Soviet censor and approved by the Sacred Congregation of Rites. In Soviet Lithuania an ecclesiastical hierarchy still survives – there are diocesan chanceries and even a liturgical commission – but it is not these which give the directions, but the completely incompetent state organs. The chanceries only retain the right of consultation.

If a priest displeases the Government, he is victimized. I suffered morally and materially. Here are the facts.

I was removed from the parish of Švenčioneliai by blackmail: "If you don't leave Švenčioneliai, you'll have to leave the priesthood," I was told by Rugienis.

The house which I had erected beside the church at Švenčioneliai was confiscated illegally . . . .

Fr. B. Laurinavičius[62]

Adutiškis,
31 July 1973.

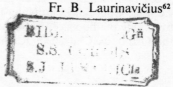

34. OVERWORKING THE CLERGY

Šeduva. On 27 August 1972 the Administrator of the Dioceses of Panevėžys and Kaišiadorys was conferring the Sacrament of Confirmation. The Government allowed only two priests to assist, but there were about 3,000 to be confirmed. Exhausted by the strain of the work, the 62-year-old rector of Šeduvos Pakrojus, Juozas Ražanskas, died in the sacristy just after he had finished preaching.[63]

35. PARISH COUNCILS: INSTRUMENTS OF STATE CONTROL (1974)

According to the Soviet Constitution, the Church is separated from the State. Yet the State interferes in the affairs of the Church at every turn through the office of the Executive for Religious Affairs and through parish councils, into which every effort is made to introduce persons as friendly to the atheists as possible, or even their trusted agents.

Church leaders immediately became aware of the atheists' scheme to paralyze pastoral work. At the moment the atheists are trying to introduce into Lithuania the same system as in Russia, Ukraine, Belorussia, and elsewhere, whereby parish councils become the real administrators of the parish and the priests merely their employees.

The parish council has to take care of financial matters and see to the necessary repairs; believers must apply to it to bury the dead, baptize children or to marry. This is an attempt to intimidate people away from religious practice. Since the parish council would hire and dismiss priests the functions of the bishop would become meaningless, or worse: the bishop would be left simply a figure-head to hide from general view the atheists' manipulations being carried out behind the scenes.

Lately, priests in Lithuania have been forced to accept new agreements concluded between district Executive Committees and the parish councils, without their bishops' knowledge. They are unilaterally and very vaguely formulated, especially as regards the closing of a church. The fourth paragraph of the agreement says:

"This agreement can be terminated . . . if, in accordance with established procedure, it is decided to close the house of prayer (the facility for worship), the use of which was permitted by this agreement."

The faithful cannot agree with any plan to close a church.

To forestall objections, the agreements are concluded secretly, at different times and even by fraud. It is regrettable that priests themselves – to say nothing of the faithful – sometimes enter into these agreements without fully thinking them over. Those priests who are not deceived by the trickery of the atheists resist signing vaguely-formulated agreements and refuse to hand over jurisdiction over their church to parish council members who have been intimidated by the atheists. These new agreements are the first step towards the final limitation of the bishops' and priests' freedom of action.

Fortunately, the bishops have until now refused to agree to the uncanonical arrangements for which the government is pressing. However, there are signs that new efforts will now be made to turn parish councils in Lithuania into all-powerful administrators of parishes. This has been mentioned by Tarasov, an official of the Council for Religious Affairs.

Actions of parish councils in line with the atheists' plan completely contravene traditional ecclesiology, in which the right to govern comes not from the people, but from Christ Himself. It is therefore not surprising that ever since the Revolution church leaders have never agreed to such parish councils. The Lithuanian Bishops, Paltarokas, Reinys and others, all refused to agree to them. Only when the widespread closure of churches and arrests of the clergy began, and when a few priests in the city of Vilnius treacherously made concessions, did the bishops accept the formation of parish councils. To date, however, these councils – with very few exceptions – have never directly interfered in the work of parish priests.[64]

36. THE TRIAL OF FR. JUOZAS ZDEBSKIS

In the large Prienai parish about 300 children are prepared every year for their First Communion. And so it was in 1971. On 16 July the children and their mothers met in Prienai church for catechism. While Fr. Zdebskis was teaching and questioning the children, a band of officials forced their way into the church. They photographed the children, asked their surnames and drew up a report. A commotion developed in the church. Angered at the behaviour of the Soviet officials, the parents themselves addressed the Party Control Committee of the CPSU:

> On 16 July of this year we the undersigned brought our children to church so that the priest could test them, to see if they were ready for First Communion.
>
> Suddenly a group of men and women forced their way into the church. Among them were the chairman of the Executive Committee, the Komsomol secretary, teachers and members of the police. The uninvited guests began to take over in the church; they photographed the children and asked their surnames. One girl became so frightened she fainted . . . .
>
> The mothers could not defend their children. In response to requests not to interrupt the proceedings, the uninvited guests answered: "The commotion is not caused by us, but by these women."
>
> Such behaviour on the part of government representatives does not bring glory upon Soviet laws. We ask that the persecution of believers be stopped.

This statement was signed by eighty-nine parents and was sent to Moscow. Unfortunately, Moscow did not answer the Catholics of Prienai.

The Procurator's Office of Prienai began to investigate the children, parents and Fr. Zdebskis. Investigator A. Pakstys searched the flat of Fr. Zdebskis.

On 26 August the former telephoned Fr. Zdebskis and asked him to call at his office 'for a moment'. Here he was arrested.

People found out about the arrest of the priest and came to the procurator's office, demanding that he be released. They said: "If you're arresting our priest, then arrest us first, since we took our children to him. It is his duty to teach and examine the children." From the procurator's office the believers went to the party secretary, but he refused to see them. A wave of anger spread through all of Prienai parish and beyond its borders. On Sunday one could see masses of people waiting their turn to sign complaints addressed to Soviet organs.

. . . .

> As a priest, he conscientiously carried out his duties. He did evil to no one. We believe that the arrest of our priest is due to some misunderstanding and therefore we ask for an investigation into the cause of his arrest, and that he be released.
>
> Fr. Zdebskis is accused of preparing children for their First Communion. If he is guilty because he fulfilled his lawful priestly obligations, then why does the Soviet Constitution guarantee freedom of conscience and religion? We believe that this arrest directly contradicts Soviet law.

. . . .

This statement was signed by about 350 people. The people of Prienai personally took it and delivered it to the Procurator of the

USSR, where they were promised that the matter would be investigated. The believers also appealed to the Procurator of the Lithuanian Republic and to Rugienis, the executive of the Council for Religious Affairs. He spoke angrily: "I know Fr. Zdebskis". The parishioners answered: "We know him even better."

On 30 August Fr. Zdebskis was taken to Vilnius. From early morning a throng of people stood near the police office, waiting for the time when he would be taken away. The KGB photographed the people and tried to disperse them. "What are you hanging around for? Do you want to bring about a miracle?" "More than a miracle!" answered the people. At 4 p.m. while crowds of people were standing there in tears, they put Fr. Zdebskis into a car and drove him away.

On 3 September Fr. Zdebskis' flat was again very closely searched. Someone spread rumours that he had been arrested not for teaching children, but because radio broadcasting equipment and other such things were found among his belongings. Since it was the government officials who spoke this way, it seems that they wanted to compromise the arrested priest even more and to discourage believers from defending him.

During the second half of September the faithful of Prienai took another statement to Moscow . . . . It was signed by 2,010 believers. This was a brave protest of the people against religious persecution.

How deeply the people reacted to the arrest of Fr. Zdebskis can be seen from several facts. On the occasion of the religious festival in Šiluva celebrating the birth of Mary about 200 people made offerings for Masses.

Since Santaikai was now without a parish priest, a statement was addressed to the General Secretary of the USSR, asking that Fr. Zdebskis be released, since the bishop did not have anyone else to fill the vacancy.

Weeks and months raced by, the day of Fr. Zdebskis' trial was delayed and kept secret with great care. On the eve of 11 October news spread like lightning through Prienai: "Fr. Juozas' trial will be tomorrow in Kaunas."

The next day would show the true face of the Soviet Government in relation to believers.

From early morning people filled the court house, the staircase up to the third storey and the yard. Many people had flowers in their hands. Everyone was waiting for the arrival of Fr. Zdebskis. The police were scurrying around. As the hour for the trial neared, they started 'to put things in order' – they forcibly ejected people and even drew blood from one woman. A large throng of KGB personnel occupied the places of the ejected Catholics. In addition to them, the courtroom held the witnesses – the children and their parents and people from various organizations in Prienai. They had to enact a charade, the spectacle of an open court in session . . . into which the

KGB allowed only atheists. Without a doubt the Government did not want to publicize this trial.

The arrests of believers began on the stairs. One young man was arrested because he asked the police why only atheists were allowed inside, while believers were not. They held him for fifteen days in the police station. A priest who accompanied Fr. Zdebskis's mother was arrested in the court-house corridor and taken away to the KGB office for interrogation.

Outside the court the crowd continued to grow. The police began to arrest those people who had flowers in their hands, and forcibly propelled them into cars. A great deal of confusion and shouting ensued. An order was given to the police to disperse the crowd, which numbered about 500-600. The order was carried out by force, and then they began to arrest individuals. A priest who happened to be walking by was arrested and charged with organizing the demonstration. Throughout the day, the police guarded Ozeskiene Street and did not permit people to gather. "Why are you standing around here like pigs?" – that is how the police 'greeted' people. Some were even chased out of nearby shops. A policeman came into one of the shops and called out, "Throw these church bigots out of here." Most of those arrested were released in the evening. One was taken to a psychiatric hospital and later held for fifteen days in prison. On this day the people demonstrated their solidarity with the priest who was on trial, while the KGB and police showed the crowd how the Soviet Government deals with the rights of believers.

In order to keep the Jewish nation in a state of fear, every month Antiochus, the king of the Syrians, killed some of those who remained faithful to the laws of God. Many chose to die rather than to give up their faith (see I Maccabees 1).

Fr. Zdebskis' trial had the same purpose – to keep the nation in an atmosphere of fear so that no one would dare to demand more freedom.

Persecution brings about fear, nevertheless we offer it up in God's name; suffering for the faith causes our people to think about and fight for the most important human values.

The People's Court of Kaunas district consisted of People's Judge, V. Gumuliauskas, presiding, and People's Assessors, Vasiliauskas and Mrs. Palaisiene. Miss Černiauskaite served as secretary. Also participating in the trial were Procurator A. Miliukas, Public Prosecutor S. Patinskas and defence council A. Riauba.

The judge read the minutes – excerpts selected by the Public Prosecutor – of a meeting held by the teachers of Prienai Secondary School. Then the judge read out the statistics of Fr. Zdebskis' life (born 1929, in Kapsukas district, in Naujiena village) and the charge against him, after which he started to question the defendant himself. The following extracts are taken from the proceedings:

"Have you ever been punished by a court?"

"Yes, I have."

"For what?"

"For the same reason as this time. Later the Supreme Court reversed the sentence."

"Have you ever been denied the right to fulfil your priestly duties?"

"I was."

"Why?"

"I can't tell the honoured court, because in my mind I still don't know why my rights were taken away."

"What do you have to say about the present charge?"

"I must state that I reject the charge that I organized the teaching of children. I didn't organize it – that would be absolutely unthinkable because of the time problem involved in going to homes or travelling among villages. The examination of children who are preparing for their First Communion goes on all year and those who want to can come at any time. However, it's more convenient for the children during the summer when they're on holiday and don't have classes; therefore, the majority of children come voluntarily."

"How many children were there in each group?"

"Sometimes one, sometimes more . . ."

"Could there have been groups of as many as a hundred?"

"Yes," he answered joyfully, "sometimes there were groups of that many. I'm happy, too, that there's a sufficiently large number of conscientious parents who prepare their children very well; they can be allowed to receive the Sacraments after only one examination. There are also some children who are not quite so intelligent and who may not be allowed to receive the Sacrament because they don't understand the tenets of the faith."

"The inspector has noted that some children attended for as long as two weeks."

"That could be."

"Is a count or attendance record kept?"

"No, I spoke with anyone who came. So that there would be no misunderstanding, those who were successfully examined received cards which permitted them to receive their First Communion. There were some children who couldn't answer the questions at first, so I would explain it all to them."

"Who told them that the Church was holding such classes for children?"

"Ordinarily, an announcement would be made in church during the sermon that parents should concern themselves with their children, should teach them their catechism and, since holidays are the most convenient time, that the children be brought to confirm their knowledge, after being prepared by their parents."

"Were you the only priest who made such announcements or did other priests also do so?"

"Whoever preached the sermon would make an announcement."

"Did you alone teach the children or did the other priests also do so?"

"Since I'm the younger at Prienai Church, I carried the larger share of the work; the parish priest has other kinds of work to do." Among all the priests, Fr. Zdebskis was charged with instigating the catechism classes.

"I wasn't the one to instigate the preparation of the children to receive the Sacraments. This would be too great an honour for me. Other priests, too, carry out this obligation to teach, which was given to us by Christ and the Church. I would be a slanderer if I said that they don't teach. Each one must answer how he fulfils this obligation according to his conscience."

After this, minors were interrogated as witnesses. The judge asked their full names and urged them: "Tell the court the whole truth. Do you know this person? Turn around and look!"

Some answered, "I know him"; others said "No." One little boy, after looking for a long time at the priest who stood smiling at him, answered: "He's changed a great deal." When the judge asked them what he had taught them, some said, "Prayers," and others said, "He didn't teach, but only questioned us." Some of the others answered, "He taught us not to break windows, not to pick pockets, not to fight, not to steal and to obey our teachers and parents." The judge asked them when the classes started and ended and when they had their holidays. Some children stated the times, others said they did not remember. When the judge asked them what books they had used and where they obtained catechisms, almost everyone answered that their mothers or grandmothers had them. The more shy children cried or kept silent. Fr. Zdebskis stood when each child entered, but the judge brought him to order every time: 'Sit down.'

After this they began to interrogate the parents. Witness R: "I prepared my child and took him to the priest so that he could test him."

"Did the child want to go on his own or did you take him?"

"Our parents brought us, so I took my children."

Defence Counsel: 'Did someone bring pressure to bear on you to take the child there, whether you wanted to or not?"

"No, I took him of my own free will?"

The parents who appeared as witnesses were questioned a great deal on how often they took their children to the priest, what the priest talked about, how many children there were in each group, and so forth.

Later the local authorities of Prienai were questioned.

Witness Kučinskas:

"At the beginning of July the Executive Committee received reports from people that the priest of Prienai was teaching children religion in the church. We went there and found about fifty children and some women. Fr. Zdebskis was instructing them. When we entered the church, he called for a pause and then we went into the vestry to talk. We notified him that this kind of behaviour was against the law, but he answered, 'I am teaching and will continue to teach. When the laws of God and the Church conflict with the laws of the State, then God must be obeyed.' He did not pay attention to our warning. A week later the commission and I went to the church once more and again we found Fr. Zdebskis teaching. A statement of the facts was drawn up."

"Was Fr. Zdebskis tactful?"

"Yes, he was. At first he even joked, 'Perhaps you came for your children? Would you like to help with the preparation'?"

"Did you make a statement of the facts both times?"

"Yes, I did."

Witness M. Naginevičius:

. . . .

"The chairman of the Executive Committee of Lazdijai District wrote that in Kapčiamiestis, as a result of the influence of Fr. Zdebskis, religious work became more active; they carry around crosses and crowns, even though they have no right to do so. They lured away Pioneers and Young Octobrists and signed them up for the Rosary Society. Fr. Zdebskis has a 'Java' motorcycle and rides around to homes. He visited a Communist family and told them he could baptize their children in their own home."

All these documents containing accusations, photographs and warnings make up fifty-three pages. After they were made public, Fr. Zdebskis asked that he be permitted to explain his motives in his final statement.

Then the legal arguments began. The Public Prosecutor, the head of Prienai Secondary Boarding School, S. Ratinskas, said in his speech that Fr. Zdebskis was aware of the laws forbidding the teaching of religion to minors, but he did not care about them, claiming he was obedient to higher ones. Breaking the law could not be countenanced Fr. Zdebskis was discrediting the teaching in the schools.

. . . .

The prosecutor ended his speech by relating a slanderous rumour about Fr. Zdebskis. The following is a summary of his address:

"Parents and guardians have a right to teach their children religion. There are penalties for putting obstacles in the way of religious ceremonies. Vatican II's declaration on Christian Education states

that, in addition to parents, the Government also has rights regarding children. Fr. Zdebskis transgressed the law on the separation of the Church and State. During July and August 1971 he organized and systematically carried out the teaching of minors – about 200-300 children; therefore, he should be punished according to the law."
. . . .

The defence council mentioned Lenin's requirement that believers should not be insulted and that the prosecutor had done just that in spreading unfounded rumours about Fr. Zdebskis. In completing his presentation, the defence counsel asked the court not to apply Article 143 of the Penal Code, but to leave it up to the Executive Committee to fine Fr. Zdebskis fifty roubles.

Fr. Zdebskis then made his final statement. The judge interrupted his speech several times, not permitting him to develop his thoughts. Therefore we present the full text of Fr. Juozas Zdebskis' intended address.

"On 26 August 1971 I was arrested and a case was brought against me because I was teaching children the catechism in Prienai church during the summer of that year. One of the statements in the charge reads: 'About seventy children and fifty parents were discovered in the church. He is charged according to Article 143 of the Penal Code of the Lithuanian SSR – the article which refers to the separation of the Church and State. The charge was made known to the person apprehended.'

"What was the reason for my behaviour? It is sufficient to repeat what was said in church when the group of atheists came in and asked me if I knew that it was forbidden to teach children. It is proper to answer with the same words which the first disciples of Jesus used to the council: 'We ought to obey God rather than men' (Acts 5:29).
. . . .

"Freedom for the Catholic Church, as a juridical entity, has meaning only if it is permitted to function. For example, if one is permitted to live, then this extends to eating, breathing and so forth. If priests are officially permitted to exist, then by the same token they are allowed to bear witness by performing their basic duties – saying Mass, forgiving sins in God's name and teaching.

"It comes to this – I am being tried for fulfilling my rightful duties.

"The problem of freedom of conscience is decided in Soviet law by the separation of Church and State. But, thanks to some atheists, the Church does not feel separated from the State, but just the opposite – she is bent to the interests of the atheists, and that frequently by means of deceit and fraud.
. . . .

"The aim of the atheists is to prevent the public – especially young people, students and workers – from participating at Mass. Surely they intuitively feel that it is easiest to know God face to face when one is deep in prayer.

. . . .

"In a number of cases, the behaviour of atheists smacks of deliberate deceit and fraud in regard to matters of conscience. Why are there no penalities? Often the conduct of atheists in relation to believers is similar to that found in the writings of Shakespeare in his portrayal of the fifteenth-century Duke of Gloucester who, in seeking to become King of England, murdered all his rivals, but then appeared before the public carrying a prayer book.

. . . .

"Honoured Judges, I would like to think that you, just like the majority of the people of the younger generation, know God today from *Biblijos Linksmybes* ('Joys of the Bible') and similar books, but that you do not know that God died for us on the cross. Even though you have diplomas of higher education in your special subjects, it is doubtful if you could pass such a religious examination as the children have before their First Communion.

. . . .

"We are obliged to forgive you for this trial and to pray to God for his forgiveness. That day, as I mentioned, when an uproar was created in the church, I asked the children: 'Children, should we hate these people?' They answered: 'No.' 'And what is the most important of the commandments of Jesus?' 'To consider no one as your enemy,' they answered again.

. . . .

"In such a situation, looking at it in a merely human and short-sighted manner, we would like to repeat words of Christ: 'Father . . . let this cup pass from me.' However, in reality, we priests should thank you for this and similar trials. These occasions force our consciences to speak, do not permit us to fall asleep, and force us to rethink our position between two alternatives.

"The first alternative – to choose the way of so-called 'peaceful cooperation' with atheists – is an attempt to serve two masters and pander to the whims of the atheists: the priest should do his duty, but he should not be a danger to atheism. He himself should drive young people from the church and not allow them to participate in rites and processions or to serve Mass; in preparing children for First Communion he should simply be satisfied with teaching them prayers, and not require them to understand the mysteries of the Mass, the centre of all Christian life . . . .

"You have shown me thousands of young people behind bars. Not one of them knows of a God whom we should love and who loves us. No one has spoken to them of such a God, no one has taught them to find happiness in doing good to everyone, even to one's enemies. I well know that if we priests do not speak about such things, then the stones will begin to cry out and God will hold us responsible for their fate!

"This is what is meant in our situation by peaceful co-operation with atheists. This is what believers living abroad cannot understand at all.

"The second possibility is to be a priest according to Christ's design, to be determined to fulfil the obligations called for by Christ and canon law. It also means accepting everything which fate permits one to suffer, as we can see in this situation: to choose windows with bars. As the prosecution said, 'You didn't want roast duck, so now you'll eat prison bread.'

"If the courts fail to judge us priests now, then our nation will judge us! After that there will be the last judgment by the Supreme Being. May God help us priests to fear this more than your judgment.

"I call again to mind those thousands of young people behind bars. In their childhood they did not know how to obey their parents . . . . the nation of the Nemunas River is dear to me. I know quite well that it will not continue to exist if its children do not have the strength to obey their parents. I have spoken to them about this, telling them that this is a commandment of God.

"If you hold this to be a crime according to your conscience, then admit that I am a fanatic and find me guilty, but at the same time, you will judge yourselves!

"I ask the court . . . . not to forget that its decision may cause thousands of believers to think that some paragraphs of the constitution are only written for propaganda purposes. Can there be respect for requirements which make one act against one's conscience? Can there be any respect for laws which forbid one to fulfil one's obligations?

"All that is left is for me to repeat the words of the first apostles which I have already spoken to the court, 'We must obey God rather than men'."

There was a two-hour recess after Fr. Zdebskis' address. Returning after a lengthy consultation, the court, in the name of the Lithuanian SSR, announced this verdict:

"Juozas Vincento Zdebskis, born 1929, is guilty under Article 143 of the Penal Code of the Lithuanian SSR and is sentenced to one year's loss of freedom, to be served in a general regime corrective labour colony. The sentence is to run from 26 August 1971," [the time of his arrest two months previously].

On 9 December 1971, the Collegium for Criminal Cases of the Supreme Court of the Lithuanian SSR upheld the verdict that Fr. Zdebskis was guilty on all counts and that the sentence was the correct punishment for the crime committed by him.

At the present time, Fr. Zdebskis is serving his sentence in Praveniškiai.

May the offering of those suffering for their faith restore the land of our fathers!

★　　　★　　　★

On 26 August 1972, the faithful of Prienai went to the detention camp at Praveniškiai to meet Fr. Zdebskis, the assistant priest of Prienai, as he emerged to freedom. However, he was released a day early to avoid 'political demonstrations'. The assembled parishioners greeted Fr. Zdebskis solemnly on Sunday 27 August. As he returned to the sacristy after Mass, children scattered flowers in his path. In the churchyard young and old alike greeted the former prisoner. There were so many flowers for him that he could not hold them all. Rugienis would not allow His Excellency, Bishop Labukas, to appoint Zdebskis to the Diocese of Vilkaviškis. Two months later Fr. Zdebskis was appointed assistant priest in Šilute, Diocese of Telšiai. This was a polite means of exile, as if to say, 'If you want to work in a parish, leave your diocese.'

★　　　★　　　★

Rugienis wanted Fr. Juozas Zdebskis, who had just come back from a term in a labour camp, quietly exiled from his Diocese of Vilkaviškis to that of Telšiai. When the plan fell through, the People's Police of Prienai gave Fr. Zdebskis fifteen days to find a job.

On 8 January 1973 Fr. Zdebskis was summoned to the Prienai police station, whence he was taken under guard to a hospital to see whether he was healthy enough to perform physical labour.

On 26 January 1973 Fr. Zdebskis received a stern warning that he had fifteen days to obtain any employment other than as a priest; otherwise he would be assigned a job at the discretion of the police.

The civil authorities gave Fr. Zdebskis permission to assume priestly duties only in the Diocese of Telšiai. What is the legal basis for such action, especially since no court has put the priest under a sentence of exile? Canon law does not recognize the sentence of exile; besides, Fr. Zdebskis never violated any canon law. The Church has registered him in the Diocese of Vilkaviškis and he had no obligation to serve in any other diocese.

In April 1973 Fr. Zdebskis was assigned to the parish of Kučiunai, located in a border area. Earlier, on the orders of the police he had taken work as a car-park attendant in Kaunas. Government agents spread the rumour that Fr. Zdebskis himself did not wish to work in a parish.

★　　　★　　　★

DECLARATION

During the 1974 trial of Petronis and others,* the final statement I made at my trial on 11 November 1971 was used as part of the evidence that the *Chronicle of the Lithuanian Catholic Church* publishes fabrications and that no such speech was delivered during my trial.

On 29 April 1972 officials played a tape-recording of my trial to a group of priests, to prove that the speech published in the first issue of the *Chronicle* was not delivered in that form during the trial. In addition, Fr. S. Tamkevičius was publicly accused before all those present of having reproduced my speech and sent it abroad.

I consider it my duty to make the facts clear: the *Chronicle of the Lithuanian Catholic Church* published my speech accurately in its written form, which I prepared before the trial. There was only one mistake: in quoting Canon Law a number "3" was omitted, Instead of Canons 1329 and 1330, it said "129" and "130".

Why are there discrepancies? At the trial when I made the speech, the judge kept interrupting me with questions or making remarks, and finally he completely broke off my statement by expounding the psychological motivation of my behaviour.

I do not consider myself competent to discuss the question of how my statement from the trial reached the *Chronicle of the Lithuanian Catholic Church.*

J. Zdebskis, Priest

Šlavantai, 25 February 1975

★   ★   ★

On 14 January 1975 an attempt was made on the life of Fr. Zdebskis. When he was driving a car down the road between Meteliai and Seiriai, in the Lazdijai district, two cars driven by KGB men tried to cause an accident. Only the car was damaged.[65]

★   ★   ★

DECLARATION

On 10 March 1976 the traffic policeman Yurevich detained the priest of our parish, Fr. Juozas Zdebskis, who was driving a car, and declared that he was drunk. He ordered the priest to go to the psychiatric hospital to establish the degree of drunkenness.

Here an indictment was drawn up without taking a blood sample, although the priest himself had asked for this. The traffic police deprived him of his driver's licence, and the district newspaper published a news item claiming that the priest had been apprehended in Vilnius for drunken driving.

*See pp. 265-270.

We, the believers of Šlavantai parish, know that our priest never touches alcohol. This is also confirmed by the three people who were travelling with him, to whom no attention was paid as witnesses at the time of the event. Such a brutal insult to the priest is also an affront to us believers. It is by such methods that atheist propaganda is to be pursued? We therefore demand that the failure of the Vilnius traffic police and psychiatric hospital employees to carry out their duties be investigated and the consequences be remedied: namely, the driver's licence should be returned . . . .

308 signatures[66]

Šlavantai,
19 May 1976

NOTES TO CHAPTER IV

1. Trevor Beeson, *Discretion and Valour*, (British Council of Churches' team study of religion in Eastern Europe), London, 1974, pp. 207-9.
2. *CLCC* 10, p. 12 (E), p. 5 (L).
3. William C. Fletcher, *Religion and Soviet Foreign Policy*, London, 1973, pp. 31-4, gives an example.
4. Bociurkiw, "Religious Dissent in the USSR: Lithuanian Catholics", p. 24, note 6, gives the probable figure as 180, but Matas Raišupis, in *Dabarties Kankiniai*, (Chicago, Ill., 1972, p. 393), gives 330.
5. *CLCC* 9, p. 5 (E), p. 2 (L) quotes several articles which Mišutis published in 1973-4.
6. *Ibid.*, p. 10 (E), p. 5 (L).
7. *CLCC* 12, p. 17 (E), p. 13 (L).
8. I am indebted to Savasis, *The War Against God in Lithuania*, pp. 86-106, for this section. He presents a fuller account, well documented from published Soviet sources.
9. Bourdeaux, *Patriarch and Prophets*, pp. 65-84.
10. Savasis, *op. cit.*, p. 100. Cf. the campaign against the Orthodox, from Bourdeaux, *op. cit.*, p. 72. See also Struve, *Christians in Contemporary Russia*, pp. 207-8.
11. Savasis, *op. cit.*, p. 102.
12. *Ibid.*, p. 103.
13. *Ibid.*, pp. 93-4.
14. *Ibid.*, pp. 94-5 and 100; cf. *CLCC* 5, p. 50 (E), p. 19 (L).
15. Savasis, *op. cit.*, pp. 95-6.
16. *Ibid.*, p. 102.
17. *Ibid.*, pp. 88-9 and 101.
18. *Ibid.*, p. 104.
19. *Ibid.*, pp. 99-100.
20. *Ibid.*, pp. 86-90. See also Chapter IX and Bociurkiw, *op. cit.*, p. 6.
21. Savasis, *op. cit.*, pp. 97-9.

22. *Ibid.,* pp. 105-6.
23. *Ibid.,* pp. 96-7.
24. *Ibid.,* pp. 90-1; cf. *CLCC* 1, pp. 23 and 5, p. 50 (E), p. 19 (L).
25. See Chapter IX.
26. Savasis, *op. cit.,* p. 91.
27. *Ibid.,* pp. 92-3.
28. *Ibid.,* pp. 91-2.
29. Bourdeaux, *Patriarch and Prophets,* pp. 196-7.
30. Bociurkiw, *op. cit.,* p. 5; *CLCC* 4, pp. 6-7 (E), pp. 8-9 (L).
31. *CLCC* 9, p. 29 (E), p. 16 (L).
32. *RCL* 2, 1976, pp. 4-10.
33. Bourdeaux, *Patriarch and Prophets,* pp. 44-6. 204-8, 344; *Journal of the Moscow Patriarchate,* Moscow, August 1961, pp. 15-17.
34. Bourdeaux, *Religious Ferment in Russia,* pp. 20-38. This book is a study of the origins of the movement.
35. *Ibid.,* pp. 20-1, 190-210.
36. *Ibid.,* pp. 83-93.
37. See Radio Liberty, *Arkhiv Samizdata,* Vol. 17, Munich 1976.
38. *CLCC* 2, p. 35 (E), p. 18 (L).
39. *CCE,* Khronika Press, New York, 17 April 1971, p. 79; *RCL* 1, 1973, p. 9; *CLCC* 1, p. 19 (L).
40. *CCE* 21, September 1971, p. 293.
41. *CLCC* 1, p. 19.
42. *Ibid.,* pp. 19-20.
43. *CLCC* 1, p. 23.
44. *CCE* 25, 20 May 1972, pp. 197-8 and *CLCC* 2, pp. 17-18.
45. *CLCC* 2, p. 20.
46. *CLCC* 3, p. 22.
47. *CLCC* 9, pp. 36-7 (E), pp. 20-1 (L).
48. *CLCC* 11, pp. 36-7 (E), 30-1 (L).
49. *CLCC* 12, p. 9 (E), p. 5 (L) and 14, p. 32 (E).
50. *CLCC* 1, pp. 17-19.
51. *CLCC* 7, pp. 23-4 (E), p. 11 (L).
52. *CLCC* 8, pp. 7-8 (E), p. 3 (L).
53. *CLCC* 2, p. 20.
54. *CLCC* 4, pp. 37-9 (E), pp. 21-2 (L).
55. *RCL* 2, 1976, p. 21.
56. *CLCC* 1, pp. 14-17; 4, p. 25 (E), p. 10 (L); 5, pp. 43-4 (E), p. 17 (L).
57. *CLCC* 15, pp. 34-8.
58. *CLCC* 10, pp. 29-31 (E), pp. 16-17 (L).
59. *Šluota* 23, Vilnius, 1962, p. 11.
60. *Ibid.,* 13, 1962, p. 2.
61. *CLCC* 4, pp. 10-12 (E), pp. 6-8 (L).
62. *CLCC* 8, pp. 23-5 (E), pp. 12-14 (L).
63. *CLCC* 4, p. 37 (E), pp. 21-2 (L).
64. *CLCC* 10, pp. 10-12 (E), pp. 4-5 (L).
65. *CLCC* 1, pp. 2-14; 4, p. 39 (E), p. 22 (L); 5, pp. 5, 51-2 (E), pp. 5, 19-20 (L); 15, p. 13.
66. *CLCC* 23, p. 38. There are several other related documents in this issue, in one of which Fr. Zdebskis himself states that he was fined thirty roubles and that he was banned from driving for eighteen months, a severe hindrance in his parish work.

V

THE CENTRAL CONFLICT

DESPITE the comparative mildness of the sentences, the arrest and imprisonment of Frs. Zdebskis and Bubnys immediately led to a chain reaction unprecedented even by Lithuanian standards.

During December 1971 and January 1972 the clandestine activity of the Lithuanian Catholics developed more widely and in a better-organized way than at any time since the immediate post-wars years. The second *Chronicle of the Lithuanian Catholic Church* devotes the first part of its issue to an account of what happened.

A group whose precise identity we do not know prepared a short text that could be conveniently reproduced on one side of a type-written sheet (Document 37). They addressed it to Mr. Brezhnev and spoke briefly of the persecution of the Roman Catholic Church in the nation of Lithuania. They complained of the illegal suspension from office of Bishops Steponavičius and Sladkevičius, the imprisonment of the two priests, the ban on the religious education of children, the limitation on the training of seminarists, the state control of clergy appointments, the illegal discrimination against believers and the difficulty of rebuilding churches. They asked for action, not "beautiful words in the press or on the radio."[1]

The organizers stated that the gathering of the signatures was not itself a clandestine activity "because the memorandum was addressed to the Soviet authorities".[2] The organizers collected signatures both in the vicinity of the churches on Sundays and during visits to private homes. They explained the text to illiterates.

The response was astonishing. Very few were afraid to sign. The campaign gathered momentum since some of the most eager signatories copied the text and gathered new signatures. In the addendum to the memorandum it was stated:

> It must be pointed out that only a small part of the believers of Lithuania signed, because the police and KGB used every available means to stop the mass collection of signatures. People collecting them in Kapsukas, Šakiai, Islauzas and Kapčiamiestis were arrested and the signatures which they had collected were taken away from them, even though the memorandum was addressed to the Soviet authorities.[3]

There are no less than 17,054 extant signatures on the petition, but it is believed that this is no more than half of those that were collected.

The rest were confiscated by the KGB. Only the Crimean Tartars, among oppressed peoples of the Soviet Union, have ever amassed more solid support behind a campaign for justice.[4]

Fearing further obstruction by the Soviet authorities, the organizers safeguarded the remaining originals by sending them abroad with all the signatures attached. They were addressed to the United Nations, with the request that Dr. Kurt Waldheim should present the whole case to the Soviet Government, seeing that repeated efforts by the Lithuanian Catholics to gain a hearing had been frustrated.

Those in the West who invited the United Nations to carry out the request of the organizers of the appeal found no response. This did not prevent their obtaining considerable publicity for the event, and thus achieving a major goal. In the words of the *Lithuanian Chronicle:*

> The foreign press, radio and television publicized this memorandum widely. World opinion supported the 17,000 Catholics who dared publicly to demand their rights. In his Easter address Pope Paul VI remembered the 'Church of Silence'.[5]

Having been singularly unsuccessful in preventing the collection of signatures under the memorandum, the KGB instigated a major campaign to negate its effect, the main aim of which was to undermine the influence of the priests whom they suspected were behind the organization of the whole enterprise. It was, and still is, asserted that the petition was organized by anti-Communist clergy abroad. A Soviet propaganda book published in 1975 in English states:

> It was not without the help of these clergymen that in 1972 the western Press carried a false report that in the districts of Alytus and Prienai some 17,000 signatures had been collected under an appeal of protest against the alleged persecution of the Catholics in Lithuania.[6]

On 11 April 1972 Rugienis and Orlov, a Moscow official of the Council for Religious Affairs, summoned all the bishops and the diocesan administrators. According to the compilers of the *Lithuanian Chronicle*, the aim of the meeting was to intimidate the church officials into signing a pastoral letter slandering the organizers of the memorandum. Two and a half weeks later (30 April) all Lithuanian priests were obliged to cancel their sermons and read the pastoral letter instead. The most controversial passage read:

> Irresponsible individuals have recently appeared in some parishes. In the name of priests and the faithful they gather signatures near or even inside churches, or sometimes by visiting homes. They do this on sheets with, or even without, a text. These request the transfer, appointment or retention of various parish priests and assistant clergy or that certain churches should not be closed. Those who gather the signatures later change or add to the text and attach this to the collected signatures. This is fraudulent. We are very surprised that there are believers who sign without knowing the text and without considering the possible results. We must remember that the

signing of irresponsible documents affects relations between the Church and State and gives rise to misunderstandings. Such activities can bring no good to the Church.[7]

Priests, say the *Chronicle,* immediately recognized the hand of the State in the formulation of this document. An examination of the full texts and signatures of the memorandum of the 17,000 demonstrates conclusively that the allegations about the text's being doctored and that signatures were written on blank sheets of paper are without foundation. Some priests managed to confer with each other on whether to read the pastoral letter or not. The shortness of time allowed was obviously a tactic by the State to prevent discussion, but a warning note was circulated to some priests correcting the allegations of the pastoral letter. The section on the doctoring of the texts was "slanderous", it said, the whole pastoral "wounds and compromises the finest daughters and sons of the Lithuanian Catholic Church" and it "irrevocably compromises the bishops themselves".[8] No priest can be bound by his vows of obedience to read slander in public; conscientious priests would rather suffer for their refusal. The message concluded:

> Fathers, we appeal to your priestly conscience: as messengers of Him who called Himself the Truth, do not bow before lies and force; do not betray your nation and Church for a mess of pottage.[9]

The KGB tried to monitor which priests read the pastoral letter that Sunday and which did not. Atheists used the bishops' text itself to dissuade the faithful from signing any further documents. The *Chronicle* reported that very few priests read the full text of the letter, though some did so under intimidation and others to keep their peace with the state. Others omitted the false passages, while yet others merely preached as usual.

By May 1972 a number of priests managed to set out a more reasoned reaction to the pastoral letter than had been possible during the few days in April before the obligatory reading. (Document 38).

In the same month the tensions in Lithuania exploded into a wave of violence* which was certainly connected with the preceding events. The Church did not herself play a role in the civil disturbances, though the memorandum of the 17,000 and the bishops' attempts to nullify its effect must certainly have been a contributing factor. In the words of the *Chronicle:*

> KGB agents looking for the organizers of the memorandum and for the channels by which accurate information about the Lithuanian Catholic Church is reaching the free world were overtaken by the tragic events of May.
>
> On the 14th of that month young Romas Kalanta immolated himself in the city park of Kaunas in protest against the persecution of freedom in Lithuania. Everyone excitedly discussed this tragic protest against national

injustices, coercion and the arbitrary policy of the Soviet Government towards ethnic groups.

The funeral of Kalanta became a mass demonstration demanding national and religious freedom. The army and police dealt roughly with the demonstrators, but government officials were disturbed, as it became obvious that freedom was the desire not only of priests but also of 'their own', the young people reared in Communism since childhood. Most of those arrested were Komsomol members born and brought up in the Soviet era.[10]

Judging by the foreign press reports, the riots in Lithuania appear to have been more widespread and serious than this account in the *Lithuanian Chronicle* suggests.

Kalanta's death had a traumatic emotional effect on Lithuanian young people. It reminded them of other self-immolations: that of the Czech, Jan Palach, in 1969, in protest at the Soviet invasion of his country; and closer to home, that of Vasyl Makukh, who burnt himself to death in 1968, on the main square in Kiev, shouting, "Long live free Ukraine!" Kalanta's suicide embodied the same sense of national outrage and protest at the violation of human rights in his country. In a Catholic country the shock of such a public suicide was all the more powerful. Paradoxically, in view of the Catholic interdict on suicide, Kalanta came to be regarded by many as a near-saintly figure, accepting suffering and a painful death for the sake of others, in order to demonstrate in his person the whole nation's resistance to the situation under which it is forced to live. There was also a penitential aspect to his death: it was seen by many as a symbolic statement that Lithuanians had not done enough for human rights, that complete self-sacrifice was needed.

At least four other Lithuanians – Andrus Kukavičius, Salis Kauskas, the worker Stonis and an unidentified young man in Varena – followed Kalanta's example over the next three months by burning themselves to death in public places. The anniversary of Kalanta's death is still often marked in some way by Lithuanian young people, by holding memorial meetings and boycotting social events.[11]

The outcome for the Church seems to have been a temporary relaxation of tension, doubtless because the authorities feared that they would gain nothing from physically counteracting the sharpened attitude which had emerged, and there was always the possibility that the discontent might spread to other republics. As the *Chronicle* put it:

> Without a doubt, this was a calculated step by the atheists to restore calm in Lithuania, to repair their image which had been damaged in the eyes of the world and, if possible, to convince everyone, including the Vatican itself, that the unrest had been caused by the tactlessness of some official or other.[12]

In support of this policy, there was a new attempt to convince the world outside that all was well. Mgr. Krivaitis was particularly active in this sphere.[13]

The removal of Rugienis as senior executive of the Council for Religious Affairs and his replacement by K. Tumenas in 1972 was doubtless also a considered concession by the regime.* Tumenas presented a more moderate face to the Church, but nevertheless he still represented the continuing Moscow policy of direct and illegal interference in the life of the Lithuanian Catholic Church.

In order to understand fully the more subtle aspects of the Soviet campaign against religion over the past two decades, it is vital not to consider the situation of any one religious group in isolation, but to draw parallels between them and see if these shed light on the darker areas, where the influence of the KGB may be suspected but is not directly provable. For example, it is illuminating to compare two instances of government interference in the Russian Orthodox and Baptist Churches. When 'New Statutes' were forced on the Baptists in 1960,[14] it gave the impression that pastors were imposing restrictions on their own people which went beyond the already severe limitations of the Soviet law. In a similar attempt to sow distrust between members of the same Church, as we saw in the previous chapter, Orthodox priests were excluded from the governing bodies of their own parishes in 1961 by the provisions of an uncanonical 'Synod of Bishops'.[15] However, pressure from believers caused the former of these regulations to be revised in 1963.

In both instances the most effective tactic has been the Soviet atheist effort to identify the centre of opposition, isolate it from the main stream of believers by any device which might lead to schism and then to discredit the activists and undermine their influence within the denomination. With the Baptists these tactics have had some influence on their own denomination abroad, though there is evidence that they have misfired internally, despite the evolution of a serious schism which still exists. With the Orthodox, the position is less clearcut; the fear of schism and the less 'activist' inclination of the average believer seems to have inhibited a widespread following of the clear lead given by some priests, though this may be primarily because the information has not circulated.

In the case of the Lithuanian Catholics there are sure indications of similar thinking on the part of the atheists, but less tangible results have been achieved. The atheists' problems here have been threefold. The Catholic Church is, in the last resort, governed from the outside, from the Vatican.† The unity of the Lithuanian clergy and people has shown a remarkable resilience. In recent years, tradition has played much more of a cementing role in the Lithuanian Catholic Church than in most other Catholic countries, with the parishioners accepting the guiding hand of the priest, and the role of the parish council – whether KGB-infiltrated or not – being only marginal.

A number of Soviet articles reveal deliberate tactical attempts to isolate the strong leadership, preparatory to undermining it. For

*See p. 32. †See p. 53.

example, P. Mišutis, head of the Department of Propaganda and Agitation of the Central Committee of the Lithuanian Communist Party, demonstrates this precisely. The disintegration of the clergy is taking place, he states, although "slowly".[16] Three divisions have emerged, he claims. Some have already left the priesthood and broken with the Church. A second group has learned to compromise. Mišutis continues:

> Others, striving to keep pace with reality, lead a Soviet way of life . . . One of the priests of Panevežys declared, "If children join the Pioneers and young people the Komsomol, there's nothing wrong in this. When young couples arrange Komsomol weddings, that's not so terrible either. What is important is that as 'true Catholics' they should not forget the Church."[17]

However, of the third group Mišutis says:

> They still occupy hostile positions, try to propagate views alien to Soviet society, play on the national feelings of the Lithuanians and often claim that the only genuine Lithuanians are "those who believe in God" and that "the Church is the only defender of Lithuania's national culture". While Soviet laws "guarantee" normal conditions for the holding of religious worship, there are also those among the servants of the cult who try to break Soviet laws.[18]

The application of legal sanctions against so-called criminals such as Frs. Zdebskis and Bubnys appears to have strengthened the unity of the Church instead of creating dissension, so the Soviet atheists have set about devising new tactics. In September 1974 Bishop Matulaitis-Labukas received an anonymous letter, copies of which went to all the other bishops, purporting to come from a group of priests from the diocese of Vilkaviškis (Document 39). The full text rapidly became known to the faithful, not least through the offices of the *Lithuanian Chronicle,* which published it in full. Its main line of argument was to pick out a group of "progressive" priests who were conforming to the precepts of Vatican II by "understanding the spirit of the times" and thus securing the rebuilding of churches in Lithuania. They do this in the teeth of opposition from priests who call them "plants" of the regime, but these others are in fact reactionaries who are trying "to turn back the wheel of history" and who are desperate to "satisfy their egotism" by appearing as martyrs on the pages of the foreign press. There is an "underground theological seminary" which has done great harm to the Church. The clergy should work in the Church herself, not "dig under her foundations". The letter ended with an appeal to Bishop Labukas to end the "schism" among the clergy and to use Vatican Radio for this purpose when he next visited Rome, thus breaking the silence which could be taken as a defence of the "trouble-makers" who produce the *Lithuanian Chronicle.*

A second anonymous letter soon followed, supposedly by an individual priest and even more extreme in its opinions that the first.[19] As its main aim was to undermine the *Lithuanian Chronicle* itself, it will be discussed in Chapter X. It claimed that this publication was a political and not a Church undertaking, that it criticised the Pope, and that because of its activities the authorities have closed down legitimate religious publishing activities. The organizers of such associated activities as the gathering of signatures under documents have intimidated priests into signing, threatening to call them "red" if they refused, and even to expose the "secrets of their life."

This campaign is not without precedent: it is reminiscent of the attempts made by the Soviet authorities to slander and discredit Georgi Vins, the Russian Baptist leader, over the last fifteen years. The defence immediately mustered against these anonymous accusations has been just as forthright and conclusive as that put forward by the friends of Georgi Vins, not to mention civil rights activists, such as Academician Sakharov, who have no religious allegiance to the cause under discussion and whose opinions may therefore be taken as even more objective. Four letters have appeared sharply exposing the arguments of the first anonymous letter,[20] as well as a short and bitter commentary interpolated into the text of the second. The space the *Lithuanian Chronicle* devotes to this issue indicates the seriousness of the challenge and the importance of unified opposition to it in the view of the editors. The critics answer the points in detail.

They show indignation at the very act of writing anonymously. The larding of the texts with Biblical quotations barely masks the political intention of the authors, who could as well be atheists as priests.[21] The fourth writer introduces his reply by saying that "behind every anonymous letter there hides a coward or a man with an unclean conscience." Even if it were any of the clergy who signed the letter, "such a priest might wear a cassock and celebrate the liturgy, but this would be as though on the stage of a theatre".[22] Those whose names do appear in the western press are not there because they have a martyr complex, but because they are true to their calling.[23]

It could be objected that the four replies in the *Lithuanian Chronicle* to the anonymous letter are themselves anonymous. However, the authors of these replies are known to the editors of the *Chronicle* and they see no reason to help the KGB to deprive them of their jobs or to persecute them in other ways. They are in danger from the authorities, whereas the writers of the letter to Bishop Labukas (if they are priests at all) are in danger only from public opinion.

The first writer deplores the terms in which the anonymous author calls for "unity". Does he mean unity with Church canons or with atheist instructions?[24] In the nineteenth century the Lithuanian people demonstrated their unity with Bishop M. Valančius, who was persecuted by the Russians, not with Monsignor V. Žilinskas, the court favourite, whose concerns were for hunting and dancing, rather than the good of the Church. The English once suborned the French Bishop Cauchon to condemn Joan of Arc, but history reversed the verdict, making her a saint and throwing him on the dust heap. The reason why Our Lord called Peter "Satan" was because he tried to prevent Christ from going forward to His suffering – but the stinging rebuke went home to Peter, who eventually made the fullest atonement by dying for his faith under Nero.

The third writer is even more succinct on the cause of the schism:

> A schism has been created among us and this is encouraged by the activities of KGB officials. However, this is not its chief cause. To our joy and satisfaction, the majority of priests have steadfastly rejected the shameful offers made to them, as being opposed to the spirit of Christianity. They have not sold themselves; they have betrayed neither other priests nor the Church.
>
> The chief internal cause of the schism is and always has been the weakness, fear, naïveté and careerism of a few priests. Some were afraid of threats: others naïvely believed the KGB when they were told that the Church and they themselves would benefit. However, some – our disgrace! – acted to advance their careers, hoping to receive a higher position or not to lose one. The first fearful priest who signed an agreement to co-operate with the KGB dealt the first, and most serious blow, to our unity. Betrayal and collaboration with the enemy have never created unity. The priests enrolled by the KGB, the deepest wound in our united body, made it necessary for other priests to warn their colleagues that so-and-so was not trustworthy. This is our greatest failure. It is just possible to excuse those who silently, but senselessly, suffer because of the situation in which they find themselves, but it is impossible to excuse those who openly flaunt their treachery.
>
> Is it not a bitter fact, now as in the past, that some priests pick out the best positions for themselves during discussions with the executive of the Council for Religious Affairs? It only remains for the bishop to confirm the 'appointment'. Where have such 'worthies', who cannot be appointed to minor positions, sprung from? Not, at any rate, from the ranks of the conscientious priests.
>
> We firmly declare that any directive from the state authorities appointing any priest whatsoever to a parish is an unlawful infraction of the bishop's rights. No priest can agree to this or benefit from it. Any priest who is defended and supported by the state authorities is our disgrace and misfortune, the destroyer of our unity.[25]

One of the principal aims of the first anonymous letter seems to have been to deflect attention from the real problems confronting the Lithuanian Catholic Church – especially the replenishment of the ranks of the clergy and their duty of teaching the young – to the subsidiary one of replenishing the churches. All four replies emphasise this. Teaching the catechism is more important than concerns with bricks and mortar – or is the building up of the living community to be considered as "turning back the wheels of history", as the anonymous writer asks?[26] The third states that local officials in some areas forbade the blessing of children on the festival of Corpus Christi in 1966 and 1967, but the priests did it nevertheless. Atheists were not strong enough to force through their ban, so now the whole Church benefits from a victory which was gained by the steadfastness of the clergy.[27] The fourth writer states that even the repair of churches is due to the determination of believers, not to the good will of the State.[28]

The arguments regarding the seminary and the replenishment of the ranks of the clergy are dealt with in the next chapter, and those on the *Lithuanian Chronicle* itself in Chapter X.

The condemnation of "underground" activity by the anonymous signatories also comes in for the strongest possible criticism. Those who are forced to work outside the official framework of the Church because of the State's interference or even persecution are the true heroes when they refuse to give up in their endeavours: "We are deeply convinced that underground priests can be an example of faith, bravery and self-sacrifice for many."[29]

The second reply draws its analogy from the missionary history of the Church:

> Church history shows there is nothing new in such events. When priests could not freely work in England, they would prepare themselves on the continent and then set out in secret for the British Isles, taking no heed of the fate which awaited them – prison or death. Missionaries in Mexico, China and other places where the Church was undergoing persecution worked in just the same way.[30]

The conclusion is that the situation of the Church in Lithuania is similar and therefore the same criteria apply now as in the past. Many priests in history have fulfilled their vocation outside the four walls of a church and criticism of those who do so now in Lithuania is slander.

The author of the first reply asks whether the anonymous writer would consider the Apostles to have undermined the Church and then sums up:

> This letter poses the question whether the Lithuanian atheists are attempting to strike a blow at the Lithuanian Catholic Church, to misinform world opinion and the Holy See, to compromise the priests in the eyes of local believers and psychologically to disarm young priests and seminary students.[31]

The third reply considers the suggestions that bishop Labukas should use Vatican Radio to criticise his own clergy to be shameful,[32] while the fourth even quotes Karl Marx back at the anonymous writer: "If you want to be on the level of cattle, you can turn your back on human suffering and care only about your own skin."[33]

The *Lithuanian Chronicle* commentary on the second anonymous letter has the last word on both documents as the work of the KGB. The alleged threat to "expose" the private lives of clergy who refuse to sign documents is a tactic, the very suggestion of which can have originated only with the KGB, not with the Church.[34] When the anonymous writer accuses the defenders of religious liberty of erring into the realm of politics, the *Chronicle* commentary counters:

To defend the rights of the Church and of believers is not politics, but the duty of every Catholic – especially of a priest. Collaborating with the KGB, travelling to various conferences organized by the Communists and proclaiming abroad that Lithuanian believers enjoy full freedom of religion – that is what dabbling in politics means in these days.[35]

The goal of those in Lithuania who have spoken out on persecution in recent years is not only to galvanize into action a more united opposition inside the country, but also to speak clearly to the outside world. The Vatican and the Catholic Church world-wide are obviously the primary audience, but they are not the only one.

The organizers of the memorandum of the 17,000 were clearly gratified early in 1972 at the success in gaining publicity when they adopted the tactic of addressing their complaints to their own government via the United Nations[36] – even though the UN did not take up their case.

The introduction to the fifth issue of the *Lithuanian Chronicle* establishes the international context, where the author reflects on the current (1973) Soviet attempt to disarm international opinion (Document 40). Here the author emphasizes how essential to the well-being of the Lithuanian Church are the efforts of fellow countrymen abroad, which the Soviets are trying to undermine, while wooing American and world opinion in order to secure the wheat purchases essential for the economy.

When the *Chronicle's* fears proved only too well grounded and the persecutions began again, Academician Andrei Sakharov presented the case of the new victims of the persecution* to the World Council of Churches, as well as to the Synod of Catholic Bishops then meeting in Rome (October 1974).

The authors of the *Lithuanian Chronicle* appear to believe that the Vatican is genuinely misinformed about the situation in the Soviet Union, and it seems unquestionable that one of the underlying motives for establishing the *Chronicle* was to provide the precise, deep-level information needed to rectify the situation.†

There is more realism in the belief that if the Vatican were better informed it would act more effectively. The most forthright expression of this opinion came in 1975. Answering the second anonymous letter, the article stated:

> The *Chronicle of the Lithuanian Catholic Church* has never maintained that the Pope did not know what he was doing, but it believes that the Holy See has for a long time been deceived and lacked objective information about the Lithuanian Catholic Church.[37]

The *Chronicle* warns the Vatican against interpreting apparent concessions as signifying any real change of heart on the part of Soviet atheism.[38]

The Vatican, it is stated, has already made some mistakes in the approval of monsignors who are in fact state-appointed.[39] The main

*See p. 265. †See p. 72.

thrust of the leading article in the tenth issue of the *Lithuanian Chronicle* (1974)* is a warning to the Vatican not to yield to further atheist efforts to promote unworthy clergy. Particularly dangerous is the attempt – so far unsuccessful – to create new bishops who would supplant those banned from office, but whom the faithful rightly hold in the highest esteem. Especially dangerous are those clergy who visit Rome, having been briefed by the atheists before they leave and intimidated into giving false advice to Vatican officials. Any such new appointments would undermine the authority of the Pope in Lithuania. New priests are more essential than new bishops, but if any bishops are to be consecrated this must be after at least six months' notice, during which the widest consultation can be held–especially with Lithuanian bishops in exile. This warning against the promotion of priests such as Mgr. Krivaitis and Dr. Butkus is repeated even more emphatically, in June 1976, in a letter to Cardinals Slipyj and Samore from the editors of the *Lithuanian Chronicle*. The promotion of such priests to the episcopacy would be "a great misfortune for the Catholic Church in Lithuania and a great joy to the atheists." The writers of the *Chronicle* do not fear open dialogue with atheism, when there is a guarantee of good will on both sides as a prerequisite, but apropos of Mr. Gromyko's visit to the Pope in 1974 they issue the sternest possible warning against current "fashionable" dialogue which is not only one-sided, but highly dangerous for Catholics living in the Soviet Union (Document 41). It is in this context that one must see the repudiation of the view expressed by the anonymous letter earlier in this chapter that those priests who compromise with the authorities in Lithuania today are merely carrying out the precepts of Vatican II.

Chronicle No. 20 is as forthright as No. 10 in voicing its fears about Vatican compromise with the Soviet authorities: it is felt that a visit by Archbishop Casaroli to Lithuania might be exploited to the detriment of the Church (Document 41).

It should be said, in all fairness, that there have been positive gains from Soviet-Vatican dialogue, although these could not have been achieved without the steadfast loyalty of Lithuanian Catholics to their church. Just after the war Lithuania had only one active bishop and the hierarchy was in danger of ceasing to exist officially. Now, at least, there are five bishops, although only two are active, and there is a minute quantity of officially-permitted Catholic literature. The Vatican is able to send some Latin-language missals to priests in Lithuania. There has also been some change in the Vatican's low-profile approach to Lithuania; this is due almost entirely to the *Lithuanian Chronicle* itself and the information it provides. In 1975 Radio Vatican broadcast the details of Nijole Sadunaite's trial in thirty-two languages. In 1976 it also broadcast a letter from Pope Paul VI to Bishop Matulaitis-Labukas, on the fiftieth anniversary of Kaunas

*See pp. 67-71

diocese (Document 42). The Pope praises the Lithuanian Catholic Church for faithfully maintaining its ancient Christian traditions and makes particular mention of Lithuanian popular devotion to the shrine of Mary at Šiluva, which he raises to the level of a Minor Basilica.

When the Pope does designate support for the persecuted Church, however obliquely, Lithuanians are quick to show their gratitude.[40] The warmest praise is reserved for those who spoke out at the Synod of Catholic Bishops in the autumn of 1974:

> In following on the radio the Synod of Bishops which has taken place in Rome, we were overjoyed that some Fathers of the Synod – Cardinal Iosif Slipyj, Cardinal Stefan Wyszynski, Cardinal Bengsch and others – so bravely defended the persecuted Catholics in Eastern Europe. In the best possible way they represented us, too, the believers of the Lithuanian Catholic Chuch.[41]

The authors of the *Chronicle* develop this in a long open letter to Cardinal Bengsch in the nineteenth issue of the *Lithuanian Chronicle* (Document 43). The Soviet authorities, it is stated, tricked Lithuanian believers by concealing from them the impending visit of the Cardinal in August 1975, so they were unable to prepare to meet him. The text of the letter contains some details as to what they would have told him about their own situation, had they been able to do so. It reveals even more clearly than before how desperate the Lithuanians are to make their situation known to the outside world.[42]

DOCUMENTS

37. MEMORANDUM

[original title]

To the Secretary/General of The Communist Party of the Soviet Union, The Kremlin, Moscow. From the Catholics of Lithuania, 1972.

It is now many years since the end of the Second World War; the nations have restored the ruins, desiring permanent peace.

But the foundation of lasting peace is justice and respect for human rights. And so we, the Catholics of Lithuania, are deeply disturbed by the violation of these rights, since the believers of our nation are still deprived of freedom of conscience, and the Church is subject to persecution.

Our bishops, J. Steponavičius and V. Sladkevičius, have now been in exile for ten years without a trial and without a defined sentence, although they have committed no crime.

In November 1971 the priests J. Zdebskis and P. Bubnys were sentenced to deprivation of liberty because, fulfilling their duty, and at the request of the parents, they explained the basic elements of the Catholic faith to children. These priests helped the children prepare for First Communion, not in school, but in church, without using any kind of coercion – only those who wanted to took part.

By contrast, atheism is forcibly inculcated in the Soviet schools in Lithuania, believing Catholic children are forbidden to speak, write and act according to their conscience, and those who perpetrate this violence do not receive warnings and are not brought to trial.

Because of the lack of a sufficient number of priests, the requirements of believers remain unsatisfied. In many places one priest now has to serve two or three parishes. Even invalid and old priests are compelled to work. This situation has been created because it is not the bishops who order the affairs of the seminary, but representatives of the authorities. Every year the authorities decide to admit only up to ten students to the seminary. It is also the representatives of the authorities who assign the priests to parishes.

There is an article in the Penal Code of the Lithuanian SSR which stipulates punishment for persecuting believers, but in practice this article is never applied. In 1970 the department of public education of Vilkaviškis district dismissed the teacher O. Briliene from work solely because she was a believer. For the same reason, the district authorities will not allow this teacher to take up any work in the town of Vilkaviškis, not even as a cleaner. The perpetrators of such arbitrary action remain unpunished, although through no fault of their own representatives of the intelligentsia struggle to practise their faith openly.

Representatives of the authorities do not permit believers, even using their own resources, to restore the burned-down churches in, for example, the parishes of Batakiai, Gaure, and Sangruda. The faithful have to try with great difficulty to get permission from the authorities to hold services in any private home, but in not a single case is it permitted to fit out even a chapel in a former church-yard. At the same time, permission was given to build a dance-hall on the site of a former church in the parish of Andrievas.

We could point to many more facts of discrimination, which grieve us and compel us to become disillusioned with the Soviet Constitution and laws. Therefore we ask the Soviet Government to safeguard freedom of conscience for us, which is guaranteed by the Constitution of the USSR, but which until now has been absent in practice. The fine words in the press and on the radio do not satisfy us, since we await from the Government such efforts as will help us Catholics to feel ourselves to be citizens of the Soviet Union enjoying equal rights.

APPENDIX TO THE MEMORANDUM

17,054 signatures have been added to the attached memorandum. It must be noted that only a negligible proportion of the believers of Lithuania gave their signatures, since the organs of the police and the KGB undertook a series of measures to stop the collection of signatures. In the towns of Kapsukas, Šakiai, Nilauzas and Kapčiamiestis several people who took part in the collection of signatures were detained. One of them was even conveyed to the police station in handcuffs. Lists of signatures found on him were confiscated, despite the fact that this memorandum was addressed to the Soviet Government.

If in future state organs are going to maintain the attitude to believers' complaints which they have held until now, then we shall be compelled to turn to international bodies: to the Pope, the head of our Church, or to the United Nations, as an authoritative institution which defends human rights.

Moreoever, we wish to inform you that the present memorandum is the result of a national calamity: during the years of Soviet rule in Lithuania, such social vices as juvenile crime, alcoholism and suicide have increased tenfold, while divorce and abortion have also assumed threatening proportions. The further we retreat from the Christian past, the more vividly are the terrible consequences of compulsory atheist education revealed, and the more widely is the inhuman image of life, deprived of God and of religion, propagated.

We are turning to you, as the highest party authority, with a request to examine the facts we have set out with all seriousness and responsibility, and to take the proper decision.

Representatives of the Catholics of Lithuania.[43]

38. COMPLAINTS AGAINST A PASTORAL LETTER

The [pastoral] letter was sent to priests a week – in some cases, only a few days – before it was to be read out. It is generally thought that this delay was deliberate and would prevent the clergy from fully consulting each other.

The pastoral letter is full of quotations from the Holy Scriptures. However, the use of Holy Scripture to twist the truth is a truly shameful act . . . .

We are firmly convinced that the unity of the Church is being destroyed by those who, while Catholics are fighting for their rights, are helping the enemies of God and the Church – those who are responsible for sending out such 'pastoral letters' . . . . This unfortunate pastoral letter has been widely used by atheist propaganda, not only in Lithuania but also abroad.

"Believers ought to obey their own pastors in matters of the faith", the letter states.

This is true only with regard to church affairs.

When senior dignitaries keep silent, the priests and the faithful speak out in their place . . . . "Each church member must love his church". But who is it that loves the Church? Those who support it with their offerings, those who risk losing their jobs, those who end up in prison for her sake – or those who spread lies in the atheist press or on the radio? Recently, Mgr. Krivaitis made a statement of the latter kind.

Perhaps it was love of the Church that inspired Mgr. Krivaitis to summon the assistant priests of his diocese some time before 30 June and to inform them that things were going badly in the parishes, that our clergy were now indulging in pastoral activities, that priests should not make any effort to examine children in the catechism, that signatures had been collected in a dishonest way and so on. It is clear to everyone that this approach has been dictated by the official Rugienis, because this priest is an obedient tool of his . . . .

This pastoral letter was dictated not by priestly advisers, but in accordance with the orders issued by Rugienis and Orlov, an official for Religious Affairs sent from Moscow . . . . They summoned the . . . . Lithuanian diocesan administrators and forced them to sign this disgraceful document, which will have serious consequences for our church, putting it on the same level as the Russian Orthodox Church.

Why do the bishops and administrators give their backing to atheist aims? The atheists want to compromise the Church, to undermine it from within. It is painful to admit this, but it is necessary to do so: they have already succeeded to a great extent in doing this. Even before 30 April [the date the pastoral letter was to be read in the churches], when he was informed of this letter libelling the believers of Lithuania and destroying the bishops' authority, Bishop Pletkus replied, "The authority of the bishops has already been destroyed."

"Some people, seeing the present difficulties the Church is undergoing, come to short-sighted personal conclusions and start losing confidence in Divine Providence itself, even in Christ" (Pastoral Letter).

. . . . Is it the believers, those who go on praying and fighting, who have no confidence in Divine Providence? But in what kind of "providence" do those whom the atheists use to destroy the Church put their trust? This situation preoccupies and grieves the believers of Lithuania . . . .

"These hunters of signatures later proceeded to make changes and additions in the text . . ." (Pastoral Letter).

How do the curias know that the signatures were falsified? In fact they have never seen them. Where did they learn that signatures had been collected on blank sheets of paper? Everyone was able to see that the full text of the Memorandum was on each page. The faithful knew quite well to what they were putting their names. Our detractors could be invited to visit the parish of Prienai, where the people have intervened more than once on behalf of Fr. Zdebskis and appealed to government representatives; these people knew why they signed and when interrogated by government officials, they did not deny that they had signed. If only one could calculate the harm done by that lamentable pastoral letter! After that mistake there is only one honourable solution: a new pastoral letter, apologizing for causing an affront to the faithful of Lithuania.

"The Church uses every means it can to serve the Gospel and the general good" (Pastoral Letter).

Perhaps slandering the faithful is serving the Gospel? Perhaps the general good is served by compromising the struggle for religious liberty?

In this letter our pastors showed their true faces to the believers of Lithuania. We feel the letter will open the eyes of Vatican diplomats. It could even be considered evident that we have had quite enough of all these monsignors and bishops appointed by the Government . . . .

"We must not lose sight of the fact that signing irresponsible documents has an effect on the relations between Church and State and is the source of misunderstandings" (Pastoral Letter).

What kind of relations are referred to here? Those between cat and mouse? How can we express satisfaction about "good relations" of this kind? . . . . The Lithuanian Church is forced to submit to the Government's yoke . . . . What do we still have left to lose? A little bit of personal well-being and a limited amount of individual liberty?

"Let there be unity as to essentials and charity in all things" (Pastoral Letter).

This is just what we expect from those who find themselves at the head of the Catholic Church in Lithuania. The combination of unity and charity is the essence of the Gospel. This means:

a) we demand at least as much liberty for religion as for Soviet propaganda;
b) we do not write pastoral letters of the kind dictated by the Government;
c) we have no fear of suffering for our faith.

In issue No. 3, 1972, of the journal *Nauka i religia* ["Science and Religion"], an article was published on the Lithuanian Church with the aid of the head of the Department of Agitation and Propaganda of the Lithuanian Central Committee. In the article* priests were classified according to three categories: those who have been defrocked or have left the priesthood; those who are "in tune with life", and those who violate Soviet laws. Thank God that the third category is the largest and enjoys the greatest authority among the faithful.

We priests of Lithuania remain faithful to the Roman Catholic Church and to the Pope, in spite of persecutions and concentration camps.

The priests of Lithuania.[44]

May 1972.

39. AN ANONYMOUS LETTER

To His Grace Bishop J. Matulaitis-Labukas, the Apostolic Administrator of Kaunas and Vilkaviškis Diocese.
Copies to: Bishops J. Pletkus, R. Krikščiunas, L. Povilonis and to the Diocesan chancellors, Č. Krivaitis and J. Andrikonis.

The only-begotten Son of God was sent by the Heavenly Father to this earth in order to redeem, renew and unite the whole human race by His sufferings and death on the cross. Before His sacrificial death, He prayed to the Heavenly Father "that they might all be one" (John 17:21), and He gave a new law to his disciples, a law to love one another, that they might all grow into one Body of Christ. If this applies to the faithful, it applies all the more to the clergy, the builders of this Body of Christ.

Nowadays this unity is badly lacking. Your Grace, you know well the mood of your priests; you are well acquainted with the behaviour of certain reactionary priests from Vilkaviškis diocese, who are acting against the will of our Saviour by destroying, not building up, the Church. They slander and vilify many excellent priests, including even the bishops, who, guided by the decisions of the Second Vatican Council and the ideas of the late Pope, are earnestly labouring in the conditions of today. It is no secret that these conditions do not make life easy for any of them. All the same, it is possible to work for the good of the Church and the salvation of souls.

In the decisions of the Second Vatican Council, a great deal of space is devoted to the question of relations between priests and their

*See p. 120.

duty of building up the Body of Christ. "This, especially in our time, makes new and varied forms of adaptation to circumstances necessary" (Decree on the Life and Duties of priests).

Thanks to hard-working priests who understand well the spirit of our times, the churches of K. Naumiestis, Pajievonis and Šakiai rose from the ruins and temporary chapels have been built in Kapčiamiestis, Bartninkai, Pilviškiai and other places. In recent years many churches have been restored to their full beauty. It can safely be said that nowadays more churches of our diocese are being restored and decorated than before the war. And who is responsible for this? Those who put themselves forward and whom even Vatican Radio calls "worthy Lithuanians"? No, indeed. It is due rather to those whom reactionary priests call "atheist plants", whom they accuse of destroying the faith and the Lithuanian Catholic Church.

What a strange paradox! The "atheist plants" decorate and beautify churches, instead of destroying and abandoning them, while the "patriotic priests", in their "fight for the Church and freedom of religion", are trying to turn back the wheel of history and long to appear on the pages of the foreign press and in radio broadcasts, to become uncrowned martyrs, to satisfy their egotism and vanity.

Everyone knows the old proverb, "divide and rule". I would not be so sad if this schism had been caused by the atheists. But how can divisions among ourselves be justified? Is this not grist to the enemy's mill?

Your Grace, you know that in some places the authorities are cancelling the permission which had been given to repair churches and refusing to assign the necessary building materials; in some places they are beginning to restrict visits by priests from neighbouring parishes. Is this not a justifiable response on the part of the authorities to the reactionary propaganda carried out by certain priests? Why has there been no reaction from our curia, our bishops and chancellors? Is such a state of affairs really beneficial to the Church?

The directorate of the theological seminary has been complaining that there will not be enough first-year students, that this year the authorities have made a more stringent choice of applicants. Again, does not the responsibility for this lie in the strenuous efforts made by the underground seminary and the reactionary priests who nominate applicants to it?

Finally, Your Grace knows what such "underground priests" (that is priests consecrated secretly by someone or other) are worth and what use they are. A priest is successful in doing his duty and being of use to the Church only when he is working within the Church, not digging beneath its foundations.

Your Grace, we know well your long years of practical work in the curia and we know equally well your views on modern life and the development of contemporary society. We know that you call things by their proper names and so now we should like you to be just as objective in assessing the present situation in the Diocese of Vilnius.

Pope John XXIII expressed the thought that we should concentrate, not on factors which divide us, but on those which unite us and which we have in common. We should like you, Your Grace, to look at the future with the eyes of this Pope and, insofar as it depends on you, that you should put an end to the schism among the clergy, which has nothing to do with the spirit of Christ, and to the baseless slander directed against those who have borne on their shoulders "the burden and heat of the day" (Mt. 20:12). We should like your pastoral advice to help us rehabilitate the words of Christ's prayer, "that they may all be one" (John 17:21).

Soon Your Grace will be visiting the Vatican. We should like to hear you speak truthfully from there, as a pastor, about our diocese and its clergy, for while you are silent the *Chronicle of the Lithuanian Catholic Church* – which represents neither the Lithuanian Catholic Church, nor the Vilkaviškis diocese – speaks for you.

A group of priests from
Vilkaviškis diocese.[45]

1 September 1974.

40. BEHIND THE FAÇADE

The present state of calm in the Catholic Church of Lithuania is temporary and deceptive. It is being maintained for the following purposes:

1. To stem the nationwide growth of discontent over the religious and national injustices perpetrated by the Government.

2. To compromise the efforts and work of émigrés in the West, which are vital to the welfare of the Lithuanian Church and nation.

3. To re-establish the Soviet Union's prestige which had declined in the eyes of the world as the result of its overt anti-religious policy. This was especially necessary in the face of the approaching meetings of the European Security Conference in Helsinki.

4. It seems probable that the Soviet Union's weak economic situation and the necessity for wheat purchases abroad had a hand in the change in policy. It is well to note the sentiments repeatedly expressed in the U.S. Congress, especially the Jackson amendment – at present supported by 75 Senators [February 1975] – which would ban the sale of U.S. wheat to the Soviet Union until the Soviets implement the provisions of the Universal Declaration of Human Rights. Rephrasing the words of Senator Jackson, the Soviet Union was the first state to sign the Universal Declaration and now remains the only State which has never made any attempt to put its provisions into effect.[46]

41. THE LITHUANIAN VIEW OF SOVIET-VATICAN DIALOGUE, 1974-5

In our times it is very fashionable to talk about dialogue. Both Communists and Catholics strive for it. A while ago the Pope's envoy visited Moscow, while on 24 March of this year [1974] Soviet Foreign Minister Gromyko called on Pope Paul VI.

What do the Catholics of Lithuania expect from future dialogue with the Communist Government?

Catholics are convinced that dialogue is necessary, but do not yield to illusions. Dialogue can be useful only when both sides show good will. The "good will" of the Communist Government is shown by the trials of priests charged with teaching catechism . . . .

To date, the Communist Government has simply made use of lies and force in dealing with believers. It seems that dialogue with the Church is needed only as a means of keeping the Vatican quiet about religious persecution in the Soviet Union, in the hope that the situation of the faithful can be eased. The purpose of the dialogue is to mislead world public opinion into thinking that religious freedom does exist in the Soviet Union.[47]

News recently [1975] spread around Lithuania that a representative of the Roman Curia, Archbishop Augustino Casaroli, was soon to visit our country. This news caused general concern amongst Lithuanian priests: if Moscow allows Archbishop Casaroli to come to Lithuania, then the Soviets must be expecting to benefit from the visit. It is now very important to Moscow that the Vatican and the whole world should be convinced that there is full religious freedom in Lithuania. If Archbishop Casaroli comes to Lithuania, then undoubtedly the Soviet Government, with the help of priests who have lost their integrity, will endeavour to show a face of the Catholic Church in Lithuania which is not a true one, but a reflection in a Soviet propaganda mirror. Moscow also wants two exiled bishops – Steponavičius and Sladkevičius – to be eliminated from church life so that bishops who are obedient and loyal to the Soviet Government down to the minutest detail will be in charge of all the dioceses. The Catholics of Lithuania are now praying that the desires of Moscow to mislead the Vatican and to obtain rulings favourable to itself from the Roman Curia are not fulfilled.[48]

42. LETTER OF MAY 1976 TO BISHOP JUOZAS MATULAITIS-LABUKAS FROM POPE PAUL VI

As it is just fifty years since the establishment of the Diocese of Kaunas – with which it is appropriate to remember other similar jubilees, for it is also fifty years ago that the Vilnius Diocese was raised to an Archdiocese – this gives Us the unusual opportunity of writing You this letter. By this We wish through You to reach all the bishops of this land who have been entrusted by the Saviour Christ with the duty of guarding his flock in this beloved Nation.

We well know, Respected Brother, that the Catholic Church in Lithuania during the fifty-year period which has just ended, as in earlier ages, has faithfully maintained its ancient Christian traditions, showing clear witness to the Faith and a close bond with the Throne of Peter.

We wish to assure You that in spirit we are always within the life of Your community, we follow its events, we feel for you with the emotions and cares of fatherly love and always remember you in our prayers.

We urge all our brothers and sons of this nation dear to us, to remain united in the community of faith and love as is fitting for the disciples of the Divine Teacher (John 13:3).

In addition We pray to the Holy Virgin Mary, who is so honoured by all the faithful of Lithuania – calling upon her particularly in the name of the Mother of Mercy of Aušros Vartai and, in Šiluva, the shrine of the birth of Mary, which we have been pleased to raise to the level of a Minor Basilica – that she should care for and protect all the dear sons and daughters of this beloved nation, preserving them in firmness of faith and confidence in Christ, her Son, who, having conquered sin and death, rose again from the dead.

Finally, to You, Respected Brother, your coadjutor and all other bishops, the priesthood and all the faithful of this Nation, We give the Apostolic Blessing as a special assurance of our benevolence towards the Church of Lithuania and our constant concern and heavenly solace.

Paul VI.[49]

43. APPEAL BY THE FAITHFUL TO CARDINAL BENGSCH, 1975

His Grace the Archbishop of East Berlin, Cardinal Alfred Bengsch.

Your Eminence,

Your visit to our country on 22-26 August of this year was unexpected, but was a very pleasant surprise to all believers. We not only saw your smiling face and heard your warm words about our faith, but the hope revived within us that more objective information about the situation of the Catholic Church in Lithuania would reach the Holy See and the world at large.

As far as radio interference permitted, we followed with interest the speeches of Cardinals Wyszysnki, Slipyj and yourself to the Synod of Bishops in Rome last year. We realised that you have the compassion and Christian courage to intercede for those persecuted for the sake of God and the Church, that you have the desire and capability to understand our misfortunes and sorrows.

The exact date of your arrival was concealed from the priests and faithful until the last moment. The bishops living in exile – J. Steponavičius and V. Sladkevičius – were not even informed of it. An announcement about your visit was made in Kaunas Cathedral only on the eve of your arrival, while the priests in the provinces knew nothing of it. The arrangements for your visit were left in the hands of priests loyal to the Government and it seems that they proved "satisfactory". All those who would have been able to describe the true situation of the Church were barred from access to you. They did not show you desecrated churches, but took you to Pirčiupis (to be objective, it must be mentioned that there are graves in Lithuania not only to Nazi hecatombs but also to Soviet ones – Pravenkiš, Rainiai woods, and others). In Panevežys the singing of hymns was not permitted, so that too great an effect should not be created and so that the displeasure of the Government should not be incurred. In Kaunas people were forbidden to hang a portrait of the Holy Father near the church door. Notwithstanding the efforts of the Government and its trusted ones, crowds thousands strong came to honour you and to demonstrate their loyalty to the Church and the Holy See.

In the name of the Lithuanian priests and faithful we apologize to you for the lack of tact shown during the visit (in the case of Pirčiupis) and that we could not greet you as we would have wished. Since we were unable to tell you personally about the difficulties of the Catholic Church in Lithuania, we would like to do this in the pages of the *Chronicle of the Lithuanian Catholic Church*.

[Here follows a short account of the Soviet occupation of Lithuania 1940-46 and the resulting persecution of the Church up to the 1950s.]

Tourists who have visited Rome say that officials of the Holy See advise them that conflict with the Soviet authorities should be avoided. We do not know if this is really the view of the Holy See, but if such a principle were maintained it would be necessary to desist from such basic pastoral work as, for example, teaching children the catechism, and to be constantly in conflict with one's conscience by remaining a "servant of the cult", which is what the Soviet authorities seek.

We are deeply convinced that it is difficult for the people of the western world to understand the conditions of our life. Only a prolonged stay in our country, and especially a spell in the interrogation rooms and prisons, makes the deceit of the Soviet authorities plain.

We believe that the Holy See wholeheartedly seeks to help the persecuted Church in its diplomatic work, but because of a lack of knowledge of concrete circumstances it can in some cases serve atheist interests. It is for this reason that we venture to warn you: do not trust the promises of the Soviet authorities, because they will not be kept. Do not believe those who come officially from the Soviet Union – they are all, to a greater or lesser degree, obliged to carry out the tasks of the Party and the KGB . . . .

We pray to God that the enemies of the Church do not force their way into the hierarchy to carry out disruptive activity from within. We do not wish to believe that our atheists will have grounds to rejoice at the spectacle of persons favourable to themselves among the hierarchy.

The present persecution of the Church is clothed in a veil of falsehood and deceit. It is for this reason that particularly stern measures are taken against those who try to lift this veil of falsehood and to bring to public notice the persecution of the faithful . . . .

When in October of this year five Spanish terrorists were executed, a wave of protest rolled over the world, but when people are tortured because of truth, freedom, their convictions and the Church, the voices of protest are weak and timid. It is just this that the Government of the Soviet Union seeks – to suffocate Lithuania's Catholics in the still of the night. He who wishes today to help us and all those in the Soviet Union who love truth and freedom should use every means at his disposal to publicise the facts about the persecution, and to tear away the veil of lies which is screening the violence.

We, the publishers of the *Chronicle of the Lithuanian Catholic Church,* ask Your Grace, in the name of many priests and believers suffering for the faith, to transmit our call for help to all persons of good will. In particular let us remember those who . . . . for the sake of the rights of Our Lord God, the Church and the future of the people, followed the way of the cross into the fortresses of the Gulag Archipelago.

The Publishers of the Chronicle of the Lithuanian Catholic Church.[50]

APPENDIX
Short List of Appeals, 1968-76

Date	From	To	Contents
31.12.1968	Priests of Vilkaviškis	Lithuanian bishops	Appeal over difficulties put in the way of seminary education of priests.
8.1.1969	63 Lithuanian priests	Kosygin	Letter on reduction of numbers at the seminary.
Aug. 1969	29 Vilnius priests	USSR Council of Ministers	These petitions are mentioned in the letter from 49 Vilnius priests in October 1970
17.10.1969	84 Panevežys priests	General Secretary of Central Committee of the CPSU	(see below).
Aug. 1969	40 Lithuanian priests	Kosygin	Appeal concerning the persecution of the Catholic church in Lithuania.
20.11.1969	56 Telšiai priests	USSR Council of Ministers	
8.9.1970	61 Vilnius priests	Brezhnev and Kosygin	Petition to restore Bishop Steponavičius to his duties.
Oct. 1970	49 Vilnius priests	Leaders of the Catholic Church	Declaration expressing dissatisfaction with Vatican policy of appeasement towards Soviet Government.
Nov. 1970	104 Lithuanian priests (72 from Vilkaviškis, 32 from Kaišiadorys)	The CPSU and the the Lithuanian CP	Appeal protesting against sentence passed on Fr. Šeškevičius.
Feb. 1971	126 Panevežys priests	Supreme Soviet of Lithuanian SSR	Petition on behalf of Fr. Šeškevičius.
Winter 1971	134 Panevežys priests	Kosygin, USSR Council of Ministers, Lithuanian SSR Council of Ministers	Appeal asking for restoration of Bishop Steponavičius to his duties.
24.12.1971	47 Vilnius priests	General Secretary of CPSU, Chairman of USSR Council of Ministers	Appeal for religious freedom in Soviet Constitution to be put into practice.

Date	From	To	Contents
Dec. 1971-Jan. 1972	17.054 Lithuanian Catholics	Brezhnev	Memorandum protesting against persecution of the Catholic Church in Lithuania.
Feb. 1972	Lithuanian Catholics	Kurt Waldheim	Appeal including the memorandum of 17.054.
Aug., Sept. 1972	1,709 Lithuanian Catholics	Brezhnev	Petition protesting against demolition of church premises by the local authorities.
Mar. 1973	16,498 Lithuanian Catholics	Tumenas [Lithuanian official for Religious Affairs]	Declaration complaining about the shortage of religious literature.
Mar. 1973	14,284 Lithuanian students and parents	Lithuanian SSR Ministry of Education	Declaration protesting compulsory lessons in atheism.
May 1973	30,782 Lithuanian Catholics	Praesidium of USSR Supreme Soviet	Petition protesting against discrimination towards religious believers.
30.7.74	45 priests of Kaišiadorys	Tumenas	Declaration calling for the restoration of Bishop Sladkevičius to his duties.
22.9.74	Priests of Vilkaviškis	1) Bishop Matulaitis –Labukas 2) Open Letter	Letters denouncing the writer of the officially inspired "anonymous" letter to Bishop Matulaitis-Labukas.
Oct. 74	Priests of Panevežys	Open Letters	2 open letters condemning the "anonymous" letter and supporting the CLCC.
11.10.74	5 Lithuanian priests	Moscow Committee of Human Rights	Appeal in defence of those arrested for producing CLCC.
28.4.75	6 Lithuanian priests	General Secretary of CPSU, etc.	Declaration protesting against lack of religious literature and "Case 345" trial.
10.9.75	19 Members of Ignalina parish council	Brezhnev	Declaration for the return of their church.
1975 Autumn	Editors of CLCC	Cardinal Bengsch	Letters asking him to publicise anti-religious persecution in Lithuania.

Date	From	To	Contents
25.9.75	66 priests of Vilnius Diocese	LSSR Council of Ministers	Declaration asking for return of Bishop Steponavičius to his official duties.
4.10.75	31 priests of Vilnius Diocese	Central Committee of Lithuanian CP	Letter denying allegations against the church made in Lithuanian press.
20.10.75	Lithuanians	Academician Sakharov	Letter of congratulation on his Nobel Prize.
(1975) Undated	Lithuanians	Intellectuals of W. Europe & USSR	Letter charging Soviet authorities with murder of M. Tamonis and other Lithuanian intellectuals.
15.2.1976	5 Lithuanian priests	Brezhnev	Declaration asking for return to his duties of Bp. Steponavičius.
6.3.1976	Parents of school-children in Viesijai and Liepalingis	General Procurator of LSSR	Declaration protesting against unlawful anti-religious persecution of their children at school.
8.4.1976	Parishioners of Simnas	Soviet authorities	Statement calling for observation of Helsinki Agreement and return of their priest.
9.5.1976	Lithuanian priests	"Our Irish brethren"	Letter appealing for support.
9.5.1976	Lithuanian priests	Cardinals Samore and Slipyj	Letters asking for publicity about the anti-religious persecution in Lithuania.
8.7.1976	212 Lithuanian believers	Comrade Griškevičius, 1st Secretary of Lithuanian CP, and Minister of Health Kleizas	Declaration protesting against the fine imposed on Fr. J. Zdebskis for drunken driving.
19.7.1976	Believers of Klaipeda	Procurator of LSSR	Declaration in support of Fr. J. Zdebskis demanding the return of his driving licence.
16.11.1976	A group of Lithuanian priests	Brezhnev	Protest against the arrest and detention of Vladas Lapienis and Jonas Matulionis for their involvement with the *Lithuanian Chronicle*.

Date	From	To	Contents
Dec. 1976	Catholics of Lithuania	The Catholics of Ireland	Letter thanking Irish Catholics for their intended gift of a statue of Mary to the Catholics of Vilnius.
1977	Lithuanian priests	Theological students	Appeal to those training for the priesthood at the seminary not to trade their principles for material security and to reject KGB attempts to recruit them as informers.
25.2. 1977	120 Believers of Žalioji congregation	K. Tumenas and LSSR Council of Ministers	Declaration demanding the return of their confiscated church and the legal registration of their congregation.
Mar. 1977	S. Kovalyov, P. Plumpa and other political prisoners of Perm labour camp, nr. Urals	President J. Carter	Telegram expressing their admiration for him as a man who believes in God and values human rights.
10.4. 1977	Lithuanian Helsinki Monitoring Group	To the Belgrade Conference	Declaration on the situation of the Catholic Church and other religious believers in Lithuania, detailing Soviet violations of freedoms written into the Helsinki Agreement.

NOTES TO CHAPTER V

1. *CLCC* 2, pp. 2-4.
2. *Ibid.*, p. 4.
3. *Religious Liberty in the Soviet Union,* Keston College, Kent, 1976, pp. 71-2.
4. A. Sheehy, *The Crimean Tartars, Volga Germans and Meskhetians,* London, 1971, pp. 7-21.
5. *CLCC* 2, p. 5.
6. Aničas, *The Establishment of Socialism in Lithuania and the Catholic Church,* p.117.
7. *CLCC* 2, p. 5.
8. *Ibid.*, p.6.
9. *Loc. cit.*
10. *CLCC* 4, pp. 4-5 (E), p.3 (L).
11. *CLCC* 14, p. 28 (E), pp. 22-3 (L).
12. *CLCC* 4, p. 5 (E), p. 3 (L).
13. See p. 59 and *CLCC* 4, p. 4, (E), p. 3 (L).
14. Bourdeaux, *Religious Ferment in Russia,* pp. 20-1.
15. Bourdeaux, *Patriarch and Prophets,* pp. 24-6.
16. *Nauka i religia* 3, 1972, p. 34.
17. *Ibid.*, pp. 34-5.
18. *Loc. cit.*
19. *CLCC* 15, pp. 8-11.
20. *CLCC* 12, pp. 8-15 (E), pp. 5-12 (L) and 14, pp. 32-43 (E), pp. 27-36 (L).
21. *CLCC* 12, p. 9 (E), p. 5 (L).
22. *CLCC* 14, p. 38 (E), p. 32 (L).
23. *CLCC* 12, p. 9 (E), pp. 5-6 (L).
24. *Ibid.*, p. 9 (E), p. 5 (L).
25. *CLCC* 14, pp. 35-6 (E), pp. 30-1 (L).
26. *CLCC* 12, p. 7 (E), p. 3 (L).
27. *CLCC* 14, p. 34 (E), p. 28 (L).
28. *CLCC* 14, pp. 39-41 (E), pp. 32-3 (L).
29. *CLCC* 12, p. 11 (E), p. 7 (L).
30. *Ibid.*, p. 15 (E), p. 10 (L).
31. *Ibid.*, p. 11 (E), p. 8 (L).
32. *CLCC* 14, p. 37 (E), p. 31 (L).
33. *Ibid.*, p. 42 (E), p. 35 (L).
34. *CLCC* 15, p. 10.
35. *Loc. cit.*
36. *CLCC* 4, p. 4 (E), p. 3 (L).
37. *CLCC* 15, p. 9.
38. *CLCC* 4, p. 5 (E), p. 3 (L), quoted on pp. 71-4.
39. *Catacombes,* Paris, January 1974, p. 16.
40. *CLCC* 2, p. 4 (L), quoted on p. 116.
41. *CLCC* 15, pp. 2-3.
42. *CLCC* 19, pp. 2-10.
43. *Religious Liberty in the Soviet Union,* pp. 71-2.
44. *Catacombes,* Paris, January 1974, pp. 13-14.
45. *CLCC* 12, pp. 6-8 (E), pp. 2-4 (L).
46. *CLCC* 5, pp. 1-2 (E), pp. 2-3 (L).
47. *CLCC* 9, pp. 16-17 (E), p. 8 (L).
48. *CLCC* 20, p. 29.
49. *L'Osservatore Romano,* Rome, No. 105, 7 May 1976.
50. *CLCC* 19, pp. 2-3, 9-10.

VI

THE THEOLOGICAL SEMINARY OF KAUNAS

TRAINING for the ministry is a key issue in the life of any church, not least where the State threatens the future by imposing artificial restraints on seminary education. The Lithuanian Catholic Church, in contrast to its neighbour in Poland, experiences severe restrictions on entrance to the seminary which, more than any other single factor, has led to a major outcry from church members. The squeeze on the seminaries has led steadily, over the years, to a rising average age among the clergy and to a declining total of those in active office.*

This decline is due not to a lack of candidates for the priesthood, but to the barring of would-be entrants – highly-qualified men among them – from the seminaries.

Immediately before the Second World War there were four theological seminaries in Lithuania with about 470 students in them.[1] During the first occupation of Lithuania in the summer of 1940 the Soviets closed the three seminaries at Vilkaviškis (62 students), Telšiai (83 students) and Vilnius (106 students), commandeering them during the vacation, and they simultaneously threatened the fourth one at Kaunas – the only one which remains open today. Nevertheless, 175 students bravely convened in Kaunas at the beginning of the next academic year.[2] They managed to work on without too many problems, but on 8 January 1941 the Soviet authorities stepped in again and broke up the seminary by physical force. The expelled students were only able to grab their personal belongings and then they had to leave between two lines of soldiers with bayonets at the ready. However, teaching continued privately wherever priests and students could meet together for study. Despite these difficulties, the ordination of twelve students took place at the end of the academic year.

The continuing efforts of the hierarchy to re-open the Seminaries were unsuccessful until the Soviets left in the summer of 1941. Under the provisional government the Church repossessed the seminary buildings, but the Nazis were not much better disposed towards the Church than the Soviets had been, regarding her as a bastion of resistance. In 1942 they closed the Vilnius seminary and deported fifty of its students to Germany.[3]

*See p. 156.

The second Soviet occupation was only slightly less severe than the first for the Seminaries, in that Kaunas remained open, while the others were again closed.[4] The bland Soviet propaganda claim that present needs are amply met and that "in post-war years 374 priests have graduated from the Inter-diocesan Seminary in Kaunas"[5] conceals the relentless pressure on the Seminary over the past thirty years.

At the second Soviet occupation the Kaunas Seminary had 400 students. Within two years the Soviets had forced out 250.[6] It is reported that four rectors were deported between 1944 and 1956.[7]

By the time of Stalin's death the number of students in the Seminary had fallen to 75. The numbers of priests in Lithuania had also fallen; during the post-war emigration 176 priests from Vilnius went to Poland and were not allowed to return later. The renewed pressure on the Church during the Khrushchev period led to a further deterioration in the situation at the Kaunas Seminary. The Seminary was one of the first religious institutions to experience the effect of the worsening situation. As the suspended Bishop Steponavičius wrote in 1975:

> The Inter-diocesan Theological Seminary experienced one of these painful 'expulsions' in 1958, when on the instructions of the local government official for religion the principal was removed, as were some of the lecturers and a significant number of students.[8]

This led to the imposition of the lowest *numerus clausus* ever for the Seminary, with an average of no more than one new student per diocese per annum. Not all sources are entirely consistent, but in the appendix to this chapter* is a table computed from them which indicates the trends of the last fourteen years.

The above-mentioned table demonstrates a slight improvement in recent years, which exactly coincides with the rise of the open movement for religious freedom in Lithuania. That the Soviet authorities did yield slightly to pressure is irrefutable, especially when one considers the centrality of the seminary question in the Lithuanian protest movement. At one point the *Chronicle of the Lithuanian Catholic Church* claimed that only after the start of the "active campaign for the rights of the Seminary did the authorities permit the intake of twice the number of candidates."[9]

Almost every appeal since 1968 and every issue of the *Chronicle* bears upon this issue at some point, directly or indirectly. It may even have been the appeal against arbitrary government restrictions on the Seminary signed by 63 priests to Mr. Kosygin (dated 8 January 1969†) which set in train the movement of events which continues today (Document 44). Fr. Zdebskis mentioned these restrictions in his defence speech at his trial in 1971[10] and they were one of the main points in the subsequent Memorandum of the 17,000.[11]

A concession followed immediately‡: the intake jumped from six to ten for the next academic year, increasing to twelve in 1973. This still

*See p. 163.   †See Table on p. 138.   ‡See Table on p. 163.

did not offset the average death-rate nor the rising average age of the clergy, but it must have been more than enough to encourage the faithful to continue the pressure for improvement. The call is for new priests, not new bishops.[12] Document 45 illustrates the way in which priests in the diocese of Vilnius long past retiring age – even up to ninety years old – have to continue to serve, as no replacements are available. The Lithuanians hear news from across the frontier with Poland and remark on the 18,000 priests there – "an increase of 4,000 over the pre-war number".[13]

A further small concession, though one which has certain over-tones, is the occasional permission which the Soviet authorities have given to young priests to study in Rome. This began as early as 1959 when Fr. (later Bishop) Romualdas Krikščiunas was sent to Rome to study at the Gregorian University. Fr. (later Dr.) Viktoras Butkus was there at the same time[14] and others have been there subsequently.[15]

Of course, only "loyal" priests or seminarians are allowed to study abroad. These are often clerics earmarked for promotion. For example, Dr. Butkus is now rector of the Seminary and a prominent figure at international peace conferences; Fr. Juozas Pranka and Fr. Pranas Vaičekonis, who studied at the Collegium Russicum in Rome in 1970-1,[16] are now lecturers at the seminary. The Russian Orthodox and Baptist Churches in the USSR are also allowed to send a few selected students to theological institutions abroad, such as the Russian Spiritual Mission (Jerusalem) and the Baptist Spurgeon's College (London).

A challenging and not wholly irrelevant contrast is provided by the numbers of students in training as atheist lecturers. The *Chronicle* gives the number of centres for such courses as 33 in 1972, with a total of 750 students attending them.[17] This is no less than twenty-three times the number of theological students in the same year.

Even today the Kaunas Seminary does not actually occupy its own buildings. The Red Army commandeered these in 1944 and the seminary church became a warehouse. The Seminary nevertheless managed to install itself in the premises of the former Salesian monastery, now abolished, where it has been ever since. The State even imposes restrictions on these premises, forcing the students to use an unventilated cellar as their chapel – a serious health hazard.[18] All the former buildings have seriously deteriorated through misuse and lack of maintenance. There are fears that, even if the Seminary should win back its original premises, the years of repair work might culminate only in a further Soviet confiscation. As the Church cannot own her own buildings, but only leases them from the State, the Government imposes a tax of 4,500 roubles per annum on the use of the monastery buildings.[19]

According to the statements of Soviet propaganda, the selection of suitable candidates for the priesthood and their entry into the Kaunas Seminary proceeds normally:

> Candidates to the seminary are selected by the Lithuanian Ordinaries from various dioceses of Lithuania.* Only graduates of secondary or similar schools possessing school-leaving certificates are eligible for enrolment to the seminary . . .[20]

One of the seminary staff, Mgr. Steponas Telksnys, is reported to have told a Lithuanian radio correspondent in 1967:

> Candidates to the Kaunas Inter-diocesan Catholic Seminary must first of all turn to their parish priest for a testimonial, then they come to the rector of the seminary who selectes suitable candidates and consults on these matters with the warden of the seminary – His Excellency Bishop Dr. Juozapas Labukas.[21]

A group of priests from the Vilnius Archdiocese vigorously refuted these statements in December 1971, just after the publication of the book by Rimaitis from which the above quotations are taken. They state that the reality is very different. The Soviet authorities engage in a systematic campaign to terrorize would-be candidates into thinking better of their desire to become priests. At school it has been known for the headmaster or the teachers to tell a would-be ordinand that it would be better for him to be a drunkard, a thief or a murderer than to become a priest.[22] The most detailed exposition of these tactics is found in No. 3 of the *Lithuanian Chronicle* (Document 46).

The *Lithuanian Chronicle* demonstrated in 1974 the continuing nature of direct interference by the State, even after the 1972 concession, in the size of the intake:

> In the spring of 1974 the principal of the Kaunas Theological Seminary informed his students that for the coming academic year the authorities had promised to allow thirteen candidates to be accepted by the Seminary. Possibly the atheists did not think that so many would come forward. The administration of the Seminary sent a list of seventeen candidates to the official on religious affairs. Tumenas, with his KGB and Lithuanian Central Committee advisers, crossed off five candidates. The Seminary itself crossed off as unsuitable a further candidate who had been confirmed by Tumenas. One decided himself not to come to the Seminary. Finally, therefore, there were only ten first-year students. Three of those Tumenas crossed off were graduates.[23]

In 1975 the suspended Bishop Steponavičius complained in a letter to the Lithuanian Government about precisely this: that the final selection of candidates for the Seminary was being made not by the Church but by atheist officials.[24]

This is no less true of the seminary staff. All seminary lecturers must have their appointments confirmed by the Council for Religious Affairs. This favours the appointment of "progressive" clergy to such posts and is a situation common to all theological colleges and

---

*This conceals a discriminatory regulation. Students from outside Lithuania have no right to training for the Catholic priesthood, except for the even smaller number who enter the Riga Seminary (see page 151).

seminaries in the USSR and Eastern Europe, though obviously the Church combats this interference more successfully in some countries than in others.

Recent evidence from Lithuania provides vivid illustrations of the sufferings of various individuals who put their names forward for seminary training (Document 47).

Even when the remaining handful of students has finally passed through all these ordeals and joined the seminary, the seminarian is still not sheltered from a continuation of the campaign against him. The atheist authorities constantly interfere, constantly intimidate and, even though they may often not carry out their threats, the aim is to produce a kind of siege mentality, a deep-seated insecurity on the part of those who should be settling down to study spiritual questions in the manner which the church decides.[25]

The average standard of health among the seminarians is reported to be low.[26] Not only do many become ill during the course of their studies, but some have not even been able to go forward to ordination. This may be due to the overcrowded conditions and bad food at the seminary. The number of seminarians may increase or fall, but the number of rooms available to them remains the same.

Entrance to the seminary is limited to graduates of secondary schools *(gimnaziya),* so that most country children, who have only studied at the so-called "middle-school", cannot apply. The seminary intake is thus mainly from the towns. Applicants include outstanding scholars and university graduates, but these are not usually allowed to enter by the senior atheist official. Usually there are twenty to thirty applicants every year. In September 1975, for example, there were twenty applicants, of whom only twelve were accepted.

The most serious problem of all for the students arises during the vacations, when they are away from the relative protection which the community of the seminary provides. Document 48 gives a picture of the way in which harassment continues unabated at a time when the student should be supplementing his academic studies by gaining practical experience or merely refreshing himself through normal holidays.

The most emotive subject of all in relation to the Kaunas Seminary is the continuing attempt of the atheist authorities either to infiltrate their own people into the ranks of the students – and thus eventually into the priesthood and hierarchy – or to recruit informers from among those with a genuine vocation. The evidence that this has happened is irrefutable. Not only has the *Lithuanian Chronicle* carefully designated the methods employed (Document 49) and differentiated between the two categories above, but, just as importantly, there is corroborative evidence that the same occurs in the theological seminaries of the Russian Orthodox Church.[27] The Russian Orthodox commentator, Anatoli Levitin, described the recruitment fearlessly in 1968,[28] doubtless one of the reasons for his subsequent imprisonment.

Considering the massive nature of the campaign, as outlined above, against a beleaguered handful of people, it is surprising that seminary training at Kaunas has continued without suffering a breakdown. The present Rector, Dr. Viktoras Butkus, took over in 1962 after the harrying and hounding of several of his predecessors. His record with the State up to July 1976 was such that he seemed an absolutely "safe" man, because he was one of the initial group of three selected to complete his theological education in Rome from 1959-60. He proved himself politically during this period and was consequently able to take over the highly-sensitive job of Rector of the Seminary. He has been able to continue his travels abroad and was used by the regime as a front-line diplomat at peace conferences and elsewhere in its efforts to prove the "normality" of Catholic life in the Soviet Union. This has led the Lithuanian faithful to urge treating him with caution and to an appeal that he should not be elevated to a bishopric.[29] As with leaders of other denominations in a similar situation, this is emphatically not the same as designating him a traitor to the faith. It is impossible from the outside – and it would in any case be wrong – to pass judgment on such supremely sensitive matters. Let it simply be recorded that under his leadership the Seminary has come through to a slightly improved situation in the 1970's.

More recently, in the summer of 1976, an episode took place which could rehabilitate Dr. Butkus completely in the eyes of Lithuanian believers. On 12 June 1976 *Moscow News* (the Soviet weekly published abroad in English and French) reported an interview with Dr. Butkus, in which the Rector was quoted as saying that religious believers in Lithuania were not hindered in practising their faith, that bishops could exercise their pastoral functions freely and that religious literature was published in adequate quantities. According to *Moscow News,* Dr. Butkus attributed the destruction of churches to the effects of the war and the scarcity of priests to emigration.[30] The interview was of the kind often given by church representatives in the USSR for foreign consumption. It was republished in No. 24 of the *Chronicle of the Lithuanian Catholic Church,* where it was severely criticised for misrepresenting the facts. There was nothing particularly surprising in any of this.

However, in 1977, an extremely interesting development took place: Dr. Butkus issued a statement denying that he ever gave any such interview to *Moscow News.* "I have been unable to find out who wrote the alleged interview with me. Unfortunately . . . . I could not check the original text of the interview, but a report on Vatican Radio contained a number of errors which no priest, particularly a seminary rector, could have made".[31] He protested to the Executive for Religious Affairs in Lithuania, K. Tumenas, asking him to find the persons responsible for writing the interview, to have it repudiated and to ensure that there should never be a recurrence.

Dr. Butkus' letter of protest was published in No. 29 of the *Lithuanian Chronicle*, accompanied by a somewhat guarded and suspicious commentary.[32] The *Chronicle's* editors suspect that the protest may be a political manoeuvre on the part of the authorities; if Dr. Butkus remains as Rector and continues to travel abroad after his statement, this becomes a more likely explanation. If Dr. Butkus is sincere, one might expect him to repudiate all his other misleading statements on the position of the Catholic Church in Lithuania. Nevertheless, Dr. Butkus' comment, repudiating as it does an official Soviet newspaper report, was unprecedented for an officially-approved church leader in the Soviet Union.

The previous Vice-rector, Vaclovas Aliulis, was popular and reportedly did a good job, but was dismissed after a year. The post is now vacant. As Dr. Butkus is often abroad, the Seminary is largely run by Bishop Povilonis, himself a graduate of Kaunas Seminary, with no supplementary education abroad.

Some of the Soviet propaganda claims about conditions in the Seminary are presumably accurate:

> Tuition is free and besides that, all the seminarists are provided with free board and lodging that is not repayable after graduation. The Seminary is maintained by voluntary contributions from believers.[33]

However, further such claims about the curriculum probably go beyond the bounds of strict accuracy. Mgr. S.Telksnys is reported as saying:

> The curricula for seminaries as well as for all Catholic universities* are drawn up by the Congregation of Seminary and University Studies in Rome. The Kaunas Interdiocesan Seminary also follows a curriculum approved by the Congregation. The term of studies at the Kaunas Inter-diocesan Seminary is five years. In the first year philosophical subjects are read, while the next four years are devoted to theology, Church Law, Holy Scripture, etc.[34]

When asked whether political subjects such as Marxism-Leninism were taught, Mgr. Telksnys answered:

> Marxism as such is not taught, the would-be priests are acquainted with state laws, including the USSR Constitution, which is read by the Rev. J. Preikšas.[35]

However, when Rugienis visited the Seminary and investigated the students' reading, he was reported in the *Lithuanian Chronicle* as "not pleased because they were not reading Marxist classics."[36]

Further evidence suggests that, while the teaching of Marxism has not become a formal part of the timetable, the students are forced to listen to some anti-Vatican lectures.[37] The seminary authorities are

---

*This statement may subtly imply to the uninformed reader that there is such a university in Lithuania. There is not._

obliged to give atheists an opportunity to lecture, supposedly on political themes. A private letter of 1971 or 1972 gives precise details:

> The single Seminary at Kaunas has not only been drastically reduced in size, but is even obliged to receive local activists who give their lectures there. For example, in March 1971 the direction of the Seminary had to receive C. Jursenas, a party propagandist who gave a lecture of a political nature to staff and students. After it one of the staff asked for elucidation on the relations between the Vatican and the USSR. In his reply the lecturer insulted Popes Pius XI and Pius XII in the most vulgar terms. The latter was supposed to have blessed the exploits of Hitler, while the priesthood had always depended on and supported the exploiters. One of the Seminary teachers, Fr. Žemaitis, then made a short speech extolling the eloquence of the lecturer, Jursenas. The clergy and the faithful in general suffer much from the penetration of the activists into the Theological Seminary and feel that the teaching body is too yielding in facing the atheist government, which interferes in problems of conscience. All this is a consequence of the excessive pliability of the church authorities.[38]

While the exposure of young students to the type of atheist argument they will inevitably meet everywhere in the course of their ministry may in itself be no bad thing, at the same time the student has the right to expect that he will have the best available teachers to put another point of view. There is current evidence that some of the best potential teachers are being barred from the seminaries.[39] However, it is certain that one small benefit from all the pressures is the amount of individual attention received by the students. The 1965 picture of the whole seminary, staff and students, published by the Soviet authorities, shows a ratio of eight lecturers and a warden of the hostel to twenty-four students.[40]

The evidence is decisive that, over the years, the authorities have either barred admission to some of the very best students or secured their removal.[41] This has led, naturally enough, to the secret ordination of some of those who were advanced in their studies, and possibly to private preparation for the priesthood in a few instances.

The best-documented case of a secret ordination is that of Fr. Vytautas Merkys. Although he was forced out of the Seminary in 1958, the case was contentious enough for Bishop Steponavičius still to be defending him in 1975:

> The official accused Merkys of anti-Soviet attitudes. After leaving the Seminary Fr. Merkys entered an agricultural college, where he was an exemplary student and later won renown as a diligent and conscientious worker in the Vilnius Horticultural Nursery. For some years now he has been functioning as a priest in the town of Khmelnytsky in Ukraine. He has shown himself to be an exemplary priest and a good and loyal Soviet citizen. When at that time I attempted to defend the wronged student, the official attacked me for defending a theological student who had anti-Soviet tendencies and threatened me with exile.[42]

There is no doubt that Fr. Merkys was secretly ordained in 1960 and that at one stage atheist officials were offering him the chance of serving as a priest if he would reveal the name of the bishop who had ordained him.[43] He must have remained firm, or Bishop Steponavičius would not have continued to defend him so vigorously. His eventual victory in the long conflict spoke eloquently for his extraordinary tenacity.

It is far from clear how much preparation for the priesthood takes place outside the Seminary. The *Lithuanian Chronicle* at one point states that "some candidates study theology and become priests outside the seminary limits",[44] but it seems more likely that this is a private arrangement with individual teachers rather than an "underground seminary" as such, even though the writer of the KGB-inspired anonymous letter makes the unqualified statement that one exists.[45] The vigorous but guarded reply to this accusation is that if there were such an institution it would be entirely worthy, even though it "probably" exists only in the mind of the accuser.[46] Whatever the situation, when the State refuses entry to some of the best candidates and keeps others waiting for up to ten years before they can become students,[47] it is natural and entirely proper that the Church should make alternative arrangements. None of this would be necessary at all, but for the direct interference of the State in the internal affairs of the Church.[48]

Priests and lay theologians who are banned from the seminary often write *samizdat* works. These form a large part of the well-organized, "self-publishing" activity in Lithuania.*

Judging by lists of confiscated literature, two-thirds of the books taken during the KGB's searches are written by Lithuanian Catholics themselves.

Although it does not strictly come within the confines of this study, we should note that there is a second Catholic theological seminary in the Soviet Union, also in the Baltic States. The Riga Seminary is even smaller in size than that at Kaunas. There is also very much less information about it. It has about eighteen students, with two or three ordinations a year.[49] A recent report by a western commentator indicates that it is under considerable pressure:

> Half the building which housed this second seminary was appropriated by the State some years ago and the seminarians feared that the remaining half would also be taken away from them, leaving them only outhouses and sheds. As it was, in 1972 with only half of the original building people were forced to sleep in corridors and the library books were stacked in every conceivable nook and cranny.[50]

The Riga Seminary accepts some students from Belorussia and Ukraine who are not accepted at the Kaunas Seminary, although some Ukrainian priests work in Lithuania. However, priests from

*See pp. 251, 253.

Belorussia have sometimes not been allowed to return home once they have been ordained.

As to the fate of the monasteries and convents, on the one hand there has been a systematic destruction and continued suppression of monasticism, which has been a guardian of Lithuanian culture and spirituality over the ages; on the other hand, Soviet intransigence has led to a rebirth of some kind of secret monastic movement, details of which are obscure, but which unquestionably exists.

With one breath, the Soviets accuse monasticism of having wrecked the morals of the nation in the past. An atheist article published in 1974 claimed that in the seventeenth century Catholic monasteries owned many breweries and inns which sold alcoholic drinks. The Dominican monastery in Skapiškis allegedly owned seventeen inns and four vodka breweries.[51] Yet in the next breath the State honours the tradition of learning which was enshrined in the monasteries. Fr. Jurgis Pabreža was an eminent nineteenth-century botanist. In October 1974 people in Vilnius were astonished to see posters going up which announced an event to mark the 125th anniversary of his birthday – to take place in the atheist museum, no less.[52]

To the Soviet authorities, there were no two ways of thinking about monasticism at the time of the two occupations in 1940 and 1944-5. Before the Second World War there were 73 monasteries, with 580 monks, over 400 being lay brothers, and 85 convents with 950 nuns.[53] By 1947 the tradition of centuries had been smashed and there was not a single monastery or convent still existing: they had all been confiscated for "military purposes". The standard Soviet pretext for this conduct is that in 1940 the monastic communities, like the seminaries, "sheltered armed anti-Soviet bands and Nazi spies".[54] The accusations relating to 1944 are even more lurid:

> One can see from priest A. Ylius's reminiscences that he was one of the organizers and ideologists of the anti-Soviet underground movement. He had turned the Kaunas Marian Monastery, the Skardupiai church with the presbytery and some adjacent buildings into a centre of anti-Soviet activities, a hiding-place of armed gangs. On the orders of Ylius and his accomplices, those gangs attacked people who were known to be sympathetic towards Soviet power, and they tortured and murdered those they caught alone and unprotected.[55]

The fact that Fr. Ylius is not only still alive, but is an active parish priest and in communication with the *Lithuanian Chronicle,* casts considerable doubt on the veracity of the events as described.[56] Fr. Ylius wrote to the *Chronicle* in 1975 to dispute an alternative reason for the closure of the monasteries which the Soviets have brought forward – that they gradually disappeared as a result of the "improved" social and economic conditions of the post-war era (Document 50).

The State has commandeered the monastic buildings for a variety of purposes, just as happened to Russian Orthodox monasteries in other parts of the Soviet Union. A favourite ploy has been to install atheist museums in them. This was the fate of the Franciscan monastery at Kretinga and the Marian monastery at Marijampole,[57] the latter being the one of which Fr. Ylius writes in particular. The former Sacred Heart Monastery in Vilnius, following the Soviet tradition originally established at Solovki in the 1920s and described so graphically in the *Gulag Archipelago* by Solzhenitsyn,[58] has become a prison which now houses 750 criminals.[59]

There is strong evidence of considerable and increasing activity among illegal nuns belonging to underground convents (Document 51). This is seen most clearly from the accusation by the atheist activist, Pranas Mišutis, published in January 1974, and the *Lithuanian Chronicle's* reply to it. Mišutis wrote that "disloyal priests . . . encourage illegal monasteries and convents".[60] Far from disputing this, the *Chronicle* confirms it:

> Mišutis mentioned illegal convents. It is strange that during the entire post-war period the atheists have never mentioned convents, as if they never existed. Yet they have existed and still do. It is actually fortunate for the convents that they are underground institutions, for in this way the Soviet Government is less able to control their activities and candidates wishing to enter do not experience the trials which must be endured by those desiring to enter the seminary. The number of vocations is not declining, but is in fact increasing. Of particular merit among the activities of these institutions is the conducting of catechism lessons and activities involving young people.[61]

The activity of the nuns is so vigorous that the bishops have apparently sought to put restrains upon it, in order not to exacerbate relations with the State.[62] The writer of the second "anonymous letter" accuses priests of "interfering" over the question of convents and pushing the nuns into various forms of illegal activity, which the *Chronicle* counters with the question of whether it would be preferable for the KGB to interfere in the life of the convents.[63]

Perhaps the most remarkable feature of the underground convents – though virtually nothing is known of their life and communal activities – is the high intellectual ability of the young nuns. Some at least of these girls have been working in secular employment and there have been several recent instances of their dismissal when their secret activities have come to light. Three girls dismissed in Vilnius in May 1973 were a senior student at an advanced teacher-training institute, a teacher of French at a secondary school and a senior research assistant at the history department of the university.[64] A fourth girl was dismissed from her job as a kindergarten teacher in Vilnius in September of the same year,[65] while yet another, a typist, met the same fate at Panevežys in April 1974.[66] Another girl who lost her job in 1974 for being a nun was Monika Gavenaite, who worked at a publishing house in Kaunas.[67]

If there are any comparable monasteries, nothing is known of them. The need for them would not be quite so urgent, because of the number of priests who are able to follow their vocations in the parochial ministry. Be this as it may, the revival of the monastic vocation in Lithuania is a remarkable phenomenon after thirty years of Soviet rule and demonstrates decisively the failure of Soviet educational policy, the aim of which is to bring up a generation of "religion-free" young people.

DOCUMENTS

44. 63* PRIESTS WRITE TO KOSYGIN (January 1969)

To: The Chairman of the Council of Ministers of the USSR

DECLARATION

We, the undersigned priests of the Lithuanian SSR, feel it our duty to you, Chairman Minister, to inform you of constantly recurring facts in our country which infringe the freedom of conscience guaranteed by the Soviet Constitution and which particularly affect the Theological Seminary in Kaunas.

Before 1940 there were 12 bishops, 1640 priests and 4 seminaries with 466 students in Lithuania, while at present there are only 4 bishops (2 of whom are persecuted), about 800 priests and only 1 theological seminary with 27 students. These numbers have fallen because officials of the civil government administer the internal affairs of the Seminary. For example, there were 400 students in the Kaunas Theological Seminary in 1944 and in 1946 the Soviet Government reduced this number to 150; only 30 students are now allowed to study there. Because of this, the Kaunas Theological Seminary graduates only five or six new priests each year. In 1969 only four priests are to complete the seminary course.

Now it is not even possible to serve the faithful fully because of the shortage of priests. A high proportion of them are elderly and some serve a number of parishes. Since about thirty priests die in Lithuania each year, it is obvious that by the use of administrative methods some

*The number is given as 63 at the head of the document but there are only 32 signatures on it now. Possibly the other signatures were lost in transit.

government officials are aiming at the destruction of the Catholic Church in Lithuania.

When in the post-revolutionary period civil government officials were closing Orthodox churches, the Central Committee of the Communist Party issued a decree in which it was stated: "The Central Committee is convinced that all these deviations are the direct result of infringement of party policy . . . and are of direct assistance to our class enemies" (Decisions of the Central Committee, 14 March 1930).

The Soviet press of today confirms the earlier Central Committee decisions: "The strict maintenance of Soviet laws and Leninist principles on religion and the believers is an important party and state requirement . . . In our country all experiments in administering religious matters are severely punished" *(Nauka i religia* 6, 1968, p. 10).

In the Kaunas Theological Seminary the following abnormal system for the acceptance of candidates is still in effect. The Rector of the Seminary is obliged to send the list of candidates to the senior Lithuanian official on religion each year. The latter can delete any candidate with no explanation, without heed to the fact that the entrant is a Soviet citizen with full rights, has never been tried and has committed no offence against the Soviet State. We do not understand why young men who have completed higher or special school studies have no right to enter the theological seminary. Why do candidates who have once been deleted because of the *numerus clausus* lose for ever their right to enter the Seminary? Why are candidates sometimes refused entry for unimportant reasons? We know that this is not done in the case of other institutes of higher education. Is this not an infringement of the Soviet Constitution? Are not the above-mentioned Central Committee decisions distorted by this?

The believers and priests of Lithuania have long been perturbed by this abnormal situation at the Kaunas Theological Seminary. Priests of the Telšiai Diocese wrote to you about this, Chairman Minister, in 1968. This year priests of the Vilkaviškis Diocese have approached the Lithuanian bishops and diocesan administrators on the subject of the Kaunas Theological Seminary.

We therefore ask you, Chairman Minister, to allow the Kaunas Catholic Theological Seminary to regulate its internal affairs independently, to allow the church authorities themselves to set the number of the intake and not to create obstacles for the candidates.

> (Signatures: Father Petras Dumbliauskas,
> resident of Garliava;
> Father Juozas Zdebskis,
> resident at Valakbudis, Šakiai district,
> and a further thirty priests)[68]

8 January 1969

45. AGED PRIESTS CANNOT RETIRE, 1975

If this were true, if we had proper conditions for our work, then why is it that in the Archbishopric of Vilnius there are at least eight priests who look after two parishes, while Father Alfonsas Merkys even has three: Turmantas, Tilže and Smalvos? Why is it that parishes in the Archdiocese of Vilnius are served by aged priests such as:

P. Bekiš, 77 years old (parish priest of the Holy Spirit in Vilnius);
L. Chomski, 90 (Baltasis Vokes);
L. Ivančik, 79 (Korvis);
L. Laucevič, 80 (Rukininkai);
A. Liachovič, 80 (Mickunai);
G. Malachovski, 77 (Eitmeniškiai);
V. Novicki, 78 (Parudaminis);
N. Pakalka, 82 (Marcinkonys)?*

These priests, with the exception of Father P. Bekiš, have no assistants.

The examples we have given show how great is the shortage of priests in Lithuania.[69]

46. INTIMIDATION OF ORDINANDS, 1972

Even at secondary school, when it becomes evident that a particular student intends to study at the Theological Seminary efforts are made to influence him to choose another profession. The school's administration, or sometimes officials of the District Executive Committee, advise the young man to move to a different school. They even promise to help. If this type of agitation is ineffective, efforts are sometimes made to impede his success in examinations. The seminary candidate would then have to repeat his course and waste a further year over his secondary education. Sometimes the school administration is reluctant to hand the exam certificate to the student and offers to send it, together with its own recommendation, to another school. If the school authorities are unable to dissuade the young man, he is sometimes asked to defer his entry to the Seminary for a few years so that another agency would then have to forward his application. In this manner the school authorities hope to justify themselves more in the eyes of the local or central government authorities against accusations of "ineffective educational work".

To delay the entry of students to the Seminary for a few years, since 1954 they have first had to complete a period of military service. There have been cases where the military command delays call-up for

*Some of these names seem to be Polish or Ukrainian; we retain the original spellings.

a few years and the candidate does not meanwhile have the right to enter the Seminary.

On the instructions of the KGB, the directorate of the Seminary has to inform them as soon as the candidate crosses the Seminary threshold. Candidates have sometimes become victims of pestering soon after first visiting the Seminary, even before submitting an application for admission.

Rugienis has outlined to the seminary directorate the type of candidate whose application is to be rejected out of hand. Into this category come the so-called "anti-soviet elements" – people who have incurred KGB displeasure for any reason, such as having parents exiled to Siberia, or a relative who in the immediate post-war years was a partisan. This means that the first screening of the candidates has to be made by the seminary directorate itself.

The KGB becomes particularly active at the stage when the seminary directorate submits the list of candidates to Rugienis for approval, and uses all available means to collect information about the candidate at his school, place of work or residence. They are mainly concerned to establish whether the young man, should he become a priest, could do much to hinder atheism and, consequently, the Soviet system itself, or whether he would merely be an innocuous opponent.

On occasion, during the course of a theological student's studies KGB officials visit his parents, pretend to be good friends of their son, and initiate a discussion on religion, enquiring about the books he has read, the priests with whom he is acquainted, and so on.

During the summer prior to joining the Seminary, the candidate is frequently visited by KGB officers. So that the security men should not be pressed for time, the seminary directorate is compelled to submit the list of candidates to Rugienis very early: for example, this year [1972] – by 26 June . . . .

In order to meet the candidate, KGB officials sometimes visit his home area anonymously; sometimes he is summoned to the military authorities or to the cadre section* at his place of work. The young men are strictly forbidden to talk about the KGB interviews to their parents, the parish priest or anyone else. During the meetings the KGB officials start by attempting to dissuade the young man from joining the Seminary and he is offered help in moving to another school. When attempts at dissuasion fail, the KGB tries to recruit the candidate as one of these agents. They argue as follows: "If we become friends, there will be no obstacles to joining the Seminary. Your faith and priestly obligations will not be affected. We'll merely meet on odd occasions and have a chat. If necessary, we'll give you material support or we will help in other ways and no one will know about our meetings".

Should the candidate be wary of KGB deceit and refuse to agree to becoming an agent, he is threatened: "You're a fanatic! You'll never

*Office of personnel files where political and domestic information on the employee is kept.

get into the Seminary. Everything is in our hands. It's clear that Soviet rule doesn't please you. Think again, so that you don't live to regret this".

In concluding the discussion the KGB officials sometimes even require the candidate to sign a written acknowledgement to the effect that should he tell anyone what was discussed, he would be answerable before the law.

If it becomes evident during the discussion with the KGB that the candidate has strong principles, his application is rejected without further ado; the KGB men draw the inference that such a person cannot be allowed to study at the Seminary, since when he became a priest he would be completely immune to their influence . . . .

The Executive of the Council for Religious Affairs, Rugienis, deletes some of the names from the candidate list submitted by the Seminary, often with the comment that particular individuals will never be able to become priests. So that Rugienis should not eliminate too many candidates, the seminary directorate is forced to submit for approval only the number of candidates laid down by government decree. At present it is permissable to accept ten candidates annually. A few years ago the permitted number was only five.[70]

47. A YOUNG MAN'S VOCATION, 1975

[To K. Tumenas]

. . . On 30 October 1974 Mrs. Skireliene was told that "the rector had influenced" her son (to apply to the Theological Seminary – Ed. of *CLCC*).

G. Skirelys [the son] knows quite well that to be a priest these days does not mean "eating white bread". Everyone, including young people, knows that atheists denigrate a priest in every way possible, calling him a "little churchman" and writing "servant of a religious cult" in his passport. Fanatical atheists mock priests, who have no rights, and write baseless complaints and reports about them, for they know they will receive only praises and promotion in their careers in return for this. If a young man sees the unpleasantness priests have to suffer and has been trying to enter the Theological Seminary since 1970, then he needs no influencing. At the young man's request I wrote him the necessary reference, but you found some "obstacles" and would not allow him to be accepted. In 1973 you promised his mother that he would be accepted in 1974, but you did not keep your promise.

The parishioners of Adutiškis often ask me why the young man has not been accepted. They have the right to take an interest in this, for every year they send in contributions for the upkeep of the Seminary.

Not knowing what to reply, I told them to go and inquire. We hear that some people are rejoicing because no one wants to enter the Seminary. This is not true. People could be found to fill the places held by ageing clergy and make up the numbers lacking, but you bar the way to many of them. A young man's vocation is decided on, not by those whose task it is, but by atheists. Just as we priests have no right to decide who should join the Komsomol or the Communist Party, so you do not have the right to decide whether a young man should enter the priesthood. It is unheard of in the history of the Church that atheists should decide which candidates are fit to become priests.

You answered the parishioners of Adutiškis by saying, "The young man himself knows why he has not been accepted". You avoided giving a straight answer, so it is obvious that you have something to hide.

On 27 November 1974 a representative from the Seminary explained to the parishioners of Adutiškis that the young man had not been accepted because, after graduating from an agricultural technical college, he had not worked a full two years for the State; he had quarrelled with his superiors at his agricultural work and he had also demanded permission to emigrate.

Without checking the truth of this slander, and without listening to the other side of the story, the seminary authorities were not in a position to make a correct decision. According to the dictates of Christian morality, I must defend the insulted party. The young man could have worked for two years and tried to do so, but because he went to church he was dismissed from his job. Having lost his job as an agricultural expert, the young man went to the Liudas Giry collective farm and was ready to pay his debt to the State by working as an ordinary labourer, but some official ordered him to be given the sack.

The farm authorities constantly became angry with him; they mocked and reproached him: "What kind of example are you showing to schoolchildren, if you, a future agricultural specialist, go to church?" J. Aničas and J. Rimaitis, in *Soviet Laws on Religion* (Vilnius, 1970, p. 31) write, "It is against the law to refuse to employ a citizen . . . or dismiss him from employment . . . because of his religious views."

The young man was dismissed from his job merely because he went to church. But it was the young man who was considered guilty, not the farm authorities for illegally dismissing him. In that case, why are such fine-sounding laws written? They are written not to defend those who are illegally persecuted, but for propaganda purposes. Look at the excellent laws we have – even the rights of believers are defended in law! This is just a mockery of believers.

This young man is accused of quarrelling with the authorities. Hoping that he would lose his vocation, they decided to make him a brigade leader. He refused the post, because he was convinced that in 1974 he would be accepted at the Seminary. His refusal to attend the leaders' classes was not an avoidance of civil duties, as everyone chooses his speciality freely.

The young man is accused of demanding permission to emigrate. This is a slander – he has never even mentioned emigration.

The seminary representative suggested that he should go away somewhere, if only to Latvia, and wait there for about three years. He has been waiting since 1970 and now must wait again for an indefinite period of time! What will happen to the young man after such a long time? But the slander will not die! The young man has lost the favour of those who do not recognize forgiveness and has earned the hatred of those who not only beat an enemy until he falls down, but have also preserved the concept of utter extermination. The aim of the enemies of the Church is understandable: they are striving to make sure that the Seminary trains only elderly and sick men. You said, "The Rector influenced him." But how is your suggestion to the young man's mother to be understood – that he should go into medicine? You do not interfere with those who wish to enter the medical profession, but only with a young man who has decided to be a priest. By not accepting him for such a long period, you hope to freeze his vocation and squeeze a "repentance" out of him. Why do you make such demands, which have nothing to do with a priestly vocation and are not even worthy of decent men? . . .

Fr. B. Laurinavičius.[71]

Adutiškis, 25 January 1975

48.   THE HARASSMENT OF ORDINANDS CONTINUES, 1972

The Christmas, Easter and summer holidays cause the greatest problem to the seminarians. The theological students have to say ahead of time where they are intending to spend their vacation periods, so that the KGB can, if necessary, find them – and the need always does arise: to talk to those not yet recruited and to train those who have been recruited, persuading them, for example, to submit information about which friends are devout and which are not, what is new in the Seminary, the feelings of the theological students, their topics of discussion, what they read and what they bring back from town on Wednesdays (half days).

Many a student on returning to his parents' home finds a letter from the KGB. Such letters convey holiday greetings and he is reminded to come to a pre-arranged meeting, for example at some suggested bus station or post office, or to ring a given telephone number in Kaunas. So as to avoid meeting too frequently with the KGB, theological students endeavour to travel as much as possible during their holidays, but they are reprimanded for this.

Meetings between the KGB and theological students are conducted under full conspiratorial rules on the assumption that, should it become generally known that a particular student has been meeting KGB officers, he would not be suitable as an agent, since everyone would beware of him. It is not advisable for theological students to spend their holidays with "reactionary" priests. Those who work conscientiously in the vineyards of Christ, particularly those who do not conform to the secret instructions of the Government which limit religious life, are regarded as being in this category. It is very desirable for a student to stay with "loyal" priests who have been recruited as security agents or who, to appease the Government, have forsaken their priestly duties and live a secular life. The KGB uses this means to try and destroy the idealism of the theological student who, on seeing examples of unworthy priests, might himself be conditioned to accept such a mode of life.

As a result of KGB interference in the internal life of the Seminary, an atmosphere of fear and suspicion prevails. To strengthen this atmosphere, Rugienis visits the Seminary from time to time and threatens to expel various of the students.[72]

49. KGB SUCCESSES, 1972

In the interests of truth it must be admitted that the KGB does succeed in recruiting some of the young men. This occurs through lack of vigilance or because of the advice of some thoughtless priest: "Don't be afraid to sign, everybody does it. Later you needn't work for the KGB". Alas, the security organs have ample means for forcing one to work for them and it is only men of exceptional spirit who can hold out.

What do the KGB organs hope to achieve in recruiting theological students as agents?

They need accurate information about the seminary's lecturers, directorates and students and about events in church life. A. Barkauskas, secretary of the Central Committee of the Communist Party of Lithuania, speaking at the Sixth Congress of the Party said:

The increased bitterness of the ideological struggle forces us to be particularly vigilant and to act thoughtfully and purposefully and reliably to close the door to any hostile influence. We must react appropriately to all the diversions prepared by our enemies, to detect them in good time and to defeat them (6 July 1972).

The KGB certainly knows that no priest with a conscience would be an earnest worker for the security agencies. However, even here recruitment has a purpose. Mistrust is sown amongst the theological students; the person recruited is afraid to appear too pious and avoids more serious discussions. The recruited youth, conscious of his dual role, inevitably suffers moral deterioration. The efforts of the KGB to recruit theological students and priests are, therefore, crude infringements of human rights.

As in the Seminary, so beyond its bounds, it is clear to all who are the true candidates and who "carry the party ticket".

There are differences amongst recruits. Many of them have the right intentions and do not want to harm the Church. They make every effort to avoid meeting KGB officers; they avoid being present at meetings of priests so as not to be faced with having to tell the KGB what had been discussed. One or two of the recruits, on the other hand, lose their clerical and human dignity and conscience and do all that the KGB officials require of them.[73]

50. A PRIEST DEFENDS HIMSELF, 1975

At the end of July or in early August 1946 I was tried under the Soviet* Penal Code, Article 58 1A, Paragraph 10, for organized efforts to make Lithuania a free, independent and democratic republic. The interrogations lasted for almost ten months. In the examination records, as far as I can recall, no instances of atrocities figure; there is no proof of terrorist or criminal actions on my part, no accusations about weapons were made. At the time of arrest there were no weapons or ammunition in my flat.

Who authorized the candidate in historical science, S. Laurinaitis, to libel me publicly in the press (*Komjaunimo Tiesa,* 2 April 1975), by accusing me of atrocities and other crimes?

When my certificate of registration as a minister of religion was withdrawn from me on 30 January 1961, I went to the Executive of the Council for Religious Affairs to ask why this had been done.

"You're a cruel man", said Rugienis.

"Please provide evidence of any cruelties that I perpetrated whilst I was parish priest of Lesčiai from 1956 to 1961."

Instead of providing evidence, Rugienis took a copy of *Tiesos Kelias*† [The Way of Truth] from a drawer, showed me an obituary of the late parish priest of Saločiai, Fr. Štombergis, and told me to read it.

*Each republic has its own penal code. Article 58 1A of the old penal code relates to treason, paragraph 10 of this article refers to anti-Soviet propaganda in war conditions.
†To be distinguished from a later *samizdat* publication of the same name (see p. 252).

"Please look and see when this article was written," I suggested to Rugienis.

The article had been written in 1939. This means that in writing this obituary I had committed a great crime against the Soviet Government, which did not even exist in Lithuania at that time. The most terrible of my crimes whilst in Lesčiai was that I had repaired and painted the church and revived the declining parish of Lesčiai.

Father A. Ylius, M.I.C.
Rector of Šiupyliai Church.[74]

51. THE WORK OF UNDERGROUND NUNS, 1976

In Lithuania there are about 1,500 monks and nuns. The nuns largely work as nurses and help to give the sick the last rites. There are no nuns in the villages. Nuns also teach children prayers and the catechism. If you ask a small child who taught him the catechism, and he replies, "sister", you can be sure it was a nun.[75]

APPENDIX

Table of Students at Kaunas Theological Seminary

Academic Year Beginning	Intake	Ordinations	Total in Seminary	Deaths of Serving Priests
1962	5	9	45	18
1963	5	18	31	13
1964	4	6	25	19
1965	5	9	24	21
1966	8	8	29	21
1967	7	9	30	26
1968	6	8	30	24
1969	10	3	30	16
1970	10	8	34	18
1971	10	4	38	10
1972	10	6	39	17
1973	12	6	54	21
1974	9	8	49	23
1975	12 (20 applicants)	8	53	19
1976	18	10	51	9 (to 1 July)

NOTES TO CHAPTER VI

1. *Lithuania: la chiesa cattolica nella tormenta*, Part 1, June 1940-June 1941, compiled by Elta Press, Urbania, Italy, 1976, pp. 53-6, to which I am indebted for this section on the seminaries during the first Soviet occupation.
2. *Ibid.*, p. 53.
3. Savasis, *The War Against God in Lithuania*, p. 23.
4. *Ibid.*, p. 27.
5. Rimaitis, *Religion in Lithuania*, p. 21.
6. Appeal of Frs. P. Dumbliauskas and J. Zdebskis of 8 January 1969, *RCL* 3, 1973, p. 50.
7. (Ed.) Marshall, *Aspects of Religion in the Soviet Union 1917-67*, p. 385.
8. *CLCC* 20, p. 10.
9. *CLCC* 12, p. 10 (E), p. 6. (L).
10. *CLCC* 1, p. 12.
11. *CLCC* 2, p. 3. See p. 115-17. 126-8.
12. *CLCC* 10, p. 8 (E), p. 3 (L).
13. *CLCC* 17, p. 24.
14. Rimaitis, *op. cit.*, p. 15.
15. *Ibid.*, p. 22.
16. *Loc. cit.*
17. *CLCC* 5, p. 5 (E), p. 5 (L).
18. *CLCC* 19, p. 9.
19. *CLCC* 8, pp. 26-7 (E), pp. 14-15 (L) and 10, p. 28 (E), p. 15 (L).
20. Rimaitis, *op. cit.*, p. 20.
21. *Ibid.*, pp. 20-1.
22. *CLCC* 14, p. 29 (E), p. 35 (L).
23. *CLCC* 12, p. 18 (E), pp. 15-16 (L).
24. *CLCC* 20, p. 10.
25. *CLCC* 2, p. 20.
26. *CLCC* 10, p. 28 (E), p. 15 (L); 3, p. 5.
27. Bourdeaux, *Patriarch and Prophets*, p. 58.
28. *Loc. cit.*
29. *CLCC* 10, p. 7 (E), pp. 2-3 (L); quoted on p. 68; *CLCC* 19, p. 6; *CLCC* 24, p. 7.
30. *Moscow News*, 12 June 1976.
31. *CLCC* 29, p. 23.
32. *Loc. cit.*
33. Rimaitis, *op. cit.* p. 20.
34. *Ibid.*, p. 21.
35. *Ibid.*, p. 21; cf. *CLCC* 3, p. 2, quoting *Vilnis*, 14 April 1970.
36. *CLCC* 2, p. 20.
37. *Elta-press*, Rome, 2 February 1969, p. 16.
38. *Ibid.*, 4 April 1972, p. 9.
39. *CLCC* 19, p. 9.
40. Rimaitis, *op. cit.*, p. 28.
41. *CLCC* 14, p. 37 (E), p. 31 (L).
42. *CLCC* 20, p. 10.
43. *CLCC* 2, p. 21.
44. *CLCC* 1, p. 21.
45. *CLCC* 12, p. 7 (E), p. 4 (L).
46. *CLCC* 14, p. 37 (E), p. 31 (L).
47. *CLCC* 2, p. 10 (E), pp. 6-7 (L).
48. *Ibid.*, p. 14 (E), p. 10 (L).

49. Paul Mailleux, S.J., "Catholics in the Soviet Union", in ed. Marshall, *op. cit.,* pp. 365-6; Beeson, *Discretion and Valour,* p. 114; *Annuario Pontificio,* Rome, 1976, p. 247.
50. Christopher Read, "Soviet Roman Catholics", *RCL* 1-3, 1975, p. 8. Unfortunately, the siting of the seminary is incorrectly given as Estonia.
51. *Tiesa,* 28 May 1974, p. 2.
52. *CLCC* 14, p. 19 (E), p. 14 (L).
53. Savasis, *op. cit.,* p. 13.
54. Rimaitis, *op. cit.,* p. 11.
55. *Ibid.,* p. 16.
56. *Loc. cit.;* cf. *CLCC* 18, p. 20.
57. Savasis, *op. cit.,* pp. 50-1, citing *Lietuviu Religine Informacija,* New York, 31 August 1963, and *Valstieciu Laikraštis,* Vilnius, 18 February 1962.
58. Alexander Solzhenitsyn, *Gulag Archipelago,* Vol. II, pp. 25-70.
59. Antanas Terleckas, appeal to Yu. V. Andropov, 23 November 1975, pp. 6-7, published as *Respect My Rights,* the Lithuanian Community in Great Britain, 14 June 1976.
60. *CLCC* 9, p. 7 (E), p. 3 (L), quoting Mišutis, *Tarybinis istatymas ir religija* ("Soviet Law and Religion"), 1974.
61. *CLCC* 9, p. 7 (E), p. 3 (L).
62. *CLCC* 4, p. 8 (E), pp. 5-6 (L).
63. *CLCC* 15, p. 9.
64. *CLCC* 8, p. 26 (E), p. 14 (L).
65. *CLCC* 9, pp. 29-30 (E), p. 16 (L).
66. *CLCC* 10, p. 33 (E), p. 18 (L).
67. *CLCC* 8, p. 11 (E), p. 5 (L); 9, p. 30 (E), p. 17 (L) and 13, p. 7 (E), p. 3 (L).
68. Bociurkiw, "Religious Dissent in the USSR: Lithuanian Catholics", p.4; full text in Radio Liberty, *Arkhiv Samizdata* 1247, Munich, 1976.
69. *CLCC* 17, p. 16.
70. *CLCC* 3, pp. 2-4.
71. *CLCC* 16, pp. 27-9.
72. *CLCC* 3, pp. 4-5.
73. *CLCC* 3, p. 4.
74. *CLCC* 18, p. 25.
75. *CLCC* 22, p. 389.

VII

THE CHURCHES

TODAY the population of Lithuania is very slightly less than in 1939 − 0.1 per cent less, according to the 1970 census, though the figures are not comparable because of several changes of frontier. Before the Second World War there were 1,180 recognized places of Catholic worship in Lithuania, one to every 2,500 of the three million population. However, for an almost identical population the number of churches in use today has fallen by just over 50 per cent to 574. The loss of parish churches is not quite as catastrophic as these figures may suggest, for two categories of churches have disappeared totally: those in monastic institutions (158 formerly) and "special-purpose" chapels in hospitals, prisons and cemeteries, of which there were once 314.[1] this means that 134 (nineteen per cent) of the 708 parish churches have gone.

Most towns have one "working" church (the Soviet term); Panevežys and Šiauliai have two each, while Kaunas and Vilnius have at least four each. However, there are no churches in new urban areas; worshippers must travel into the older part of towns to find a church. Some priests have to serve two or more parishes.

Even so, the overall picture is considerably better for the average Lithuanian Catholic − especially in the countryside − than for his Orthodox counterpart in the Soviet Union generally, where over half of all churches have been closed within the last twenty years, leaving only about fourteen per cent of the 54,000 before the Revolution, located in a much smaller area.[2]

Interestingly, the statistics for the Catholic Church in Lithuania are more precise than those available for any other Church in the Soviet Union − a factor which may be explained by the extraordinary determination of Lithuanians to make their situation known to the outside world.

The fact that Lithuanian Catholics have relatively more churches than the Russian Orthodox is due partly to history (Lithuania was not within the Soviet Union during the catastrophic purges of the 1930's), and partly to the greater determination of the Lithuanian Christian people to keep some place of worship open in their area, whatever the consequences might be.

The most serious wave of church closure in Lithuania came immediately after the second Soviet occupation, at a time when the situation was improving for the Russian Orthodox Church. It was then that the Soviet regime disbanded every ancillary church and chapel in the land. Approximately one hundred parish churches were closed at the same time. The losses were particularly severe in the large towns. Document 52 gives precise details of the names of over fifty churches in Vilnius and Kaunas so affected, together with an indication of the way in which the State now exploits the buildings for other uses.

The situation was made worse by the fact that churches destroyed in the war were rarely given permission to rebuild: some continued to exist as registered congregations in "temporary" buildings, while others were refused registration altogether.

A further thirty or so churches have closed since then, most of which were victims of the nationwide anti-religious campaign of the early 1960's under Khrushchev.[3] However, the Russian Orthodox and Baptist Churches suffered much more severely at this time and Lithuania escaped more lightly than almost any other area of the Soviet Union.[4]

In Lithuania, though, the Russian Orthodox Church has an almost privileged status:[5] no Orthodox churches were closed after 1944 in Vilnius or Kaunas. This is partly due to immigration, as Russians form the overwhelming majority of Orthodox parishioners, but the Russian population growth in Lithuania has been far smaller than in its neighbouring republic of Latvia. The Orthodox Church in Lithuania is sometimes seen – and with some justification – as a bastion of Great Russian expansionism, while the Catholic Church is the refuge of Lithuanian nationalism.

If we look at the situation of one local Christian community, we can see the type of difficulty which confronts those who want to benefit from the one legal right which the Soviet Christian does possess: that of worshipping God in a convenient building. We choose the situation of the believers in Ignalina, not because it is better or worse than that of thousands of others, whether Catholic, Orthodox or Protestant, scattered round the Soviet Union, but because the Catholics in Ignalina have supplied detailed information through the pages of the *Lithuanian Chronicle*.[6]

Ignalina is a small town of 4,000 people, of whom the majority are practising Catholics, but it is also a district administrative centre, so there is a constant coming and going of people from other places, some of whom naturally wish to attend church while they are there. The present building used for worship will accommodate a maximum of 300 people, but at this point conditions become highly inconvenient, possibly even dangerous. The faithful there claim they have every right to a far more adequate church.

Local people made great personal sacrifice to build a proper church under the Poles; Ignalina is in that region of Lithuania which was part of Poland from 1918-39. However, the work was interrupted by the outbreak of the Second World War. After the second Soviet occupation the new administration took over the building, promising to complete the construction, but instead they requisitioned it as a "house of culture" – a sort of clubhouse which is the focus for local arts, theatre and lectures, all of which are organized by the local Communist authorities. However, the church building was manifestly unsuitable for this purpose, so the local authorities planned a new house of culture. These plans were cancelled and instead they began to remodel the church and build an extension. Not unnaturally, the local Christians rented a house conveniently situated nearby while the dispute over their own premises continued. The activities of the house of culture extensively and deliberately interrupt worship, making the maximum noise with blaring music while services are going on. Once the director of the house of culture even threw stones at the windows of the house where the Christians were worshipping and broke the windows. The building of an extension will bring the disturbance six metres closer, and to do this the presbytery is being demolished.

Meanwhile, conditions for the worshippers are becoming intolerable. Condensation is so serious in cold weather that moisture drips from the ceiling. The majority of the people cannot find even standing room inside, so they have to remain out in the open in all weathers.

Repeated attempts by the faithful to rectify the situation have met with no response whatsoever. 1,026 people signed an appeal to the central Lithuanian authorities in March 1971.[7] Rugienis even visited Ignalina in person, but no action ensued. The Ignalina believers continued their campaign into 1975, but fruitlessly. While they did so they reflected on other registered congregations lucky enough to enjoy reasonable facilities for worship, but they may well also have been aware of others less fortunate than themselves, such as the Eastern-rite Catholics, for example, who are totally barred from any legal existence whatsoever.[8]

Even congregations with a registered status – and therefore a theoretical guarantee of a reasonably settled prospect, insofar as this is possible for any Christian community within the Soviet system – may find their situation radically altered overnight. For example, in 1971 the church at Sangruda burned down. Arson was suspected, but in Soviet conditions no proper investigation was possible.[9] The energetic parish priest managed to convert a private house into a church, so there was no serious interruption in the life of the parish, and soon (in 1975) people were coming in droves from all over the surrounding countryside to celebrate the fiftieth anniversary of the establishment of the parish.

In the Russian countryside the Orthodox Church was often the only stone building. When the regime began its programme of enforced atheism the temptation to commandeer the most secure and solid building as an agricultural store or village hall or club was strong. Some became workshops or factories.[10] In Lithuania, as we have seen, the atheist campaign commenced later and the results for the country churches were not devastating. Nevertheless, where there were concentrations of churches in the larger population centres the losses to the Church were still considerable. Document 52 demonstrates this conclusively: churches have been turned into warehouses, restaurants, clubhouses, archives, gymnasiums and museums. As well as the widespread desecration of minor shrines, two churches have been torn down in Kaunas and the area of one of them used as a sports ground. Vilnius Cathedral is now an art gallery.[11] However, the worst example is the conversion of the Church of St. Casimir, Vilnius, into a museum of atheism in the early 1960's under the impulse of the Khrushchev campaign.[12] This is an affront to the feelings of believers, even though the building itself has been well restored.[13] Although this was the first such museum in the Baltic States, Leningrad had long housed a similar one in the imposing Kazan Cathedral on the Nevsky Prospect. Document 53 is a revelation showing – as has never happened with similar institutions in Russia – how the authorities gather materials for the exhibits and how the general public reacts. There is also a singular lack of interest among students, who are supposed to see it as a supplement to their compulsory atheist course.[14]

Even those buildings which are apparently safe under the tutelage of the ecclesiastical authorities are in fact under constant threat which may long remain latent, but which may break out at any time in the form of vandalism or burglary. While the law protects church property in theory, some would claim that in practice it has encouraged – or at least has taken insufficiently vigorous steps to prevent – the desecration of churches. This is a typical problem in a country where the judiciary is not independent of the state ideology. Consequently, a wave of burglaries has plagued the Lithuanian churches for years.

There have indeed been trials of people caught breaking into churches, and even this is an improvement over the rest of the Soviet Union, where there do not seem to have been many such trials after similar occurrences. The culprits have received sentences, but so mild that no one has been discouraged from following suit.

In Kaišiadorys there have been a number of such burglaries. In one case the accused, though found guilty, received a suspended sentence on the grounds that she was receiving psychiatric treatment.[15] In an earlier case (1964) the authorities apprehended a man who apparently had a considerable record as a robber of churches and had already broken into the Orthodox Church in Riga (Latvia). When the Lithuanian court heard his case, the judge, according to the

Lithuanian Chronicle, used every method to exonerate the criminal, saying that he was a man who needed money, so that what he had done was understandable. The judge even turned to the offensive against the wronged party – the church – upon which the local priest made a vigorous defence of the church in court. "Who is on trial here, anyway" he asked, "this criminal or we representatives of the church?" The guilty party received no more than a suspended sentence and was released forthwith.[16]

The authors of the *Chronicle* connect the burglaries with the financial blandishments of the atheist museums in Leningrad and Vilnius, which offer sums of money for religious articles.[17] Similar robberies have recently been reported from Soviet Georgia, for example.[18]

The church authorities have naturally done what they can to safeguard their treasures. In 1972 Bishop Labukas sent an instruction on this matter to all the priests under his jurisdiction. In it he asked priests whose churches were not guarded by night watchmen to remove the Blessed Sacrament to the security of the sacristy overnight and to put all the church plate there as well, or to bring it into the presbytery.[19] This did not prevent the wave of burglaries which began in 1974[20] and became even worse in 1975, with one at Tubaušiai in February [21] and a connected series of four in five days at Panevežys in September, which must have been either officially inspired or condoned.[22] In some instances there was not even a pretence at robbery. The atheist authorities confiscated the keys of the church at Staloriai in July 1974 and then removed pictures and other treasures to the atheist museum. A similar incident occurred at Satraminai in September 1975.[23]

Some of these robberies may well have been the work of hooligans, rather than premeditated acts for financial gain. The problem is that the aggressive nature of Soviet atheist propaganda whips up hatred against the Church and louts look on the churches as one of the few possible recipients for their attention, knowing full well that the penalties for destroying regular State property could be severe – far more so than for similar offences in other countries. But they can attack the Church with impunity. Document 54 describes these young people physically attacking churches, not even stopping short of violence against defenceless old people who want nothing other than to worship in peace. One is reminded of Alexander Solzhenitsyn's essay, *The Easter Procession,* in which he depicts the scene outside a Russian Orthodox church at the most solemn moment of the Church's year, when a procession of the faithful is attacked by a group of young hooligans who humiliate them without injuring them physically. The so-called guardians of law and order look on impassively.[24]

Very often the disruptions are less physical but more systematic. One tactic particularly used is to establish any source of loud and

disruptive noise close to the church and to ensure that it is working at
maximum volume when church services are in progress. Dance music,
sporting contests – Document 54 demonstrates that anything will
serve to achieve this end.

The Soviet authorities also keep constant watch on the inside of
churches to ensure that no improvement is made which would make
them more attractive to the worshippers. For example, at Jurbarkas
the local authorities demanded the removal of a new statue of the
Virgin Mary which a local sculptor had just completed and donated to
the church (Document 55).

There is no absolute ban on the ringing of church bells, as there
appears to be with the Russian Orthodox Church elsewhere in the
Soviet Union.[25] Nevertheless, the churches encounter extreme
difficulty over this question. For example, it was also at Jurbarkas that
the local authorities banned bell-ringing in 1964, on the pretext that
this made children in a kindergarten next door want to go to church.
After a decade of campaigning the local priest persuaded the
authorities to rescind the order in 1974.[26]

Standing physically on the frontier between the Church and the
world, churchyards, precincts and cemeteries have always been the
object of special attention by the atheists. What occurs there in the
open air can be an act of witness, even of evangelism, to casual
passers-by who have no intention of entering the church itself, but the
defences of the churchyard are less easy to maintain than those of the
building. Nevertheless, the *Lithuanian Chronicle* does not report
many acts of vandalism, which would seem to indicate the widespread support which the Church still retains in Lithuania.

At Pievenai an ancient cross stood outside the church porch. From
time immemorial the faithful used to rest the coffins of their dead here
for a moment on the way into the church for the funeral service. A
local official ordered its destruction because it was close to the road.
The faithful resisted these plans and appealed to their own diocesan
authorities. The atheists changed their tactics and offered to put it in a
less visible place, but the faithful, in fear of losing it, removed it themselves and put it into the church porch.[27]

As the church precincts have been nationalized, only the church
building can be used for "cult purposes". Often the fence between a
church and the neighbouring cemetery is removed, to make it secular
property.

The *Chronicle* contains records of church successes rather than
failures in this area of conflict. In April 1974 the parishioners at Šates
put up a statue of the Virgin Mary outside their church. The local
authorities ordered its removal. The people resisted by claiming that
the Telšiai Curia had stated in 1954 that it was permissible to erect
crosses in churchyards, cemeteries and in believers' own gardens.
Despite this, Mgr. Barauskas of the Curia advocated the removal of

the statue, but the faithful held out even against the threats of the local authorities to hire some thugs to do the demolition job for them. Eventually a Vilnius official representing the Council for Religious Affairs, came and yielded to the pressure of local parishioners, even allowing himself to be photographed beside the statue.[28]

At Jurbarkas the local priest repeatedly requested permission to re-dig the well outside his church. Finally, tiring of the refusals, he did it anyway in 1973. The local council ordered him write and explain what he had done and to fill it in again. The priest complied with the first request, but not the second. The well remains in working order.[29]

Desecration of graves seems to have taken place in the crypts of requisitioned churches rather than in cemeteries, and there are complaints of this occurring in Vilnius and Kaunas.[30]

The Soviet laws on religion ensure that there is a permanent and official means by which the State can interfere in the normal running of a parish. With the Russian Orthodox and Baptist Churches the main vehicle for this inteference has been the parish council, consisting of three people, into which the state could infiltrate its own agents.[31] This is made easier by the fact that the parish council and the three-man auditing commission are elected by a show of hands, so that it is clear who voted for which candidate. As we saw in Chapter III,* these methods have been far less successful with the Lithuanian Catholic Church, because its more autocratic tradition has always put the priest in charge of running his own parish. While unending problems were caused in the Russian Orthodox Church in 1961, when the parish priest was barred from his own council and thus removed from the administration of his own parish, such a move would have been irrelevant to the Church in Lithuania, because the faithful would have simply ignored any decision of the parish council which went counter to the wishes of the priest.

The Lithuanian officials of the Council for Religious Affairs attempt to keep the closest watch over the material situation of the churches, as the following extract from the *Lithuanian Chronicle* demonstrates:

Ignalina. When the new Soviet Executive for religious affairs, K. Tumenas, was appointed in 1973, he visited the churches of the Ignalina region in person or through his deputies, accompanied by officials of the local government executive committee. He inspected church interiors, altars, organs, electricity fittings, liturgical vessels, vestments, financial records, electric meters, and asked where the money was kept, what the relation-ship between the parish council and the priest was, and whether young people served at the altar. Where they did serve, the chairman of the parish council was reprimanded and ordered not to allow children near the altar.[32]

The most constant form of state control over the parish church is financial. As everywhere else in the Soviet Union, the State seized the

*See pp. 55-6.

title to church property after the Communist take-over, so in order to have an official place of worship at all the faithful have to apply for registration and, where this is granted, the State leases their own building back to them, but at a price which can be considerable.[33] Before 1960, taxes ran at between 1,000 and 1,500 (new) roubles a year – about £750-£1,130 ($1,450-$2,230) at the current rate of exchange.[34] The authorities justified their action by classifying the church as a place of entertainment. Kaunas Cathedral now has to pay 6,000 roubles a year to the State[35] on top of running costs, a figure which might not seem high to an affluent American congregation which for some reason does not own its own church, but which is extortionate when one considers Soviet wage-levels with an average monthly income of 150 roubles (£113 or $220). This point is elaborated by the faithful themselves in No. 26 of the *Lithuanian Chronicle* (Document 56).

In addition, churches must pay compulsory contributions to the Peace Fund. Fire insurance is mandatory, but in at least three cases – at Santaika, Batakiai and Vilkaviškis – when churches were burnt down no insurance money was paid to rebuild them. Gifts to the Church are taxed at exorbitant rates, so that priests often receive gifts in kind – for example, a parish might buy a car for its church and parish priest. There are no reports of churches being closed because of failure to pay their taxes. Small parishes are not legally allowed to receive aid from larger parishes, but it is almost impossible to stop this happening. Priests themselves have their salaries taxed at a rate of fifty to sixty per cent, but they are helped out by gifts of produce from their parishioners. Stipends (fees) for Masses are distributed by the bishop, ten roubles per intention going to the priest. One way of transferring money from one parish to another is for priests in small parishes to say Masses for larger parishes. This is also a way in which the Lithuanian clergy can make contributions to the Vatican: they say a number of Masses free, then ask the Vatican to contribute the sum to missions.

Often there are difficulties in obtaining connections with the public services such as water mains and electricity.[36] The authorities force the churches to pay for their electricity at a punitive rate. Collective farms have to pay one kopek per kilowatt for electricity used on common enterprises, while the domestic rate is four kopeks. Churches frequented by the very same people must pay no less than twenty-five kopeks per kilowatt.[37]

All these penalties pale into insignificance beside the unending bureaucracy and red tape which prevents believers from securing the repair of their churches at the proper time. The delays, sometimes even outright refusals, deliberately ensure that deterioration is rapid and sometimes very serious. This is just another subterfuge which the authorities use in the hope that ultimately this will lead to the closure of churches – perhaps by having them classified as dangerous structures – without having to take the provocative step of closing a well-maintained building.

The only time during the last thirty years at which it has been possible to repair churches with reasonable safety from state interference was the period 1954-7.[38] This means that some repairs are now twenty years overdue. There is in fact some state-sponsored repair taking place, but this seems to be confined to those churches which have been taken over as museums,[39] despite the presence on the walls of some open churches of a plaque proclaiming that the State maintains their structure. In his propaganda book J. Rimaitis makes the quaint claim that "a great many churches have been repaired, and some of them have never before looked so cosy,"[40] but a reading of the evidence suggests that many of them, very far from being "cosy", are in a state of imminent collapse.

The church at Mielagenai would not survive unless something was done immediately, stated Fr. Vladas Černiauskas, the parish priest, in November 1974. Being refused permission, the faithful took the matter into their own hands and worked at it during their spare time.[41] In many other places, repairs to the church or its associated buildings have either been prevented or halted once they have begun, despite complaints to which in some instances thousands of believers from the local community have added their signatures.[42]

At Akmuo in 1974 two workmen were engaged on repairing the church, when a local Communist official appeared and halted the work, threatening them with five years' imprisonment for what they were doing. Later he said that, as this was their first offence, he would be lenient and have them fined, provided they gave an undertaking never to repair a church again. Accordingly, they received a fine of twenty-five roubles each on 8 January 1975. The *Chronicle* states that they were totally innocent men and that there is no Soviet law they have broken.[43]

These hindrances, serious though they are for the hundreds of thousands of practising Catholics affected by them, are nevertheless not without their occasional touches of unconscious humour. For example, at Šilale in 1975 a dispute arose over the repair of the church clock, which culminated in an ascent of the tower by the local man responsible for atheist propaganda. He wished to be sure the clock was not working properly, because it would harm the cause of atheism if it showed the correct time.[44]

The most significant and best-documented clash between the Church and the atheists over a church building since the Soviet takeover concerns the one new church built in Lithuania during this period – the Church of Our Lady Queen of Peace at Klaipeda on the Baltic coast, which was consecrated in 1960. Document 57 tells the story of the building, consecration, expropriation and sentencing of those responsible for the enterprise with such vividness that no commentary is necessary. It is itself the most eloquent commentary on freedom of religion in a country whose constitution proclaims "freedom of religious worship."

DOCUMENTS

52. THE DESECRATION OF THE CHURCHES, 1975

In a very short period of time (by 1950 – the tenth anniversary of Lithuania's incorporation into the USSR), about fifty Catholic churches and semi-public chapels had been closed down in Vilnius and Kaunas alone; the authorities forbade the use of cemetery chapels, later they destroyed some of them in the process of annihilating the graves, and they blew up the Church of Three Crosses at Vilnius and knocked down crosses and chapels in the streets and squares. On the eve of the twenty-fifth anniversary of Lithuania's incorporation, they blew up the thirty-five stations of the cross at Vilnius and cleared away the ruins immediately, so that nothing was left to remind people of their existence.

Beneath we list the churches and chapels that were closed in Vilnius and Kaunas alone, with brief, though incomplete, explanations of how they have been used since their closure.

VILNIUS CHURCHES

1. Cathedral	picture gallery.
2. Augustinian Church	rebuilt into warehouse for electrical equipment
3. St. Bartholomew's Church	first, a warehouse; now a sculptors' workshop belonging to arts collective; in summer 1975 a huge Lenin monument was completed there
4. Basilian Church	first, a warehouse; now a material resistance laboratory belonging to the Institute of Civil Engineering
5. Bernardine Church	warehouse of Arts Institute; sculptors' workshops
6. St. Ignatius Church	first reconstructed as film studio, stage-properties storehouse; now the "Bočiu" restaurant.
7. Sacred Heart of Jesus Church	rebuilt as a builders' club-house

8. Church of SS Philip and James	store for opera and ballet theatre stage decorations
9. St. John's Church	first, a paper store for *Tiesa* newspaper; now being restored to house "museum of progressive thought" and auditorium for meetings and concerts administered by the university
10. St. George's Church	book store for book department
11. St. Catherine's Church	first, a food store; now empty; but to be restored and converted into arts museum
12. St. Casimir's Church	first, a warehouse; since its restoration in 1961, a Museum of Atheism
13. Holy Cross or Bonifratre Church	first, a warehouse; now being restored and scheduled for use as a concert hall
14. The Benefactors' Chapel	rebuilt as a book-trade warehouse
15. The Church of the Assumption of Mary or the Franciscan Church	rebuilt to accommodate central state archives
16. St. Michael's Church	first, a warehouse, damaged by fire; after restoration, permanent civil engineering exhibition
17. Missionaries' Church	warehouse supplying medical institutions with equipment and goods
18. St. Stephen's Church	store for cement and other building materials
19. Holy Trinity Church	first, a gymnasium; after wall collapsed, became workshop for Museum of History and Ethnography; in 1975 a model of the Kaunas ninth century fort was manufactured there
20. Trinity Church	military depot
21. Trinapolis Church	hospital store; a driver has constructed a flat for himself above vestry
22. All Saints Church	first, a food store damaged by fire; after partial restoration in summer 1975 opened for Arts Museum permanent exhibition of folk art
23. Visitandine Church	first, a warehouse; now premises adapted as juvenile prison

KAUNAS   CHURCHES

1. Aušros Vartai (Dawn Gates) in Aukstieji Sančiai	first rebuilt as barracks and occupied by Russian families; later, a cultural club-house, then salt store; now food packaging warehouse

2. Freda Church	first, a gymnasium for the Michurin agricultural institutute in Kaunas; now abandoned. In summer 1975 homeless family squatted in porch
3. St. Gertrude's Church	medical store
4. Garrison Church	museum of stained glass and sculpture
5. St. George's Church	first, a military depot, now warehouse for the general supply of medical equipment, stocks and building materials, attached to Medical Technology Centre
6. Church of the Adoration of the Cross	demolished; in its place small sports ground constructed
7. Church of the Visitation of Mary in Pažaislis	first, a mental hospital; now being restored as a branch of the Arts Museum
8. Benedictine Church	store for old books from Kaunas public library. Inhabitants of neighbouring houses say it contains the "yellow press" – pre-Soviet publications
9. St. Francis Xavier Church	first a book-store; now a gymnasium
10. Church of the Resurrection	rebuilt as a radio factory
11. Holy Sacrament Church	cinema
12. Holy Trinity Church	book-store No. 10 of republican book centre
13. Chapel of Seven Sorrows of Mary in Žaliakalnys	destroyed
14. Church of Mary the Immaculate Mother of God	warehouse of shop for specialised medical equipment

The following semi-private chapels that were a part of buildings serving other purposes were closed in Kaunas:

1. Guardian Angels
2. St. Antony's
3. St. Luke's Church of Christian Love
4. Mary the Support of Christians
5. Franciscan Chapel
6. St. Stanislov Kosta
7. St. Zita's
8. Prison Chapel

There is only one chapel functioning in Vilnius – that of the Mother of God at Aušros Vartai. The authorities destroyed the others, of which there were many, and closed down all the Evangelical churches in both cities. The Vilnius Evangelical churches are being used as film theatres or gymnasiums. The oldest one in Kaunas became a food store, then it caught fire and today it is no longer in use. Another church is a gymnasium. The newest one contains a police school club, a gymnasium and a dining hall.[45]

It is interesting to note that the authorities did not close a single Orthodox church in either of the towns (in Vilnius they are particularly numerous), in spite of the fact that only a few people visit them.

These thirty years, while the Lithuanian Church was being violently destroyed from both inside and outside, have seen inestimable damage done to the art treasures of the Lithuanian people. In all the above-mentioned Vilnius and Kaunas churches, and in other chapels not listed which have been closed down, an enormous collection of pictures, sculptures, old frescoes, memorial plaques, stained-glass panels, organs, various church articles, liturgical vestments and vessels of great artistic value have been destroyed, some dating back to between the fifteenth and eighteenth centuries. The valuable architectural interiors of many old churches have been greatly damaged or even completely ruined by the treatment they received. All that had been carefully preserved by generations over the centuries has been lost forever in three decades of "the peaceful construction of Socialism and Communism" in Soviet Lithuania.[46]

53. HOW TO SET UP AND RUN AN ATHEIST MUSEUM, 1974

In 1965 the authorities turned St. Casimir's Church in Vilnius into a museum of atheism.

There is a permanent advertisement in *Vakarinese Naujienose* ("Evening News") stating that the museum of atheism is willing to buy any object of exclusively religious significance from the public. Similar advertisements appear in the pages of local papers. It is often emphasized that objects bought will not be destroyed but preserved for the future. It seems that the museum of atheism even buys up prayer-books, which were formerly printed in large quantities. For handing in a prayer-book students at Kaunas Polytechnic Institute and at the Agricultural College receive marks for atheism. Museum officials organize excursions all over Lithuania, only they travel not as atheists, but under the guise of "ethnographers", led by officials of the Ethnographical Museum. Their conversations give the impression that they consider a prayer-book to be a most precious discovery. More than one Catholic has given these people religious books, with the aim of helping others so that young people could read them and tell others about them – but only later did they find out that they had been deceived by the atheists. The atheists themselves ask the local authorities to keep their secret and not to tell anyone that an expedition has arrived from the museum of atheism. Its officials are armed with credentials from other institutions. In order to acquire objects of religious art they use even deception and force. An example of this was the behaviour of museum officials in the village of Mosedžiai, where they obtained the keys of the cemetery chapel and with the help of the local authorities attempted to confiscate an icon. When a woman started to protest, the museum officials tried to remove it by force.

In an attempt to attract more visitors, the museum puts on exhibitions which have nothing to do with atheism, such as, for example, the "Kupiškenai" (folk-lore) evenings. On one occasion the traveller, A. Poška, was to have shown a film on India.* However, when they began to show an atheist film instead, all the spectators started to whistle and shout. Then the show was stopped and they were told that the projector had broken down.

Entrance is free to the museum of atheism, but the number of visitors is small. But of course school children are always dragged into it when they go out on excursions.

In spite of all their efforts, the exhibition has not succeeded in avoiding vulgarity and giving offence to the feelings of believers: anti-religious caricatures are exhibited, together with sacred liturgical vessels and so on.

The comments in the visitors' book show that many people are dissatisfied with the conversion of St. Casimir's Church into a museum of atheism. In 1812 Napoleon used it as a military depot, but he desecrated it less than our atheists.

"I came, I saw – and only here did I first feel that I believed in God. A.R.", was a typical comment in the book.[47]

54. THE ASSAULT ON CHURCH BUILDINGS AND SERVICES

On 13 April 1974 hooligans threw lumps of brick at the church in Varena during services. The police refused to intervene, since there was "no bloodshed".

On 20 April 1974 during an atheist evening for students they mocked a figure of Christ crucified, which had probably been torn from a cemetery crucifix. The correspondent of the regional newspaper, *Raudonoji Veliava (Red Flag)* (28 May 1974) rejoiced that the young were being properly educated to ridicule religious ritual. By such "education" a child's respect for everything that is good and holy is destroyed. Will such children not become inmates of penal colonies?[48]

*Poška was a pre-war traveller and author who reached India on a motor cycle.

A Petition from the Executive Committee of the Catholic Parish of Plutiškes

On 5 May 1974, while devotions were taking place during a religious festival, J. Jakštas, headmaster of the Plutiškes secondary school, burst into the church precinct and harassed the faithful by his aggressive behaviour. With no police representative present and unbeknown to our executive committee, he made a search of the belfry and the church vestibule.

Immediately after the departure of Jakštas, a group of pupils from the secondary school of Plutiškes forced their way into the precinct and began seizing rosaries and other religious articles from some old ladies. From one they even stole her money. An uproar ensued and the youths were expelled from the precinct. Then they caused a disturbance in the street and began to throw stones at those praying outside the church. Mrs. Deltuviene, an elderly lady, received a sharp blow from a stone.

Apparently the youths must have been instructed by someone, since they never used to behave this way before. It should be noted that this was not the first time Mr. Jakštas had behaved in such a fashion.

We request the Ministry of Education to reprimand Mr. Jakštas, since his behaviour does not bring honour upon the Soviet school system, nor upon the sort of ideal to which a Soviet citizen should attain.

Plutiškes

10 May 1974.[49]

★   ★   ★

The atheists will frequently make use of any means to divert people from the practice of their religion. Here are a few examples from the present and recent past.

On Palm Sunday 1972 crowds of people were packed into Kaunas Cathedral and its precincts. When the service began, those working at the Žilvinas youth club across the street opened the windows, began playing popular dance music and created a considerable disturbance on the club balcony. As a result, people who had gathered in the churchyard were unable to follow the service.

Every year those attending the Palm Sunday services at the cathedral used to purchase palms in the precinct which had been brought and prepared by the children. The faithful were grateful for what they did.

In 1973 the atheists were determined to disrupt these solemnities. When the service began, the police arrived and began arresting those selling palms. Some were taken to headquarters. On the Sunday after Easter the police again turned up at the cathedral and began arresting those selling religious articles. They did not even spare a crippled old lady, who was arrested and taken to the local headquarters.

During the Khrushchev era the Government set up a loudspeaker near the church of Žiežmariai. This installation carried local radio broadcasts. For years local worshippers put up with the disturbance from the loudspeaker. No one paid any attention to requests from the parish priest and his parishioners that the installation be moved away from the church.

On the first Sunday of July 1969 the present author had occasion to participate in the annual religious festival in Žemaičiu Kalvarija. Pilgrims from all parts of Lithuania filled the church and precincts. When the church bell announced the beginning of the principal Mass, a whistle was blown in the stadium next to the churchyard to signal the start of an athletic event.

A group of semi-clad youths played and screamed, making so much noise that it was impossible to pray in the precinct. The people were shocked by the disturbance organized by the atheists. Usually the participants at such athletic or other events sponsored by the atheists are herded in by force. Few people participate voluntarily.[50]

55. NEW RELIGIOUS WORKS OF ART CONFISCATED

In 1972 the former lecturer and artist, Verbickas, now a pensioner resident in Jurbarkas, carved a wooden statue of Our Lady for the church in his own town. On the occasion of its consecration, Fr. V. Byla's sermon expressed his joy at the beautiful new statue. Immediately afterwards the parish priest, Fr. Buožys, was visited by a commission headed by Chairwoman Tamošiuniene of the Jurbarkas District Executive Committee, who demanded that the statue should be removed, as it had been erected without a permit. The parish priest stated that no permit was needed to decorate the inside of a church; further, Mr. Verbickas had given the statue to the church, so he would not remove it. Then the commission demanded that Verbickas himself should remove the statute. The artist stated that he had promised his parents to make a statue for the church and so he had erected it in accordance with their wishes, and would on no account take it out of the church. The commission declared that they would force the parish priest to remove the statue from the church.

Quite recently Mr. Verbickas made a statue of the Sacred Heart of Jesus for the church in Jurbarkas. The Executive Committee has so far said nothing about it.[51]

56. THE REGISTRATION OF PARISHES, 1977

In 1948 the Soviet Government ordered each congregation to choose a group of "twenty"* who, in accordance with an agreement prepared by the Government, were to be allowed to rent their own churches which had been appropriated by the State. Those "twenties" which did not sign the agreement were threatened with the closure of their churches. No one doubted that Stalin could indeed implement this threat. The country was being terrorised: people were being exiled to Siberia; prisons and cells were full of innocent people; the defiled corpses of partisans were lying in public places in towns, a third of the priests were in the Gulag Archipelago. The only bishop then remaining in Lithuania, Kazimieras Paltarokas, wishing to preserve the lives of priests and believers, did not strongly oppose the signature of these compulsory agreements.

The following is an example of the agreement that was forced upon the believers of Lithuania:

1. We, the undersigned citizens, accept the responsibility of preserving the chapel and all the property attached to it and promise to use it solely for the purpose for which it has been handed over to us. We accept responsibility for the maintenance and security of all the property handed over to us and for the implementation of all the obligations to which this agreement binds us.

2. We accept the obligation to use the building and also to give all other members of the denomination the opportunity to use it solely for the requirements of religious worship, and not to permit the performance of religious rites to ministers of religion who are not registered with the Lithuanian Executive of the Council for Religious Affairs under the Council of Ministers of the USSR.

3. We accept the obligation to do everything necessary to ensure that the property handed over to us is not used for any purposes not in accordance with paragraphs 1 and 2 of this agreement.

4. We accept the obligation to pay from our own resources all the expenses for the maintenance of the chapel and also all the expenses which will be necessary for repair, heating, insurance, local taxes and the like.

5. We accept the obligation of keeping in our custody an inventory of all ritual objects which will list all newly-acquired articles . . . .

6. We accept the obligation, at times when worship is not taking place, of allowing persons authorised by the town Executive Committee or the Official for Religious Affairs to check and inspect the property.

7. We accept a collective responsibility for the loss or damage of property leased to us with regard to the losses incurred.

8. In the event of having to return the property we accept the obligation to return it in the same condition as when it was taken into our custody and protection.

*See p. 37, footnote.

9. For any breach of the regulations which are laid down in this agreement we bear responsibility in law: in addition, in such circumstances the town Executive Committee has the right to cancel this agreement.

. . . .

Soviet propaganda constantly condemns the capitalists who by unjust means appropriate the material wealth of others. Is there any capitalist in the world who would take everything from a person and then rent his own property to him, forcing him to pay the expenses and appropriating what the tenant may in future acquire or be presented with?

. . . .

The atheist government boasts that it gives the church to believers for their use without payment. But that is a lie. Paragraph 4 of the agreement obliges the believers to pay for insurance and local taxes, and to pay six times the normal price for electricity – twenty-five kopecks per kilowatt. These payments result in huge sums accumulating to the Government.

In this agreement only the tenant accepts obligations, but the "owner" – the Soviet Government – has no obligations. Such a one-sided agreement mocks and robs the faithful. They would willingly enter into a decent bilateral agreement, but this would be inconceivable. In recent years the Government has wanted to bring in an even harsher "agreement". For five years now the Government has been forcing parish committees to sign a new one. Some have signed, others attempt to resist. The text of the new agreement has not been co-ordinated either with the church leaders or with the faithful.

. . . .

In the new agreement the executive body of the religious community is obliged to inform the financial supervisors how much the priest receives in donations for his religious services. There is no doubt that the Government aims at introducing into Lithuania the same system that already exists in the whole of Russia. For example, parents wishing to baptize a baby do not come to a priest, but to the treasurer of the religious community. The parents have to write out a declaration that they want their baby to be baptized and submit their passports; certificates of birth are completed and, upon payment, a receipt is issued. With this receipt they go to the priest who then baptizes the child. The Government is interested not only in the priest's income, but in whoever makes use of his religious services. Are matters of a person's conscience going to remain secret if they have to be revealed to all sorts of treasurers and chairmen, when the atheist government endeavours to infiltrate people favourable to itself into these posts? The decree of 28 July 1976, Paragraph 14, empowers an executive committee to remove from the ranks of a religious community any person considered undesirable by the Government.[52]

In forcing believers to sign the new agreement the Government obliges them to agree that "in accordance with established procedures" the church may be closed . . . . Who knows whether in a few years the Soviet Government will not, as in Belorussia, force members of the religious community to be stationed at the doors of churches to prevent students and young people up to eighteen years of age from entering the church because, "in accordance with established procedures" the church might otherwise be closed? Being forced to sign such an agreement is equivalent to having to put a rope round one's own neck.

According to the new agreement and the new decree, in the event of the church being closed the faithful must hand over everything to the Government, even sacred liturgical vessels, which can then be used in atheist museums or for other profane purposes. Is it possible to insult and debase the faithful any more than this?[53]

57. KLAIPEDA: A CHURCH BUILT AND CONFISCATED

Just as the war was coming to an end in 1945, Hitler's army mined and destroyed the brick Catholic church in Klaipeda, an act witnessed by the local inhabitants.

After the war the number of Lithuanians increased rapidly, and today Klaipeda has a population of 85,000 Lithuanians and 43,000 Russians (1970 figures). The majority of the Lithuanians are practising Catholics. For example, during the Lenten Retreat in 1972 about 8,000 people received Holy Communion.

After the war the Soviet Government allowed the Lithuanians to use the small church belonging to a German sect located on Bokštai Street. It was so crowded during services that people fainted; Catholics then began to request permission to build a larger church.

In 1954 Fr. (now Bishop) Povilonis, the pastor of Klaipeda, received permission to build a new church. At that time Malenkov was the supreme ruler of the Soviet Union and the persecution of believers in Lithuania had somewhat lessened. Believers were urged to join in establishing peace throughout the world. Permission to build the church in Klaipeda was unquestionably given for propaganda purposes; many foreign seamen visit the city. The government representatives said, "Build it so that the steeple can be seen from the sea."

Even though at that time there was a great shortage of construction materials in war-torn Klaipeda, the Government permitted material reserves to be used for the construction of the church. During the first stage of building it appeared that there was no illwill on the part of the Government, and no plans to take over the rebuilt church later for secular purposes.

On 30 June 1957 Bishop P. Maželis, the Administrator of Telšiai Diocese, blessed the foundation of the Catholic church being built in Klaipeda. The following document was placed in the foundations: "The Catholics of Klaipeda and of all Lithuania, dedicating themselves to the care of Our Lady, by their own offering are building a church to the Queen of Peace, whose foundation was blessed on 30 June 1957 by Bishop Petras Maželis, Administrator of Telšiai Diocese."

In its proclamation to the Catholics of Lithuania, the church committee of the Klaipeda Catholic Parish stated: "We are building the church in honour of the Queen of Peace. By this action we want to emphasize that never again do we want to see the fires and destrucion of war on the shores of the Baltic."

Offerings were collected throughout Lithuania for the construction of the church. The Catholics of Klaipeda joined in the enterprise with joy and enthusiasm. Even though the site was very boggy, within a few weeks the people had filled in the marsh, using small carts and even baskets of earth. After returning home from work, believers hurried to help in the construction and worked late into the night. Drivers brought the necessary materials in their own time and collected bricks among the ruins in the city. Even inspectors turned a blind eye as drivers helped in the work and some officials would come to help the believers. Among the helpers were people who had never previously been to church.

The believers collected about three million roubles for the church building fund. Even poor Catholics gave joyfully of their savings. One worker who brought a considerable sum of money said, "Put my heart among the bricks in the walls of the church." It turned out that this man, who had a large family to support, had contributed one month's wages. When people sold anything, they allocated part of the money for the church. The church was completed during the summer of 1960 and the consecration ceremonies were to be held on the Feast of the Assumption. Alas, a second "explosion" similar to Hitler's took place; the faithful who had gathered for the consecration ceremonies found that the church gates were nailed shut with boards.

"The Government is not permitting the church to be opened!"

"The atheists have taken away our church!"

Shouts such as these echoed around the church, expressing their unbearable grief. Everyone felt crushed and duped.

Why was the church closed?

Some party workers explained it in the following words: "When Nikita Khrushchev found out that a church had been built in Klaipeda, he went out of his mind and shouted, 'I forbid it to be opened!' The order was given to the Government of the Lithuanian Republic and the opening of the church was stopped."

Without a doubt, the complaints of atheists to Moscow also had a part in closing the church. They suggested that their atheistic propaganda would be weakened.

The atheists acted in total disregard of people's feelings. During the night the army knocked down the church steeple with tractors. They defaced the Stations of the Cross and threw them into the mud. The people's only defence against the whims of the army and police was tears. Policemen hunted them down and took them into custody. Others were taken by lorries forty or fifty kilometres out of town and told to walk home.[54] Such harsh conduct towards the church and believers is unimaginable in any nation which respects basic human rights. The believers, by whose contributions and physical exertions the church was built, were bitterly wounded.

"This is the true face of an ungodly government," said the people through their tears.

"We must complain to higher authority . . ."

"To whom can we complain when believers are considered to be outside the law? The godless government won't defend our rights."

The government, fearing a riot by the believers, sent in about 200 police.

At the beginning of 1961 two priests of Klaipeda, Povilonis and Burneikis, were arrested and sentenced to prison. Father Talaišis was exiled from Klaipeda.

At present the new church in Klaipeda is used as a public concert hall. At first no people holding religious beliefs, whether Lithuanians or Russians, would go to the concerts. There were times when fifty artists performed on stage, but there were only five people in the audience . . . .

So the Catholics continue to make do with a small church. During services on Sundays and holy days one can often see people who have fainted being taken out of the church. At the beginning of this year [1972], after hearing persistent talks by the atheists stating that the rights of believers are not infringed and that people of all beliefs should be respected, it was decided to address the authorities of the Soviet Union and to ask them to return the church to the people. Over a period of several months, signatures were carefully collected, but then this move was stopped because of persecution by the KGB.

[An appeal was sent to Moscow dated 19 March 1972 with 3023 signatures.]

So far only the KGB has responded to the appeal of the citizens of Klaipeda. Because it was sent with the address of Jonas Saunorius on it, the KGB called him to their offices three times, trying to find out who were its organizers. Rugienis summoned Saunorius to Vilnius for the same reason.

During the services on the first day of the Easter festival, the KGB arrested two photographers – amateurs who wanted to take a picture of the crowd praying outside. They were charged with taking the photographs with the intention of sending them abroad.

Security officials reprimanded them with the words, "People abroad are waiting with outstretched arms for such pictures."[55]

. . . .

Mrs. Gražiene, who sent the request [of March 1972] was summoned to appear before the local Executive Committee on 25 August. Rugienis came from Vilnius, showed Mrs. Gražiene the believers' petition with 3023[56] signatures, and told her:

"You won't get the church back, since the building is needed by atheists as well as believers. You've got a church – so pray. No one is preventing you. You're not as much concerned about the church as about sending information abroad. If not everyone can get into the church at Easter, it's not our fault."

Mrs. Gražiene was questioned about the organizers of the petition and those who collected the signatures. The government officials reprimanded her for becoming enmeshed in 'politics' and threatened to turn her over to the KGB.[57]

★   ★   ★

On 14 July 1973 the church in Klaipeda was visited by Tarasov, another official of the Council for Religious Affairs, in the company of Tumenas, Ruginis, vice-chairman of the local Executive Committee,* and a security official . . . .

Hearing that Tarasov had said that the church in Klaipeda was no smaller than the Catholic church in Moscow and that it was entirely adequate for the needs of believers, the Catholics of Klaipeda were very annoyed.

The parish of Klaipeda has about 6,000 parishioners. Every year about 800-900 children prepare for First Communion. The faithful must crowd into a church with no precinct measuring 288 square metres (17 metres square), the size of a living-room. At festivals the faithful must stand in the street, since it is impossible for many to get into church.

When the priest pointed out to Tarasov that if the sheds built against the end of the church were torn down, the church itself could be extended, he replied, "We'll see later."

The Soviet press reports that the city of Klaipeda is growing, that there is new building construction and that living conditions are improving. Only the faithful wait in vain for the Government to pay

*Not to be confused with Rugienis.

some attention to their hard lot and to return their Church of Mary, Queen of Peace, which has been unjustly confiscated.

Can the faithful of Lithuania respect a government which has desecrated a church dedicated to the Queen of Peace, and which for propaganda purposes sends its builder, His Excellency Bishop Povilonis, to a peace congress in Moscow?[58]

NOTES TO CHAPTER VII

1. These statistics are taken principally from Savasis, *The War against God in Lithuania*, pp. 13 and 82 and ed. Marshall, *Aspects of Religion in the Soviet Union 1917-1967*, p. 395.
2. Beeson, *Discretion and Valour*, p. 53. The Soviet Union annexed a large area of western Ukraine, western Belorussia, as well as the Baltic states at the end of the Second World War.
3. Savasis, *op. cit.*, p. 82, names four.
4. Bourdeaux, *Patriarch and Prophets*, pp. 119-55; Bourdeaux, *Religious Ferment in Russia*, p. 2.
5. *CLCC* 18, p. 6
6. *CLCC* 2, pp. 15-17; 19, pp. 17-20.
7. Text in *CLCC* 2, pp. 15-16.
8. See Bociurkiw, *Religion and Atheism in the USSR and Eastern Europe*, 1975, pp. 101 f.
9. *CLCC* 19, p. 29.
10. See Alexander Solzhenitsyn, "Along the Oka", in Bourdeaux, *Patriarch and Prophets*, pp. 154-5.
11. *CLCC* 8, p. 6 (E), p. 2 (L).
12. Savasis, *op. cit.*, p. 48.
13. *CLCC* 14, p. 40 (E), p. 33 (L).
14. *Ibid.*, p. 23; see also p. 242.
15. *CLCC* 7, pp. 28-9 (E), pp. 12-13 (L).
16. *Ibid.*, p. 29 (E), pp. 12-13 (L).
17. *CLCC* 9, p. 33 (E), pp. 18-19 (L).
18. *RCL* 1, 1976, pp. 49-50.
19. *CLCC* 5, p. 44 (E), p. 17 (L).
20. *CLCC* 14, p. 16 (E), p. 12 (L).
21. *CLCC* 16, p. 15.
22. *CLCC* 19, p. 30.
23. *CLCC* 20, pp. 30-1.
24. Solzhenitsyn, *Stories and Prose Poems*, London 1971, pp. 121-6.
25. Bourdeaux, *Patriarch and Prophets*, pp. 120, 148.
26. *CLCC* 15, p. 25.
27. *CLCC* 19, pp. 27-8.
28. *CLCC* 12, pp. 24-5 (E), pp. 21-2 (L).
29. *CLCC* 15, p. 25.
30. *CLCC* 18, p. 7.
31. Bourdeaux, *Patriarch and Prophets*, p. 17.

32. *CLCC* 6, p. 32 (E), p. 13 (L)
33. Bourdeaux, *op. cit.,* pp. 19-20.
34. Savasis, *op. cit.,* p. 84.
35. ed. Marshall, *Aspects of Religion in the Soviet Union, 1917-1967,* p. 381.
36. *CLCC* 5, p. 33 (E), p. 14 (L); 6, p. 32 (E), p. 13 (L); 14, pp. 14-15 (E), pp. 11-12 (L).
37. *CLCC* 9, p. 38 (E), pp. 21-2 (L).
38. Marshall, *op. cit.,* p. 387, quoting the declaration of Bishop Brizgys to the Second Vatican Council.
39. *Sovetskaya Litva,* 9 October 1975, p. 2.
40. Rimaitis, *Religion in Lithuania,* p. 28.
41. *CLCC* 14, pp. 13-17 (E), p. 11 (L).
42. *CLCC* 3, pp. 11-12; 5, pp. 39-41 (E), pp. 13-15 (L); 6, pp. 31-2 (E), p. 13 (L).
43. *CLCC* 15, pp. 23-4.
44. *CLCC* 16, p. 16.
45. Cf. Savasis, *op. cit.,* pp. 83-4.
46. *CLCC* 18, pp. 3-7.
47. *CLCC* 12, pp. 31-2 (E), pp. 28-30 (L).
48. *CLCC* 11, p. 23 (E), p. 19 (L).
49. *Ibid.,* p. 37 (E), pp. 31-2 (L).
50. *CLCC* 9, p. 10 (E), p. 5 (L).
51. *CLCC* 15, p. 24.
52. For a criticism of the same practice in Russian Orthodox churches, see Bourdeaux, *op. cit.,* p. 192. There it has been in force at least since 1929.
53. *CLCC* 26, pp. 39-46.
54. Cf. a similar tactic in the early 1960's at Ternopil in Ukraine: Bourdeaux, *Patriarch and Prophets,* p. 105.
55. *CLCC* 2, pp. 6-9.
56. *CLCC* 2, p. 9 gives the numbers as 3023, *CLCC* 3, p. 13 gives the numbers as 2023.
57. *CLCC* 4, pp. 33-4 (E), p. 19 (L).
58. *CLCC* 8, p. 45 (E), p. 25 (L).

VIII

THE FAITH OF THE PEOPLE

THE story of the Lithuanian people is that of a national identity, culture and faith which have become as hard and bright as a diamond under the increasing pressures of recent centuries. Like the Jews, they have a diaspora in many countries. An enduring Christian faith and the Lithuanian language are the principal factors which unify them. Over thirty years of Sovietization have failed to achieve the planing down of the chiselled face of the Lithuanian social landscape into the featureless unit which this term implies. Even more signally in Lithuania than in some other places of the Soviet Union, the "homo sovieticus" has failed to emerge.

Nowhere did the faith do more to hold the people together than during the deportations to Siberia, where 300,000 faced death and only a fraction survived to return to Lithuania after the death of Stalin.[1] There are many references to this, but we will limit ourselves to two brief examples. Dmitri Panin, a former companion of Solzhenitsyn in the camps, describes the Lithuanians' daily evening prayer:

> They knelt facing the wall, crossed themselves and prayed for five to ten minutes. Before long we came to imitate them, because the example they gave us made us blush with shame at not having the bravery to bear witness to our faith. Moreover, these brave country-folk openly wore their baptismal crosses on their necks, thus making a silent testimony to their belonging to Jesus Christ.[2]

Panin goes on to describe how other believers also began to make crosses for themselves out of wood or anything available and to wear them. The rosaries which the Lithuanians managed to make also impressed many non-Catholics in the camps. There is a passage in Solzhenitsyn's *Gulag Archipelago* describing how they were made:

> While I was in the Kuibyshev transit camp, I saw how the Catholics (Lithuanians) made prison rosaries by hand. They used bread which they soaked in water, kneaded into balls and then coloured (burnt rubber for black ones, tooth powder for white, red streptocide for red); then they threaded them, while still moist, on to wet threads of cloth and let them dry out on the window.[3]

Among the Lithuanians exiled to camps in Siberia were four young girls, Lione, Vale, Levite and Adele (surnames unknown) who wrote out by hand a book of prayers they had composed in prison. The book, *Marija, gelbek mus* ("Mary save us") was later sent back to Lithuania. The prayers in the book express not only the anguish and fears of the exiles, but their spiritual strength, their power to forgive and trust in God:

> Jesus, my Lord,
> Come to me,
> Comfort me, console me,
> Visit the hearts
> In strange lands
> Yearning for you.
> Visit the dying and those
> Who have died without you.
> Jesus, my Lord,
> Visit also those
> Who persecute you.
> Lord Jesus, you are my light
> In the darkness.
> You are my warmth
> In the cold.
> You are my happiness
> In sorrow . . . .[4]

Those who returned from Siberia to a more normal existence in Lithuania still found their faith threatened in all sorts of ways.

One of the enduring features which the Soviet regime has tried hard to erase, but with no success so far, is the Christian calendar, which paces the year, giving additional colour and character to the succession of seasons. The Soviet authorities have attempted to substitute for this their own secular atheist framework for the year, attended by a barrage of propaganda in the Soviet press, very often under the catch-phrase, which is a solecism, "Let us introduce new traditions."

For example, festivities are organized at Easter, Shrovetide and Christmas, incorporating all the traditional folk elements – painted eggs, traditional dishes and folk-plays – but without any religious content. On the contrary, it is usual to include actively anti-Christian propaganda, such as a lecture on how Easter is "really" only a pagan spring festival, or a "folk-play" ridiculing God, the angels and devils, who appear on stage together with pagan gods.[5] The emphasis on folklore and the authorized wearing of Lithuanian national dress at these ceremonies would seem to indicate an attempt to make use of national feeling to combat religion and thus to destroy the present identification of religion and nationalism. It is only in such "controlled" conditions that the authorities permit anything which smacks of nationalism. The atheists, rightly, emphasize that many of the

Christian festivals had pagan origins, but their attempts to de-Christianize them are singularly clumsy, showing very little tact and understanding of people's feelings.[6]

At the same time, official atheist literature attacks the Church for trying to modernize its rituals since Vatican II in order to identify religion with national character and to make religion a continuing part of family life:

> A clear aspect of Catholic liturgical reform in Lithuania is the attempt to
> give it a national character. In this connection, believers often hear of the
> 'Catholic traditions of our country' in their churches . . . .
>
> The Church would like to use liturgical reforms to bring believing families back into its fold . . . . trying to impart a religious character to new secular traditions which have become part of Soviet life. The Church would like to take even such new traditions under its wing, though earlier it used to pay no attention to them.[7]

Obviously, the new atheist traditions are being rivalled and often left standing by the Lithuanian Church's "old traditions". It would be hard to imagine huge crowds of Lithuanian people gathering to follow some relevant pursuit on, for example, Cosmonaut Day. But this does happen on important saints' days, even when they do not fall on a Sunday. It is common practice for believers to work extra hard to finish their allotted work ahead of time, so that they can be free to go to church, but this does not shield them from bitter criticism.[8] Even during the worst years of the Khrushchev persecution crowds flocked to church. People from surrounding villages trying to reach Rumšiškes on the festival of the Nativity of the Blessed Virgin Mary in 1963 (Sunday, 8 September) found road blocks preventing them. Many were in horse-drawn carts and they were turned back after being told that there was an outbreak of foot-and-mouth disease. Yet the next day the authorities restored free movement to the area.[9]

Sometimes when a new Communist holiday falls in the week, the authorities "abolish" the following Sunday.[10] Presumably this practice annoys non-believers, too, because it denies them any real holiday at all. Neither can the Soviet authorities particularly enjoy the enforcement of such decrees, which can be either local or national. It involves them in an unending tug-of-war, which they may win by intimidation on a given occasion, but they know they will have to pull just as hard again the next time the conflict emerges. An incident at Salos on 25 May 1975, a Sunday, illustrates their pettiness.

The local *sovkhoz* management declared it a working day and warned that they would punish any who went to church. A member of the church council and his wife broke the ban, for which they were prevented from pasturing their animals close to their house (collective farmers are permitted to own some cattle privately) and forced to use land much further away. Some other farm workers also failed to turn up for work, but they were not punished, for they had merely taken the day off, and had not gone to church.[11]

The conflict is likely to be at its sharpest when the abolished Sunday happens also to be a high festival. Easter has often been the atheists' special target. Declaring Orthodox Easter Sunday a working day in 1975 led to one of the most impassioned defences of Christian rights ever to be made by an Orthodox believer, when Fr. Gleb Yakunin wrote a declaration condemning the authorities for forcing Christians to "pull the flagging train" (of Communist ideology) on the most sacred day of the Christian year.[12] Roman Catholic Easter usually falls on a different day from the Orthodox festival, but the Soviet authorities in Lithuania have not been slow to apply similar sanctions, though with a singular lack of conviction because of the manifest impossibility of enforcing the decree properly. When this happened at Panevežys in 1974, the scenes described by the *Lithuanian Chronicle* belong almost as much to the world of comic opera as to the repression of a basic human right, which they in fact represented (Document 58).

The great festivals are the occasions on which the Church most notably crosses the frontier into secular society, as it were, bears public witness, and therefore breaks the discriminatory constitutional ban on religious propaganda.[13] Lithuania has a lively tradition of religious processions, both for celebration and for mourning, which naturally take place outside the church building and are therefore an increasing cause of conflict with the authorities, especially when children take part. The authorities often try to force priests themselves to forbid the traditional modes of observance[14] and they fine people who organize the processions.[15]

Despite all the pressures, the faithful perpetuate their traditions. Nowhere is this more evident than in the way they continue to demand the association of the Church with the most solemn moments of their personal lives: birth, coming of age, marriage, death – what the sociologists call the *rites de passage*.

It is a moot point whether Communism has succeeded at all in lessening this adherence, despite its claims to have done so. Communist holidays, even on their strictest enforcement, hold the promise of a day off work. The attempted substitution of new rituals affecting people at the deepest level of consciousness is something quite different.

It is very noticeable that the official atheist substitute rituals often follow closely the original Christian customs and order of service – the god-parents, the "baptismal vow", the lighting of candles on graves – emphasizing the more pagan elements of these ceremonies, but omitting any mention of God.

An atheist survey published in 1962 claimed that church attendance had fallen by fifty per cent, but the reduction in baptisms, church weddings and funerals was no more than ten to fifteen per cent.[16] Even if this figure is accurate, it is far from impressive when one considers the massive resources which the State has been able to devote to popularizing its own ceremonies. There is, furthermore, the distinct possibility that the authorities doctor their own statistics, and, where the data depend on the voluntary help of the people, that the latter might be intimidated into giving figures which are acceptable to the interrogator.

There seems to have been very little success in combating church ceremonies in Lithuania, in comparison with the successes the Soviet authorities claim to have achieved in this respect in the other two Baltic republics. For example, in Estonia the number of baptisms is said to have been reduced to 11.8% of babies born.[17]

The Soviet press, especially in the early 1960's, gave a lively impression of the new substitute rituals for baptism (Document 59) in which a stork figures prominently. Storks or no storks, people, often even party members, want to continue having their children baptized in church. Typical is the campaign waged against a young couple who asked for the Sacrament at Bagaslaviškis in 1974. The father, a party member, was a *kolkhoz* driver and his wife was a book-keeper. The authorities kept up the pressure for months and even made them state in writing the untruth that there had been no baptism.[18] For another example of such persecution, see Document 60.

In the early 1960's the Soviet authorities tried to increase the controls on baptism generally in the Soviet Union, requiring written application to be made in advance to the church council in a Russian Orthodox church.[19] This was to prevent, for example, believing grandmothers from taking the child secretly to the priest while fulfilling their normal duty of babysitting. There is no evidence that these sanctions have decreased the number of Russian Orthodox baptisms and it appears that attempts at greater control in Lithuania at the same time did not achieve even temporary success.[20] From the administrative point of view it was easiest for the authorities to prevent the baptism of sick infants by barring the access of priests to hospitals and making documentation essential even for emergency baptisms.[21] However, according to the Soviet press, the authorities have been unable to enforce even this control absolutely and when a child in danger of death recovered after baptism, this compounded the "offence" by giving grounds to the populace for attributing miraculous powers to the age-old ritual.[22]

We shall treat confirmation (or "coming-of-age" in the secular idiom) in the next chapter dealing with education and young people, but we come here to another point of conflict: marriage. Because the overwhelming majority of people now being married in Lithuania were not only educated but even born under the Communist system, according to the logic of party proclamations church marriage should now be something of the past. The truth is very different. There are, of course, new Soviet ceremonies dreamed up by the atheists to provide, as the baptism rituals are supposed to do, a solemnity equivalent to the church milieu.[23] Nevertheless, there would probably not be a lecture to Komsomol members on the subject where the speaker would not admit the continuing prevalence of church weddings.[24] There are, of course, sanctions against young people who break the injunction, but they seem to be feeble and ineffective, doubtless due to the continuing prevalence of reception of the Sacrament, which makes it difficult for the authorities to dole out punishment on such a broad scale in the Soviet Union as it is today. There are reports, however, of young people being dismissed from their jobs after church weddings[25] and of children losing good-conduct marks for merely being present as guests at the ceremony.[26]

The attempt by the Communist Party to supplant the Christian view of marriage by an alternative morality has led to a more vigorous defence of traditional teaching than that now being made in some other areas of the world. The *Lithuanian Chronicle* reports a debate on this matter in Vilnius in 1972, where the lecturer not only failed to dent the Christian position, but even made himself look ridiculous in the process (Document 61).

A man may live as an examplary Communist and yet at his death still feel the need for contact with the supernatural. Or new-style secular burial rites may fail to satisfy the deep-seated psychological needs of his relatives. Here, again, the arena is set for never-ending conflict,[27] especially when official funeral parlours forbid the performance of religious rites on the premises (Document 62).

In February 1975 an old party member and atheist died on a *kolkhoz* in the Plunge district. The *Lithuanian Chronicle* reported the circumstances as follows:

> Before her death she invited a priest in, received the Last Rites and died as a Catholic. When the active party cell of the *kolkhoz* found out about this they rushed to the daughter of the dead woman, the director of the house of culture, and demanded how she could permit her mother, who had been a member of the Party for twenty years, to invite a priest in. "It's unheard of. It's an insult to the Party," the atheists cried. The daughter stated that her mother had herself decided how she would behave on the threshold of death and did not ask her daughter's advice. But the party activists disregarded all this and gave Lučinskaite an atheist funeral anyway.[28]

It is not unknown for Communist Party members also to be Catholics. This again leads to conflict over their funerals. On 8 October 1975 Vitautas Ivonis, a well-known local Communist worker, died in Švenčioneliai. His wife arranged a church funeral, in spite of opposition from her atheist brothers-in-law. The priest, Fr. J. Baltušis, was summoned to the district Party headquarters.

"Do you know who it is you're burying today?"

"Yes."

"But he was a Communist, you know; he must have been an atheist, so you can't give him a church funeral."

"What sort of atheist was he, when he got married in church, had his children baptised and also came to confession? I can't refuse to preside at his funeral."

The priest went ahead with the funeral, in spite of further attempts by Party officials to dissuade him. The dead man's wife was threatened with expulsion from the Party for allowing this.[29]

Because of its "possession of the body", the State has been successful in preventing priests from administering the Last Rites in numerous instances, despite the known wishes of patients (Document 63). The ban is not absolute everywhere, however, and the *Lithuanian Chronicle* quotes the 1975 regulations of a senior doctor at Utena which designate the carefully-controlled conditions (as if they were bringing in some infection) under which the priest may be admitted to his hospital.[30] The authorities try to ban priests from access to old people's homes,[31] but this is not always successful, either, and the clergy have vigorously defended their traditional rights in this area.[32]

Naturally, the funeral of a child or of a young person is especially contentious, but it seems that in practice believing parents usually manage to carry out their wishes when they lose a child. Examples are recorded of the opposite, however, as at Debeikiai in April 1975, where a child died in a motor accident. The boy's teacher issued threats, after which she tore the ribbons (presumably containing dedications or religious texts) from the wreaths under the eyes of his classmates, and then the mother yielded to the violence and agreed to a secular funeral.[33] The Christian funeral of a 29-year-old veterinary surgeon who was known as a believer went ahead at Alytus in November 1974, despite intimidation.[34]

A funeral procession is, in its way, a public act of Christian witness, so the authorities have sometimes attempted to prevent priests from participating.[35] However, the physical fact is that not even the Communists have been able to devise a method of invisibly transporting a body from its place of death to its final resting-place. As long as people die and the Church endures, Christian burial is an act of faith which it will be impossible for the authorities to confine to the four walls of a registered church.

The death of a well-known Christian figure continues to provide an opportunity for a major act of witness. The funeral of Canon Rauda* is a particularly notable example: a working day, 40 cars, even after many taxis and lorries had been denied access, crowds lining the streets, 180 priests and 4 bishops – not many funerals in the West would attract such a massive display of sympathy.

Communist propaganda has often claimed that the continued adherence to the most ritualistic part of religion is a residue of the past

*See pp. 93-5.

which is on the way to extinction. The Lithuanian example does not bear this out. On the contrary, there is considerable evidence that the ritual is only one aspect of a continued widespread personal commitment to the faith in Lithuania.

Everywhere in Lithuania the churches continue to attract huge crowds of worshippers. There is no evidence of falling away, except in the pages of atheist propaganda.[36] In July 1973 Bishop Povilonis visited the parish of Veisiejai for a confirmation. There were 2,600 candidates – some doubtless were adults – and 10,000 people present altogether, of whom over a third received communion. The *Lithuanian Chronicle* many times refers to large numbers of people, often overflowing the inadequate facilities for worship.[37] The overcrowding is worse at Klaipeda than in most other places, because of the confiscation of the new church.* Here the church has 6,000 members, with 800-900 taking First Communion every year – and yet those who can must crowd into a building barely seventeen metres square.[38] Sometimes the physically unpleasant conditions are made even worse by malicious interruptions from local atheists.[39]

Even where not actively disrupting their services, the local atheists keep the churches under observation. It is probably true to say that the authorities have a good idea of who goes to church and who does not in Lithuania. As elsewhere, discrimination occurs against some who do and it is not confined to children. Even some adults in a relatively menial position – such as a postwoman – have been dismissed from work for their religious practice.[40] Yet others in more exalted positions apparently continue to worship unscathed.

Those who attend church are not, in the main, passive or curious onlookers. Vast numbers of people make their confession and the *Chronicle* sometimes describes the priest as being "besieged" by crowds of people seeking his personal office for this Sacrament.[41] In an open letter to the Soviet authorities written in 1974, Fr. Laurinavičius, writing of the town of Adutiškis, asks:

"Could three priests take care of all the confessions we heard during this year's retreat – 3,105 people?"[42]

In Lithuania retreats usually preceded Easter; these were three-day events, incorporating special prayers, sermons, fasting and confession. Little is known of these retreats today, once a universal feature but now inevitably controversial because of the legal ban on any religious gathering other than a service of worship in a registered church. As there are other references it is certain that they continue, however.[43]

Coupled with the survival of popular faith is the need for religious devotion. There is unofficial buying and selling of rosaries in Lithuania. The worst fate to befall those engaged in this trade has been rough handling and administrative fines,[44] but the attempted

*See pp. 184-8.

import of rosaries and statuettes has led to a number of scenes with customs officials (Document 64). Living rosary groups have become popular among young Catholics. In 1963 A. Šaltis was imprisoned for two years for forming such a prayer-group for young people.[45]

The secret layers of this private faith fold upwards and break the surface most insistently not only with church-going, but perhaps even more imposingly with the public devotions at national shrines, to which people throng from all over Lithuania and beyond.

The widespread devotion to the cross in Lithuania begins in the private house or just outside it. There is an old tradition that individuals should raise crosses in the immediate surroundings of their own houses and this, not surprisingly, has led to an almost endless series of clashes with the authorities (Document 65). There is even an instance recorded in 1974 when the authorities removed a widely-respected scholar from her position as head of the local museum for showing to her public pictures of Lithuanian crosses and of folk sculpture, including a group of the Last Supper.[46]

One of the great places of devotion in Lithuania used to be the seventeenth-century Stations of the Cross at Vilnius. There would be huge influxes of 150,000 pilgrims at a time from as far away as Belorussia and Ukraine, especially on festivals of the Holy Cross. This continued up to 1962, but in that year the authorities dynamited the thirty-six chapels without warning, under the pretext of making way for a new road (Document 66).

One of the greatest national shrines is at Šiluva, where the week-long devotions on the Nativity of the Blessed Virgin Mary in early September traditionally attract huge crowds from all over the country. In recent years they have been harassed by the police, who hold up their buses and turn them back, making even old people trek miles to the town itself.[47] Recently an atheist writer publicly claimed that as few as 1,300 people came for the devotions in 1972 (the church holds three times that number).[48] The *Chronicle* was not slow to produce evidence to the contrary and stated that in 1974, as in other years, the total was approximately 50,000 people.[49] The next year the crowds were even greater and blocked the streets to such an extent that all traffic came to a virtual standstill.[50]

At another famous shrine, Žemaičiu Kalvarija, 15,000 people took communion in July 1975. These Lithuanian holy places can stand comparison with Polish shrines such as Czestochowa. Indeed, Polish pilgrims are often among the crowds of pilgrims at Šiluva and Žemaičiu Kalvarija.

Perhaps even more remarkable among places of popular devotion is the Hill of Crosses near Šiauliai. In its original state it was a remarkable sight – a hummock rising from a flat cornfield, the top of which bristled with a burgeoning of crosses in their thousands, wedged thicker than the trees of a forest. Perhaps no events better symbolize the endurance of the faith in Lithuania under persecution than the destruction of the Hill of Crosses on 5 April 1961 under the Khrushchev persecution, then its gradual "replanting", followed by a further total devastation in April 1973, and then a most solemn nocturnal procession culminating in the erection of a new cross during the night of 20 May 1973.

In November 1975 the Hill of Crosses was raided again and a large maple tree on the hill was chopped down, as its branches were hung with crosses. However, it is certain that this new attempt by the authorities to destroy the shrine has been no more successful than the others.

With the constant raids by the authorities and the determination of the faithful to resist them, the number of crosses on the hill obviously fluctuates. The *Lithuanian Chronicle* in 1977 quotes the number as being 360 (Document 67). Visual and other evidence – for example, two Russian airmen who celebrated a miraculous escape by placing a cross there – suggests that Russian Orthodox crosses occasionally appear among the Catholic ones.[51]

The State might try to destroy places of pilgrimage hallowed by the prayers of centuries; but it also has to cope with the emergence of absolutely new places to compensate for these losses. In July 1962 a girl is reported to have seen a vision of the Virgin at Skiemonys.[52] At first the faithful had no means except by word of mouth to pass on the story – but the job was immediately done for them by the Soviet press, when the main Lithuanian newspaper described what was alleged to have happened in order to criticize it. Doubtless the faithful reflected on the mysterious ways in which God works. There are reports of similar visions from Ukraine.[53]

DOCUMENTS

58. THE ABOLITION OF EASTER

Before Easter 1974 Mrs. J. Kalačiuviene, secretary of the Panevežys Party District Committee, told *sovkhoz* director Valaitis to declare Easter Sunday a working day. Trembling with fear before the district authorities, Valaitis told the farm managers to drive everybody out to work on Easter Day and to make them work in the open, so that people could see from the road that sowing was in progress. Anyone who had nothing more important to do had to gather stones in the fields.

The managers Kripaityte and Vasiliauskaite showed unwonted zeal. Kripaityte wept, saying, "Have pity on me and go out to work, or I'll be dismissed." The workers were given beer as an inducement to work on Easter Day. Vasiliauskaite even demanded signed promises from people that they would come to work. Office staff had to work, too. Some of the tractor and lorry-drivers obeyed, but not many workers turned up.

The anger of the believers knew no bounds: even in the days of serfdom people did not work on church festivals, but nowadays believers are insulted.[54]

59. COMMUNIST STYLE BAPTISM, 1963

On an agreed date, in a beautifully decorated office of the local registrar, a pram adorned with roses is placed on a rug. The best orchestra in the area plays a march in honour of the 'name-parents' [god-parents], who are prominent local Communists. The chairman and the deputies of the Executive Committee address the name-parents, asking them to bring up the child to be a good Communist. The name-parents then sign the registry book wherein the following pledge had been inserted:

A new person has been born. It is a day of jubilation for our collective farm and the entire district. There has come into our community still another builder of Communism, a new member of Communist society. Whatever he will be – collective farmer, doctor, engineer – our primary duty is that he grow morally sound . . . We accept the duty of protecting him, so that the mouldy fingers of the outworn relics of the past do not touch him and the shadow of the cross does not darken his life's bright dawn. We will guard his first steps carefully, so that he does not stray from the single path that leads to Communism.

A certificate is then made out with the infant's name and date of birth, set into an artistic folder and handed to the name-parents for presentation to the child's actual parents. A card attached with a ribbon to the folder bears the inscription, "In remembrance of your birth." Inside is the following note:

You are born at an unusual time, when an uncommon life – that of Communism – is being established on earth. You are very much needed in the ranks of its builders, for you come to take our place and to complete what we have begun. We believe that when you grow up you will justify the hopes we have placed in you and you will be worthy to be a member of Communist society.

After this, girls in national costumes present the name-parents with flowers. Flowers are also given to the happy father for him to present to the mother. Then the entire group goes to the parents' home for entertainment, speeches and singing.[55]

On a Saturday afternoon [at Pasvalys] Pioneers and Octobrists hurry to the registrar's office . . . They settle down and make a neat line formation in the room of the festivities . . . The orchestra is playing a march. The name-parents step out of an automobile. They are carrying the infant son of Zaliauskas, who is a construction worker. Suddenly, approaching them in measured steps, on tiptoe, his long neck bobbing up and down, there comes a stork. He flaps his black wings, points the way and leads the entire solemn procession indoors.

The march becomes even livelier when the stork and the name-parents step into the decorated festivities room. The long-necked creature comes to the table, bows before the waiting staff of the registry office, points with his beak at the infant and steps aside. He has completed his assignment.

"Remigijus" is solemnly announced as the name of little Zaliauskas.

The director of the registrar's office has scarcely finished her speech, when the stork gives a signal and we hear the young Pioneers. The best speakers of the group deliver their orations and offer their congratulations to little Remigijus. They wish him to follow in their footsteps and be even better than they are . . . Finally they are quiet. Now several Pioneers leave their group and . . . present a gift. It is accepted by the name-parents, who then turn to the door. Stretched out across their path, with the children lined up on either side, is a 'ribbon of happiness'. An eleven-year-old hands the name-parents a pair of scissors. Let them cut the 'ribbon of happiness' and let little Remigijus begin his life's journey accompanied by every success.[56]

60. PARENTS PERSECUTED FOR BAPTIZING SICK CHILD

It was a dark night on 22 October 1966. A cart stopped near Žaiginiai church. Juozas Mockus had brought his ailing child to be baptized.

After the baptism the parents were leaving the church when they saw that the cart was no longer there. People began to search for it and they found it in the garden of the party secretary, Vincas Montvila. Ignoring both the men's pleas and the mother's tears, Montvila unharnessed the horse and said, "I'm not giving you any horse for a baptism." The unfortunate people had to wade home down five kilometres of muddy track with a sick child in their arms on a dark, wet night.[57]

61. A NEW MORALITY

At the end of 1972 two debates for young people were held [at the
Museum of Atheism] on topics dealing with love, dating and the
family. Professor K. Daukša affirmed that love was a passing biological feeling and that there could be no faithful couples. What was
important, according to the professor, was that the other partner
should not know; and if he did, to be forgiving. The professor said that
he had been in love "four and a half times" in his life . . .

There were many questions from the audience:

"Is it normal for a couple to have intercourse before marriage?"

The professor replied, "Is sex normal? Of course it's normal! There
can be no question about it."

"How does the speaker feel about virginity?"

"That's a religious anachronism. The man who wants to marry a
virgin is an egoist."

"Professor, are you in favour of free love?"

"In a socialist country there is freedom: you can live in a legal
union, or you can have a private arrangement."

"Then, perhaps you're in favour of houses of prostitution?"

"Perhaps they should be allowed, but their form could be different
– socialist."

"Free of charge?"

"Professor, you've made everything seem banal: art, poetry, love.
What's the purpose of life then?"

"Purpose? Who knows? There's a will to live, so we live; but when
that drive weakens, we hang ourselves, take poison, drown or shoot
ourselves. Anyone who thinks too much about the meaning of life will
end up in a psychiatric hospital."

More than one member of the audience wondered who had put
Professor Daukša up to encouraging delinquency of minors. Perhaps
the atheists no longer believe that they can convert the young without
undermining their morality?[58]

62. ATHEIST FUNERAL PARLOURS

At 14 Santakos Street in the old town of Kaunas, the regulations for
use of the buildings are displayed within. They include the following:

"Inside the funeral parlour it is forbidden to:
- alter the decoration arrangements in the rooms
- make use of religious pictures or any other religious objects
- sing religious hymns

- use the services of the clergy
- organize funeral ceremonies using religious rites on the premises."

These regulations were approved by the Executive Committee of the Kaunas *soviet* on 21 February 1957.[59]

63. THE BAN ON THE LAST RITES

A Statement to the Minister of Health of the Lithuanian SSR

By the Rev. Petras Budriunas

For some years in the city hospital of Anykščiai believers have not been allowed to summon a priest to take in the Blessed Sacrament. Their requests receive a variety of replies: "The patient is not in critical condition"; "he doesn't need a priest; you do"; "there's no special room"; "once you take the patient home, you can have the priest as often as you like," and so on. Those who ask for the priest are deceived and mocked.

On 7 October 1973 the mother of Valentinas Kovas, of Daujočiai, and the daughter of Juozas Grižas, from the village of Čekoniai, requested Šinkunas, the senior registrar, to allow a priest to visit the ailing patient, but he would not give permission. Some hours later Valentinas Kovas died.

. . . .

In the press it is always emphasized that in the hospitals nothing prevents performance of religious observances which are requested by the dying or the seriously ill . . . .

In Anykščiai priests are not allowed to visit patients even when they are in a private room.

. . . .

On 17 July 1972 Petras Katinas and Šukys were alone in a ward and asked for a priest, but their request was not heeded. When I tried to visit the patients at their request, Šinkunas intercepted me in the hospital yard and ordered me to go back.

A few years ago I appealed about this matter to the former vice-chairman of the Executive Committee of the Anykščiai District, K. Zulona. He promised to look into it, but I never received any positive reply from him. On 17 September 1972 I requested the present vice-chairman of the Executive Committee of the Anykščiai district, A. Baltrunas, to come to a decision on this serious question. He replied that people had more than once come to him and he promised to

speak with the senior registrar. It seemed that the problem would be
solved, but once again someone blocked the road.

. . . .

On 9 January 1974 I was summoned by Baltrunas, who admonished
me in writing for administering the Sacrament of Extreme Unction on
25 December 1973 to Julius Vitkevičius, of the village of Lagedžiai,
without the permission of the hospital administration. I had visited this
patient for about three minutes just before his death.

This situation has existed in Anykščiai for more than fifteen years.
Hundreds of people have been seriously deprived, in the moral sense,
since their final wish was not carried out at the most critical moment
of life – the hour of death.

I respectfully request you, Mr. Minister, to see that the law regarding religious cults be observed in the hospital at Anykščiai, so that
believers might be able to take advantage of the right to receive the
Blessed Sacrament.

The Rev. P. Budriunas.[60]

Anykščiai,
2 March 1974

64. CUSTOMS OFFICIALS CONFISCATE RELIGIOUS ITEMS

A resident of Žibikai village, Jadvyga Grabiene, went to the USA in
1973 to visit her son, who is a priest. Whilst in Rome, Mrs. Grabiene
bought rosaries for herself and her relatives. Customs officials on the
Soviet border searched Mrs. Grabiene's luggage minutely and
smashed the rosaries which they found. The officials wanted to
deprive her of her last rosary, which she held in her clenched fist. "I
will never let you have this treasure," the old lady said in tears, "even
if you wrench it out of my hands."

A few years ago the present author witnessed a similar scene of
plundering in a border customs building when Russian officials filled
sacks with confiscated rosaries, pictures and statuettes. "Why do you
want these devil-charms?" the officials taunted. One woman asked:

"Where do you put the holy things you confiscate?"

"We throw them on the rubbish dump," replied the officials.

The travellers all became depressed. Some wiped away their tears.[61]

65. THE STRUGGLE FOR THE CROSS

To the Prosecutor of the Lithuanian SSR

Copies to: His Grace the Bishop of the Kaunas Archdiocese
and Vilkaviškis Diocese, The Executive of the
Council for Religious Affairs.

From: Citizen Ignas Kazio Klimavičius, resident in Lazdijai
District, Buckunai village.

DECLARATION

A year ago I erected a wooden cross on the staircase of my house.
Such a tradition is of long-standing in Lithuania – Catholics honour
the cross and erect it in fields and by their houses, they hang it on the
walls of their homes, wear it around their necks and so on. I was
certain that, as no government permit was necessary to wear a cross
around one's neck or hang it on a wall, it was also unnecesary for
putting up a cross on one's own staircase. The officials of the Lazdijai
District Executive Committee decided, however, that I should be
instructed to demolish the cross. Naturally, as a Catholic, I can only
honour the cross and not desecrate it, so I did not pull it down. To
issue an order to a Catholic to tear down the cross I regard as being
itself an offence. What would be said if I were to tell a Communist to
tear up a portrait or to pull down a statue of Lenin?

On 25 July this year, while I was at work, a representative of the
Seirijai police, Alberov, the Žagare district secretary, and A.
Gereltauskas, administrator of the Buckunai section of the Mateliai
Fish farm, drove up to my house, looked around for half an hour
and drove away again. An hour later the Lazdijai fire engine arrived.
Inside it, according to the statements of witnesses, were two drunken
men: the Chief of the Lazdijai fire brigade, Vincas Janušauskas and
the Lazdijai Executive Committee employee, Markevičius. These two
men frightened my wife and children, pushed the cross over, threw it
on to a flower bed and hurriedly departed.

That same day I approached the Lazdijai District police department to find out who had come to knock down the cross and whether
they had really been drunk, because by the next day they would have
sobered up and it would not have been possible to establish this. At
the police station I heard officials talking to each other: "What a nerve
this old man's got – he's come to write a statement to the police chief.
He should be locked up, then he'd know what's what!"

The deputy chairman of the Executive Committee, Jurkevičius,
told me that the Soviet Government had never given permission to
anyone to erect crosses and would never do so. In addition, I would

have to pay those drunkards fifty roubles for demolishing the cross. I then asked them if there could really be a government in the world that would force its citizens to pay drunkards for the crimes they had committed. Even if they forced me, I would not pay. They had better take my jacket, my cow or something else.

I ask the Prosecutor's office to investigate this offence committed by officials of the Lazdijai district and to take appropriate action. I also ask for clarification on the following points:

1. Does the Soviet Government really forbid the erection of a cross near a house or on the staircase of a private house? If it is forbidden, then on what grounds is this refusal based? If it is allowed, then who is able to issue the permit?

2. Did the Lazdijai District Executive Committee have the right to send two drunken men to knock down the cross erected on the staircase of my residence (not even in my fields) without my knowledge? But perhaps it is possible to treat Catholics just as one pleases and that no laws defend their rights?

Ignas Klimavičius.[62]

Buckunai,
30 July 1975

66. THE DESTRUCTION OF THE STATIONS OF THE CROSS, 1974

Fanatical atheists took great pains to prevent the faithful from going to the Stations of the Cross of Vilnius in particular. In 1961 the present author witnessed such efforts. On Pentecost morning notices appeared on the bulletin boards of the taxi garage announcing that travel on the road to the shrine was prohibited. Taxi drivers categorically refused our request to take us, on the grounds that the police were stopping cars on the road and confiscating the licences of drivers heading in that direction. The taxi driver suggested that we go by way of Antakalnis and cross the Neris River by rowing boat at Valakampiai. However, when we arrived at Valakampiai, police prevented us from crossing the river. Local residents tried to assist the pilgrims. They advised us to go through the bushes along the river bank towards Nemenčine, where there were no police. But even here, after we had been rowed across the Neris, the boatman was beaten by auxiliary police, who warned him not to bring anyone else across.

These methods proved ineffective and the forests along the banks of the Neris were filled with the sound of hymns and litanies. In 1962 the atheists, with military reinforcements, dynamited the Stations of the

Cross of Vilnius and carried away the rubble that very night. The site was bulldozed and levelled.

From that time on attendance decreased, but it did not cease. Pilgrims from all over Lithuania gather here on Pentecost and walk the seven kilometres of pathways where the stations once stood. The sites of the former stations are marked by crosses fashioned of loose stones placed there by prayerful hands, which also decorate the sites with flowers.[63]

67. THE HILL OF CROSSES

If you want to know the real mood in Lithuania, travel along the road from Šiauliai to Joniškis. After twelve kilometres there is a sign pointing to the right which says: Daumantai 2 km. Going down this stretch of road, you will see a small hill covered with crosses. This is the Hill of Crosses. You go up a small path to the top of the saddle-like hillock. There is a large stone on the northern side, with the date 1861-4 carved on it – the years of the uprising [against the Russians] and the repressions that followed. These dates now mean a great deal to every Lithuanian.

The local inhabitants tell a vivid story of how a small chapel once stood at the foot of the hill. The Lithuanian revolutionaries came there to pray during the uprising. The Cossacks locked the doors and buried the chapel with the Lithuanian revolutionaries inside by covering it with earth. In time the roof rotted away and caved in, which is why the hill has a hollow in the middle.

At first people put up crosses there in honour of the revolutionaries, but later they put them there as petitions or acts of thanksgiving to God.[64]

. . . .[There were] no less than 3,000 large crosses, not to mention a countless number of smaller ones. Each cross had its own history. Here is what one priest recounts:

"Once I was on my way to the Hill of Crosses to bless a newly-erected cross. At that moment a military vehicle drove up to the hill. Two Russian airmen asked me to bless a cross which they had brought. I honoured their request. One of them described how on a flight his plane had caught fire. It is practically impossible to escape in such circumstances. Suddenly he remembered the story of the Hill of Crosses and resolved that if he survived he would put up a cross there. The cause of the fire was never known, but it went out unexpectedly."

Many people used to come on foot carrying the crosses to erect them. Several of them had been brought from Latvia, Estonia, Belorussia and even from America. People say, "How many sufferings, how many illnesses we have brought to this hill. One wonders how the mound can bear all that trouble. It's a real Lithuanian Golgotha."

Early on the morning of 5 April 1961 a group of cars arrived at the Hill of Crosses. Unknown men began knocking the crosses down. The Hill of Crosses was being destroyed by the army, police and prisoners. They broke up the wooden crosses and hauled them off to Šiauliai. It is said that they used the pieces for building work. They carried away two lorry-loads of crosses to Bubniai. They burned some of them and threw others which would sink into the water. All the crosses were destroyed in a single day. At the cross roads near the hill police used to stand guard to stop people turning off towards the Hill of Crosses. Not far from it an armed guard was on duty. Apparently they were afraid of the people's anger. The guard remained for some time, so as to keep people from re-erecting the crosses.

In the midst of this barbaric operation, Rugienis visited Siauliai. After the crosses had been destroyed, he summoned the parish priest of Šiauliai, Mazanavičius, and asked:

"Have you heard what happened to Meškuičiai Hill?"

"No, I haven't."

"The crosses have gone up to heaven in smoke," Rugienis said, and he ordered the priest to use his influence with his people to prevent any disorders.

On 14 September 1970 Fr. Algirdas Mocius walked sixty-five kilometres from Lauksodžiai to Meškuičiai with bleeding, bare feet, carrrying a wooden cross; on the Feast of the Exaltation of the Holy Cross he erected it on the spot which had been vandalized by the atheists.[65]

★   ★   ★

The Hill of Crosses had just about recovered from damage suffered during the devastation of 1961. However, at the end of April 1973 it was once more destroyed; not a sign of the crosses survived. The desolate, denuded hill seemed to be waiting for believing hands and loving hearts once more to crown its desecrated head with the symbol of the redemption.

At midnight on 19 May 1973 an unusual procession appeared at the edge of the city of Šiauliai. A small, solemn group of young men and women were carrying a cross and praying. They went quietly, meditatively, praying the rosary. From time time the cross, measuring three metres and weighing 99 pounds, would be transferred from one pair of shoulders to another. The cross was decorated symbolically: a heart pierced by two swords. On the handle of one sword was a swastika, and on the other, a five-pointed star [emblem of the Soviet Union].

✓ Young Lithuanians were carrying the cross not for the good of their health, but to atone for the desecration of the cross and make reparation for the sins of our nation against the Redeemer. They also carried the cross as a symbol of victory. On the night of 19 May many knew of this procession with the cross and devoted an hour to prayer and the veneration of the cross. During that hour many joined their hands in prayer and carried the Cross of Christ in spirit.

All the cross-bearers received Holy Communion the evening before. As preparations were being made for this Way of the Cross, it was discovered that someone had informed the KGB what was to happen. Throughout the night KGB men patrolled the proposed route from Šiauliai to the Hill of Crosses. To the cross-bearers the success of the procession seemed a miracle. By 2.30 a.m. on 20 May 1973 the Hill of Crosses boasted a beautiful new cross. Around it were planted flowers and a candle was lit in front. Everyone knelt and prayed: "Christ our King, may your kingdom come to our country."

At 6.45 a.m. the sound of a car was heard. The KGB men rubbed their eyes. All night they had been chasing after the cross and here it was! Angry hands tore the cross down and hauled it off. But by noon another one stood in its place. The more the atheists destroyed them, the more the crosses seemed to sprout from the ground.

On the evening of 20 May 1973 the KGB arrived at the home of Mečislovas Jurevičius, a resident of Šiauliai, born in 1927, and hauled him off to the KGB headquarters for interrogation. Did he carry the cross? What route did they follow? How many people carried the cross? What priests encouraged the demonstration? Jurevičius told them that he had made the cross and carried it himself.

Then they asked Jurevičius why he had been tried previously.

"For Stalin's errors," he replied.

"Stop maligning Stalin!" the interrogator shouted, "He should be here now!"

They asked Jurevičius what priests he knew, who served at Mass in the church and who his contacts were. He refused to answer any more questions. The interrogators called him a fanatic and threatened that he would be given a longer prison sentence than the first time, that they would send him to an asylum, give him injections, and so on. Finally they ordered him to stand against the wall. Undaunted by the threats, Jurevičius was ordered to sit down. In this way the night passed.

In the morning they resumed the interrogation: who teaches boys to serve at Mass? What priests do you speak to most often? Who serves at Mass? . . . .

In the afternoon the prosecutor came and demanded why he would not answer. "You're going to give me ten years anyhow," Jurevičius said. In the evening they allowed him to return home, with orders to present himself again on 23 May. That day more interrogations and threats followed, but he remained silent. He was ordered to re-appear on 29 May. A KGB man ordered him to write everything down and then went on to claim that there was freedom of religion, that the priests deceived the people, and so on.

Jurvevičius exclaimed, "If I'm guilty, put me on trial!"

"It's easy to condemn someone," stated the interrogator, "but we must rehabilitate you." As he allowed the prisoner to go home, the interrogator stated, "We know that you carried the cross in honour of Kalanta."

★   ★   ★

At noon on 20 May 1973 KGB men came and dragged of Zenonas Mištautas, a fourth-year student at the Polytechnic Institute of Šiauliai. They took him to their headquarters and grilled him about what he had done the previous night, whether he served at Mass, what church he attended, who else served at Mass, who took part in adoration of the Sacrament and what the priests had said in their sermons.

At about 4 a.m. the security people brought Zenonas home, and searched the place without a warrant. They went through all his books and note-pads. In the course of the search they seized exposed film and a note-book containing religious material. They developed the film and returned it, but kept the note-book. They went back to the KGB headquarters and continued the interrogation.

Zenonas was asked how many people had carried the cross, who made it, what route was followed, what time the cross was erected, and so on. When they failed to get anything out of him by cajolery, the KGB turned to threats. Four interrogators surrounded him, shook their fists and showed him the kind of "sausages" that would be left on his back if he were beaten with the "banana".

Three times they came out with the words, "Now we're going to bring in the 'banana'. When we take down your trousers and give it to you, you'll tell us everything." The interrogators had all kinds of nonsense to say about the Hill of Crosses, much of it unprintable.

On 10 October KGB again took Mištautas off to their head-quarters. The interrogation lasted three hours, but he remained silent for the most part. So far, Zenonas Mištautas has not been expelled from the Polytechnic Institute . . . .

. . . .

This persecution by the KGB has not only failed to intimidate people, but has even inspired them with more courage. One woman who carried the cross wrote: "Lithuania, be aware of your strength! It lies in Christ and in our unity with one another! Stand immovable and courageous, on guard for what is sacred and dear to your heart! Do not let them desecrate the Hill of Crosses. Do not leave it lying bare. Take your joys and your sorrows, your hopes and your victories there;

take your love of God and your loyalty to him there: carry your own cross to the Hill of Crosses!"

The desecration of the Hill of Crosses had inspired a new idea: "If it is impossible for us to erect a cross on the Hill of Crosses, we should begin erecting crosses in our gardens, in our homes, in our hearts and in the hearts of others."[66]

On 18 November 1975 at 6 p.m. a pupil returning from school was detained near the Hill of Crosses. The policeman asked him where he was coming from. When the boy told him he was coming from school and that his home was nearby, he was released. As he was passing the Hill of Crosses, the boy saw a group of people who were pulling down crosses on the hill and piling them into lorries. One lorry had already been filled with crosses taken from the hill and a second was being loaded, while other lorries were still empty.

The enraged atheists of Meškuičiai are not content merely with crosses, of which the majority were hanging on a fine maple standing in the middle of the hill. On one occasion the atheists made bonfires of the crosses, statuettes and other devotional objects near this fine maple standing on the hill. As a result, the tree has more than once been seared and damaged, but it has continued to sprout leaves while crosses hanging on the tree showed out among the foliage. This time the atheists behaved even more harshly; they felled the tree which was festooned with crosses, rosaries and holy pictures.

Some of the cross-destroyers are beginning to come to their senses – one or two did not take part in this last act. One of them said: "My wife is very devout and suffers because of the desecrating of the cross. She is now in hospital and I will not be her murderer." A second became ill as he was preparing for this dishonourable task. Stepas Česnauskas, the Communist fourth secretary, Simonavičius, a Communist driver, and Timofeyev, a policeman, are particularly zealous organizers of the desecration and destruction. All are from Meškuičiai.

Perhaps the fine maple on the Hill of Crosses was found to be a hindrance by the atheists this time because it had been planted by young people in 1918 to commemorate the restoration of Lithuanian independence.

★　　★　　★

In October, 1975, the present author happened to observe the following scene at the Meškuičiai Hill.

At 8 a.m. a bus arrived at the hill and a large group of young people – university students and senior schoolchildren – swarmed out. The young people took a cross from inside the bus and together they put it at the foot of the hill. The girls then decorated it with flowers of rue. They all then carried it up the hill, each trying to play his part in bear-

ing the noble burden. Candles were lit around the cross after its
erection and all knelt in prayer:

"Lord, give us the strength to confess our faith courageously and to
show that we love you!

"Lord, help us to conquer the present evils of our nation: lack of
faith, immorality and drunkenness!

"Lord, help the young people of Lithuania, both of our town and
of the whole nation!

"Lord, be merciful to those who with blasphemous hands destroy
the crosses we erect and desecrate Lithuania's holy places."[67]

★   ★   ★

The famous Lithuanian Hill of Crosses which has weathered many
storms, by the grace of Divine Providence, has been left unravaged
and avoided new attacks last year (1977). The hill is gradually recover-
ing from the wounds of the atheists, but the scars remain. On 2 May
1977 there were already 360 larger or smaller crosses. What inscrip-
tions are to be found there! Here there is a message of thanks for the
blessing of good health, a request for a prayer for the motherland;
elsewhere there is a prayer for the re-conversion of those who have
strayed. One cross has even been brought from Siberia.

The wounds of the most recent devastation (November 1975) are
still evident: the visitor is met by the remnants of an iron fence which
still protrude – a memorial to the hatred of the atheists. At the end of
the hill three fragments of iron with twisted ends protrude – here there
had also been crosses.

In the centre there stands a blackened tree-trunk surrounded by
crosses, the remains of a maple tree which had been planted during
the independence period and which was cut down during the last
atheist desecration. The tree has been cut down but the roots remain
. . .

The atheists have not succeeded and will not succeed in rooting out
the faith from the hearts of the people. Alongside the trunk a large
beautiful cross with a metal depiction of the torment of Christ has
again "grown up". It is apparently made from the same felled maple
found at the foot of the hill. It has the inscription: "2 May 1977. So it
is regulated by God: if the roots remain the tree will shoot up again.
Atheists are helpless here!"

Crosses continue to "sprout". Some one has also carved a cross on
a stone to commemorate the uprising of 1863. Love is inventive![68]

APPENDIX

Table of Confirmation Figures
(from a private source)

1970 1,500 confirmed in Vilnius every Sunday in July, August, September
8,000 confirmed in Joniškis
30,000 confirmed in Panevežys (where there had been no confirmation for many years)

1972 9,664 confirmed by Bishop Povilonis

1975 9,117 in Kaunas
1,417 in Zarasai
924 in Biržai
1,400 in Akmene

1976 617 in Kaunas cathedral

NOTES TO CHAPTER VIII

1. In 1970 there were still just over 150,000 Lithuanians living in other parts of the USSR. (See *Itogi vsesoyuznoi perepisi naseleniya*, 1970, Vol. IV, Moscow 1973, pp. 9, 14.)
2. *Catacombes*, September 1975, p. 5.
3. Solzhenitsyn, *Arkhipelag Gulag III*, Paris 1975, p. 108 (Russian edition).
4. *Mary Save Us*, Immaculata Press, Putnam, Conn. 1963, p. 65.
5. *Nauka i religia*, February 1976, pp. 52-3.
6. Savasis, *The War against God in Lithuania*, pp. 72-3.
7. *Katolitsizm v SSSR i sovremmenost*, Vilnius, 1971, p. 89.
8. *CLCC* 8 p. 39 (E), pp. 21-2 (L).
9. *CLCC* 9, p. 12 (E), p. 6 (L).
10. Savasis, *op. cit.*, p. 73.
11. *CLCC* 18, p. 29.
12. *Sunday Telegraph*, London, 11 May 1975, p. 2.
13. Ed. Bourdeaux, *Religious Minorities in the Soviet Union*, London 1970, p. 7.
14. *CLCC* 4, pp. 19-20 (E), p. 11 (L).
15. *CLCC* 2, p. 19.
16. *Komunistas*, Vilnius, April 1962, quoted in Savasis, *op cit.*, p. 75.
17. *RCL* 4-5, 1973, p. 32.
18. *CLCC* 16, p. 23. Cf. *Komjaunimo tiesa*, 26 July 1974, p. 2.
19. Bourdeaux, *Patriarch and Prophets*, p. 171.
20. Savasis, *op. cit.*, pp. 78-9.
21. *CLCC* 11, p. 19 (E), p. 15 (L).

22. Savasis, *op. cit.*, p. 79.
23. *Loc. cit.*
24. *CLCC* 9, p. 15 (E), p. 8 (L).
25. *Ibid.*, p. 33 (E), p. 18 (L); *CLCC* 19, p. 28; cf. *CLCC* 16, pp. 23-4.
26. *CLCC* 15, pp. 26-7.
27. Savasis, *op. cit.*, pp. 79-82.
28. *CLCC* 16, p. 15.
29. *CLCC* 22, p. 390.
30. *CLCC* 16, pp. 16-17.
31. *CLCC* 7, p. 51 (E), p. 20 (L).
32. *CLCC* 14, pp. 7-11 (E), pp. 3-6 (L).
33. *CLCC* 17, p. 31.
34. *CLCC* 16, p. 24.
35. *CLCC* 4, p. 30 (E), p. 17 (L).
36. E.g. *Komunistas,* April 1962, quoted in Savasis, *op. cit.*, p. 75.
37. *CLCC* 9, pp. 10-11 (E), p. 5 (L); *CLCC* 16, p. 22.
38. *CLCC* 8, p. 45 (E), p. 25 (L) (see p. 187).
39. *CLCC* 9, pp. 10-11 (E), p. 5 (L); *CLCC* 16, p. 22.
40. *CLCC* 17, p. 21.
41. *CLCC* 9, p. 12 (E), p. 6 (L).
42. *CLCC* 11, p. 22 (E), pp. 17-18 (L).
43. *CLCC* 7, p. 57 (E), p. 22 (L).
44. *CLCC* 8, pp. 45-46 (E), p. 25 (L); *CLCC* 17, p. 26.
45. *CLCC* 22, p. 62 (MS).
46. *CLCC* 14, p. 22 (E), p. 17 (L).
47. *CLCC* 4, pp. 31-32 (E), pp. 17-18 (L); *CLCC* 8, pp. 35-6 (E), pp. 19-20 (L); *CLCC* 9, p. 12 (E), p. 6 (L).
48. *CLCC* 9, p. 12 (E), p. 6 (L).
49. *CLCC* 12, pp. 18-19 (E), p. 16 (L).
50. *CLCC* 19, pp. 28-9.
51. *CLCC* 4, p. 32 (E), p. 18 (L). See also photograph opposite
52. Savasis, p. 132-3.
53. Bociurkiw, *Religion and Atheism in the USSR,* p. 111.
54. *CLCC* 12, p. 23-4 (E), pp. 20-1 (L).
55. *Tiesa,* 10 August 1963, as quoted in Savasis, *War Against God in Lithuania,* pp. 76-7.
56. *Lietuvos Pionierius,* Vilnius, 28 December 1963, quoted in Savasis, *op. cit.*, pp. 77-8.
57. *CLCC* 21, p. 325-6.
58. *CLCC* 6, pp. 29-30 (E), p. 12 (L).
59. *CLCC* 21, p. 322.
60. *CLCC* 10, pp. 31-3 (E), pp. 17-18 (L); cf. *CLCC* 7, pp. 30, 51 (E), pp. 13, 20 (L).
61. *CLCC* 18, p. 32.
62. *CLCC* 18, pp. 17-18; cf. *CLCC* 7, p. 49 (E), pp. 19-20 (L); *CLCC* 19, p. 27; *CLCC* 18, pp. 19-20; *CLCC* 20, pp. 32-33.
63. *CLCC* 9, p. 13 (E), p. 6 (L); cf. Savasis, *op. cit.*, p. 74.
64. *CLCC* 12, p. 13 (E), pp. 27-8 (L).
65. *CLCC* 4, pp. 32-3 (E), p. 18 (L).
66. *CLCC* 8, pp. 27-33 (E), pp. 15-18 (L).
67. *CLCC* 21, pp. 320-2.
68. *CLCC* 29, p. 28.

Nijole Sadunaite

Teofilius Matulionis, Bishop of Kaisiadorys

Bishop Matulionis in a Siberian prison camp

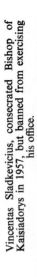

Vincentas Sladkevicius, consecrated Bishop of Kaisiadorys in 1957, but banned from exercising his office.

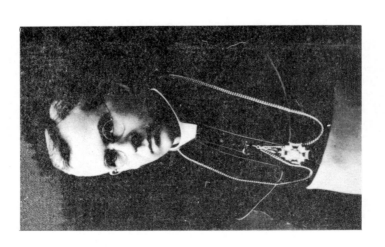

Vincentas Borisevicius, Bishop of Telsiai, condemned and shot in 1946.

Bishop Povilonis conducting an ordination on 25 May 1976 in Kaunas Cathedral.

The trial of the priests who constructed the church in Klaipeda.

Vilnius Cathedral—now a picture gallery.

V

The church built and confiscated at Klaipeda

The Hill of Crosses at Siauliai: a close-up view

A hand-written prayer-book, composed by Lithuanian girls
in a Siberian prison.

A Lithuanian wayside cross.

Nukryžiuotojo pietų pertrauka.

"The crucified having a lunch
break", *Jaunimo Gretos*, 1964,
No. 9.

IX

THE BATTLE FOR THE MINDS OF
THE YOUNG

THE battle for the minds of the young – the minds of Lithuanians born and brought up under the Soviet regime – is probably considered the key point of conflict by both Church and State: the outcome will determine the situation in the twenty-first century and has implications, by analogy, for the whole of East-West relations and the future of man. For Catholics, whether they are parents, children or teachers, the school has become a front-line battlefield. According to the Law on Family and Marriage of 1968, parents must educate their children in "the spirit of the Moral Code of the Builders of Communism". As it was presumably intended by those who drafted the law, the authorities take this to mean education in an atheist spirit and parents may be threatened with the deprivation of their parental rights if they oppose the atheist education of their children at school. There is discrimination against children at school if they are seen to be religious believers: they may receive bad conduct marks and bad school reports and they may be prevented from going on to higher education. Every subject taught must have an "atheist content". At institutes of higher education courses in scientific atheism are compulsory.

Religious education of a juvenile by anyone other than the parents, even if it is with their consent, is a crime. Before 1929 the Soviet Constitution still allowed freedom of both "religious" and "anti-religious" propaganda, but after that date only anti-religious propaganda was permitted.

In the USSR military service is compulsory for all men, the minimum period being eighteen months. This is often used for atheist indoctrination of the young men concerned, through compulsory lectures in a controlled environment. Lithuanians usually serve their term outside their own country in an army unit where all conversation is in Russian, and where they have no opportunity of attending Catholic services.

However, despite all the efforts by the Soviet authorities atheism does not seem to be winning the battle for the minds of the young. Those tried in 1974-5 for producing and distributing the *Lithuanian Chronicle* were mostly young people brought up under the Soviet system. Nijole Sadunaite was two years old when Soviet rule was established in Lithuania; Virgilijus Jaugelis was born in 1948. Perhaps the most revealing part of the *Chronicle*, in this respect, is the section in every issue devoted to the "Soviet school". This consists of reports of discrimination in schools against religious believers, schoolchildren and teachers; the majority of these reports are of children persecuted by atheist teachers. This information, giving the names and addresses of pupils concerned, could come from only one source – the children themselves: it could almost be described as the *Chronicle's* junior section. They and their parents are protected from prosecution under the libel laws first and foremost by the certainty that the *Chronicle* writes the truth. Secondly, the authorities cannot rely on the evidence of the other children to contradict the *Chronicle's* evidence. Thirdly, there is the knowledge that further proceedings would bring even more adverse publicity to Soviet policy in Lithuania. The *Chronicle* evokes the battle going on in the schools and universities in minute detail, rendering commentary virtually superfluous. The material below, selected verbatim from the first 22 issues, speaks for itself.

All the material included from here to the end of the chapter is taken from documents, many in short extracts. For simplicity of presentation, they are grouped together and not given individual titles, except where necessary. Some of these titles, where indicated, are from the original documents, while the rest are editorial. The document numbers continue the sequence from the previous chapter.

DOCUMENTS

68. ATHEIST ORGANIZATION AND AIMS IN EDUCATION

In October 1974 the schools of Vilnius district all received twenty typewritten pages of: "Methodical recommendations on strengthening scientific atheist education among pupils in secondary schools". It was not stated where, how and by whom these recommendations were issued. They were in Russian . . . . Some characteristic extracts are quoted below:

> In scientific atheist education the main deficiencies in the struggle are the lack of any attack against the religious outlook on life and the weakness of individuals' work with believing members of pupils' families.
> Teachers, the instruments of popular education, are not always in time

in coming to the aid of children whom believing parents, or leaders of religious sects, force into participation in religious rituals and drag into a religious atmosphere. In such cases Soviet laws on the defence of children's rights and on . . . . the elimination of the evil influence of the clergy are not properly used . . . .

In the atheist upbringing and education of pupils, most attention should be devoted to questions which unmask religious morality . . . . The proclamation of love towards all, including the exploiters of the working class . . . . is a hypocritical philosophy. Such teaching conceals and does not recognize the fact that in today's world two hostile classes exist, irreconcileable in their interests; it also disguises the existence of two opposing ideologies – socialist and bourgeois . . . . In schools with older pupils various forms of out-of-school atheist activity should be used: talks, lectures, atheist circles and clubs.

With regard to believing parents who encourage a religious outlook in their children, it is sensible to begin individual work with contacts who inspire trust. It should be explained to them what difficulties parents thus create for their child's development, emphasizing that the contradictory influences exerted by the school and the family turn children into hypo-crites and liars, and that it also leads to emotional disturbance in children (fear of punishment at home, mockery at school).

. . . . In individual work, in order to destroy the religious opinions of parents it is important to have links with unbelieving family members, with the aim of exerting atheist influence through these relations.

. . . . Teachers often say that it is difficult to establish contact with a believing adolescent or to hold a conversation with him: he does not accept atheist proofs and retreats into himself. Here we are talking of a believer's outlook which is prematurely negative. A teacher's main task must be to win him over. This is usually achieved by a variety of means: by attracting the pupil into the system of real relationships, from which he, as a believer, has "escaped" . . . . His membership of the collective must begin with some activity against which he does not have an inner resistance. Activities must be chosen which answer to the inclinations, interests and needs of the pupil . . . .

Believing pupils must be attracted into groups which satisfy their aesthetic needs above all – choral, drama, dance and music groups; they should become members of committees which organize school evenings and exhibitions, and at the same time the teacher should explain to them the link between religious rituals and religious ideology, encouraging the pupils to make a decision about the principles underlying their behaviour.[1]

★   ★   ★

A. Barkauskas, the secretary of the Central Committee of the Lithuanian Communist Party, stated in an article in *Tiesa*.[2]

The goal of the school is to see the facts presented in the learning process become firm beliefs. The duty of each educational collective and each teacher is to educate ardent atheists.

M. Gedvilas, Minister of Education of the Lithuanian SSR, asserts:

Noting the existence of the ideological struggle in the world, we should always search for better ways and means of producing well-rounded and

educated people who are spiritually rich and have a materialistic outlook
on life, Communist beliefs and a strong civic consciousness.[3]

What are the methods used to instill atheist beliefs in the minds of
students?

Students are forced to study atheism. Teachers in all fields, as for
example, physics and astronomy, are compelled to teach atheism. Its
elements are to be found even in mathematics classes. In their guide-
book for teachers entitled *Scientific Atheistic Education in Schools,* A.
Gulbenskiene and V. Petronis state:

> For example, third and fourth year students can be given assignments in
> which they have to calculate the unnecessary expense of maintaining
> churches and paying priests . . . . It is absolutely essential that the
> students be shown how this same money could be used to improve the life
> of the working man.[4]

Each secondary school is required to list an active atheist club
among its extra-curricular activities. Some teachers make it compulsory for Christian students to participate in the activities of such
groups to supplement a small voluntary membership.[5]

★   ★   ★

The *Lithuanian Chronicle* quotes an atheist source:

> Some insist that in the process of the atheist education of students one
> should not use satirical criticism against students who practise their
> religion. The material we have accumulated seems to indicate that this
> assertion cannot be accepted categorically in cases involving religious
> adolescents . . . . An adolescent does not want to be the butt of the
> group's jokes and this phenomenon frequently has more influence on him
> than the urging of his parents that he perform his religious duties.[6]

★   ★   ★

Parents must remember that the children belong to the State more
than to them. "Once the child is born, he's no longer yours," Vaitonis
parroted in an official lecture at Ignalina in March 1974.[7]

★   ★   ★

Father Zdebskis was discrediting what the schools were teaching.
The students cannot assimilate the programmes and doubts arise in
their minds . . . .

[from the prosecutor's speech at his trial][8]

69. RELIGIOUS TEACHERS.

The Reflections of an Old Teacher

[original title]

I studied at secondary school in Tsarist times. The teachers tried to indoctrinate me with their own brand of patriotism and so denigrated Catholicism. With the uncritical mind of youth, I was then receptive to all that they offered. I was fascinated by the positivist ideas then fashionable – that only that which is tangible and physical is real.

I left secondary school as a confirmed materialist and, naturally, an atheist . . . . The various twists and turns of life with the trials they brought subsequently made me review my ideological outlook . . . . God then appeared to me to be the only sensible answer to the problem of life and I said farewell to atheism. This step was taken by many of the people of my generation – among them even the great professor of physics, V. Cepinskas . . . .

Today I have one foot in the grave. A ten-year odyssey in the Gulag Archipelago by courtesy of the new "liberators" was an opportunity to come into deeper contact with God. Today it is unspeakably painful to me that I devoted my best and most fruitful years to conflict with Him . . . . Only one thing troubles me – that I will be unable to repair the damage I did in sowing the seed of godlessness in the hearts of my compatriots.[9]

★   ★   ★

In the Soviet School, 1940-70

. . . . Persecution of teachers who were believers began after the second Soviet invasion. In the Rokiškis district alone more than fifty teachers were dismissed. The order from the director of the Education Department would contain the conventional phrase, "Dismissed for religious superstitions".

The persecution produced noble individuals, too.

"You're a good teacher. Renounce your superstitions, stop going to church and I'll asssign you to the best school in the entire district," Chmieliauskas tempted Mrs. Šlepštiene.

"I will not sell my convictions for a mess of pottage. Without religion or the church I would not be a good teacher."

Mrs. Šlepštiene was soon assigned to a small village school . . . .

★   ★   ★

One teacher describes her impressions of the postwar years:

"When they took Teacher X off to Siberia, I was left to work alone.

With the children, we decided to say the Lord's Prayer before school and the 'Hail Mary' after. It was extraordinarily beautiful and no one betrayed us . . . .

"On Sundays we used to go with the village children to church. The school was established in a building belonging to a farmer who had been sent to Siberia.

"I let the village children set up an altar to Mary in the storeroom . . . . However, someone reported us and I was dismissed from my post."

★   ★   ★

. . . . At the end of August 1952 teachers gathered for a regional conference. The speaker addressed himself mainly to the problem of religion, saying that many students went to church. He reminded his listeners that there were still teachers who believed in God. One of the teachers was invited up on the stage. A deathly silence came over the auditorium, which held 300 teachers from the district.

The secretary of the Komsomol demanded, "Well, now, do you believe in God?"

"Yes, I believe," the teacher replied.

"Leave the conference and pick up your papers at the Education Department. We have no need of such teachers."

The teacher was discharged, even though she had performed her duties conscientiously.[10]

★   ★   ★

Aldona Matusevičiute was a teacher at Vilnius Kindergarten No. 81. On 27 September 1973 the Education Department charged her with being a nun and forced her to sign a statement that she was "voluntarily" resigning her position. On 13 October Miss Matusevičiute was dismissed from her position.[11]

★   ★   ★

[In 1970 Mrs. O. Briliene appealed against her dismissal from teaching.]

The judicial cross-examination began.

"You are a believer and you openly go to church?"

"Yes, I am a believer. I do go openly to church. I have had enough of secrecy. I hid this for 21 years, but now that my religious beliefs have been made public I see no reason to dissemble any further."

"What did you say to the children during the final lesson?"

"I told them that I would not be teaching them any more, and that I had been dismissed from employment for believing in God."

Mrs. Briliene turned to the court and asked:

"If the Education Department had the right to dismiss me because of my beliefs, have I not the right to say why I have been dismissed after twenty-one years of work? Was it for drunkenness?"

"Did you say anything else to the children?"

"I said that a person must have firm beliefs, that it's better to die standing than to live crawling . . . ."

At this point another man intervened:

"Even though I am not a believer, I say this teacher has been dismissed unjustly. It is an infringement of the law. Soviet law guarantees freedom of conscience, but what sort of freedom is it when they had a long consultation and then threw her out of her job because of her religious beliefs?" . . . .

At this juncture the judges returned from their deliberations and read out their verdict to the effect that the teacher was to be reinstated in her work. Incensed, the Prosecutor declared:

"I will not allow this!"

The head of the Education Department said despondently:

"All the atheist work will now collapse . . . ."

After the ruling of the Supreme Court reinstating Briliene, the Prosecutor's office in Vilkaviškis invited the pupils' parents who had written a complaint in October to come and sign a statement to the effect that Mrs. Briliene had been reinstated in her work . . . .

Nevertheless, she did not return to her work. When she arrived at the school with the bailiff, the head of the Education Department barked angrily:

"I won't accept you. Come back at 3 p.m."

Obviously the matter had to be discussed with someone. After lunch Šačkus signed the decree and told Briliene to go to the school . . . .

At the school the situation was unbearable. The teachers would not greet or talk to her. Every day the headmaster informed her:

"There won't be any lessons for you today. You're free to go!"

It is certain that the headmaster was not acting on his own initiative in keeping her away from lessons. Someone was afraid that a Christian teacher would "corrupt" Soviet pupils.

In December there was a local trade union committee meeting at which Mrs. Briliene's case was again discussed. The secretary of the teacher's party organization, Mrs. Urboniene, spoke with particular venom. In conclusion, all voted in favour of dismissing Mrs. Briliene and this was done on 23 December.[12]

★   ★   ★

The headmaster of the eight-year school, Vaičiulenas, dismissed the school cook, Mrs. Petrikoniene, because she had helped to decorate the altar of the Smilgiai Church (Biržai District).[13]

★   ★   ★

More than once teachers known to be believers have been assigned to lead atheist groups in school. Thus it is felt that they can be forced to speak and act against their inner convictions. Not wishing to lose their position or even to put up with unpleasantness, educated people sometimes give in and become auxiliaries of the atheists. It is impossible even to approximate how many teachers, terrorized by the atheists, have spoken against their faith, how many students they have recruited for atheist organizations . . . . It is no accident that one often hears in Lithuania that it is the teachers who have contributed most towards making the nation godless and, by the same token, to its assimilation.[14]

70. ATHEIST TEACHERS

On 25 May 1973 the little second-year children [eight-year-olds] were told to sketch caricatures making fun of religion. Many did so, failing to understand that this was wrong, but others were scandalized at such behaviour on the part of the teachers. One girl said, "It was so terrible that I couldn't look. I asked for permission to go to the lavatory and stayed there for half an hour, so that I shouldn't have to do the sketch."[15]

On 23 December 1974 girls in the dormitory of the secondary school in Šilale decorated their room. The teacher, Mrs. Auškalniene, tore everything down, called the girls monsters and banned them from the party around the new-year tree as a punishment. The essence of their crime was the use of Christmas motifs in the decoration of their room.[16]

At the secondary school in Šilale the teacher, Mrs. Šerpitiene, has organized an atheist circle and tries to bring up her pupils as unbelievers.

The form-mistress of the second class, Mrs. Račkauskiene, once cried out in front of the whole class: "If God exists, let him cut my tongue out!"[17]

★   ★   ★

In 1970 a teacher at the primary school at Šilute, Mrs. Arlauskiene, spent a long time demonstrating to the sixth year [thirteen-year-olds] that there was no God and that only the ignorant believed in Him.

"Let's all shout together three times, 'There's no God!' urged the teacher. However, the only one to shout was Mrs. Arlauskiene, with a few hesitant little voices chiming in.

One seventh-year pupil says that at the time he knew nothing about God, since his father was a strict atheist. However, the boy went on: "But now that I've found out about religious truths, I would boldly cry out, 'Miss, you're mistaken – there is a God' ".[18]

71. COMMUNIST YOUTH ORGANIZATIONS

Soviet press admits Komsomol church-going

A number of students from the school of Valkininkai attended church and participated in religious ceremonies this summer. Some went so far as to assist the priest at ceremonies; among these were members of the Pioneers and the Komsomol. Even the most active members of these organizations at Valkininkai have become so complacent that "they saw nothing wrong with such activities." Others, alas, began asserting their "belief in God" and their determination to continue going to church. Most painful is the fact that the ranks of these "others" included a number of Pioneers and Komsomol members.[19]

★   ★   ★

Pressure on parents

Terrorized by the atheists, uninformed Catholic parents often undermine religion. When a child is in doubt whether or not to join the Komsomol, Christian parents often advise him or her to join, fearing that otherwise the child might be harassed.

There are parents who, from fear of reprisal or just from indolence, are afraid to stand up for their children, when the latter are pressurized to act against their beliefs. On the other hand, there are very determined parents who speak out: "Don't terrorize my child, or I'll be forced to keep him home from school."[20]

"If you allow your son to go to church and serve at Mass, you'll be deprived of your mother's rights."

"I do not and will not forbid my son to go to church," replied Mrs. Kleiniene. "Since my son started to serve at Mass he has become a better boy, more obedient and more hard-working at lessons. Take away parental rights from those whose children are being brought up badly. What about the hooligans who recently shattered our school windows, vandalized the medical room and broke the benches? Have parental rights been taken away from the parents of those children?

My son commits no offences. Why, then, do you want to deprive me of parental rights?"

"This is none of my business," said the inspector. "I received my orders to warn you and I've done my duty."[21]

★   ★   ★

On November 28, 1973, Juozas Šileikis and his son Leonas were summoned to a meeting of the Šiauliai City Committee for the Employment of Juveniles, where about twenty-five persons from various agencies were in attendance.

The members of the committee asked about the leaflets which Leonas had distributed, and about church attendances. Some members of the committee said that such a father ought to have his rights of parenthood taken away, since he contributed to the delinquency of his son. The committee decided to expel Leonas from school, but later satisfied itself with fining the father thirty roubles. Sileikis told the committee, "If going to church is forbidden, then you should write on the church door that entry is strictly forbidden" . . . . Teacher Misiuniene explained to Šileikis the damage religion does to children.

"It is not true that religion is harmful," retorted Šileikis. "Today religion is trodden underfoot, and the pupils do not respect their teachers; they smoke, drink, and even fornicate: those are the fruits of atheism."

"Nowadays very few people go to church, so one must go along with the majority," explained teacher Jakimciene.

"Only a dead body is carried along by the current, but a live person can always swim against the stream."

"You will block the road to higher studies for your children by your beliefs," teacher Misiuniene tried to convince him.

"It is not I who will block the road, but you, the atheists. Why, in the long run, is education necessary, if one must renounce the most valuable thing, one's faith? You, honourable teachers, should be punished according to Soviet law for persecuting the child for his religion."

"We will make your child an atheist yet!" exclaimed Misiuniene.

"As much as I have been in your sessions, I have become convinced that you are more concerned about making the child a hypocrite than an atheist, since you have more than once emphasized, 'Believe as much as you want, but in our presence, renounce God'."[22]

★   ★   ★

Pupils join through indifference

Many students who join the Pioneers or the Komsomol no longer see this as a definite evil. Growing up in an atmosphere heavy with lies and insincerity such as developed in post-war Lithuania, students are unable to understand fully the harm in hypocrisy and lack of principle. Many students who are forced to take lessons in atheism and write atheist essays fail to see the harm in this. Their disorientation in the area of faith and morals and the severe coercion to which they are subject are the true reasons why students demonstrate great offensiveness towards religion and fall into inexcusable errors.

Special responsibility for such mistakes and lapses by students must lie on the conscience of their parents. Some of these neglect their own religious life; others fail to defend their children when young people are pressurized in matters of faith. A third category mistakenly advise the children, "Join the Komsomol – but just remember not to renounce God in your heart".[23]

★   ★   ★

Forced enrolment

Christian students are forcibly enrolled as members of the atheist Pioneer and Komsomol organizations.

New pupils are signed up as Little Octobrists or Pioneers without their own or their parents' consent. The children are simply told to buy the insignia – red neckerchiefs and stars. A number of teachers buy the emblems themselves and then tell the children to bring in the money for them.

After forcibly enrolling them in the Pioneers, teachers instruct their children not to be hypocrites and to stop going to church, since a true Pioneer is always an atheist. The teachers do not usually coerce the children on their own initiative, but under pressure from the Ministry of Education. In many Lithuanian schools the Pioneers' red neckerchief is unpopular and children avoid wearing it.[24]

★   ★   ★

Mrs. Kuneikiene, teacher of the seventh class [fourteen-year-olds] at Gargždai Secondary School No. 2 selected pupils for an atheist group at a class meeting in spring 1975. She asked those who went to church to stand up. At first half the class stood up. The teacher looked angrily at the pupils who went to church and then addressed those still seated. As soon as the teacher mentioned a pupil's name and wished to enrol him in the atheist group, the pupil stood up and said: "I also

go to church and I'm not suitable for the atheists". Finally the whole
class of 32 pupils unanimously declared that they went to church and
would not enrol in an atheist group. The teacher became furious and
began to scold them all. In the end Mrs. Kuneikiene selected four
pupils and forcibly enrolled them in the atheist group.[25]

★   ★   ★

Refusal to join

According to a Soviet book, "the religious belief of the parents and
of children themselves stands as the main, if not the sole reason, for
the latter's reluctance to join the Pioneers. On occasions when a child
refuses to join, we may presume that it is the child of a religious family
who itself has a religious inclination."[26]

★   ★   ★

"Join the Komsomol or we'll expel you from school for good." The
girls were suspended for a week "to think it over". They had the sympathy of their schoolmates and even the faces of some teachers
showed compassion. When a week had gone by, the approach
changed; district Party representatives carried on with the threats. "If
you don't join the Komsomol we'll put your parents out of work, we
won't let you take the examinations, we won't give you your report,"
shouted the government officials. The girls stood all day in the staff
room, but would not fill out the application. In protest against such
unfairness, the entire class went to church together at Easter . . . .
The headmistress, unable to control her anger, ran from the staff-
room, while both girls went off to May day devotions. They had with-
stood the pressure.[27]

★   ★   ★

In 1972 large numbers of non-members [of the Komsomol] went on
to college education. It seems that the goal of 100 per cent student
membership will with time become harder to achieve . . . . Young
Catholics in Lithuania realize increasingly that membership of the
Komsomol is a great mistake.[28]

★   ★   ★

Komsomol undermines morality

Soon the fruits of the new education became obvious. On the night
of 7 January 1975 three of teacher Račkauskiene's pupils, Komsomol

members Karžinauskas, Belitsa and Moroz, stole a car in the town of Taurage. When they tried to make off with a fire-engine in Laukuva, they were stopped by a guard and a policeman. Karžinauskas severely wounded the policeman with a knife. The offenders are soon to be tried. In the opinion of residents in the town of Šilale, their teachers should be tried together with them, as they have destroyed the good seed that their parents had sown in them.[29]

72. DISCRIMINATION AGAINST RELIGIOUS CHILDREN

Teachers and the KGB

On 14 April 1974 at Easter detectives visited all the churches in the Moletai District to observe which schoolchildren went to church. The teachers, on being informed which pupils were involved, began to visit their homes and to browbeat the parents because their children were going to church.[30]

★   ★   ★

Questionnaires

On 19 October 1973 a survey was distributed to fifteen-year-olds of the secondary school at Kuršenai, with the following questions:

1. Are your parents religious?
2. Do your parents make you take part in religious rites?
3. Do you take part in religious rites, go to church, pray, observe obligations on holy days?
4. Do you still sometimes think that our lives may be ruled by supernatural forces?
5. Do you consider yourself as believing or not believing in religious dogmas?
6. Are you convinced that religious superstitions are harmful, that the work of enlightenment must go on and that an atheist outlook should be fostered in people?
7. Have you had occasion to explain how religion contradicts science? How did it go? Do you have the necessary information?
8. Have you read any scientific atheist literature and how much of it can you remember?
9. Do you think that religious superstition will disappear of itself, so that no one will be interested in it any longer?[31]

The faithful are deeply annoyed at these "sociological" investigations, which are simply heavy-handed interference in matters of conscience. Many are of the opinion that only the first question should be answered – "Do you believe in God?" – and not any of the others, since the purpose of these surveys is to find out who influences the children, who teaches them, who gives them religious books to read, and so on. Some of the answers could be out-and-out betrayal, which the atheists would use in their war against religion.[32]

★   ★   ★

[The following is the text of a letter sent by a religious pupil to the Editor of the *Chronicle of the Lithuanian Catholic Church.*]

When I was eleven, the teacher put a lot of pressure on me, from the very start of the school year, to join the Pioneers. All the pupils in the fourth year had to be Pioneers, but I had not joined. The teacher told me that if I did not join this year, then I would have to become a Pioneer next year. As I did not want to join, he threatened to give me low marks and to make life unpleasant for me in various ways. And that was how it turned out, of course. Certain teachers consistently gave me low marks.

My form-master often saw me going to church in the evenings. Once he asked me where I went every evening and I gave him the answer, "to church".

After this the teacher kept telling me every time he met me, "Stop this church-going once and for all!"

In class questionnaires were distributed, containing such questions as:

"Do you go to church? Where did man come from? Did the human race evolve from apes or was it created by God? What makes you go to church? Do you observe religious feast-days? Are the Church's activities good or bad?"

I answered the questions on the form as follows:

"I go to church. Man was created by God. I god to church because I want to. We do observe religious feast-days. The Church does only good."

One day the teacher summoned me and said: "I know that you go to church. All right, go there! But if a commission comes here and asks if you go to church or if you believe in God, say that you don't go and that you don't believe." At home, however, my parents advised me never to deny God.

In class we were always being given essays on atheist themes. This is how my form-master tormented me for my faith throughout the school year.[33]

★   ★   ★

Interrogations

On 14 December 1973 Procurator Venckevičius from Vilkaviškis visited the secondary school in Vištytis. A rumour spread among the pupils that he was going to interrogate those who went to church. Trembling with fear, the pupils G. Balčiunas, Rita and Vilma Aleknavičiute, O. Dulskyte, V. Uldinskaite and others went one by one into the headmaster's study, where the Procurator, dressed in uniform, was waiting for them. The children were asked how the rector, Fr. Montvila, had prepared children for First Communion, whether he had given them prayer-books and catechisms, if he had written down their names or noted down how well the children had learnt the catechism, and so on. The Procurator tried to find out which children were acting as servers during the liturgy and if they received any payment for this from the parish priest. They mocked Gintis Balčiunas because he served at the liturgy, although he was a Pioneer. The boy replied that he believed in God and that no one would stop him from going to church or serving at Mass.

G. Saukaitis heard that the Procurator had come to the school and was carrying out an investigation into children who went to church, so he ran away.

The Procurator interrogated the pupils about the church choir: who sang, who taught them, what kind of songs they sang, and so on. The frightened children replied that the parish priest's housekeeper had persuaded them to join the choir; others said it was the priest himself who had done so; still others said they had come by themselves. If any of the pupils kept silent, the teacher went up to them, smacked them on the face or pulled their hair and made them answer.

After the interrogation each child had to sign his statements.[34]

★   ★   ★

Prevented from attending funeral

In September 1973 an eleven-year-old named Andrijauskas at the primary school at Kašučiai died. His parents, devout people, buried their son with a religious ceremony. The headmaster, Povilaitis, forbade pupils to accompany their friend to the cemetery.

"Where the church is, we have no place," stated the headmaster.

When the pupils heard strains of the funeral music, they wept during the entire period, but they were not allowed to leave the class.[35]

★   ★   ★

Forced to organize atheist lesson

[An official Soviet statement reads:]

"We shall touch on some methods used to draw the students into atheist activity. Among these is a public address which the religious student delivers in defence of an atheist subject . . . . It is most important that the student should be urged to accept an atheist opinion. Now his action must suit his words, otherwise his classmates would consider him a hypocrite, a charge to which a young person is usually very sensitive."[36]

★   ★   ★

Mocked by school newspaper

During the Easter procession in 1973 in the parish of Kuktiškes, girls scattered flowers. Meškauskas, the head of the eight-year school at Kuktiškes, reprimanded the girls for his "misbehaviour". Caricatures of some pupils appeared on the wall-newspaper of the school.[37]

★   ★   ★

Insults

Mr. Šerkšnys, headmaster of the secondary school at Baisogala, and Miss Šidlauskaite, the senior form-mistress, berated and insulted the eighteen-year-olds, Regina Jagelaite and Vanda Aleksandra-vičiute, simply because they had been flower-girls in an Easter procession.

The teacher tried to shame them before the entire class. When the girls stated that their mothers had told them to go to church, Miss Šidlauskaite exclaimed, "Perhaps your mothers will also tell you to go to bed with the priest!" Even though the girls had a perfect attendance record and were good pupils, their conduct marks were lowered for the flower-strewing incident and the following entry was made in their records:

"Even though the girls were members of the Komsomol, their atheistic outlook has not been developed, since in the top class they have still been going to church."[38]

★   ★   ★

Confiscation of personal property

Teachers frequently confiscate crucifixes and religious medals worn by believing students. Mrs. Rimkiene, the headmistress of Kaunas Secondary School No. 2, is an example of an administrator well versed in such activities. After tearing a religious medal from around the neck of a student in January 1973 she declared, "I've got a drawer full of such trinkets."[39]

★   ★   ★

District Chairman Kmieliauskas ordered members of the orchestra to turn in their instruments – apparently they had dared to play in church at Easter.[40]

★   ★   ★

Physical violence

During class the headmaster [Povilaitis at Kašučiai] would seize upon some pupil and demand, "Are you going to join the Komsomol?" If the pupil refused, the headmaster would seize his or her hand and strike it against the bench. He sometimes made their knuckles bleed.[41]

★   ★   ★

During the 1973-4 school year, Leonas's teacher, Mrs. Valera-vičiene, another atheist, began to "educate" him. She ridiculed him in front of the class for going to church with his mother. Upon his return home from school the boy frequently complained that he had been pushed around and beaten up by his classmates . . . .

On 5 October Leonas returned home from school after taking a beating. He was pale and complained of a headache. His mother called an ambulance which took him to hospital. The doctor called the police and informed them of what had occurred at the school. Though the youths responsible for the beating-up were taken to the juvenile police station, they went unpunished.

Leonas stayed home from school until 15 October and was unable to resume physical education classes until December.[42]

★   ★   ★

School reports

Frequently students who attend church find their marks lowered, particularly for conduct. Aurelia Račinskaite of Rageliai Secondary School (Rokiškis district) received "fives" [the highest possible mark] in all of her subjects during the second term of 1972, except for conduct, which was marked "satisfactory". A note at the bottom of the report card states: "The conduct mark during the second term has been reduced to 'satisfactory' because she attends church."[43]

★   ★   ★

Impartial investigations

[Thousands of Lithuanian complaints have been unanswered, but we give one of the few examples of a positive outcome.]

On 9 March [1972] a commission came to Lukšiai from Vilnius to investigate the allegations made in the complaint. The members of the commission said they were from the Ministry of Education. They remained in Lukšiai for three days; children, parents, teachers and others were questioned.

They asked a seven-year-old, J. Naujokaitis, "Did the teacher reprimand you severely for serving at Mass?"

"Yes, she did."

"Did the teacher frighten you by telling you to take your trousers off?"

"Yes, she did," confirmed the boy.

The members of the commission stated that the teacher did not have the right to do that and that religious freedom was permitted; those who want to go to church do and those who do not stay away. They told Vitas Pavalkis, "If you like, you may go to church and serve at Mass; no one will punish you for that and no one will suspend you from school." The boy returned from school happy now that no one would mock him . . . .

It would be a cause for joy if all complaints were handled in this manner; but alas, it was the only example of its kind over several years.[44]

73. CHILDREN HOLD ON TO THE FAITH

The fact that the atheist clubs in most Lithuanian schools are on the wane or are alive only to the extent that such activity is "required" serves to prove that atheism is unpopular among Lithuanian students.[45]

★   ★   ★

The battle for the inculcation of an atheist outlook upon students is constantly intensifying, which indicates that the majority of them believe in God.[46]

★   ★   ★

In May 1973 at a Middle School in Panevežys, sixth-year pupils [thirteen-year-olds] were asked to answer questions such as "Why do men exist on earth?" Many pupils replied in the words of the catechism. On reading the answers, the teacher made the children responsible leave the classroom. In response to another question, "What name would you give to a new Pioneer's group?" some children answered, "St. John, since he was the best man in the world."[47]

In September 1974 the Pioneer leader at the secondary school in Kartena asked the fourteen-year-old Pioneers, "Stand up all those who believe in God and go to church." The whole class stood up, except for three children.[48]

When other Pioneers attempted to knot a Pioneer neckerchief around the girl's neck, the child would not give in, saying, "I'm the mistress of my own neck."[49]

At a secondary school in Klaipeda a history teacher, Miss Keturakaite, claimed to her pupils that Christ did not exist and that this was just a story thought up by someone.

One pupil remarked, "Miss, there are many stories, but no one counts the years from them, but only from Christ." The class burst out laughing and the teacher was glad to be saved by the bell.[50]

[The Soviet press admits the continuation of the faith among the young:]

During the summer the effect of atheist teaching weakens and the church people, religious old women and others who are prone to spread religious superstitions, exploit this situation. Their first glance is directed at the most junior pupils, those at primary schools who are furthest from their influence during the summer. Using sweets and other pleasant temptations for the young children, the religionists try to ensnare them in the spider's web of religious superstition. This is often done without the knowledge or approval of their parents and guardians . . . . We are disturbed when young and delicate hearts are injured, when infants are taught hypocrisy, when their minds are enmeshed in veils of darkness . . . .

During the summer holidays, therefore, every form teacher, everyone in education – especially primary school teachers in the village –

must maintain close contacts with the parents and take scrupulous care that not a single child falls into the toils of the church people . . . . Atheist education conducted throughout the school terms must not be broken off in the summer.[51]

74.   TEACHING RELIGION TO YOUNG PEOPLE

The law and its application

[A legal commentary states:]

"In those cases where the participation of juveniles takes the form of camouflaged religious teaching (such as the systematic singing of psalms and hymns by children during services, holding group discussions with children on religious subjects, and organizing activities with children while preparing them for confirmation) the offenders are subject to criminal liability in accordance with Paragraph 143 of the Penal Code of the Lithuanian Republic."

Signed: Kuroyedov, Chairman of the Council for Religious Affairs.[52]

★   ★   ★

On 13 January 1972 at Naujoji Akmene the People's Court tried the case of seventy-year-old Kleopa Bičiučaite from the village of Žagare. She had violated Soviet law by preparing children for their First Communion. Twenty-seven witnesses, most of them children between seven and fourteen, were called together to prove her guilt. Because Miss Bičiučaite pleaded guilty to teaching prayers to children over a period of six days in July 1971, these witnesses were not necessary – they only upset the plan for the trial by giving testimony very favourable to the defendant. Seeing that the children were contradicting what others had stated, the judge began to investigate the children's political awareness. He asked how many of them belonged to the Pioneers. Only four said they did.

The prosecutor noted . . . . that the defendant had taught children the following in an organized manner: the Lord's Prayer, Hail Mary, the Creed, the Angelus and the Ten Commandments. The Soviet regime could not permit this. It could not allow a system of teaching which was different from that which prevailed at school . . . .

In her final statement to the court Miss Bičiučaite said that she had been asked by the parents to teach the children; those who could not teach their own children should be permitted to ask another person for help. She gave such help to parents. Besides, she taught the children good things: not to steal or lie, and to obey their parents.

The court announced its decision: Miss Bičiučaite was sentenced to one year's imprisonment.[53]

Four days later the defendant was transferred from Akmene to Šiauliai prison. The Supreme Court of the Lithuanian Republic reduced the sentence to a fine of one hundred roubles. Miss Bičiučaite spent a month in Šiauliai prison and returned home on 17 February. Kleopa Bičiučaite had previously been sentenced for teaching religion to children. She had been dismissed from her job at a kindergarten and was given no other work. Her brother supported her.

★   ★   ★

In June 1973 in the villge of Vingininkai an old lady, Miss Eidukaite (born 1887), was teaching catechism to sixteen children at their parents' request. Suddenly there burst into the room Mikučis, chairman of the *kolkhoz,* Martinkus, an agricultural expert, Brigadier Vidmantas and several other local officials. They snatched catechisms, prayer books and rosaries from the children's hands. The children hid the catechisms and ran weeping from the room. The intruders searched them and took away everything. They wrote down the names of the children and their mothers . . . . The prosecutor interrogated the old lady several times and threatened her with imprisonment.

"To go to prison for a crime is shameful," retorted the old lady, "but for saying the Lord's Prayer I'm not afraid."

They interrogated the children and their mothers. Some of the children were so disturbed that they could not sleep that night.[55]

★   ★   ★

Harmful influence on youth

On 3 December 1971 Fr. Petras Orlickas, parish priest at Margininkai, was sentenced because he had violated Paragraph 143 of the Lithuanian Penal Code – he had played volley-ball with a group of children! . . . .

Atheists and party officials acted for a long time as though they could not see the children who played insolently and swore at each other in the yard of the *kolkhoz* office. But the priest did see it and set up a volley-ball court. Now even the worst trouble-makers stopped swearing.

What caused the Kaunas party officials and some teachers to become alarmed? It was noticed that during the funeral of a student there were many young people in church . . . . Fr. Orlickas was charged with harmfully influencing Soviet youth and was fined fifty roubles. When the priest explained that even his doctor advised him to participate in the sports, the chairman of the commission, S. Jančiauskas, answered: "You can play with the housekeeper" . . . .

As expected, Fr. Orlickas was immediately removed from the parish.[56]

★   ★   ★

Karsakiškis . . . . For three years the authorities have been trying to force the parish priest to move out of this tiny house somewhere into the country. The main reason was that he lived too close to the school.[57]

75. CONFIRMATION AND FIRST COMMUNION

Undoubtedly a very negative effect resulted from a letter which Dr. J. Stankevičius, Administrator of the dioceses of Kaunas and Vilkaviškis, wrote under pressure on 31 May 1961:

> "According to a directive from Rugienis . . . . young men and women may participate publicly in services of worship when they have attained the age of eighteen. Younger children may not serve at Mass, nor sing in the choir and carry banners, nor scatter flowers in procession; children may be present at the liturgy only in the company of their parents."[58]

After this decree some priests began to excuse themselves more readily, although recently children have begun to take an active part in religious services in many parishes – and it is very difficult for Rugienis to fight this development.[59]

★   ★   ★

Government officials decide where and how many times a year the sacrament of confirmation may be conferred.[60]

★   ★   ★

In the summer of 1972 some relaxation of tension was evident. Children preparing for First Communion were harrassed in only one or two places . . . . A few priests were given administrative sentences for not turning children away from the altar.[61]

★   ★   ★

In spite of the obstacles, about 7,000 people gathered at Ratnyčia. Approximately 2,700 children and young people received the Sacrament of Confirmation [1973].[62]

★　　　★　　　★

"In 1972, 20,000 children made their First Communion, though more than a quarter of a million were in their first four years at school," (P. Mišutis, "The Church and Religious Adherence Today").[63] In this instance Mišutis has lied. For the 1972-3 school year about 57,000 children were registered in the first four years (see *Lietuvos TSR gyventojai* ["The Population of the Lithuanian SSR"] V, 1973, p. 175) – much less than a quarter of a million.

It is also a fact that in each year only children in a single age bracket are prepared for their First Communion. Twelve per cent of the children living in Lithuania are non-Catholic: Russians, Jews, Latvians and others. About 50,000 children should be prepared for their First Communion each year, and in fact the Sacrament is conferred on at least 44,000 annually. The figure of 20,000 which Mišutis gives is absolutely incorrect, since it was calculated before 1973 when the Government first began to require priests to present statistics on children preparing for their First Communion.

Government statistics, however, will be incorrect in the future too, since some priests do not hand over the figures on the religious instruction of children, while others, "hoping to ease the atheists' heartaches", present the kind of figures the atheist government desires.[64]

★　　　★　　　★

On 22-3 July [1972] the Sacrament of Confirmation was administered at Kalvarija. The authorities of the Kapsukas district ordered the priest to take down the outside loudspeakers for the occasion. There was no sermon on 22 July, "so as not to anger the authorities". About 4,000 children received the Sacrament of Confirmation.[65]

★　　　★　　　★

Large numbers of children are prepared to receive First Communion each year. In Anykščiai, for example, approximately 150 children are prepared for the Sacrament annually; in Svenčionys, 200; in Prienai, 300; and in Marijampole, 500. Between 100 and 120 children per annum are prepared in larger parishes and between 15 and 30 in smaller ones.[66]

★　　　★　　　★

In 1974 thousands of children and young people received the Sacrament of Confirmation in Lithuania. Here we give some statistics to demonstrate that religious life continues to be active, despite all the efforts of the atheists.

At Dotnuva 1,526 children were confirmed; at Tituvenai 2,456; at Prienai 2,702; at Šilale 5,100; at Alanta 2,000; at Griškabudis 1,200; at Obeliai 2,860. [Total: 17,844].[67]

1,400 schoolchildren received the Sacrament of Confirmation at Akmene in 1975.[68]

★   ★   ★

Bezusparis, the investigator of Zarasai district procurator's office, and Police Lieutenant Bagdonavičius came to the Aviliai Eight-Year School during classes on 17 December 1971.

In the teachers' room the following students were interrogated one by one because they were prepared for the reception of First Communion during the summer of 1971: Bakutis, Razmanavičiute, and the two Jezerskaite sisters. The students were asked: did the priest teach you? How long did he teach? What did he teach? Did the priest give you a catechism? Did he give you a prayer book? What did the priest talk about?

The children were questioned about an hour each; before they were released they had to sign a document which had already been drawn up. When he returned to class, Bakutis cried throughout the entire lesson.

Other children were taken into the physics office, where the investigator had written on the board "To the Procurator of Zarasai district". The children had to write down how many times they had seen the priest, who taught them religion and how they were taught it. Then they had to sign these statements. The investigator took away with him the statements and eighteen children. The children were shaken by the interrogation and some of them were still crying when they got home. Finding her daughter in tears, Mrs. Pupeikiene went to the headmaster to express her dissatisfaction with the questioning of the children, unknown to their parents, regarding the reception of First Communion. The next day, Mrs. Mažeikiene went to see the headmaster, complaining that her son woke up at night because of his fear.

On 20 December the women went to the Procurator's office at Zarasai to make their protest. They demanded that children should not be questioned without the parents' being present, since the children would write anything the investigator told them to out of fear, and they presented the Procurator with a written protest. Later the Procurator and the investigator questioned all of them.

At the very time that the women were being questioned in the Procurator's office, the children, who were being guarded by the teachers, were again being questioned about their First Communion. Several of the mothers whose children did not return home after lessons hurried back to school. Forcing their way into the office, they found their children being interrogated. The police officer and one teacher were still in the room. A hidden tape recorder was under the table. Complaining that their children were being questioned without the mothers' being present and that they had not been fed all day, the mothers took their children home. At that point, the children who had not been questioned were also released. As the workers of the Procurator's office were leaving, they promised to return . . . .

The parents met the headmaster and sharply criticized him for permitting their children to be interrogated and so frightened that they could not sleep at nights and trembled when they saw any kind of a car: it might be the interrogator again!

It is shameful that eight- to ten-year-old children are interrogated as if they were thieves or hooligans for receiving First Communion.[69]

76. PARENTS AND TEACHERS

The *Chronicle of the Lithuanian Catholic Church* contains dozens of texts of and references to petitions by parents concerning the atheist education of their children.[70] We include just one, more individualistic than the others, which encapsulates all the philosophical, moral and emotional problems which the atheist regime has forced on Lithuanian families.

A letter to a teacher

[original title]

Dear Teacher of My Child,

We are both offspring of the same Lithuanian nation; we are both bound not only by blood, language and cultural inheritance, but also by our common concern for the future of our nation, which lies with our children. We both look to them with hope, concern and love. I look after my children; you look after yours, mine and many others who gather every day in your classroom. The future of our nation depends on what we give these children, how we prepare them for life and what kind of people we make out of them. Hence a great responsibility for their future rests on our shoulders.

Since I deeply feel my great responsibility and am well aware of a parent's duties, I try to instil into my children from their early days such principles as would help them to remain honest, decent and strong-minded human beings. I received these principles from my own parents. I have verified and confirmed them through the experiences of a life-time, I have mulled them over and reasoned them out in my own mind and decided to make them my own in accordance with my conscience, which obliges me to transmit to my children whatever I consider good and necessary.

Furthermore, I also have the right to do so. We parents brought these children into the world, we bring them up, clothe them, feed them and nurse them when they are ill. No one forbids me to dress my children this or that way, no one interferes with my feeding them the food which in my judgement is necessary for them. Hence no one has the right to prevent me from handing on to my children those ideals and moral principles which I am convinced are the most necessary for humanity. I know that it is not right to lie, steal, cheat or kill and I try to instil this into my children, too. I know that it is good to act decently, to be honest, to love one's neighbour; and I want to make my children understand this. I also know that if one wishes to remain an honest human being one must wage a constant fight against one's own weaknesses and vices and against external temptations. I am preparing my children for this struggle. From my experience of life I am convinced that such a struggle is most successful when a man feels responsible not only in the eyes of human beings, but also in the sight of God; when he is convinced that his actions and deeds have not only a temporary, transient value, but also an eternal worth; when he obeys not only the law, but also the voice of his conscience. Hence I consider it an essential duty to bring up my children in a religious way and I do not want anyone to interfere with this duty of mine. Moreover, you as a teacher agree that parents have a duty to bring up their children . . . .

I am not on my own in bringing up my children. I send them from my home to school. There I turn them over to you to be educated. However, I want you to carry on my work, not to destroy it. I want you to equip my child's mind with scientific information and to teach him to make use of this in his life. That, in my opinion, should be the task of a school. However, it pains me greatly when, instead of building, you begin to wreck what I have begun. Instead of teaching scientific knowledge and its principles objectively, you begin to denigrate my convictions and those of my child. You call my beliefs religious superstitions, my education compulsion, while considering the atheism you foist on my child by force to be a free and normal thing.

If you do not respect my convictions, leave them alone, just as I do not attack or insult yours. Teach my child to read and write; explain to him the rules of mathematics and the principles of physics; but do not turn these things into attacks on the principles which my child and I respect. I do not fear objective facts of science, but I do not want you to present them in a warped and tendentious manner, with the sole aim of inculcating an alien outlook upon my child. When you attack my beliefs and those of my child, you not only use class material which has been deliberately distorted, but even in extra-curricular activities you try to find ways of rooting out of my child's mind what I have sown there. Disregarding my wishes, you force him to join the Pioneers, the Komsomol and atheist groups. You make fun of his beliefs in the wall-newspaper, on bulletin boards, at atheist evenings and lectures. You compel him to answer various questionnaires and force your way into his conscience. And if my child were weaker or if I were unable to strengthen him in every possible way, you would cripple him morally and teach him to be hypocritical and to mistrust either his parents or his teachers – most likely both.

Will my child then not begin to look elsewhere, will he not start to deceive both you and me, will he not begin to seek questionable entertainment, shallow pleasures, will he not take a direction which neither you nor I want him to follow? Will higher ideals be important to him? Will he be concerned with the future of his nation? With the people's good? Perhaps he will become a common egoist, without higher goals, without higher ideals, concerned only with personal pleasures? Will such a youngster give much satisfaction to you or to me? Will he be useful to the nation and to other people? Our nation is not large, so every one of its members is valuable and important. So much the more should each young person, each opening bud of the nation be whole and fair! Yes, dear teacher, our children are our future, the future of our nation, and we must consider seriously how we are going to treat this future. True, you try to justify yourself, saying that you are told to act in this way, that you are carrying out someone else's directives. Perhaps you do not want this yourself and would not act so, if it were left to you. I firmly believe that. Nevertheless, remember that my child belongs to me and not to those who have ordered you to educate him in a way contrary to my own. Remember your great responsibility to your nation. Its future, its vital demands ought to influence you, too. Would you not be afraid to stand trial before your nation? Would you be able to answer with a clear conscience that you have never exchanged those things most sacred to the individual and to the nation for the sake of a higher salary and peace of mind?

Finally, on the question of money: the salary which you receive for your work was earned by me and the parents of other pupils. However, you are unwilling to listen to the wishes of the parents regarding the way in which their children should be educated.

I do not wish to tell you how to do your work. That is your affair as a teacher. Certainly it is not easy to work with young people. To educate a child or young adult, to shape his character, is truly a great responsibility and a difficult task. Therefore there should be no place or time in such work for destroying what I have already built up. On the contrary, in this matter we must co-operate, reinforcing each other's work and collaborating as closely as possible. This is our common duty: it is required of parents and teachers, this is the duty of the sons of the small Lithuanian nation.[71]

The atheists characterize parents who defend their children's religious rights as fanatics. The real fanatic is the person who cannot tolerate anyone who disagrees with him. Is it not from fanaticism that the present persecution of religious young people stems?[72]

77. UNIVERSITY STUDENTS

The course on atheism at the Medical School of Klaipeda in 1969 was given by B. Juškevičius, a director at the Klaipeda Theatre. To pass his course a student had to answer several ideological questions. The lecturer was particularly shaken by the following answer presented by a female student:

> It has been asserted that the various religions originated from human helplessness and ignorance, but this is not true. The origin of religion is much more sublime . . . Scientists discover various scientific principles. Doesn't this lead man to question that some higher being must have laid down these principles? Man is more than a hunk of meat and a pile of bones: he has an immortal soul. Christ actually lived and the calendar is calculated from the time of his birth . . . Life would be ideal and beautiful, even heaven-like, if all men were true and loyal Catholics. No army, police or prisons would be needed, but now . . . I think the Catholic faith is correct. I have been of that opinion for a long time; the atheism courses have served only to confirm my thinking.[73]

In the 1973 academic year the Museum of Atheism attempted to attract at least some of the uninterested students at the Arts Institute by announcing, with the co-operation of the institute authorities, a competition for artistic works on atheist themes. In spite of the fact that money prizes were promised, the competition had to be widened. Later, when some of the works were exhibited in the Museum of Atheism, it was noted that their atheist content was somewhat obscure.

That students are not interested in the atheist museum is further shown in a speech delivered in Vilnius on 19 October 1972 by V. Kojala, Secretary of the Vilnius Communist Party Committee, at a conference of party activists in higher education in the Lithuanian Republic. Here is an extract from Kojala's speech:

> All higher education institutes stipulate a course in atheism, but how many students have visited the Museum of Atheism, for example, in the first half of this year? One group of 18 people from the university, one group of 9 from the Institute of Construction Engineering, two groups of

31 from the Pedagogical Institute, and no visitors from the Arts Institute. Only the State Conservatory sent three groups of 84 in all. Only 58 people came from all the other institutes of higher education. Such a situation is clearly abnormal . . . .

(from the archives of the Lithuanian Higher Education Conference, 1972, pp. 72-3).

In the same speech Kojala stated, "In the higher education institutes of Vilnius alone there are more than 30,000 students, including external students . . . . There are over 12,000 Komsomol members . . . ."[74]

★   ★   ★

ORDER NO. 20

Rector's Office of the Vilnius State Pedagogical Institute, Vilnius
14 February, 1975

The responsibility of lecturers organising and accompanying student excursions

Recently incidents have been noticed which, in defiance of the elementary rules governing the organization and conduct of student excursions, have had a harmful influence on the ideological education of students and the formation of their Marxist convictions.

Between 29 June and 12 July 1974 a group of fourteen students from the History Department under the leadership of lecturer R. Šaluga was carrying out practical studies in education, archaeology, ethnography and folk-lore in the districts of Joniškis, Akmene and Mažeikiai. While in the Akmene district, this group humiliated itself before the clergy by asking for permission to enter the wooden church at Klikuoliai, as an architectural monument; they listened to the anti-scientific comments of the local rector (Jonas Paliukas, who graduated from Kaunas Seminary in 1969 – Ed. of *CLCC*), and looked at privately-produced films and pictures, mostly on religious themes. It goes without saying that none of this was included in any practical study plan.

Šaluga's services are no longer required by the institute, as he did not justify the trust put in him, and he no longer works there. The group's student leader was relieved of his responsibility. It was necessary to interview the students on this subject.

On 27 October 1974 a group of second-year students from the same department, under the leadership of senior lecturer A. Gaigalaite, went on a one-day educational excursion along the route Pilaite-Kernave-Musninkai-Čiobiškis-Žasliai-Elektrenai-Vievis-Lentvaris. In

Kernave, without the lecturer noticing it, the students went on their own initiative to visit the church, in which an unscientific and unhistorical museum had been installed. When she learned of this, the lecturer immediately led the students out of the church and gave an explanatory talk. However, on her return, she did not inform the head of the department about the incident . . . .

Aldona Gaigalaite, senior lecturer of the Soviet History department, has received a reprimand for failing to inform on the improper behaviour of some students during the excursion . . . .

V. Uogintas,
Rector of Vilnius
State Pedagogical
Institute.[75]

NOTES TO CHAPTER IX

1. *CLCC* 15, pp. 29-32 (L).
2. 26 February 1972.
3. *Tiesa,* 18 August 1972.
4. *Mokslinis ateistinis auklejimas mokykloje* ("Scientific Atheist Education in Schools"), Kaunas, 1959, p. 33; *CLCC* 5, pp. 8-9 (E), p. 6 (L).
5. *CLCC* 5, p. 15 (E), p. 9 (L).
6. B. Bitinas, *Religingi mokiniai ir ju perauklejimas* ("Religious students and their re-education"), Vilnius (?), 1969, p. 122 – quoted in *CLCC* 5, pp. 18-19 (E), pp. 8-9 (L).
7. *CLCC* 11, p. 18 (E), p. 14 (L).
8. *CLCC* 1, p. 8.
9. *CLCC* 17, pp. 33-6.
10. *CLCC* 11, pp. 6-9 (E), pp. 3-5 (L). For a 1958 example, see *CLCC* 10, pp. 43-5 (E), pp. 25-6 (L).
11. *CLCC* 9, pp. 29-30 (E), p. 16 (L). Cf. 10, p. 36 (E), p. 20 (L); 14, pp. 27-28 (E), p. 22 (L).
12. *CLCC* 3, pp. 5-11.
13. *CLCC* 20, p. 30.
14. *CLCC* 4, p. 13 (E), p. 8 (L).
15. *CLCC* 7, pp. 48-9 (E), p. 19 (L).
16. *CLCC* 15, p. 29.
17. *Ibid.,* p. 28.
18. *CLCC* 8, p. 67 (E), p. 26 (L).
19. *Lietuvos Pionierius,* 1971, quoted in *CLCC* 5, pp. 7-8 (E), p. 6 (L).
20. *CLCC* 4, p. 13 (E), p. 8 (L).
21. *CLCC* 18, pp. 32-3.
22. *CLCC* 12, pp. 19-20 (E), pp. 16-17 (L).
23. *CLCC* 5, pp. 23-4 (E), p. 11 (L).

24. *CLCC* 5, pp. 12-13 (E), pp. 7-8 (L); cf. 5, p. 36 (E), p. 11 (L); 7, p. 41 (E), pp. 16-17 (L); 8, p. 50 (E), p. 28 (L); 12, p. 27 (E), pp. 24-5 (L).
25. *CLCC* 21, p. 346.
26. B. Bitinas, *op. cit.,* p. 128, quoted in *CLCC* 5, p. 13 (E), pp. 7-8 (L).
27. *CLCC* 11, pp. 11-12 (E), pp. 7-8 (L); cf. *CLCC* 10, p. 35 (E), p. 20 (L); 11, pp. 12-14 (E), pp. 8-10 (L); 12, p. 26 (E), pp. 16-17 (L).
28. *CLCC* 5, pp. 14-15 (E), p. 8 (L).
29. *CLCC* 15, p. 28.
30. *CLCC* 11, p. 38 (E), p. 32 (L).
31. *CLCC* 8, pp. 47-8 (E), pp. 26-7 (L). For a longer questionnaire, see *CLCC* 6, pp. 43-5 (E), p. 18 (L).
32. *CLCC* 10, pp. 41-2 (E), pp. 23-4 (L).
33. *CLCC* 22, p. 400.
34. *CLCC* 14, pp. 24-25 (E), pp. 19-20 (L).
35. *CLCC* 8, p. 46 (E), pp. 25-6 (L). Cf., among many other examples, *CLCC* 5, pp. 17-18, 35 (E), pp. 9, 14 (L); 11, p. 38 (E), p. 33 (L); 15, p. 28; 17, p. 31.
36. B. Bitinas, *op. cit.,* p. 165, as quoted in *CLCC* 5, pp. 16-17 (E), pp. 8-9 (L).
37. *CLCC* 7, pp. 61-2 (E), p. 24 (L). Cf. *CLCC* 10, p. 43 (E), p. 24 (L).
38. *CLCC* 8, pp. 36-7 (E), p. 20 (L); cf. *ibid.,* pp. 48-9 (E), pp. 27-8 (L).
39. *CLCC* 5, p. 22 (E), pp. 10-11 (L); cf. *CLCC* 7, p. 39 (E), pp. 16-17 (L).
40. *CLCC* 11, p. 29 (E), p. 24 (L).
41. *CLCC* 8, p. 46 (E), p. 26 (L).
42. *CLCC* 9, pp. 32-3 (E), p. 18 (L).
43. *CLCC* 5, p. 22 (E), pp. 10-11 (L); cf. *CLCC* 12, pp. 26-7 (E), p. 24 (L); 17, p. 31.
44. *CLCC* 2, pp. 14-15.
45. *CLCC* 5, p. 16 (E), p. 9 (L); cf. *CLCC* 15, p. 31.
46. *CLCC* 5, p. 8 (E), p. 6 (L).
47. *CLCC* 7, p. 45 (E), p. 18 (L).
48. *CLCC* 14, p. 31 (E), p. 26 (L); cf. *CLCC* 9, p. 10 (E), p. 4 (L).
49. *CLCC* 5, p. 25 (E), p. 11 (L).
50. *CLCC* 10, p. 34 (E), p. 19 (L).
51. *Tarybinis Mokytojas* ("Soviet Teacher"), 30 May 1975, quoted in *CLCC* 17, pp. 36-7.
52. *CLCC* 3, p. 21.
53. *CLCC* 1, p. 24. Cf. the defence of Fr. Zdebskis by the children in the court, (p. 106).
54. *CLCC* 2, p. 19.
55. *CLCC* 7, pp. 46-7 (E), pp. 18-19 (L); cf. *ibid.,* pp. 52-3 (E), p. 21 (L); *CLCC* 6, p. 41 (E), p. 17 (L); 20, pp. 24-5.
56. *CLCC* 1, pp. 20-1.
57. *CLCC* 14, pp. 22-3 (E), p. 18 (L).
58. See similar decrees at the same time for the Russian Orthodox Church (Bourdeaux, *Patriarch and Prophets,* p. 201) and for the Baptists (Bourdeaux, *Religious Ferment in Russia,* p. 20).
59. *CLCC* 4, p. 10 (E), p. 6 (L).
60. *CLCC* 7, p. 20 (E), pp. 9-10 (L).
61. *CLCC* 4, p. 5 (E), p. 3 (L).
62. *CLCC* 7, p. 22 (E), p. 10 (L); cf. *ibid.,* p. 57 (E), p. 22 (L); *CLCC* 14, p. 31 (E), p. 26 (L); 18, p. 26.
63. *CLCC* 9, pp. 8-9, 14 (E), p. 4 (L).
64. *CLCC* 9, pp. 8-9 (E), p. 4 (L).
65. *CLCC* 4, p. 37 (E), p. 22 (L).
66. *CLCC* 5, p. 7 (E), p. 6 (L).

67. *CLCC* 12, pp. 22-3 (E), p. 27 (L).
68. *CLCC* 20, p. 35.
69. *CLCC* 2, pp. 18-19.
70. E.g. *CLCC* 1, pp. 16-17; 2, pp. 9-10; 4, pp. 28-30 (E), pp. 15-17 (L); 7, pp. 25-7 (E), pp. 11-12 (L); 8, pp. 40-4 (E), pp. 22-3 (L).
71. *CLCC* 7, pp. 1-5 (E), pp. 2-4 (L).
72. *CLCC* 5, p. 28 (E), p. 12 (L).
73. *CLCC* 5, p. 26 (E), p. 11 (L).
74. *CLCC* 14, p. 29 (E), pp. 23-4 (L).
75. *CLCC* 16, pp. 33-5.

X

CHRISTIAN PUBLICATIONS

IT WAS in the early 1970's that unofficial Lithuanian publications became known to the outside world. However, Lithuanians have behind them well over a century of experience in producing Christian literature in defiance of Russian government policy, both in the nineteenth century and during the last thirty years.

Before the sixteenth century Lithuanian was hardly ever written, as the official language of the State and Church was Latin; however, from then onwards church schools began to teach in Lithuanian, as well as Latin and Polish. It was in the eighteenth and early nineteenth centuries that Lithuanian literature really began, but just as Lithuanian poetry, history and religious works were starting to spread into print there was an attempt by the Russian Tsarist government to put an end to this national desire for self-expression.

From 1864-1904 there was no proper Lithuanian press at all within the Tsarist empire. The maximum which the Russians permitted under the hated Governor-General, Mikhail Nikolaevich Muravyov, and his slightly more liberal successors, was the printing of some books in a newly-devised Cyrillic script strait-jacketed on to the Lithuanian language, which has always been written in the Latin alphabet.[1] Curiously, Tsarist Russia's unfortunate Lithuanian experience of this colonialist tactic did not dissuade its Communist successors from enforcing the same upon the Turkic languages of Central Asia, even though Lithuania was spared this policy the second time. Stalin is reported to have been in favour of reintroducing a Cyrillic alphabet for Lithuanian, but apparently he abandoned the idea in the face of united support for the Latin alphabet from the Lithuanian Communist Party.

Lithuanian printing survived, with added determination injected into it by the insult, through one of the most massive operations of external printing and clandestine distribution that the world has seen. Exiles in Tilsit (East Prussia) – now Sovetsk in Kaliningrad region – printed 1,442 titles to a total of nearly four million copies for this tiny nation in the years 1864-1904, and those in the U.S.A. added a further 721 titles. Also there was clandestine printing in Lithuania itself, with books bearing a pre-1864 date in order to trick the police.

Bishop Valančius became a key figure in the opposition, particularly in the organization of a nationwide network of colporteurs. He urged Lithuanians to resist russification by rejecting the books printed in the Cyrillic alphabet:

> Even if secretly, teach your children Lithuanian from your old books. They may be expensive, but buy them, give them to your children and tell them to pray from these books to the end of their lives.[2]

The bishop was himself a prolific writer of both secular and religious books for the Lithuanian press in Tilsit; he was seen as not only a religious, but a national leader. He contributed 25,000 roubles to the Tilsit press, out of the 1,384,109 roubles spent on the production of Lithuanian literature there.[3]

In the 1880s and 1890s it became increasingly obvious that the attempt at russification of the Lithuanian language was a complete failure. In 1880 Russian educational establishments were allowed to print a few books in Lithuanian, but this was merely a token gesture by the Tsarist government. In 1903 the Governor-General of Vilnius, Svyatopolk Mirsky, recommended that the Cyrillic alphabet should be abandoned and Lithuanian books printed in the Latin alphabet, as the authorities were quite unable to stop the flow of books from abroad and as the whole policy was merely producing an upsurge of Lithuanian nationalism.[4] After two lawsuits by Lithuanian citizens appealing against the ban on Latin lettering, in which the courts were forced to admit the illegality of the ban, the Tsar finally revoked the imposition of the Cyrillic alphabet in 1904.

The upsurge of Lithuanian publications after this change showed just how much of a failure the previous policy had been. By 1914 no less than twenty-five regular newspapers and journals were being published in Lithuanian and hundreds of books were being printed by the Society of St. Casimir, founded in 1906.

After the 1917 Revolution and the declaration of Lithuanian independence in 1918, Lithuanian became the official language and almost all publications were in Lithuanian.

One of the first acts of the Soviet authorities after their June 1940 occupation was to seize control of that part of the press which they needed and to shut down the rest, which of course included the religious press. A decree of 6 August further expropriated all book-shops from the control of the Church and the Soviets destroyed all the stocks.[5]

The clandestine printing of literature played a role of importance in crystallizing the opposition, both during the first Soviet occupation[6] and the subsequent period of Nazi rule. During the later part of the war underground journals began to appear in a flood, with over a dozen titles.[7] They not only criticized policies of the Nazis, but openly listed their crimes. Catholic organizations played their part in the production and distribution of the underground press. There was even a clandestine radio station, partially supported from the U.S.A.

After the second Soviet occupation it was quite logical that the Partisans should continue the underground press. Although it was more difficult than under the Germans, they continued it until the end of 1951. There were no specifically Christian publications,[8] but the Christian faith was mentioned as part of the national heritage in most of them.

For years it looked as though the Soviet authorities would never permit the printing of a single Christian book in Lithuania, not even a rigidly-controlled official journal, such as is permitted for the Russian Orthodox Church and the Baptists. Even during the period of "the thaw" there was no concession, though the Russian Orthodox Church managed to publish a very small edition of the Bible in 1956.[9]

The first sign of a modification in this policy did not come until 1966, when a Lithuanian prayer-book, written by Mgr. Stankevičius, administrator of Kaunas diocese, was published in three editions of 30,000 each.[10] In 1968 this was followed by a Latin-Lithuanian missal. Both were later re-typed or photocopied as *samizdat*. At the beginning of 1977 a prayer-book, *Always with God,* which had been in preparation for two years, was published in Lithuania. The number of copies produced is not known, although there had been a promise of 60,000. The prayer-books are said to be badly bound and often fall apart when first opened.[11]

There could be no question of an equitable distribution of any of these books and their appearance immediately created a black market, with copies of the prayer-book changing hands for thirty roubles or more (£22.60 or $38 at the 1976 rate of exchange).[12] Often black market copies have appeared months before the official publishing date. The New Testament can be sold for as much as one hundred roubles. Plans for subsequent printings have been delayed and meanwhile the faithful have to make do with such disintegrating pre-war copies as still exist. Certainly the Soviet authorities enforced the export of a large number, as they did of religious books subsequently printed, in an effort to "prove" the freedom of religion in Lithuania.[13]

As late as 1972, years after the Russian Orthodox and the Baptists had received similar concessions, the Lithuanian Catholic Church, in co-operation with Lithuanian Evangelicals, was able to bring out the Scriptures, in an edition of 30,000, though this was limited to the New Testament only. Even then, the Soviet authorities attempted to discredit the translator, Fr. Kavaliauskas, by forcing him to write a series of articles for a Communist newspaper published in the U.S.A. The *Lithuanian Chronicle* stated:

The series cast aspersions on Lithuanian émigrés, active priests, the faithful in Lithuania and the programmes transmitted by Radio Vatican. It also
praised the "beautiful and thriving" living conditions in Lithuania.[14]

20,000 copies of the Lithuanian New Testament, or two-thirds of
the edition, were immediately taken by J. Rugienis and the CRA for
distribution abroad, although plenty of Scriptures in Lithuanian are
already available there. The New Testaments, once sent abroad, could
not be officially sent back to the Soviet Union. However, the text was
reproduced in small format in Mexico and according to some reports
10,000 of these are now back in Lithuania.

The distribution of that portion of the 10,000 copies which was not
exported took place in February 1973. Even the largest parishes
received between ten and twenty copies, while smaller ones had far
fewer – probably an overall average of five per parish[15] or one for
every two hundred believers.[16] The *Chronicle* provides some most
interesting sidelights on the printing and distribution (Document 78).

A further small concession has been the publication of the decrees
of the Second Vatican Council in 1968. Each parish received one copy
only, for the priest. Although the edition was of course very small,
even this was not without its benefit to believers, because the
Chronicle circulated an analysis by a layman, Vitautas Vaičiunas, in
which he quoted various extracts and sharply contrasted them with
the situation in Lithuania, as governed by Soviet law.[17]

More surprising was the publication in 1972 of a two-volume
edition in five thousand copies[18] of the works of Bishop Valančius.*
Not only are his works permeated with religious ideas, but he is, for
Lithuanians, a potent and emotional symbol, for he was in the very
forefront of the campaign to preserve the Lithuanian language under
the Tsars. It was he who instructed his people never to take into their
hand any book printed in the Cyrillic alphabet.[19] In 1973 a small
edition of the psalter was published; *samizdat* editions of this are confiscated during searches.

Soviet policy is to make this restricted activity appear to be religious
freedom. Such is the purpose of the 1971 publication, *Religion in
Lithuania*, by J. Rimaitis. Its appearance in English and Italian is itself
eloquent commentary on its purpose and the *Lithuanian Chronicle*
was not slow to condemn its "mendacity", criticizing particularly
those priests who allowed themselves to be quoted in it.[20] There is
special criticism of Bishop Krikščiunas, who appears to have given the
impression to foreigners that the five religious books so far published
constitute a library.[21]

Naturally, the faithful have been urgent in their petitions for more
titles and larger editions, indeed, for the right implied by the constitutional separation of Church and State to organize the Church's
own printing of her needs. The most basic Catholic book totally un-

*See p. 248.

published since 1940 is the catechism, and present Soviet policies would render a concession on this subject inconceivable. In 1973 no less than 16,498 people appended their signatures to a document addressed to the Soviet authorities asking for this, more Bibles and other books.[22] The *Chronicle* also documents the experiences of a priest when he attempted to acquire a copy of the Scriptures (Document 79).

The suppression of partisan clandestine literature did not end the unbroken tradition. In the 1960's, long before any Lithuanian *samizdat* became available in the West, the Soviet press was complaining about the activities of priests who circulated religious literature in an attempt to retain their hold over the faithful (Document 80). Leaving aside secular *samizdat,* there are four main types of underground writing and publishing activity which concern us here: the circulation of petitions on religious liberty for people to sign before submitting them to the Soviet authorities or sending them abroad; the reproduction of permitted books (such as the prayer-book), of which the Soviets have allowed the printing of an insufficient quantity; the reproduction of other Christian books, copied from pre-war or imported originals; and the production of new Christian literature, including the *Chronicle of the Lithuanian Catholic Church.* In practice, it is impossible to consider these separately because the same people are involved in producing and circulating them and the KGB unquestionably intends to stamp out the whole activity.[23] Recent technical improvements, such as widespread use of tapes and photocopiers, have been of great help to *samizdat,* although attempts have been made by the Soviet authorities to register all photocopying machines and even all typewriters. However, believers include technicians who can build photocopiers: Petras Plumpa, for example, was tried for building an "Era" photocopier.* There have been secret printing presses built and run by religious believers: a Baptist publishing house was discovered in Ligukalns, Latvia, in October 1974.[24] There has even been a case, in Lviw, Ukraine, when a state publishing-house was used to print Uniate literature.[25] Tourists from the West are another source of religious literature.

The new emphasis on public protest, allied with the writing and signing of petitions, which began in 1968, has already been mentioned.† This became more and more massive, since the petition of the 17,000 in 1971-2 was followed by the collection of 30,782 signatures over two petitions in 1973,[26] but the KGB terrorist operation against the *Chronicle* itself, to be discussed in the next chapter, does not seem to have had a deterrent effect.

Not only has the number of petitions increased, but even the *samizdat* journals now number ten: The *Chronicle, Aušra* ("Dawn"), *Dievas ir Tevyne* ("God and Fatherland"), *Lietuvos Balsas* ("Voice of Lithuania"), *Laisves Šauklys* ("Herald of Liberty"),

*See p. 275. †See pp. 138-141.

Varpas ("The Bell"), *Rupintojelis* ("The Guardian"), *Aušrele, Alma Mater,* and *Tiesos Kelias* ("The Way of Truth" – a journal designed to meet the needs of priests, especially in the field of theological and philosophical developments).

In November 1973 the KGB mounted a massive search operation designed to confiscate every piece of Christian literature they could lay their hands on. The *Lithuanian Chronicle* records no less than 36 house searches on 19-20 November in a nationwide co-ordinated swoop.[27] Probably not all the incidents were reported to the editors of the *Chronicle.* While the main purpose of this campaign was to isolate those responsible for the production of the *Chronicle* itself and to suppress it, in the process the vast extent of other underground literary activity came to light.

The evidence does not permit us to establish the total extent of this unofficial publication production in Lithuania, but there is proof that the undertaking has been extensive. The main emphasis has been on prayer-books.

The raid on the Vilnius home of Zenon Urbon uncovered not only a home-made printing press and religious pictures, but the matrices of a prayer-book.[28] It was no ordinary one: it was *Mary, Save Us,* the collection of prayers expressing the suffering of four girls during their Siberian exile in 1953.*

The search at the home of Kazimieras Gudas at Šlenava, near Kaunas, uncovered a home-made duplicating machine, together with 2,500 unbound prayer-books (the *Chronicle* does not state their title). Like everything found in the raids, they were confiscated by the KGB.[29]

A raid on the home of an unnamed person at Kaunas produced 250 kilograms of unbound pages for a book entitled *A Youth's Outlook* and a prayer-book, *Lift Up Your Hearts.* The KGB discovered a further thousand unbound copies of the latter at another address in Kaunas.[30]

Two of the victims of the raids were Boleslovas Kulikauskas and Jonas Ivanauskas. Nearly a year later (18 September 1974) they appeared in court on charges of "stealing state property". In fact, they had been producing the prayer-books, *Mary, Rejoice* and *Let Us Pray.* The former, on trial for the second time for a similar offence, received a sentence of three and a half years of strict-regime imprisonment, while the latter's sentence was two years of ordinary regime.[31]

During the trial in December 1974 of those responsible for producing the *Lithuanian Chronicle* it also emerged that they had been extensively engaged in printing prayer-books. Povilas Petronis admitted that he had printed 20,000 books, of which he had distributed 16,000.[32] Some of these were copies of the prayerbook, *Jesus and I;* others were copies of the book, *A Young Person's Religion.*[33]

*Quoted on p. 191.

Additionally, the KGB have been keeping watch near the churches and confiscating prayer-books from the hands of the faithful.[34]

The accounts of the searches give a long list of other religious books confiscated. The titles of such underground publications give some indication of the subjects that interest Lithuanians today: a great many are obviously religious in content: *Lift up Your Hearts, Jesus and I, At the Altar, What Modern Scholars Say about God;* there is a strong emphasis on titles appealing to young people: *A Young Man's Struggle, A Youth's Outlook, The Religious Education of a Young Soul;* books dealing with Lithuanian history, usually pre-war editions, are also popular, as are works attacking alcoholism.[35]

About two-thirds of the books confiscated were produced inside Lithuania; the rest were either pre-war editions or had been brought into the country by tourists. During searches official Soviet editions of the Bible and New Testament were confiscated. The *Chronicle* states that the search of Fr. A. Keina's home produced "about eighty religious books reproduced by typewriter or electrograph", of which it names twelve.[36] The reactions of a priest to the searches is given in Document 81. Vladas Lapienis sums up the situation in a letter to the KGB:

> In Lithuania we are experiencing a famine of religious literature. This forces people to type out religious books brought in by tourists, to reproduce them on an Era photocopying machine or to write them out by hand.[37]

A letter written by V. Lapienis to Leonid Brezhnev, asking for his personal intervention to ensure that religious literature confiscated from him by the police is returned to him, has remained unanswered.[38] Lapienis was later arrested.*

The *Chronicle of the Lithuanian Catholic Church* became the lynchpin of the whole movement for human rights and religious liberty in Lithuania from the moment the first number appeared on 19 March 1972. We may not ask the basic questions. Who started it? Who edits it? How is it distributed? Even if we knew the answers, the KGB would love to share the knowledge and there is no evidence yet, despite the investigations and the trials which have taken place, that the authorities have broken the inner circle of organization. Whatever its theoretical status, the *Chronicle* appears to speak authoritatively for a broadly-representative mass of the priesthood and laity of the country. It has never officially claimed to do so, but came near to this admission in the 1975 editorial to No. 19, written as an open letter to Cardinal Bengsch of East Berlin.[39]

Nothing could be simpler than defining the reason for the existence of the *Chronicle:* it is to put the record straight. For decades the Soviet authorities had mobilized every resource to slander the faithful and to discredit the Church. At last, possibly influenced by the unofficial

*See pp. 273-4, 291-2.

Russian civil rights publication in Moscow, the *Chronicle of Current Events*, which preceded it by three years, the Lithuanians also decided to set up a single united publication to cover the whole field of religious liberty and human rights in their country. In the Moscow journal the emphasis is on human rights, with religious liberty taking its natural place within this framework. The Lithuanian journal puts these the other way round.

The *Lithuanian Chronicle* usually begins with a long article concentrating on a particular issue, such as a trial or a petition from a large number of religious believers. The journal always includes a number of petitions or declarations addressed to Soviet authorities or international bodies from Lithuanian Catholics who feel their rights have been infringed. The *Lithuanian Chronicle* usually concludes with a number of short reports from dioceses and schools, and there is a strong emphasis on national values, as well as religious ones. In the more recent issues there has been evidence of close co-operation between the *Moscow Chronicle* and the *Lithuanian Chronicle* on issues of human rights. However, the latter has very little discussion of non-Catholic matters inside Lithuania.

In February 1974 A. Barkauskas, Secretary of the Central Committee of the Lithuanian Communist Party, stated at the Eighteenth Congress of the Lithuanian Komsomol:

> The enemy is stubbornly trying to maintain a torrent of lies about alleged violations of human rights in the Soviet Union, trying to arouse discontent and encouraging religious fanaticism.[40]

The aim of the *Lithuanian Chronicle* is to show where the truth lies. It is, of course, a "cry for help from the suffering Catholics, the children of the Church in Lithuania,"[41] but it is more than this. A group of six priests from the Archbishopric of Vilnius, who identify themselves by name, rightly emphasize that the *Chronicle* "writes nothing against the Soviet system, it raises only the facts about offences against believers, the truth of which no one will deny,"[42] but the attentive reader will legitimately raise the question of whether these basic denials of human rights which have persisted in the Soviet Union since 1917 have now become such an integral part of the system that they are ineradicable so long as Soviet power persists.

Beginning almost unnoticed in 1972, the *Chronicle* rapidly gained an influence and an importance both at home and abroad beyond the original hopes of its editors, as they stated in the twelfth issue (1974).[43] In an editorial postscript to the fifteenth issue (1975), the editors offer a brief but very warm word of thanksgiving on the third anniversary of the publication, confidently expecting that God would reward those who had helped with it in any way.[44]

Clearly, the editors are well aware of the importance of the *Chronicle* outside the Soviet Union, as well as inside. One of their objectives must certainly be to inform the world-wide Lithuanian diaspora – and all other Christians of good will – though it never actually says so. Very possibly, the aim may be even more precise: to inform the Vatican of the true situation in a country where it commands loyalty to a degree almost unknown elsewhere in the world today.

There is evidence that Soviet atheists are coming to recognize the fact that Lithuanian believers can successfully publicize their troubles in the *Chronicle*. At a district teachers' conference in Šakiai on 26 August 1975 a delegate from Vilnius, A. Sinkevičius, stated that he had read sixteen issues of the *Chronicle* "published by Lithuanian nationalists" and warned the other teachers:

> Every tactless action committed by a teacher in the course of talking to a religious pupil or his parents is published in minute detail, without exaggeration, giving people's surnames, the name of the school and the date and is circulated everywhere in this journal, not only at home, but also in the outside world. The journal is translated into English, French, Spanish and other languages. And what will foreigners think? What will they bring up when searching for something to criticize?[45]

One notable feature of the Soviet *samizdat* journals on human rights and religious liberty is their faithfulness to the facts. A church newspaper published in Britain or America would find it hard to vie with the record consistently achieved by the *Chronicle of Current Events* or the *Bulletin* of the Council of Baptist Prisoners' Relatives. The achievement of the *Chronicle of the Lithuanian Catholic Church* is on this level. For this there must be careful co-ordination with a network of informants and the tightest editorial control. The instructions printed at the end of several issues of the *Chronicle* indicate that these exist, but naturally the publication is totally silent about the techniques and personalities involved. Further, the editors state that they have an archive to draw on and they use it to illustrate the continuity of persecution from Stalin,[46] through Khrushchev[47] and up to the present. There is some evidence that, in early issues, the *Chronicle* changed the names of some persons mentioned, such as children, but as this was used to try to discredit it by the authorities, names are now precisely indicated.

While the editors set their standard with the first issue, which dealt mainly with the trial of Fr. Zdebskis,* their instructions to the network became more precise as time went on. They first appeared in the second issue, where the instructions were threefold: to "gather appropriate data from present-day life", to "protect the *Chronicle* from the KGB" and to pass it on from hand to hand.[48] For this, the fifth issue states, the *Chronicle* "needs the assistance of all conscientious Catholics".[49] The seventh issue made these requirements even clearer:

*See pp. 101-111.

Vague information and incorrect material is unsuitable for the *Chronicle of the Lithuanian Catholic Church*. Such material is not printed in the pages of the *Chronicle*. Every news item, fact or event connected with the situation of the Catholic Church, the history of our nation past or present, the arbitrariness of government agencies, repression or other forms of discrimination, must be carefully verified, clear and specific. Numbers, dates, names of people and places and other information must be especially clear, correctly recorded and checked.[50]

This does not exclude the right of the informant to request that the editors withhold individual names for security reasons.[51] The eleventh issue instructed those who copy the *Chronicle* and pass it on to be meticulous in their proof-reading and not to disseminate unclear copies.[52] The sixteenth issue makes it clear that the editors are seeking information not only on Soviet persecution of religion and enforced atheism, but also on Lithuanian resistance to russification ("denationalization", the meaning implied by the term *nutautinimas*).[53] The seventeenth issue stated for the first time that it had not included certain information because it did not fulfil the requirements of precision and factual detail. Excluded material should be resubmitted to conform to this standard.[54]

The primary method of reproducing the *Chronicle* has been typing. The originals in the West are carbons* stapled together between plain white covers of thicker paper. At the trial in December 1974,† one of the witnesses admitted using an Era photocopying machine in the work and producing twenty copies of each of two consecutive issues.[55] One of the defendants admitted distributing one hundred copies of the sixth issue.[56] The present author has not seen any of these mechanically reproduced numbers and it is not possible to guess the total production for any issue. As far as is known, the organizers of the literature have used their secret printing facilities only for the production of prayer-books, not the *Chronicle*. Similarly, the Russian Baptists used their clandestine press primarily for printing the Bible and *Bratsky Listok* ("Fraternal leaflet"), which has theological content, not their *Bulletin* (which lists prisoners), though some appeals have also appeared from the press.[57]

A distinguishing feature of the *Lithuanian Chronicle* is that it is the only regular *samizdat* in bilingual form. Most issues have appeared in Russian as well as Lithuanian. The Russian has some linguistic and orthographical peculiarities which identify it as the work of a person or persons whose native language is Lithuanian. The reason for the Russian version is clearly to make the text available to other than Lithuanian people both at home and abroad. There have also been cases of Lithuanians reproducing Russian-language *samizdat* for Russians. In 1974 KGB agents discovered 2,000 prayer-books and catechisms (in Russian), reproduced in the copying department of the Vilnius Republican Library by Matulionis, a resident of Vilnius.[58]

*Some are in the possesion of Keston College.   †See pp. 265-70.

Although the *Lithuanian Chronicle* has not yet become nearly as well known in the West as it deserves to be, not even in Roman Catholic circles, and although there is no evidence on record, at least until the election of Pope John Paul II, that the Vatican has taken sufficient note of what it is saying, it has already played a role of the highest importance in Lithuania itself, not only informing people, but unifying them in their struggle for their rights and setting them a goal to achieve. Apart from the campaign of a Muslim people, the Crimean Tartars, to return from the exile in Central Asia and Siberia to which they were assigned under Stalin during the Second World War, no other nationality in the Soviet Union has yet attained such unity in the statement of its rights. The movement represented visibly by the *Chronicle* could not have attained the momentum it has without massive backing – and the inference is that this has come from the laity, parish councils, priests and very probably senior clergy representing a much broader social base than any other religious protest movement. These developments have presented the KGB with a major challenge.

DOCUMENTS

78. THE NEW TESTAMENT PRINTED

It is said that in printing the New Testament at the Vaizdas Press workers were picked exclusively from party ranks. In spite of their loyalty to the regime, more than a few copies of the Scriptures disappeared from the printing house.

Upon the appearance of the Holy Scriptures some atheists of Vilnius pretended to be Catholics and tried to purchase the book from priests, so that as few copies as possible should fall into the hands of the faithful. Some Catholics rejoiced over the printing, others criticized the translation and still others said: "We've won one rouble's worth and lost ten." Such a small edition will have almost no practical effect, but the Soviet Government will exploit it for its own propaganda, saying, "See what freedom of the press there is in Soviet Lithuania!"

Very many copies of the Holy Scriptures were taken by the Central Committee of the Party (no accurate figure is available), and many copies were sent for propaganda purposes to Lithuanians and to senior dignitaries of the Catholic Church abroad.

His Excellency, Bishop R. Krikščiunas, speaking at a general meeting of the Lithuanian Committee for Cultural Relations with
Lithuanians Abroad, said, "The Catholics of Lithuania publish the
religious books they need . . . . Here, hot off the press, is a most
essential publication, *The New Testament of the Holy Scriptures.*" The
bishop's speech evoked the reaction from Catholics, "We haven't got
any religious books at all!" . . . .

From various corners of Lithuania orders poured into the offices of
Knyga paštu [a mail order book service], "Send me a Bible". However, the response to them all was negative.[59]

79.   A PRIEST SEEKS A BIBLE, 1976

To the Representative of the Council for Religious Affairs, K. Tumenas

A DECLARATION

On 30 August 1974 you told parishioners P. Burokas, V. Trečiukas,
I. Burokiene and V. Steponiene of Adutiškis parish, "Re-educate your
priest." This means, bring influence to bear on him so that he will no
longer be guided by the Church and his conscience, but only by the
atheists. If you suggest that the ordinary workers of the Adutiškis
sovkhoz should re-educate me, then permit me to suggest that perhaps
the watchman on your street or the cleaning woman in your office
should re-educate you.

I was brought up and educated by teachers and professors of high
culture and moral principle. In forming my outlook on life, they
allowed and sometimes even recommended me to become acquainted
with Marxist-Communist ideas. My outlook did not evolve by order,
but freely. I also had to read the works of free-thinkers. Does such an
opportunity exist today for those forming their outlook on life to read
books by people who do not share Communist opinions?

In 1966 I asked for a copy of the Bible in a Moscow bookshop. The
bookseller answered me honestly, "We have never had it here. If you
want to read it, go to a library, but even there you'll get it only if you
have got special permission."

If such a restriction operates, then there is no hope at all of obtaining or reading works of a non-communist character. However every
person must, in the process of forming his outlook on life, come to
know the opinions of those who think differently from himself.
Molotov rightly said, "The truth turns out to be somewhere between
two opposing points of view."

In the distant past I was attracted by Communist ideas and slogans, but experience later convinced me that all they wrote and said was just a dead letter and that life was pointing in the opposite direction . . . .

Article 125 of the Soviet Constitution guarantees freedom of the press. If this freedom existed, believers would not today be paying out sixty roubles for a prayer-book . . . .

Fr. B. Laurinavičius.[60]

80. THE SOVIET PRESS ATTACKS NEW CATHOLIC METHODS, 1970

. . . . As we have already said, the Church wishes to adapt itself to contemporary conditions, while remaining unchanged in essence, and thus is modernizing its political, social-philosophical and economic doctrine and reviewing its attitude to the achievements of science and technology. These tendencies and the increased activity of the Church in our country are clearly noticeable, especially in the activities of the Catholic clergy. The servants of the cult try to adapt to national characteristics, and to revive in the daily life of the believers religious traditions which have either already died out or are in the process of dying out, traditions which the Church made use of as part of a system of exploitation. The new tactics of the clergy are noticeably more subtle, sometimes disguised in order to influence the faithful both ideologically and politically. Some of them search out illegal contacts with reactionary émigrés or try to interfere in social life and support the remnants of bourgeois nationalism. Some individuals, the better-trained priests, sometimes write and try to disseminate so-called memoirs, lectures, tracts on theology or religious poetry, regarding this "creative work" as spiritual food for young people, inexperienced priests and some believers.

In recent years the Vatican has embarked on a series of hostile actions, intended to encourage religious and nationalist activity in Lithuania. It has issued a special anti-Soviet proclamation to the clergy and believers, which perceptibly emphasizes the specifically national characteristics and aims of the Lithuanian Catholic Church. On the one hand, the Vatican preaches cosmopolitan ideas and invites all Christian religions to unite, on the other hand it eagerly fans the flames of the question regarding the so-called inequality of Catholics and the Catholic Church in the USSR in comparison to other religions, calculating that this would inflame the nationalist sentiments of believers. Attempts have been made to send us religious literature, church vessels and vestments. The Vatican radio-station, together with the radio-stations of other western countries, carries on active propaganda in Lithuanian and often transmits instructions to the clergy in this way.[61]

81. THE SEARCH OF A PRIEST'S HOME

On 20 November 1973 the KGB of the Biržai District, under the command of Captain Jasinskis, searched the church, the sacristy, the adjacent buildings and my living quarters in the sacristy. I live there because both the old and new rectories built by the parishioners for their ministers have been confiscated by the Biržai District Executive Committee.

Much of my religious literature, hymnals and typing paper were confiscated during the search, as were my typewriter and all my recording tape, both new tapes and recordings of hymns. All the hymns of the religious community of Smilgiai were also confiscated.

I consider the search completely illegal for the following reasons:

1. It was conducted without any witnesses, because those listed as such were part of the search team and I was not permitted to call in anyone else to serve as a witness.

2. My confiscated property – religious literature – was taken illegally because natural law and the constitution permit anyone to profess any religion and freely to use any religious literature, no matter how it is produced, whether in pencil, ink or by typewriter.

3. The warrant you issued did not authorize the confiscation of the materials removed under its pretext by the officials conducting the search. Two months have passed since the search and yet the confiscated materials still have not been returned. For this reason, I address you with the request that you remind them of the elementary principles of the law and that they return my property, since I cannot see any legal basis for their actions.

Who can be hurt by the simple possession of religious literature and hymns, something safeguarded by the constitution and natural law? On this basis, I consider the confiscation of my literature and hymns to be robbery.

What is the legal basis for the confiscation of my recording tape which can freely be purchased in shops? I do not understand it. I have reason to consider the confiscation of my late mother's recorded words (the box bore the title "Mother's Statement", it was one of our family's most cherished treasures and the only recording of her voice left for the five children whom she brought up) as an unprecedented act of barbarism by the officials involved, an act for which I can find no words.

What blame can be attached to plain white typing paper and carbon paper which can freely be purchased in shops? Perhaps we can tell you the answer in the words of the officials who conducted the search: "It's hard to get carbon paper. There will be enough for a number of offices." It is easier for officials to steal from a citizen than to look for paper in the shops.

I was surprised by the rumours about what they found which have been started by those who participated in the search. I consider that all this is due to the immaturity and lack of manners on the part of some of the officials who conducted the search.

On 22 January 1974 I was called in to see A. Tumenas, Chairman of the Biržai District Executive Committee, who threatened to raise my income tax because I was still able to pay it. He then enumerated the items which had been noted in the search and turned over to him, starting with my bank-book and ending with two pairs of gym shorts found in my room. This just proved the unwritten rule that any conduct – even the coarsest – is permissible towards a believer, especially a priest. He can be attacked, discriminated against and, as on this occasion, even robbed. Such actions lead one to presume that with a priest anything is permissible.

The confiscation of hymns belonging to the religious community of Smilgiai was an example of completely arbitrary conduct, because the hymns were the property of the church of Smilgiai. The search was conducted in the absence of any representative of the religious community of Smilgiai, one of whom could have been found a few steps away – not kilometres – in the village of Smilgiai.

On the Sunday after the search the representatives of the religious community could not find their hymn books, and they came to me asking for an explanation. They were very surprised and shocked by the arbitrary actions of the government officials. They began collecting signatures on a petition, in which they complained that their church had been robbed. I requested that they wait, in the expectation of support from the prosecutor's office, since your agency is run on the basis of law and not according to the arbitrary behaviour of a few officials.

On this same basis and in the belief that the State is run under the rule of law, I appeal to you to correct the injustice and order the officials involved to return all the confiscated religious literature, hymns, tapes and typewriters.

At the same time, in an effort to alleviate the people's anxiety, to relieve them of the strain of collecting signatures and of sending delegations to officials, I request that you return their hymn books.

Smilgiai, 24 January 1974   Rev. Balys Babrauskas.[62]

NOTES TO CHAPTER X

1. For a detailed account of the struggle for the Lithuanian printed word under the Tsars, see Juozas Vaišnora, *The Forty Years of Darkness,* Brooklyn, New York, 1975.
2. J. Vaišnora, *op. cit.,* p. 22.
3. *Ibid.,* pp. 22-3.
4. *Ibid.,* pp. 47-8.
5. Ed. Vardys, *Lithuania under the Soviets,* p. 217.
6. *Ibid.,* p. 63.
7. *Ibid.,* pp. 77-8.
8. *Ibid.,* pp. 99-100.
9. *RCL* 6, 1975, p. 9.
10. Private information; *CLCC* 19, p. 8; Rimaitis, *Religion in Lithuania,* p. 19.
11. *CLCC* 29, p. 24.
12. *CLCC* 4, p. 18 (E), p. 10 (L).
13. *CLCC* 19, p. 7; confirmed by Rimaitis, *op. cit.,* p. 19.
14. *CLCC* 5, p. 5 (E), p. 5 (L).
15. *CLCC* 6, p. 22 (E), pp. 9-10 (L).
16. *Ibid.,* p. 10 (E), pp. 5-6 (L).
17. *CLCC* 15, pp. 17-19; cf. his interrogation before TV cameras, pp. 21-2.
18. *CLCC* 5, pp. 42-3 (E), p. 17 (L).
19. Vaišno a, *op. cit.,* p. 20.
20. *CLCC* 4, p. 11 (E), p. 7 (L); cf. *CLCC* 18, p. 7.
21. *CLCC* 6, p. 10 (E), pp. 5-6 (L).
22. *Loc. cit.*
23. *CLCC* 8, p. 6 (E), pp. 2-3 (L).
24. *CCE* 34, 1975, p. 51.
25. *Zhovten,* Lviw, No. 4, April 1974, pp. 90-6.
26. *CLCC* 6, pp. 1-11 (E), pp. 2-6 (L).
27. *CLCC* 8, pp. 6-16 (E), pp. 2-8 (L) and 9, pp. 17-22 (E), pp. 9-11 (L).
28. *CLCC* 8, p. 13 (E), p. 6 (L).
29. *CLCC* 9, p. 19 (E), p. 10 (L).
30. *CLCC* 9, pp. 19-20 (E), p. 10 (L).
31. *CLCC* 13, p. 48 (E), p. 44 (L).
32. *Ibid.,* p. 12 (E), p. 7 (L).
33. *Ibid.,* pp. 23-24 (E), p. 22 (L).
34. *CLCC* 17, pp. 24-5.
35. *CLCC* 9, pp. 17-21 (E), pp. 9-11 (L).
36. *CLCC* 8, p. 7 (E), p. 3 (L).
37. *CLCC* 15, pp. 14-15; cf. *CLCC* 7, pp. 5-6 (L); 13, pp. 9, 16, 32, 37 (E), pp. 5, 20, 33, 35 (L).
38. *CLCC* 23, pp. 24-34.
39. *CLCC* 19, pp. 2-10.
40. *CLCC* 9, p. 15 (E), p. 7 (L).
41. *CLCC* 17, p. 15.
42. *Loc. cit.*
43. *CLCC* 12, p. 5 (E), p. 2 (L).
44. *CLCC* 15, p. 39.
45. *CLCC* 20, p. 34.
46. *CLCC* 15, pp. 34-6.
47. *CLCC* 10, pp. 43-5 (E), pp. 25-6 (L).
48. *CLCC* 2, p. 23.
49. *CLCC* 5, p. 53 (E), p. 20 (L).

50. *CLCC* 7, p. 62 (E), p. 24 (L); cf. 9, p. 42 (E), p. 24 (L).
51. *CLCC* 6, p. 51 (E), p. 20 (L).
52. *CLCC* 11, p. 39 (E), p. 33 (L).
53. *CLCC* 16, p. 39.
54. *CLCC* 17, p. 42.
55. *CLCC* 13, p. 14 (E), p. 10 (L).
56. *Ibid.*, p. 19 (E), p. 15 (L).
57. *RCL* 6, 1975, p. 11.
58. *CLCC* 10, p. 15 (E), pp. 7-8 (L).
59. *CLCC* 6, pp. 22-4 (E), pp. 9-10 (L).
60. *CLCC* 16, pp. 24-6.
61. *Partiinaya Zhizn,* Moscow, May 1970, pp. 58-9.
62. *CLCC* 9, pp. 33-6 (E), pp. 19-20 (L).

XI

CASE 345
THE KGB'S PURSUIT OF THE CHRONICLE
OF THE LITHUANIAN CATHOLIC CHURCH

IN THE face of the new challenge which the *Lithuanian Chronicle* presented, the KGB set itself the task of identifying its editors and chief distributors and destroying the whole enterprise. They gave the operation the laconic title, Case 345.[1] Additionally, they intended to discredit the *Chronicle,* with the hope of reducing opposition to their campaign.

It seems that a decision had also been taken at the end of 1971 to suppress all *samizdat,* a growing phenomenon disturbing the authorities' peace of mind. In January 1972 there was a KGB crackdown on the *Chronicle of Current Events* and the *Ukrainsky Vistnik* ("Ukrainian Herald"). The former survived; the latter was suppressed for two years, appearing again for a while in 1974. It was at this most difficult time that the *Chronicle of the Lithuanian Catholic Church* was launched.

We have already quoted* an official Soviet instruction indicating that an intensification of the campaign against the Catholic Church was being planned in the 1960's. At the beginning of 1973 the criminal investigation agencies began to reveal the extent of their efforts in this direction. The Executive Committees of some districts issued instructions about typewriters, which were sent to every office where there was likely to be one – including church offices. One typical letter read:

> Please send in to the Executive Committee by 22 March samples of typing from machines at your headquarters (factory, farm, organization, private house). Two originals must be typed on standard size paper, according to the enclosed specimen text. Further, please tell us what other typewriters you have of which you are unable to send in samples because the machine is out of order, being repaired or for any other reason. With the sample typescript you must also indicate the number and make of the typewriter.[2]

Undoubtedly these specimens would have been analyzed by computer and stored up in a memory bank, from which it would be possible to trace the origin of any typewritten copy of the *Chronicle* or of any other Lithuanian *samizdat.* It is no wonder, then, that the editors of the *Chronicle* expressed anxiety about having it typed on machines which could be identified.[3]

*See pp. 46-8.

Later that same year (19-20 November), obviously after months of careful preparation, the police carried out a simultaneous raid on dozens of Lithuanian homes.[4] The purpose was to confiscate copies not only of the *Chronicle*, but also of every other example of *samizdat* which they could find. Almost immediately the net began to close around some of the key figures. All those arrested in early 1974 were lay people. The State began to prepare a series of trials against them, which would take place later in 1974 and in 1975.

At the same time the attempts to discredit the *Chronicle* in the eyes of the faithful intensified. While the Soviet Lithuanian press has apparently not dared to mention the *Chronicle* by name, for fear of increasing its popularity, representatives of the Lithuanian Church sent abroad on diplomatic missions did mention that there was a campaign to suppress the *Chronicle*.[5] However, in Lithuania itself the KGB did not manage to persuade church leaders to denounce it.[6] Tumenas, of the Council for Religious Affairs, is reported to have demanded that Bishop Povilonis throw his weight behind the effort to suppress the *Chronicle*, but the bishop replied that as he had not initiated it, he could do nothing.[7]

More insidious was the campaign to discredit the *Chronicle* through "anonymous letters". This was apparently the tactic adopted after it had proved impossible to secure a condemnation of the *Chronicle* by the bishops. The *Chronicle's* vigorous defence of its own position seems to have been successful in preventing an atheist wedge from being driven in to church life at this point.*

On 18 September 1974 the first trial of persons connected with the *Chronicle* took place in Vilnius. Hardly any details are known, but Boleslovas Kulikauskas received a sentence of three and a half years strict regime and Jonas Ivanauskas two years general regime for printing prayer-books.[8]

On 11 October 1974 five Lithuanian priests addressed an appeal for those awaiting trial to Academician Andrei Sakharov's Human Rights Committee in Moscow. He immediately forwarded it to the World Council of Churches and to the Synod of Catholic Bishops which was meeting in Rome at that time, asking these bodies to support those who had been arrested for their religious convictions.[9] The appeal stated in no uncertain terms that the *Chronicle*, on account of which the arrests had taken place, was not "libellous literature", but rather would help to do away with the abuses which were destroying respect for the Soviet legal system.[10] Sakharov's action caused the world press to pay serious attention to the persecution of the Church in Lithuania for the first time.[11] However, the Soviet authorities continued with their plan of bringing the case to trial and in December it opened.

For twelve days the five faced the Soviet Court,[12] from 2-24 December 1974, interspersed with recesses. The casual observer, had any such been permitted inside, might have concluded that the charge

*See pp. 120-4, 131-3.

must have been at least high treason or armed rebellion. Each accused
was led in by an armed guard – two in front and one behind.[13] If two
prisoners had to move at one time, a soldier always separated them.
At no time during the proceedings were there less than six soldiers
maintaining constant guard over the accused, with further patrols on
both the inner and outer doors of the courtroom itself. The trial was
conducted in open violation of Soviet criminal law. Secret, closed
trials may be held only in cases involving state secrets, sex crimes or
crimes involving minors. Verdicts must be given in open court. Witnesses must remain in the courtroom after giving testimony. This
procedure was not observed here. The so-called "public" at this trial
was composed of KGB men, while friends of the accused and the
general public were kept out. Precautions, obviously not completely
successful, were taken against secret recording of the trial. Apart from
the KGB, hostile Soviet newspaper correspondents and various
officials, only the most immediate relatives of the accused could gain
access.

On the first day the State set out its case against the five accused. It
was as though a cross-section of Lithuanian manhood was in the dock.
The eldest was Povilas Petronis, aged 63 at the time of the trial. But
alongside him was Virgilijus Jaugelis, a mere 26, born after Lithuania
had lost its independence, who should have been, because of his
education, a prime example of what the authorities would like to call
"the new Soviet man" – someone totally free of "bourgeois",
nationalist or religious prejudices. Also there were Petras Plumpa,
aged 35, Jonas Stašaitis, aged 53, and A. Patriubavičius, aged 39.

All of them faced the accusation of being key figures in the production and circulation of seven numbers of the *Chronicle of the
Lithuanian Catholic Church*, "the aim of which is to denigrate the
Soviet system",[14] according to the wording of the indictment – an
accusation vigorously refuted at every subsequent opportunity by the
defendants, who claimed that it was a journal which records the facts
concerning the persecution of the church in Lithuania. Legally
speaking, there is nothing criminal in copying written material, either
on a typewriter or by hand, unless this is done on a printing press for
monetary profit, which would infringe the privilege of the state-owned
press and could then be classified as "speculation". The grounds for
prosecuting producers of *samizdat,* under Soviet law, must be that the
material reproduced was "anti-Soviet" or "libellous". It has become
usual to charge *samizdat* writers with libelling government institutions; in a one-party state it is very difficult to prove that statements
criticizing state institutions are not libellous. It is even easier to
"prove" that *samizdat* publications are anti-Soviet, as the term "anti-
Soviet" is not defined in law.

The indictment went on to name Plumpa as the ringleader of the
group. During the trial his life-history and personality emerged with

impressive clarity. This was not his first appearance before a Soviet court. Indeed, it emerged that his imprisonment at eighteen years of age in 1958 had marked a change in the whole direction of his life from one of aimlessness to that of service to God and the Church. He had merely been a teenage rowdy, but after being arrested his house was searched and in it the police found a few useless fragments of military paraphernalia gleaned from the Lithuanian battlefields of the Second World War. For this he was sentenced to no less than seven years imprisonment for alleged involvement in Lithuanian nationalist activities.

Prison cured him of any excess that he may have felt in this direction (see Document 82). Indeed, in his prison camp he met people who had actually committed atrocities in the name of nationalism and he felt that their ideology had serious shortcomings. While still in confinement he began to seek more profound principles by which he might orientate his life. This did not lead him to renounce his attachment to Lithuania. On the contrary, he could now place it in a broader context: that of supreme loyalty to the God whose goodness he discovered there in the camp. His did not come as an overnight conversion. He learned French, in order to read French philosophers in the original: some of their writings were available in the prison library. He found his faith in 1961 – a faith Plumpa proclaimed from the dock of the courtroom, using it like a pulpit to preach to the armed guards and the assembled handpicked ranks of hostile observers. In the camp itself he had discovered a key to life which was not to be found in nationalism or politics alone.

Plumpa is far from being the only person to discover the faith in a prison camp. Many other instances are known.[15] It is no surprise that such people have subsequently come in for pointed repression from the KGB.

Plumpa felt impelled to serve God in a special way. To publish the truth and defend His Church in the *Lithuanian Chronicle* became the practical outreach of his faith. So severe did the campaign against him become during his years of so-called freedom after his release that he felt he had lost all his rights as a Soviet citizen, even though his work on the *Chronicle* was secret. He even took his wife's surname, Pluira,* in order to seek a cover from the persecution. Had he given up every ideal and become a common criminal, life would have been easier for him, he stated.

After the interrogation of himself, his co-defendants and many witnesses, and after the final statement of the accused, he received his sentence on Christmas Eve: no less than eight years of imprisonment for his work on behalf of religious freedom as embodied in the *Chronicle* and for writing a preface to Zhores Medvedev's *A Question*

*Pluira – this name is given in three different versions in various issues of the *Lithuanian Chronicle*, as "Pluira", "Pliura" and "Pliuira". We have chosen "Pluira", as a common form, which appears in the most recent issues.

of Madness.[16] He was destined to face conditions of imprisonment so severe that they can only be described as torture. In spite of this, Plumpa's letters from the camp show that he is unbroken: if anything, he has gained in spiritual strength (Document 83).

Plumpa was not the only one to receive a heavy sentence. The other four in the dock were also found guilty. Virgilijus Jaugelis was sentenced to two years for his part in the affair. These sentences were imposed for the vaguely-defined crime of "anti-Soviet agitation and propaganda". A Soviet newspaper described this offence as "producing and distributing literature which was full of hatred for Soviet society, which incited people to act against the State and which was also published abroad".[17]

During the trial Jaugelis turned out to be just as interesting and outstanding a character as Plumpa, perhaps even more outspokenly dedicated to the cause of religious freedom in Lithuania, though several years younger (see Document 84).

From the dock he challenged the KGB over their interference in church life and said that if there were any justice in this world his accusers should be up there in his place. When challenged on the sharpness of his attitudes, Jaugelis stated that he himself had once had the ambition of becoming a priest, but the authorities had prevented it. Little did the KGB realize that by blocking the young man they were in fact channelling his energies into something which from their point of view was far more harmful. Instead Jaugelis threw himself into more "secular" activities as an expression of his faith. For example, he was one of the people who helped collect signatures for the Memorandum of the 17,000. In court he freely admitted that he had duplicated and circulated about one hundred copies of the *Lithuanian Chronicle*. Although in serious ill health – he was suffering from a polyp of the large intestine and was in urgent need of specialized medical attention – he refused to recant and to petition the court for leniency. Instead, he ended his part in the trial by turning his final statement into one of the most impassioned appeals for religious freedom and national liberation that can ever have been heard in a public place (as the court theoretically was) in the Soviet Union:

> What do you understand by the word 'freedom'? Perhaps the closure of Catholic churches and their conversion into warehouses and concert halls? Perhaps the fact that priests are being imprisoned for giving religious instruction to children? . . . .
>
> All this is happening in a country where liberty, equality, brotherhood, justice and other ringing words are loudly proclaimed.
>
> However, today there are many people working for justice, liberty and the general welfare of the people. How many such have perished in the snows of Soviet Russia, how many have suffered hunger, disease, torture?

. . . .

For Christ, for the truth He proclaimed, millions of martyrs have suffered and died. Let the atheists not think that today there is no one left who would be prepared to suffer for truth, for religion and the Church (see also Document 84).

A few weeks after his sentence Jaugelis became the victim of an atrocity – very probably the KGB's revenge for these provocative words.[18] He had quarrelled with no one, but on the night of 10-11 February 1975 a bunch of criminals, among whom this young Christian had been thrown in the camp at Praveniškis, set upon him while he was praying and beat him almost to death. Despite a broken jaw, he was kept for a week in the camp with no qualified medical attention. Then he was sent to the prison hospital at Lukiskes, but another group of criminals robbed him of his personal possessions *en route*. The doctor immobilized his jaw with a plaster cast, but even more serious was the pre-existing intestinal problem, which was diagnosed as third-stage cancer. They said that an immediate operation was necessary and it would be too late after his release. Jaugelis refused in writing, presumably being unwilling to submit to prison doctors.[19]

On 7 March 1975 his mother wrote an appeal from her home in Kaunas to the Lithuanian Procuracy, complaining at the way in which the camp authorities had failed to protect her son from the criminal prisoners, but the reply was negative.[20]

On 28 March Jaugelis himself wrote an appeal to the procuracy, threatening a hunger-strike if his stolen possessions were not returned and unless he were put alongside political prisoners.[21] This was effective, for a commission considered his case immediately after he began the hunger-strike on 2 May. He was released and had an operation on 20 June.[22] This was probably due to a desire by the authorities to prevent his becoming a martyr. He was arrested yet again in December 1975 when he tried to attend the trial of Sergei Kovalyov, but he was soon released because of ill health.*

Povilas Petronis, despite ill health and a good defence by his lawyer (so unusual in Soviet conditions), received the second-longest sentence: four years. In court he stated that he had been drawn into the work because of the lack of religious literature. He admitted producing 20,000 prayer-books and distributing 16,000 of these,† for which he had bought the paper and paid the helpers. Witnesses testified to his calibre: years of dedicated work in an isolation hospital and a spirited campaign against drunkenness. He gave up all this and disappeared when he became absorbed in the printing. In the past he had dreamed of becoming a missionary abroad, but eventually came to realize that Lithuania must be his mission field. He further admitted listening to Vatican Radio and transcribing important broadcasts.

Patriubavičius, who was on a strange and barely-explained charge concerning a car accident in which two girls were injured, as well as

*See p. 252.   †See pp. 316-17.

being accused of reproducing the *Chronicle*, emerged as a man of much lesser stature, almost illiterate, who had done what he did because he was paid for it and without fully understanding its significance. His sentence was thirteen months, but he was released at the end of the trial because he had already been in prison this length of time.

Although Stašaitis defended his role in attempting to provide literature for Lithuania, he said he felt that the *Chronicle* itself did not open a way to dialogue, but rather exacerbated relations with the Communists. His experiences in an isolation cell during the period of investigation had convinced him that some other way must be found. Doubtless his attitude of partial repentance was the determining factor in his lenient sentence: one year, which meant his immediate release because he had already been in prison longer than this time.

On 25 February 1975 Fr. Juozas Zdebskis wrote to the Supreme Court of the Lithuanian Republic, claiming that the State had falsified certain details in the case against the five. He complained that the *Chronicle* – and this was a cornerstone of the State's case – had been accused of printing untrue information. In particular, the prosecution claimed that it had printed a falsified version of Fr. Zdebskis's defence speech at his own trial. Fr. Zdebskis refuted this allegation in his letter, stating that the *Chronicle* had in fact been more true to his intentions than what occurred in the court-room. It had printed his original text, which he had not been permitted to deliver in its prepared form due to constant interruptions, cross-questioning and improper comments on the psychology of the accused from the judge.[23] Fr. Zdebskis continued his commitment to the defence of the five in more practical terms in 1976 by accompanying Petras Plumpa's wife on a harrowing visit to her husband in the camp where he was imprisoned (Document 83).

Lithuanian Chronicle No. 13 concluded with the statement that the authorities had now liquidated "almost all the centres for the preparation of prayer-books and catechisms".[24] The purpose of the trial had been to demonstrate the smashing of the *Chronicle* itself. This was the end of "Case No. 345" . . . . except that all of these events were recounted in No. 13 of the *Chronicle* and that since then issues have continued to appear.

Although several others were still being held in prison awaiting trial on similar charges, the last days of the December trial coincided with a further co-ordinated series of searches, not only in Lithuania, but in Moscow also. *Chronicle* No. 15 lists a further twenty people in Lithuania who were either searched or taken in for interrogation on or about 23 December 1974. The KGB widened its net to include Moscow. They searched the flat of Sergei Kovalyov, the Russian human rights activist, on the same day, which was followed by his arrest four days later and his immediate transfer by plane to Vilnius.*

*See pp. 301-2, 314-17.

The intensification of the savage repression in 1975 was marked by a series of trials – those of Gražys, Sadunaite, Kovalyov – which could fill a book between them; indeed, two of them have already formed the subject of separate pamphlets.[25]

This was the third time that Gražys had faced a Soviet court, the first two occasions also being on "political" charges.[26] During his second imprisonment he had begun to suffer from an incurable kidney complaint. The authorities excluded even the immediate relatives of the accused and not even a partial transcript of the trial has become available. The *Lithuanian Chronicle* merely records a few details. Petronis and Stašaitis were among the witnesses. The accusation was that Gražys had bound some of the early numbers of the *Chronicle* and about twenty of No. 7. He had also retyped sundry other *samizdat* publications, several not connected with religion. His only "original" work seems to have been the translation of an article on nationalism from Russian into Lithuanian. Gražys refused to name the contacts from whom he had received this material and to whom he had distributed it.

He was accused, under Article 68 of the Penal Code of the Lithuanian Republic, of anti-Soviet agitation and propaganda, corresponding to Article 70 of the RSFSR Penal Code. The prosecution asked for six years of strict-regime camp, but the sentence was only three years of general regime. His typewriter and various items of reproducing equipment were confiscated, but his money was returned.

Captain Markevičius and other KGB officials were prominently present through the trial, states the *Chronicle*.

The *Lithuanian Chronicle*[27] was able to include much more about the trial of Nijole Sadunaite, who was also charged with reproducing and disseminating the *Chronicle*. These few pages (Document 85) are sufficient to establish a previously unknown woman as a person of heroic and saintly character, totally dedicated to others in her life.

She was born in 1938 in Dotnuva. Her father was a lecturer at the Agricultural Institute; her parents were firm religious believers and passed their faith on to their daughter. Nijole Sadunaite completed secondary school in Anykščiai; although religious pupils suffered discrimination at school, she never missed Mass on Sundays and openly knelt in respect before the Blessed Sacrament, even on school excursions. For five years she nursed her sick mother, until her death in 1970. Her father had died in 1963, so her only close relative now is her brother Jonas. She looked after Canon Rauda for several years before his death.* "Any person's sufferings touched a chord in her heart," says the *Chronicle*. "She tried to keep her own needs to a minimum so that she could help others. She sometimes gave away to others what she herself most needed."[28]

When she was arrested, on 27 August 1974, a copy of the *Chronicle*

*See p. 82

of the Lithuanian Catholic Church was found in her typewriter. She could not deny her technical "guilt", but she made it clear at her trial that she did not consider herself morally guilty of any crime: "The truth does not need to be defended, as it's omnipotent and invincible! . . . . for the truth I'm prepared not only to lose my freedom, but would joyfully even sacrifice my life."[29] The *Chronicle,* she stated, was fighting for the right to freedom of conscience which was guaranteed in the constitution. "The *Chronicle* is like a mirror which reflects all the crimes of atheists against those who believe in God. Nothing evil likes to look at its own image, it hates its own reflection. That's why you hate everyone who tears off the veil of falsehood and hypocrisy behind which you are hiding."[30]

Nijole Sadunaite protested in court at the intimidation and threats to which she had been subjected during the pre-trial investigation. Her KGB interrogators had threatened to put her in a psychiatric hospital. She also protested at the fact that witnesses were kept in a separate room and not allowed to stay in court after giving evidence.

She emphasised that she felt no enmity towards her judges and interrogators, although she thought she had the right to reprimand them for their unjust and hypocritical conduct. "I love you all as if you were my brothers and sisters and I would not hesitate to give my life for each of you. Today you don't need my sacrifice, but you do need to hear the truth spoken to your faces."[31]

The judge sentenced her to three years in a labour camp, to be followed by three years in exile. In her final statement, she expressed her sense of privilege at being allowed to suffer as a Christian for human rights. "This is the happiest day of my life," she stated. "Today I am standing at the side of Eternal Truth, Jesus Christ, and I remember the fourth beatitude, 'Blessed are they which hunger after righteousness, for they shall be filled'. How can I not be happy, when Almighty God has shown that light triumphs over darkness and truth over lies and falsehood?"[32]

More recent issues of the *Chronicle*[33] have provided evidence of Nijole Sadunaite's unbroken spirit in the camps of Mordovia (Documents 86, 87) despite a four-week journey by railway, during which she was kept in damp cells swarming with bedbugs, in the company of hardened criminals. In the camp, although she had already spent one period in the hospital and had to work from 6 a.m. to 10 p.m. in a workshop full of glass dust, she was still cheerful: "How good it is that the small craft of my life is being steered by the hand of the good Father. When he is at the helm, nothing is to be feared . . . . We have a lot of old women and sick people here, so I rejoice that I have been brought here in accordance with my calling – to nurse and to love."[34]

The censors removed Christmas and Easter cards from the letters Nijole Sadunaite received. Over three hundred letters sent to her from well-wishers in England were returned to the senders, while some of her own letters to other people were confiscated.[35] Nevertheless, it seems that the amount of interest demonstrated by the letters sent to her by people abroad had its effect on the authorities: according to the latest information received (Document 88) she has been released early and is now in exile in Boguchany, Krasnoyarsk Territory. She was given work, first as a cleaner in a secondary school, then as an orderly in a hospital. She suffered from chronic bronchitis in the camp, but her health is now improving. Perhaps the most impressive aspect of her letters is the complete lack of self-pity and the spiritual security they express: in almost every letter she thanks God for His goodness to her and rejoices at the beauty of the Siberian landscape and the friendliness of her fellow workers.

Although the trial of Sergei Kovalyov took place in Vilnius in December 1975 and was clearly intended partly as a deterrent to those responsible for the *Lithuanian Chronicle*, it was quite different from the trials listed above, and since in fact the Lithuanian aspect of the case turned out to be a very minor one it will be considered in the next chapter, which discusses the relation of the Lithuanian dissent movement to that in the Soviet Union as a whole.

Vladas Lapienis, Jonas Matulionis and Ona Pranckunaite, three Lithuanian Catholics, all of whom were involved in the production and distribution of the *Lithuanian Chronicle,* were arrested in October 1976 after a series of searches by the police at their homes and places of work. Vladas Lapienis, a pensioner with a heart condition, was already known to have written letters to the authorities protesting at the confiscation of religious literature from him by the police in 1973; his letter to Brezhnev on this subject was published in the *Lithuanian Chronicle* No. 23.[36]

He and Matulionis were arrested after a copy of the *Chronicle* was found by police at his home. Ona Pranckunaite was detained by the police after quantities of religious *samizdat* literature were found at her place of work, together with a typewriter and an Era photocopying machine. The KGB interrogator accused her of being a secret nun, threatened her with physical violence and told her she would be locked up with prostitutes. He jeered at her, saying she did not know what Siberia was really like. It turned out, however, that Ona Pranckunaite was well acquainted with the camps of Siberia. In 1951, when she was 15 years old, she had been given a ten-year sentence for writing an anti-Soviet poem.[37]

The trial of the three began on 20 July 1977. They were charged with circulating libellous anti-Soviet literature – the *Chronicle* itself. Their friends were scarcely allowed into the courtroom except to hear the inevitable verdict: Lapienis was sentenced, in spite of his advanced age, to three years in strict-regime camps and two years exile; Matulionis, who expressed his repentance, got a two-year conditional sentence; Pranckunaite was sentenced to two years in an ordinary-regime camp.[38] According to an eye-witness, all the defendants looked pale and ill and their voices could hardly be heard.[39] Nevertheless, Vladas Lapienis managed to put a copy of his final statement to the court into the hands of the *Chronicle*, which published it in No. 29 (Document 89). It expresses his defiant refusal to admit any "guilt": he had acted according to the original Soviet Constitution and the International Declaration of Human Rights; it is rather the Soviet authorities who should be ashamed of their actions. Citizens have a right and a duty to speak the truth and to defend their religion.

The KGB, having been apprised in no uncertain manner of the survival of the *Chronicle*, continued their campaign. Issues continued to appear and reached the West rapidly up to No. 20, and a gap after this proved to be only a hold-up in the communication with the West. By January 1979 36 issues had appeared, the last few of which could not be considered in detail in this book.

In October 1975 the authorities searched and interrogated Fr. S. Tamkevičius at Simnas, in connection with the *Chronicle*, but at the time of writing he has not been arrested.

Whatever the fate of this man and of others linked in some way with the *Chronicle*, the KGB seems powerless totally to suppress the freedom movement in Lithuania.

There are still people in Lithuania, prepared to identify themselves publicly and by name as supporters of the *Chronicle*, and who continue to campaign for the release of those imprisoned for producing it. In the prevailing climate of repression, the Vilnius priests who signed an open letter on 28 April 1975 making these points showed themselves to be men of outstanding bravery.[40] With such men to lead there are always others to follow.

DOCUMENTS

82. PLUMPA'S DEFENCE

"Before beginning to speak", said Plumpa, "I should like to emphasize that the charges should not be brought against me . . . . When I returned from the camp, the authorities constantly persecuted me after having me dismissed from employment . . . .

"If I haven't got the right to work", said Plumpa, "It means I haven't the right to live, and I can't consider myself as a citizen of a state which gives me no rights . . . .

" . . . . When I was about to get married, I had to obtain a residence permit, but so that I could live in peace with my family I changed my surname from Plumpa to Pluiras. Besides, I thought that if this falsification were discovered I would receive a two-year sentence, but that after serving it I would be left in peace."

[Some time later Plumpa changed his mind and then was left once more without either job or documents.]

"In 1972 when my wife was unable to work because of her two infant children", Plumpa continued, "I determined to get some kind of work to feed my family. When I received an offer to construct a duplicating machine, I agreed to do this."

"Who made this offer to you?" asked the judge.

"I have no moral right to answer that, as I don't wish to make trouble for that person."

"On what model did you contruct the machine?"

"I was brought about thirty drawings. It wasn't a very big duplicating machine but it was of a special design."

Plumpa described how he constructed the machine at the home of Semaška-Semaškevičius in a small attic room he had rented.

"Who brought you the parts?"

"The man who made the offer."

"Did you finish the work?"

"I completed seventy per cent of it" . . . .

"We know from the evidence of Patriubavičius that the first time you visited him it was to decide which room in his house at Ežerelis would be the best for the duplicating machine; the second time you came to set up the Era machine and taught Patriubavičius how to use it. On the third occasion you came to repair it and instruct people how to use it. The fourth time you brought with you Nos. 6 and 7 of the *Chronicle of the Lithuanian Catholic Church*, you took a religious book out of the machine, and then you set it to print about twenty copies of the *Chronicle*."

"Yes."

"Who gave you these issues of the *Chronicle?*"

"I have no moral right to betray these people" . . . .

"What were you tried for on the previous occasion?"

"For a political offence."

"Describe it in more detail."

"It was in the time of Khrushchev . . . . I was involved in some riots which took place on All Souls Day. (Each year at the Kaunas city cemetery the police would disperse, detain and arrest young people for lighting candles on the Tomb of the Unknown Soldier . . . . *CLCC* Ed.) That All Souls Day I was arrested at the cemetery and my home was searched. There they found a knife used for killing pigs, a rusty barrel and a grenade without a detonator. The court ruled that I had 'wanted to overthrow Soviet power by taking up arms against it.' I was given a seven-year sentence. I was then eighteen years old and all children and young people were in the habit of collecting and examining objects like the incomplete grenade and the rusty rifle, out of curiosity.

"When I was in prison my belief in chauvinistic nationalism declined, as a result of a sharp impression I received. There were a few nationalists imprisoned with me who had formerly shot Jews; in the camp they vied with each other in informing on others to the authorities, and they wore the red badge of administrators. Then I understood that a man who has no firm principles will strive only to satisfy his basest instincts, power, money and ambition for his career. Therefore I resolved to develop a firmer base for my outlook on life; I began to read the works of philosophers, especially the French thinkers such as Diderot, Rousseau and others . . . . At the same time I learned French. In reading these philosophical books I noticed the constant battle waged by atheists against God. I began to think: 'If there is no God, then why do they fight against what is non-existent? But what if He does exist?' . . . . Wanting to hear the other side, I began to read religious books. Thus I found God and the faith. Until 1961 I had looked on religion with suspicion, I never went inside a church and understood nothing about God, but since that year my faith has never betrayed me and I firmly believe to this day."

. . . .

Plumpa asked how long he would have to keep on being punished for the same offence, even though he had served his sentence. Ten, fifteen years, or all his life?

"Is the punishment I was given and served really insufficient? Or perhaps I should accept what the Vilnius police told me – that I had ruined my whole life? Perhaps they were right to ask me during my interrogation: 'Why did you marry? Why did you have children?'

. . . .

"According to the charges laid against me, it would appear that I have been campaigning against the Soviet system, slandering it and organizing others against it. Allow me to ask: Where? When? To whom? Where is the evidence? Where are the witnesses?" demanded Plumpa.

Plumpa said that the KGB had told him they would deprive him of his parental rights and that the State would bring up his children as atheists . . . .

He ended his speech with the request that his family should not be persecuted.[41]

83. PLUMPA IN PRISON

At the beginning of April 1975 it became known that Petras Plumpa has already been sent to a place of detention after his sentence. His present address is: Perm Region 618263, Chusovoi District, Kuchino, VS 389/36-2. The journey to this camp took two months. The Lithuanian KGB wanted to leave Plumpa in Vilnius for a while to be a witness in the case of J. Gražys, but as he could not give any evidence against him he was sent off to Kuchino.

Plumpa will only be able to receive food parcels after four years. He will be allowed to write two letters a month.

Plumpa is enduring his imprisonment in a thoroughly Christian spirit. In his opinion, the Christians of today should follow in the footsteps of the suffering, not the rejoicing, Christ; they should grow in charity, forgiving their persecutors and betrayers. Plumpa asks for help in prayer.[42]

Before being taken to Russia, Plumpa was held in a punishment cell for a week. When they removed him from Vilnius, they threw him into a wagon beside criminals despite the fact that political prisoners are supposed to be held separately. For two whole months Plumpa was pushed around between various murderers and thieves who showed their animal instincts in a variety of ways.

Some stole his warm, imported boots which his wife had given him in Vilnius, others tore off his padded coat, a third snatched his hat, gloves and other articles. A group cornered him and tried to interrogate him about details of his trial; when he refused to talk, they undressed him down to his underclothes and threatened to slit open his stomach. Plumpa was also deprived of all the food which he had with him and had hoped to take to the camp. He was kicked around in the process. All this was done with the knowledge of the supervisors, since he had pointed out that he had been sentenced under the political paragraphs of the Penal Code and should be transported separately.

In Minsk the guards displayed an even greater hatred of him than the prisoner-bandits. When they learned that Plumpa had been sentenced for his religion, they shouted furiously that religious papers and articles were forbidden items. They even confiscated little pictures of Jesus, Mary and Joseph. In their fury they pushed him around in such a way that even the thieves were surprised, since the guards had acted much more gently towards them.

Wishing to break Plumpa physically and morally, the KGB placed him in the same cells as murderers for two months; in a whole year in the Vilnius security prison he had not undergone a single medical check, despite the fact that he suffered throughout from high blood pressure and a chronic eye infection. Nevertheless, a certificate from the KGB had been read aloud during the trial to say that he was in good health. On what basis was this certificate written, if no doctor had ever examined him? It would seem that all this was part of an attempt to inflict the maximum punishment possible. When Plumpa arrived at the camp his blood pressure was 90 x 165. He pointed out to the camp authorities that he suffered from hypertension, eye infection and a constant cough which was the result of three bouts of pneumonia. Notwithstanding this, the head of the camp labour force assigned Plumpa to work which was seriously harmful to health – he even had to wear a mask to protect himself from the injurious dust. Because of shortage of oxygen, however, his eye veins began to protrude, while a constant infection of his eyelids and the dust caused trachoma. He began to see things as if through a mist, with no sight at all in the mornings. The infection was so serious that it spread all over his face.

After the trial and up to July Plumpa received no news from home. On 25 May of this year (1975) he sent an appeal to the Praesidium of the Supreme Soviet of the USSR, in which he formally renounced his Soviet citizenship and requested permission for himself and his family to go to Argentina. He gave as his motive the fact that believers were being deprived of their basic rights and that he was being held in conditions fit only for animals. On 2 July he received notification from Moscow that his appeal had been transmitted to the Prosecutor's office of Lithuania. There is a danger that he may receive an additional sentence. There is another prisoner serving with Plumpa who was given an extra five years because he renounced Soviet citizenship and asked permission to go abroad.

Aldona Pluiriene, Plumpa's wife, received no news from her husband's place of detention for six months, and so she sent a letter of enquiry. She was told in reply that her husband was well and that letters arriving at the camp were not registered, so it was impossible for the camp administration to explain why Plumpa had not received her letters. Soon after this query had been raised, Plumpa received three of his wife's letters written over a period of several months.[43]

FROM A PRISON LETTER BY PLUMPA

May Jesus Christ be honoured!

. . . . No matter where you may live the same important problems and questions always arise – those concerning the salvation of souls – and it is not always easy to know the most suitable field for us where we could bring most benefit. Only the King of Souls knows that, whilst we are left to bloom where He has sown us. If He has sown us in the field of sorrows – let us bloom in sorrow; if in that of solitude – let it be in solitude, for the Creator sows even the most beautiful of flowers on inaccessible tracks between mountain paths, and they have their value even though nobody sees them. In these days it is impossible for us to live without being seen: only the anguish of the soul can be unseen

and, like blossoms, it can be constantly plucked and offered to the
Saviour. This is the most beautiful decoration for the Altar of Jesus.
Without decorations of this kind even the finest churches are sad
places; without that kind of donor even the greatest of nations are
poverty-stricken . . . .

23 August 1976.[44]

In September 1976 Mrs. Pluiriene visited her husband in Perm
strict-regime camp. Sarunas Žukauskas* and Sergei Kovalyov are also
serving their sentences with him at Perm. As Mrs. Pluiriene was
accompanied on her long journey by Fr. J. Zdebskis, the camp
administration expressed the greatest annonyance and allowed
Plumpa's wife to be with her husband for barely twenty-four hours.
Before seeing her husband, she was minutely searched. During the
search she was stripped naked . . . .

At Easter Mrs. Pluiriene sent her husband greetings on a religious
picture, but the camp administration did not pass this on to the
prisoner. His wife wrote a complaint. When Plumpa demanded the
release of the religious picture, the camp administration locked him
up in solitary confinement. In the camp regulations governing what
may not be sent in to prisoners, there is no reference to a ban on
religious pictures.[45]

84. JAUGELIS IN COURT

Jaugelis at first spoke very quietly. The judge immediately interrupted him and asked him why he was speaking so angrily.

"It's offensive to me that believers don't enjoy the same rights as
atheists, that they have no freedom of speech or of the press. The very
fact that I'm on trial here is itself certain proof that believers don't
enjoy these freedoms. Really the roles should be reversed: my
accusers should be sitting here in the dock."

The judge interrupted Jaugelis and asked him to answer the
charges.

"What proof have you that believers do not have the same rights as
atheists?" the judge asked.

"Churches are being closed and turned into warehouses and
cinemas. We have no prayer-books, we aren't allowed to publish the
catechism, there is a famine of religious books in general and the
KGB hinders those who wish to enter the theological seminary."

"What proof have you that the State Security interferes with
entrance to the theological seminary?"

*See p. 297.

"While I was still working in Kaunas as a driver, I applied to enter the Kaunas Theological Seminary.* Some days later I was summoned to the police station and from there I was taken to KGB headquarters, where officials told me, "It all depends on us whether you get into the seminary or not.""

"So you conclude from this that the KGB has up to now prevented you from entering the seminary?" asked the prosecutor.

"Well, what would you have concluded, if KGB officials had said this to you?"

"You were detained in Šakiai, when you were gathering signatures for the so-called Memorandum?"† asked the judge.

"Yes."

"You were detained in the Prienai district for the same reason?"

"Yes."

"When you approached people, did you read them the Memorandum or did you tell them about it in your own words?"

"I only read them the Memorandum."

"What was your basic aim in doing this: to gather as many signatures as possible or to publicize the contents of the Memorandum as widely as possible?"

"I aimed to do both."

"Who gave you the Memorandum?"

"I don't remember."

"We know that one member of the family signed on behalf of the whole family."

"No. I fulfilled my task conscientiously."

"Stašaitis says that you made copies with him of the *Chronicle of the Lithuanian Catholic Church* No. 6."

"Yes."

"How many copies did you make?"

"About a hundred."

"Who distributed them?"

"I did."

"Where did you distribute the *Chronicle*?"

"Everywhere. I don't remember."

"Was this on your own initiative?"

"Yes."

"Stašaitis stated it was done on his initiative."

Patriubavičius's lawyer asked Jaugelis:

"How old are you?"

"27."

"Aren't you in bad health?"

"I'm not in the best of health, I have a polyp of the large intestine."

"Can that be cured?"

"No. Better living conditions could help a little."

. . . .

*Jaugelis was secretly ordained in 1978, after returning from prison camp.
†See pp. 115-17, 126-8.

Jaugelis conducted his own defence. He declared that in the Soviet Union believers were the poorest of the poor.

The judge interrupted him, saying that Jaugelis only had the right to defend himself at this moment, and that he could keep this speech for his final statement. Jaugelis then said that he would not defend himself.

. . . .

In his final statement Jaugelis accused the Soviet authorities and atheists of persecuting Catholics.

"Who are we, in the eyes of the atheists?" asked Jaugelis. "Fanatics, idlers, people who have failed to keep up with life. That's what atheists call believers. There is a popular saying that if you tell a man a hundred times that he is a dog, the hundred and first time he'll start to bark. Perhaps that's why believers can't imagine that they could have a religious press, that they could send their children to religious schools or elect their own representatives to government bodies.

"Who'll defend our interests if all the posts in the state machine are taken by atheists and we, the believers, are left on the very lowest level of the proletariat?"

According to Jaugelis, only people whose brains had frozen from fear could assert that there was freedom of religion in Lithuania and that believers were not persecuted.

. . . .

"What do you understand by the word 'freedom'? Perhaps the closure of Catholic churches and their conversion into warehouses and concert-halls? Perhaps the fact that priests are being imprisoned for giving religious instruction to children? Perhaps the fact that religious children are being turned against their parents? Why are basic human rights not being observed?

"Everywhere there are lies, deceit, the use of physical force against innocent people", said Jaugelis.

"All this is happening in a country where liberty, equality, brotherhood, justice and other ringing words are loudly proclaimed.

"However, today there are many people working for justice, freedom and the general welfare of the people. How many such have perished in the snows of Soviet Russia, how many have suffered hunger, disease, torture?

"They died as martyrs, enslaved but unconquered. Today, no less, the best hearts, the brightest minds are rotting in prison. How many such people are being 'cured' in psychiatric hospitals? Here we stand before the Supreme Court. Here the most just people should be in charge. And what do we see, in fact? Corruption, lies and violence . . . The thought even occurs to one that some are born slaves and others to enslave them.

"For Christ, for the truth He proclaimed, millions of martyrs have suffered and died. Let the atheists not think that today there is no one left who would be prepared to suffer for truth, for religion and the Church."

Jaugelis expressed the desire of all believers for equality with atheists, for parents to be allowed to educate their children in accordance with their beliefs, and for churches not to be closed.

Jaugelis ended his speech with the words: "Lithuania, land of our birth, our own dear country . . . How many times have the boots of foreigners trodden you down? How often have you been bathed in tears and blood? But you have always had many noble hearts which have not feared to suffer and die for you. Such hearts will be found even now."[*46]

85. THE TRIAL OF NIJOLE SADUNAITE, JUNE 1975

Nijole Sadunaite was arrested on 27 August 1974. The charge brought against her stated that the eleventh issue of the *Chronicle of the Lithuanian Catholic Church* was found on Miss Sadunaite's type-writer when the Soviet KGB searched her flat.

During the preliminary interrogation Miss Sadunaite refused to provide any evidence; the interrogators therefore threatened to put her in a psychiatric hospital. She was not allowed to receive food for two months.

At the end of January 1975 she wrote a complaint to the prosecutor's office, protesting against the abuse of authority in the conduct of the interrogators and their threats to detain her in a psychiatric hospital.

In March the members of the investigating committee contacted two of the local psychiatric hospitals in the city of Vilnius, inquiring whether Nijole Sadunaite had ever been a patient there. The answer from both hospitals was negative.

In April Nijole's case was transferred from No. 345 to a separate file numbered 416.

On 16 June the Supreme Court of the Lithuanian Republic opened Nijole Sadunaite's trial at 10 a.m., with Kudriašovas presiding and Bakučionis as state prosecutor.

The following witnesses were summoned by the court:

Jonas Sadunas – Nijole's brother.
Vladas Sadunas – Nijole's cousin.
[Mrs.] Regina Saduniene – Vladas's wife.
Povilaitis – school headmaster.
Kušleika and Miss Brone Kibickaite.

*In the original Lithuanian this last paragraph is in the form of a poem, written in the style of the old Lithuanian national anthem, which begins with the same words: "Lithuania, land of our birth . . ."

During the trial the witnesses were kept in a separate room. After giving evidence they were led out of the courtroom so that they could not hear the proceedings.

In the courtroom there were only six soldiers and five security men (Pilelis, Jankauskas, Platinskas and others). The chairman of the court allowed only Nijole's brother, Jonas, to remain in the courtroom. No observers were allowed in. The KGB men announced to anyone asking to be admitted that the courtroom was closed to the public.

Nijole Sadunaite refused to reply to the question of the court, " . . . since it is not I but you who are the criminals, who infringe the most elementary of human rights guaranteed by law, by the constitution and by the Universal Declaration of Human Rights." She went on: "You defend falsehood, repression and violence in slandering and sentencing innocent people. You torture them in prisons and camps. I will not, therefore, reply to any questions put by the court any more than I did during my interrogation, and by this means I register my protest against this trial."

Sadunaite explained why she refused the services of a defence counsel.

"My eyes were opened by the trial of Fr. Šeškevičius in 1970. He was sentenced for having fulfilled his priestly duties; because I had engaged a counsel for him, I was threatened by KGB Lieutenant Gudas, who said he would make out a case against me similar to that against Fr. Šeškevičius and put me in prison. In Room 225 of this very building the former KGB man Kolgov threatened my brother and relatives with punishment if I didn't stop interesting myself in the defence of Fr. Šeškevičius. It seems that to engage a counsel for a priest is a 'great crime'. Since, according to you, I'm a particularly dangerous state criminal and as I don't wish to bring your terrorist measures upon the heads of those who engage a counsel for me, I decline to have one. That's one side of the coin. The other side is that truth doesn't need to be defended, as it's omnipotent and invincible! Only treachery and falsehood, being powerless against truth, require arms, soldiers and prisons to prolong their vile domination – and win their temporary triumph. It's been well said that a one-sided government digs its own grave. I'm in the right and for the truth I'm prepared not only to lose my freedom, but would joyfully even sacrifice my life. There's no greater happiness than to suffer for justice and for humanity. That's why I don't need a lawyer. Instead, I'll speak for myself.

"I'd like to tell you all that I love as if you were my brothers and sisters and I wouldn't hesitate to give my life for each one of you. Today you don't need my sacrifice, but you do need to hear the truth spoken to your face. There's a saying that only he who loves has the right to reprimand. I make use of this right in addressing you . . . .

"You know very well that anyone who contributes to the publication of the *Chronicle* loves his people and that's why he's fighting for their honour and liberty, for their right to freedom of conscience which is guaranteed to all citizens by the constitution, by the laws of the land and by the Declaration of Human Rights. These aren't supposed to be just pretty words on paper or false propaganda. They must be enforced. The words of the constitution and of the law are powerless if they are not enforced. At this very moment legalized discrimination against believing citizens is the order of the day in our lives.

"The *Chronicle* is like a mirror which reflects all the criminal acts of the atheists against those who believe in God. Nothing evil likes to look at its own horrible image, it hates its own reflection. That's why you hate everyone who tears off the veil of falsehood and hypocrisy behind which you're hiding. But the mirror doesn't lose its worth for all that! A thief takes a man's money, but you rob the people of what's even more valuable – a person's right to be faithful to his convictions and to hand them on to his children.

"On 14-15 December 1960 the 'Convention Against Discrimination in Education' stated in Chapter 5 that parents must be able to bring up their children according to their convictions. However, in the records of my case a teacher, Mrs. Rinkauskiene, replied to a question: 'There's only one Soviet school system, so there's no need to confuse children or to teach them to be hypocrites.' Who's teaching them to be hypocrites? Is it those teachers or the parents who are free to bring up their children according to their convictions? When the school has destroyed the authority of the parents over their children, for some reason the parents are blamed, not the teachers, when children go off the rails.

"In Secondary School No. 10 at Klaipeda, a teacher, Miss Keturakaite, writes in the record of her interrogation: 'Since I'm a history teacher, I have to explain religious matters to my students. In presenting the development of Christianity, I also explain the myth of Christ . . .' How can this teacher talk of matters beyond her field of competence, when even in her own subject she doesn't show much competence by affirming the truth of a lie perpetrated by atheists – that Christ is a legend? It is incompetent people such as these who are bringing up and teaching our young people and using their authority as teachers to make their students believe lies.

"My interrogators, Lieutenant-Colonel Petruškevičius, head of the interrogation subdivision, Rimkus, head of the interrogation division, and Kažys, his assistant, often threatened to put me in a psychiatric hospital, because I refused to answer their questions, even though I explained to them that my silence was a protest against this whole case. When I got tired of their threats, I wrote protests to the prosecutor general of the Republic, and to the head of the KGB and of the interrogation division, asking that my letters be filed with the rest of the records concerning my case. This did not happen and the prosecutor general's assistant, Bakučionis, who is sitting right here, replied in writing that they have the right to order psychiatric tests to be carried out, but that the members of the investigating commission had not recommended it. But I was not talking about that in my letter, I was protesting against the manner in which the investigation was being carried out – threatening the person under investigation to make him betray his conscience.

"In that letter of protest I wrote (and I quote):

Does an interrogator have the right to threaten an accused person with detention in a psychiatric hospital or with having to submit to psychiatric tests, if the person will not give up his own opinion and will not betray his conscience? During the interrogations, because I refused to answer his questions Colonel Petruškevičius repeatedly threatened to put me into a psychiatric hospital where, he said, it would be much worse than in prison. Kažys, the assistant to the chief of the interrogation division, who saw me for the first time, immediately diagnosed me as being schizophrenic; my thinking was schizophrenic; he would ensure that the commission which determined psychiatric cases [of which he was a member], would examine me.

The chief of the interrogation division, Major Rimkus, also repeatedly threatened to have psychiatric tests carried out on me. Is the Soviet system of justice based only on fear? If I am a psychiatric patient, I need medical attention, not threats about my illness. Why threaten a sick person? Where is his guilt? But my interrogators don't believe this, because for five months now they have been threatening to put me in to a psychiatric hospital, since they want to break my will. This is the kind of behaviour that insults a person's dignity, and this is the cause of my protest.

. . . .

"You're not interested in having wrongs righted: on the contrary, you tolerate and condone them. This is easily proved by the fact that the witnesses who were called to testify in my case, and who were aware that the information in the *Chronicle* was true, were asked such questions as: 'Who gave this information to the publishers of the *Chronicle*? To whom did you talk? Who saw or heard you?' and so on. That's what you're afraid of: the truth! The interrogators didn't summon any of those who, in their hatred of anyone with different convictions, dismissed the secondary-school teacher, Miss Stase Jasiunaite of Kulautuva, for wearing a cross. And not only that: they mocked and insulted her and wouldn't even give her an ordinary job in the kitchen for a long time. Neither did they summon Markevičius, the chairman of the Executive Committee, nor Indriunas, the head of the financial section of the local *soviet* in Panevežys, for dismissing the typist, Miss Maryte Medišauskaite, because she went to church. This happened in spite of the fact that she had worked as a secretary for nine years. Yet everywhere you declare that religion is the private affair of all citizens and that each has equal rights, no matter what are his personal convictions. How noble is your propaganda and how ignoble is the reality!

. . . .

"The interrogators have never reprimanded doctors who have refused to allow their patients to have a priest at their deathbed, even if they and their relatives had requested one. Even criminals are granted a last request. But you dare to mock a person's most sacred beliefs at the most difficult moment of his life – the hour of death. Like a gang of bandits, you rob thousands of religious people of their moral and human rights. That's Communist morality and ethics!

"Who gave you atheists the right to tell pastors which priests they can invite to give retreats and missions to their parishioners? The formal decree on the Separation of the Church from the State and of the School from the Church declares that the State should keep out of internal religious activities. In Lithuania the Church is not separated from the State; it's oppressed by it. In the most illegal and insulting manner government personnel dictate in religious matters, not even excluding the realm of canon law. They order priests about and punish them according to their own biased opinions, paying no attention to the law.

"These and hundreds of other facts clearly show that you atheists are seeking to enslave people spiritually by forcing them to accept your opinions, and you justify any means to attain this end – lies, slander, terrorist tactics.

"And are you happy with your triumph? What have you triumped over? You have achieved the moral ruin of the country, you have killed millions of unborn children, people have been robbed of their human dignity, poisoned by fear and evil passions. That's what you have achieved, these are the fruits of your labours. Jesus Christ truthfully said: 'By their fruits shall you know them.' Every day your crimes are bringing you closer to the dust-heap of history.

"Thank God that not everyone has succumbed. We haven't got strength of numbers on our side, but we do have quality. We're not afraid of your prisons or concentration camps and we consider it our duty to denounce your accusations, which bring about injustice and degradation, which sow inequality and repression. To fight for human rights is everyone's sacred duty. I'm happy to have the privilege of suffering for the *Chronicle of the Lithuanian Catholic Church,* for I'm convinced of its truth and of its importance and I'll remain faithful to my convictions until my last breath. You may pass any laws you like, but keep them for yourselves. One has to discern what belongs to man and what God has commanded. Caesar can be given whatever is left over from what we owe to God. The most important thing in life is to

free one's heart and mind from fear, for to let evil go on raging
unchecked is a great sin."

. . . .

FINAL STATEMENT

"This is the happiest day of my life," Nijole began. "I'm being tried
for the *Chronicle,* which is a protest against the physical and spiritual
tyranny to which my people are being subjected. This means that I'm
being tried because I love our people and desire the truth. Loving men
is the greatest love and fighting for their rights is the most beautiful
love-song. May it echo in everyone's heart and never stop! I'm
privileged, my fate is an honourable one: not only have I fought for
human rights and justice, but I'm being punished for doing so. My
sentence will be my triumph! I'm sorry only for one thing – that I have
not been able to do as much as I would wish for our people. I will
gladly lose my freedom for the freedom of others and I'm willing to
die so that others may live.

"Today I'm standing on the side of Eternal Truth – Jesus Christ –
and I recall his fourth beatitude: 'Blessed are they that thirst after
righteousness, for they shall be filled.' How can I fail to be happy
when Almighty God has shown that light triumphs over darkness and
truth over lies and falsehood! In order to bring this about, I'm willing
not only to be imprisoned, but also to die . . . .

"So let's love one another and we'll be happy. The only man who is
unhappy is the one who doesn't love. Yesterday you were surprised
that I was in such good spirits at such a tragic hour of my life. This
proves that my heart is burning with love for all people, since only love
makes everything seem easy! We have to condemn evil as harshly as
possible, but we must love men, even if they are wrong. And we can
learn to do this in the school of Jesus Christ, who is our Way, our
Truth and our Life. May your kingdom, Jesus, come into every soul!

"I have one last request of this court: free all prisoners and all those
who have been taken to psychiatric hospitals for fighting for human
rights and for justice. You'd thus show your goodwill and it would be a
good beginning toward a new and better life, so that your beautiful
motto, 'A man is a brother to his fellow man', would become a
reality."

In the afternoon session the verdict of the court was read out:
"Nijole Sadunaite is charged under Article 68 I(d) of the Penal Code
of the Lithuanian Republic with the reproduction and circulation of
the *Chronicle of the Lithuanian Catholic Church.* She is sentenced to
three years deprivation of liberty, the sentence to be served in a strict-
regime camp, followed by three years exile."

On hearing the verdict, Nijole Sadunaite asked the court: "Why
have I been sentenced so lightly?"

In accordance with the court verdict, Miss Sadunaite's typewriter was confiscated.

On 20 June 1975, after lunch, the KGB confiscated all her notes and writings and after a detailed search removed her to a camp at the following address:

Mordovskaya ASSR
pos. Javas, uchr. Zh. Kh. 385/3.[47]

86.   NIJOLE SADUNAITE'S JOURNEY TO THE CAMP

On 20 June 1975, soon after the trial, Nijole's brother took some warm clothes to his sister, but the head of the Vilnius KGB isolation prison, Petrauskas, refused to accept them. On the evening of the same day Nijole Sadunaite was taken off to Mordovia.

She was held in a Pskov prison cell for seven days. It was underground – damp, cold, dark and airless. Only a dirty mattress was thrown in for her to sleep on, there were no pillow or bed-clothes. In this cold and damp cellar Nijole caught a chill, and when she asked the supervisor for cough medicine the latter barked back angrily: "You can cough away to your heart's content". After such a reply Nijole did not ask again for medicine, although she was greatly in need of it.

She was then held for one and half days with a female criminal in a cell in Yaroslavl, she spent seven days in a basement cell in Gorky with female criminals, and one night in a cell in Ruzayevka. In Potma she stayed five days in a cell with female criminals. Every night was spent sleeping on the floor. The cell was full of bugs, as merciless as the cell supervisors themselves. In Potma Nijole spent two days in an isolation cell.

The journey from Vilnius to Mordovia lasted from 20 June to 18 July. In trains she was usually transported with criminal prisoners, locked in iron cages. For food she received bread, very salty fish and water. She did not take the bread or fish and only drank the water. In all the above-mentioned cells she was provided with a very small prisoner's ration, which she ate.

In the autumn of 1975 four KGB men from Vilnius arrived at the camp in Mordovia. They questioned Nijole Sadunaite as to whether she had given her speech and final statement in court to someone in the Vilnius isolation prison, *en route* to Mordovia, or in the Mordovian camp.

She replied: "Haven't you learned that, since I made no reply to your questions during nine and a half months of preliminary investigations in the Vilnius KGB isolation prison, I am not going to answer you now?" The KGB men said that they were not asking her to whom she had given her speech, but only where she had passed it on. Nijole did not reply to this question either. Having gained nothing, the KGB men said that they had only called in to see her in the course of their other duties, since they had other business. They asked her about her state of mind – whether she was bored, how she was getting on in the colony, then they left.

During the whole period of her imprisonment Nijole Sadunaite has not received a single letter from the U.S.A., although her relatives and others have written to her. Neither has she received any letters from England or other countries, nor do all the letters sent from Lithuania reach her.

Some chocolate was sent to Nijole from Norway, but this was not given to her. She only learned about this parcel when eight roubles were deducted from her tiny prison wages for it. Three months later the camp administration allowed her brother to have the parcel.

In July 1975 the Ukrainian poet Vasyl Stus was badly beaten in the Mordovian camp. When she learned of this incident, Nijole, together with four other female political prisoners, staged a hunger strike from 1-5 August as a sign of protest against the arbitrariness and brutality of the camp administration.[48]

87. NIJOLE SADUNAITE'S LETTERS FROM THE CAMP

. . . I am grateful to those whose efforts have led to my being here. I have learned and experienced much, and it is all to my benefit. The good Lord truly knows best what I need.

In six days time it will be six months since I was brought here from Vilnius, but it all seems so recent, as though it were yesterday. And everything stands before my eyes: my guard of 'honour', my fellow victims, of whom there were many (every one of them criminals, I was the only political prisoner), the final farewell glance at the town or, more accurately, the railway platform, and all the romance of the journey which is indescribable, for one has to undergo it oneself to be able to experience life and understand the need and value of love. I shall have the opportunity to live through that romantic journey a second time – when they take me to my place of exile . . .

How good it is that the small craft of my life is being steered by the hand of the good Father. When He is at the helm nothing is to be feared. Then, no matter how difficult life may be, you will know how to resist and love. I can say that the year 1975 has flown by like a flash, but it has been a year of joy for me. I thank the good Lord for it.

There is not a great deal of dust in our section, although the material from which we sew gloves is dusty with glass powder. The work is oppressive in its monotony, and frequent mechanical defects add to this – patience is needed. The mechanic does not come every day and we often have to wait until he does his repairs, but the norm does not wait for us . . . We have to produce seventy pairs of gloves in a day.

I came back from hospital on 3 March. Finally, it seems, I shall be well and on my feet again. Your diagnosis is the most accurate – a great loss of strength. My 'holiday' lasted a longish time: it began on 18 October. I worked only six days in November, spent the whole of December in the hospital, and only at the end of the month did I sew for four days. January fell into two parts – I worked one half and not the other. All February and the first three days of March I was in hospital. I now sew a little, at intervals; whenever I feel weak, I go into the yard to enjoy the fresh air and sun. I complete my norm because we work a single shift. I can begin sewing at 6 a.m. and finish at 10 p.m. In this way everything is going excellently at present. Everyone likes me and I try to return their kindness. I am fortunate and contented.

We have many old women and sick people, so I rejoice that I have been brought here in accordance with my calling – to nurse and to love. Although I long greatly to see you all, it will be hard for me to leave here. It will be distressing to leave people who have become so near and dear to me, but the good Lord does indeed care for us most of all . . .

I receive letters not only from acquaintances, but also from some whom I have never met. I am so moved by people's desire to help in any way possible. How much feeling and sincerity there is in people's hearts. How encouraging is all this, how it raises one's spirit and stimulates one to be better, to be worthy of such great love.

Ten girls from Kaunas write: "We are with you and intercede for you with God. Do not give way! Everything on earth can be borne by people of great spirit. Best wishes from our nation!"[49]

88. NIJOLE SADUNAITE'S LETTERS FROM EXILE

Most Respected Birute!

I thank you most sincerely for the beautiful postcards, paper and for the even more beautiful words and your affection. May the good Lord provide a most adequate reward.

The love and goodness of people is not affected by distance, as it reaches me, and that bright warmth of people's hearts provides me with so much joy and strength!

May the Almighty increase your strength, may He provide the pure joy and inner peace which the world cannot give!

With gratitude, respect and love.

Nijole

23 May 1977.

Most Respected and Beloved Birute!

I send you my most sincere greetings and thanks for your good words and beautiful postcards which I received in Barashevo. May the Almighty reward you a thousand-fold!

I flew from Krasnoyarsk to Boguchany on 19 September. Thanks to good people I now have a job as a cleaner in a secondary school. I live on the shores of the Angara river and the taiga surrounds the place. Very beautiful views. Thanks be to the good Lord for everything!

I live with another cleaner who is bringing up three children and I now have no reason for being miserable. The children like me and we get on very well together. The people are also good to me.

From the bottom of my heart I wish you the greatest blessings from the good Lord! Stay well and happy! God be with you!

Your greatly loving and thankful.

Nijole

2 October 1977.[50]

Dearest Ones!

Since 2 November I have been working at the Boguchany district hospital as an orderly. I have a room in a hostel. People are considerate and friendly towards me. Thanks to Almighty God, love and goodness are alive even in Siberia. I have everything I need and rejoice at the beautiful landscape. I am grateful to all who remember me in their prayers. This is the support that I need the most.

May the good Father bless and look after you all!

With love
Nijole.[51]

89. FINAL STATEMENT OF VLADAS LAPIENIS

[original title]

I detest injustice, lies, cunning, deceit and coercion. So when I see these evils I cannot pass them by with an easy conscience. However, some government officials describe a struggle against such evils, and criticisms of them, as anti-Soviet agitation and propaganda, an attempt to oppose the Soviet Government and the like . . . .

During my interrogation I was asked more than once why I saw only the worst in Soviet life. This is untrue. I bring evil into the open, not because I see nothing good, but because evil brings people trouble, misfortune and suffering. If we want to aspire to a better life, we must struggle against evil. It is unquestionably much more pleasant to rejoice about our achievements, and for this the Government will praise and might even reward you. To bring errors and injustice into the open, to criticize some of the government officials, means "disturbing their peace". This requires self-sacrifice, it involves risks and sometimes results in the temporary loss of one's freedom . . . .

How would it seem to the Marxists if the Soviet public announced to the Communist Party that freedom of anti-Communist propaganda was acknowledged to all citizens, but pro-Communist propaganda forbidden? The Communists would surely say that this was not freedom but abominable demagogy . . . . The Communists would not merely fail to rejoice over such "freedom", but would condemn it as a mockery of the most elementary human rights and basic freedoms. Why, therefore, do the Communists proffer a form of "freedom" to others which they do not themselves acknowledge as freedom? . . . .

Apart from obligations to the State I, as a Catholic, have a duty to my religion and Church, placed upon me by my conscience. The defence of the rights of believers and the Church is not a question of politics but the sacred duty of every Catholic.

When there is no longer any persecution of believers there will be no motive for the promotion of discontent, indignation or opposition and, by the same token, no *Lithuanian Chronicle* . . . .

We, the Catholics of Lithuania, are determined to fight for our faith, for true equality and for our rights which should be guaranteed not only verbally and on paper, but also in everyday life.

To be condemned for doing my duty is not only no shame to me, but it is an honour. I stand on the side of the Eternal Truth who said: "Blessed are they which are persecuted for righteousness' sake: theirs is the kingdom of heaven. Blessed are ye when men persecute you and say all manner of evil against you falsely for my sake" (Matt. 5: 10-12).

We ought to obey God rather than men.[52]

NOTES TO CHAPTER XI

1. *CLCC* 10, p. 14 (E), p. 7 (L).
2. *CLCC* 6, p. 21 (E), p. 9 (L).
3. *CLCC* 11, p. 39 (E), p. 33 (L).
4. *CLCC* 8, pp. 6-16 (E), pp. 3-8 (L); 9, pp. 17-21 (E), pp. 8-11 (L).
5. *CLCC* 17, p. 14.
6. *CLCC* 12, p. 5 (E), pp. 1-2 (L) (quoted on p. 57).

7. *CLCC* 17, p. 13.
8. *Loc. cit.*
9. *Arkhiv Samizdata,* Vol. 17, No. 1915.
10. *Ibid.,* No. 1916.
11. For example, *The Times,* 24 October 1974, p. 6.
12. The information on the build-up to the case in *Chronicles* 8-12 is frag-
    mentary. However, No. 13 devotes all its 49 pages (English text) to Case
    No. 345, the main body of which is a partial transcript of the trial by an
    eye-witness. This account is based on that issue of the *Chronicle.*
13. See the plan published in *CLCC* 13, p. 38 (Russian MS).
14. *CLCC* 13, p. 9 (E), p. 5 (L).
15. See, for example, Vasili Kozlov, "How a Criminal Became a Christian in
    a Russian Prison", *Church Times,* 1 January 1971, available from Keston
    College, Keston, Kent, in brochure form.
16. London, 1971.
17. *Sovetskaya Litva,* 29 December 1974.
18. *CLCC* 15, p. 20.
19. *CLCC* 16, p. 4.
20. *Ibid.,* pp. 4-5.
21. *Ibid.,* pp. 5-6.
22. *CLCC* 17, p. 12.
23. *CLCC* 15, pp. 13.
24. *CLCC* 13, p. 49 (E), p. 45 (L).
25. *No Greater Love . . .* The Trial of a Christian in Soviet-occupied
    Lithuania, The Lithuanian Roman Catholic Priests League of America,
    120 Front Street, Baltimore, MD, 1975; *Delo Kovalyova* (The Case of
    Kovalyov), 16 pp., Khronika Press, New York, 1976.
26. *CLCC* 16, p. 2.
27. *CLCC* 17, pp. 1-11. The substance of this account has also been printed
    in *No Greater Love* (see note 25 above).
28. *CLCC* 17, p. 11.
29. *Ibid.,* p. 3.
30. *Ibid.,* p. 4.
31. *Ibid.,* p. 3.
32. *Ibid.,* p. 9.
33. *CLCC* 23, pp. 44-6 (MS); *CLCC* 24, pp. 14-15 (MS).
34. *CLCC* 23, p. 44.
35. *CCE* 46, pp. 66-7 (MS).
36. *CLCC* 23, pp. 24-34.
37. *CLCC* 25, pp. 8-9.
38. *CLCC* 29, p. 10.
39. *Ibid.,* pp. 11-12.
40. *CLCC* 17, pp. 14-17.
41. *CLCC* 13, pp. 14-18, 43-4 (E), pp. 10-14, 39-40 (L).
42. *CLCC* 16, pp. 6-7.
43. *CLCC* 18, pp. 9-11.
44. *CLCC* 25, pp. 39-40.
45. *Ibid.,* p. 38.
46. *CLCC* 13, pp. 18-19, 42, 44-5 (E), pp. 14-15, 38, 40-1 (L).
47. *CLCC* 17, pp. 1-11.
48. *CLCC* 24, pp. 14-15.
49. *CLCC* 23, pp. 44-6.
50. *Teviškes Žiburiai,* Mississauga, Ontario, Canada, 1 December 1977.
51. Private letter to Jonas Sadunas, undated, but received by him 3 January
    1978.
52. *CLCC* 29, pp. 4-9.

XII

RELIGION, NATIONALISM AND HUMAN RIGHTS

IT IS the purpose of this study to concentrate on religion. Nevertheless, in Lithuania religion was – and still is – intertwined with so many other strands of life, both public and private, that it is impossible to keep it in a separate compartment. It is not possible to retain the perspective of our subject without looking at the relationship between nationalism and religion.

It is by no means unusual in Eastern Europe for nationality to be identified with religious affiliation. The position of the Catholic Church in Poland is very similar to that in Lithuania, and for much the same reasons: Catholicism in both countries has for hundreds of years been the religion of the people, rather than of the government, and of an oppressed non-Russian nation, as opposed to the Russian colonial power. In both countries Catholicism has been the uniting factor, keeping the nation together even when the national territory was split between warring great powers; in both countries Catholicism pervades national literature and is closely identified with the national language itself. In Lithuania the Catholic Church is the only purely Lithuanian institution that cannot be assimilated into the Party totalitarian structure. Attempts have been made by the Communist Party to split up the synthesis between church and nationality in Lithuania by emphasizing class links with the "brotherly" Russian nation and by propagating the concept of a new "Soviet nation", but these attempts have failed. In Lithuania that failure has been far more resounding than in some other national areas of the USSR, although the new "Soviet nation" is not exactly popular there either.

An analysis of *samizdat* documents from the Soviet Union for the year 1976[1] showed that exactly a quarter were from various national groups dissatisfied with their situation in the USSR. In Ukraine, for example, russification of the language, the press, education and literature has gone much further than in Lithuania. Most "national" republics have a national representative as the nominal head of government in the republic, but the deputy head is almost always a Russian, who is the real person in charge. The same analysis noted that about a third of the 1976 *samizdat* documents were from religious groups protesting against government persecution. Lithuania thus combines the two strongest trends in the human rights movement inside the USSR: religion and national feeling. It is this synthesis that has given the *Chronicle of the Lithuanian Catholic Church* its authoritative position.

The *Lithuanian Chronicle* mainly, though not exclusively, confines its reporting of nationalism to the religious aspect, but one can detect a strengthening stand on nationalism as the periodical develops its personality. Lithuanian nationalists who have achieved international publicity through their actions in life or death, but who do not have any particular relation to religion, are treated with restraint in the *Chronicle*. This is the case with Romas Kalanta, who immolated himself in a park in Kaunas in May 1972,[2] and Simas Kudirka, who jumped ship in the U.S.A., was returned by the Americans to the Soviet authorities, but was finally allowed to emigrate after a period in a prison camp,[3] – probably as a result of large-scale demonstrations on his behalf in the U.S.A.

If, however, we look at issues 10, 17 and 20 of the *Chronicle,* we have clear evidence of an increasing attention paid to nationalist questions which are only marginally religious. Thus No. 10 reports extensively on the Vilnius trial of five ethnographers in February-March 1974,[4] while No. 17 has an important article on religion and nationalism, "Thoughts on Victory Day",* followed later in the same issue by a long selection of miscellaneous items on the state of the nation.[5]

No. 20 has an extended article on pollution which is not connected with religion at all.[6] Mostly, however, the *Chronicle* confines itself to relatively brief reporting on a variety of nationalist manifestations: a strike,[7] a boy in school persecuted for doubting whether "freedom" exists for Lithuania,[8] the circulation of anti-Soviet leaflets in Vilnius and Kaunas on "Victory Day", 1975.[9] Only a brief reference is made to the *samizdat* publication, *Naujasis Varpas* ("New Bell")† in the context of the trial of the ethnographers. However, by the time the more openly nationalist journal *Aušra* ("Dawn") made its appearance in *samizdat* (perhaps one should say its re-appearance : there was a nineteenth-century anti-Tsarist publication of the same name) the *Chronicle* was prepared to summarize its contents more fully (Document 90).

Although the *Chronicle* expressed its joy at the appearance of a third *samizdat* journal in Lithuanian, *Dievas ir Tevyne* ("God and Fatherland"), it published a letter from one of its readers severely criticizing the new journal for its intolerant and insulting tone towards its opponents, which was reminiscent of the way atheists wrote about believers. "Let us respect others if we also wish to be respected," the *Chronicle* reader comments.[10]

*See pp. 297.   †Presumably the same as *Varpas* (p. 252).

On looking at the nationalist "crimes" which the authorities are concerned to stamp out, one is struck by the very pettiness of so many of them. One reads of incidents so trivial that they would be laughable, if it were not for the major campaign against human rights and national identity of which they are symptomatic.

The singing of folk-songs is a dangerous undertaking, because if they are Lithuanian they will more than likely extol some aspects of Lithuania's past not acceptable to the Soviet authorities.[11] A museum official has even been dismissed for permitting such old songs to be sung in the museum.[12]

Communist Poland permitted the publication of a fifteenth-century map of Lithuania, but to display this on your walls in Lithuania itself can lead to a furore among those conducting a house-search.[13] Old books may be confiscated from second-hand bookshops, leading to the dismissal of the manager. When a large cache of pre-war stamps was found in a bank vault in February 1975, the authorities confiscated and burned the whole lot, both those which the employees had kept themselves and those they had handed over to a museum.[14]

Although the revered nationalist leader of the nineteenth century, Bishop Valančius, has had his books republished and has a museum to his memory at Nasrenai, the village of his birth, it is not permitted to write favourable comments in the visitors' book – or at least this is the implication of its confiscation.[15]

Even travel to archaeological sites can arouse the hostility of the authorities, both because of their symbolical meaning and because people have criticized the destruction of these places.[16]

While it is impossible psychologically to eradicate the past of a nation, it is only slightly easier to remove all the corresponding visual signs. Nevertheless, the authorities try to remove any slogan which harks back to the independent past[17] and they prevent the erection of any memorial to people associated with Lithuania's past heroism.[18] Naturally, any singing of the old national anthem or showing of the flag is banned.[19]

Sporting occasions make the authorities especially nervous. Where no local team is competing in an international tournament in Lithuania, the local people are perfectly capable of giving vent to their feelings by supporting anyone against a Russian team – so the authorities have to try to recruit "more loyal" spectators, by distributing tickets to selected people.[20]

Where Lithuanians attempt to contact their own exiled nationals in Siberia, for example, or the leaders of other nationalist groups, such as Armenians or Georgians, the KGB is much more seriously concerned,[21] as it must be by contacts with Lithuanian émigrés abroad.[22]

There was an instance in April 1975 of the dismissal of a senior politician, Povilas Kulvietis, deputy chairman of the Lithuanian

Council of Ministers, for his suspected favourable disposition towards Lithuania.[23] A Russian succeeded him.

Clearly, the professions of historian and ethnographer are dangerous ones, obviously attracting people of a certain temperament who may well wish to find some legitimate expression for their feelings about their country. One recent Soviet definition of the ethnologist almost obliges him to ignore the very groundwork and scientific basis of his own profession:

"By not collecting all kinds of ethnological material, but only that which reeks of the past, we turn away, whether we like it or not, from the most important problems of life . . . The first task of the ethnologist is to record everything in the life of the working people today, all that the Soviet Government has given them."[24]

It is not surprising, therefore, to find representatives of this profession in very serious trouble, comparable to that which has overtaken the producers of the *Lithuanian Chronicle*. The long trial of five ethnographers in February-March 1974 led to the imposition of sentences of up to six years (the youngest, Š. Žukauskas, 24, receiving the longest sentence).[25] The charges against them included "establishing an underground organization to inform the public of the criminal activities of the Soviet Government against the Lithuanian nation" and "the dissemination of contraband literature".

While some of the manifestations outlined above may seem trivial, they are in fact the expression, on a variety of levels, of the most deep-seated malaise over the welfare of Lithuania. It is the contention of a number of outspoken Lithuanians that, far from bringing new morality and new opportunities to the many, the advent of Soviet power is the direct cause of a moral decline in the standards of the nation.

The addendum to the Memorandum of the 17,000 spoke of a "tenfold increase in juvenile delinquency, drunkenness, suicide, divorce and abortion" since the Soviet take-over.[26]

In the opinion of one writer represented in the *Chronicle,* the nation is "drowning in a river of millions of litres of alcohol" – and the Government is unwilling to allow campaigns against it because of the potential loss of tax revenue. There is a similar worry over the decline in sexual morals, represented by the enormous increase in the number of hospital beds allotted to cases of venereal disease and in the budget to fight it.[27] The anonymous author of "Thoughts on Victory Day" reflects also on the decline of the Lithuanian population as a symptom of malaise.† There are now fewer Lithuanians in the country than there were at the turn of the century, the most serious ravages arising not through the Second World War but from the deportations and murders after the second Soviet occupation. Lithuania even has to export its political prisoners.

A ban on original historical writing is an attempt to cut the country off from its own past,‡ a clear prelude to russification. The present

†See p. 295.   ‡See p. 18.

plan to create a "Lithuania without Lithuanians" is more subtle in
form but no different in ultimate goal from that which pertained at the
time of both the German and Soviet deportations. This is not the place
to study the effect of the corresponding colonialization – the import of
Russian people who are designated to provide the leadership of the
republic. However, we should note that in Lithuania the percentage of
Russians is lower than in the other Baltic republics. The exaggerated
attention paid to proficiency in Russian at school[28] is merely one
manifestation of the indoctrination which inculcates upon the young
the cultural and ethnic superiority of the conquering race.

But if a true appraisal of their heritage has become difficult for
young Lithuanians living in their own country, the situation is even
more serious for those living elsewhere through enforced migration or
the accident of geography. However great the concentration of
Lithuanians in a particular locality, Lithuanian schools are totally
banned except on the territory of the republic itself, while the Soviet
press criticizes the closure of such Lithuanian schools in the U.S.A.[29]
Yet Russians living in Lithuania have a plethora of their own schools.

This affects not only pockets of Lithuanian people scattered
through deportation, but, more seriously, approximately 50,000
Lithuanians "cut off" in Belorussia through the re-alignment of the
frontiers after the Second World War. The *Chronicle* has several
references to this, including the statement that in the whole of this
area there are only two Catholic churches;[30] when a confirmation
service was allowed in one of these, it was swamped by thousands of
parents and children from all over Belorussia. Although the Soviet
press condemned the closure of the last Lithuanian language school in
the U.S.A. and offered to send American Lithuanians books to
educate their children, Lithuanians in Belorussia have appealed in
vain for their children to be educated in their own language; they even
find it difficult to order Soviet Lithuanian periodicals.[31] However, the
most important account of the problem resulting from these circumstances is contained in a little-known appeal from people living in
Belorussia. Here is an issue which is almost totally unknown, smaller
in scale than that of the Jews, the Crimean Tartars or the Volga
Germans, but of the same moral order. Document 91 extracts those
portions of the letter most relevant to religion and these indicate the
tone and urgency of the whole appeal.

A detailed and impassioned outcry against the physical pollution of
the land of Lithuania by the projected building of a new oil refinery
turns out to be an indictment of Soviet policy which is among the most
outspoken passages of the *Chronicle*. The pages vibrate with indignation against the Russians, but their motivation is love of the country
and the desperate concern to preserve its unique but disappearing
countryside against the ravages of colonialism under the guise of
economic progress.[32]

In one of the more recent *Lithuanian Chronicles* a wise old teacher reflects with sadness on the present state of Lithuania and of its Church. Most of all he regrets his own many years of active atheism in the past, during which time he expressed ideas which others took up and which have contributed to the present decline in morality and responsibility in society. Ten years of labour camps powerfully guided him back to the path of faith. Now he is able to see why it was that the Tsarist empire considered that the first step towards the denationalizing of Lithuania had to be the removal of the influence of the Catholic Church. It is not surprising that the Soviet authorities have discovered the same truth. The Church, more now than ever, keeps the key of Lithuania and anyone who fights her is a "grave-digger" of his own nation.*

There seems to be an increasing number of people in Lithuania willing to say this publicly. Jaugelis and Plumpa put it forthrightly in their different ways at their trial.† Juozas Šileikis, in defending his right to bring up his children as Christians, reveals the interlocking of religion and nationalism in his mind which is wide-spread in Lithuania today and may well be becoming even more so, as people reflect more deeply on current trends in Soviet policy and the moral state of Lithuania (Document 92). There are, for example, reports of women beginning to wear Lithuanian national costume to church again – a small but significant and defiant gesture.[33]

It is hard to obtain any concrete evidence that the hierarchy is giving a lead in the direction of emphasising the unity of Church and nation. Naturally, it would be highly dangerous for the bishops to do so, but they have not made any pretence of saying the opposite and people would probably therefore draw their own conclusions. One receives occasional glimpses, though, of the Church sublimating nationalism in an impressive way.

On Holy Saturday 1972, two young atheists came into the church at Plunge and began to cause a disturbance. They pulled down a crucifix from the wall and smashed it. The *Lithuanian Chronicle* reports:

> The priest, in his Easter sermon, declared that he who insults a nation's flag offends every citizen of that country. 'The crucifix is the flag of the faithful and today it has been insulted'. The whole church wept.[34]

Apart from the trial of Jaugelis and Plumpa, one of the most moving accounts in the *Chronicle*, highlighting the relationship between religion and nationalism, is the life-story of Mindaugas Tamonis, an engineer brilliant enough to have gained entry into the *Concise Lithuanian Soviet Encyclopaedia* while still in his thirties, before his death in 1975. The case of Tamonis has remained almost totally unknown outside Lithuanian circles at the time of writing, in spite of its similarity to other incidents in the Soviet Union when dissidents have been incarcerated in psychiatric hospitals. Tamonis' original

---

*Quoted in part on p. 219.   †See pp. 274-6, 279-82.

crime was his refusal to renovate a monument to the Red Army until a memorial had been erected to Stalin's victims. He was declared abnormal and after being "treated" with dangerous drugs for almost two years he was driven to suicide. The *Chronicle* calls his death murder:

> He was not shot, not made to rot in prison, he was not even summoned for interrogation. He was being healed. Moditen-B is a medicine – if you give it to someone who is ill. Given to a healthy person, it is an instrument of death (Document 93).

The Catholic Church has become the focus of the human rights movement in Lithuania because of her central position in the life of ordinary Lithuanians. Political restrictions are always irksome and, for nationalists, a permanent thorn in the flesh, but restrictions and harassment in everyday personal life over matters such as attendance at Mass, the religious education of one's child by a friend, the wearing of a cross, open discussion of religious matters with colleagues or co-workers – these are daily reminders of the insults to freedom of speech and conscience in Soviet legislation and government instructions on religion. The Soviet Constitution provides for the separation of Church and State, but almost anything connected with the Church – religious services, baptism, confirmation, marriage, funerals, last rites, even the church buildings and priests – must have government sanction or registration to be legal. This situation is of course common to religious denominations in the Soviet Union as a whole, but the Russian Orthodox and Baptist human rights movements are less united, both ideologically and territorially, than the Lithuanian Catholic movement.

Like other human rights groups in the Soviet Union, Lithuanian Catholics have concentrated on pointing out the discrepancies between Soviet legislation, the Soviet Constitution and Soviet practice. Nijole Sadunaite typified this attitude when, at her trial, she pointed out that her judges were themselves ignoring the law: "It is not I, but you, who are the criminals, who infringe the most elementary of human rights guaranteed by law, by the Constitution and by the Universal Declaration of Human Rights."* At their interrogations and trials human rights activists often now make use of a *samizdat* book giving instructions on "How to behave during interrogation", and quote the laws they can use to their advantage.

It could well be that the united religious base for human rights in Lithuania will give the current movement to establish justice a firmer and more reliable ground for future action than the sometimes diffuse "democratic" movement in the rest of the Soviet Union. While the main strength of the Lithuanian movement is an internal one, it is only natural that the activists should wish to contact people in sympathy with them both inside and outside the Soviet Union.

*See p. 283.

The internal links at the outset were weak. To this day there is very little in the *Lithuanian Chronicle* about non-Lithuanian *samizdat*. There is no evidence of organized anti-Soviet activity linking the three Baltic States.* There has, however, been a keen concern in recent years to establish contacts with prominent human rights activists based in Moscow and through them (or directly) with the world outside. An indicator of the original lack of contact as seen from Moscow is to be found in the pages of the *Chronicle of Current Events*. The first four-teen issues[35] do not include the Church in Lithuania in their subject matter. Only in the last three numbers for 1970 (15-17) did the situa-tion in Lithuania first receive the attention it deserved from the editors of the Moscow *Chronicle*.[36]

On its part, the *Lithuanian Chronicle* is at first extremely reticent in its references to anyone outside Lithuania (except the Vatican) from its first issue in 1972 up to No. 12 in 1974, after which such references become much more frequent. By No. 15, a year later (1975), the editors are ready to publish a vibrant appeal in support of Sakharov and other Russian dissidents, addressed to a broad section of Soviet and world opinion, no doubt gaining inspiration from the reaction to earlier feelers in this direction (Document 94).

One cannot at the moment say whether Sergei Kovalyov was the only or even the chief link between the Lithuanian and Moscow activists. Certainly, however, the Soviet authorities behaved as if he was. After his arrest in Moscow on 27 December 1974, he was immediately sent to Vilnius to face investigations[37] and, a year later, was tried and sentenced: his sentence was a savage one of ten years, of which the last three were to be spent in exile. A transcript of this trial has been published in the West.[38] A careful examination of this and of the associated documents published with it reveals a curiously low proportion of Lithuanian relevance, in view of the Soviet action of despatching Kovalyov to Vilnius with such rapidity. While no one denied that Kovalyov had inserted Lithuanian material into the *Chronicle of Current Events*, it was at no time claimed that this was one of his main activities. The suspicion arises, therefore, that the KGB was concerned primarily to remove such an important case from the added glare of publicity it would have received in Moscow, with its resident corps of foreign correspondents, and merely chose Vilnius as a convenient alternative. Whether or not the KGB achieved its objectives, these events certainly caused an increase in Lithuanian sympathy for Kovalyov and those whom he represents. *Chronicle* No. 15 devotes three pages to him;[39] No. 20, issued just before the trial began in December 1975, reciprocates consideration earlier shown by the Moscow *Chronicle* by reprinting the latter's account of the pre-trial investigation,[40] while No. 21 gives a spirited account of the events surrounding the trial itself (Document 95). The Soviet plan to avoid publicity for Kovalyov's trial by holding it in Vilnius backfired when

*Written before information came on the establishment of a "Baltic National Committee" (possibly by V. Petkus). Cf. *Elta*, Sept. 1978, pp. 4-5, 12.

Academician Sakharov conspicuously journeyed to Vilnius to attend the trial; the subsequent scenes outside the courthouse, when Sakharov was barred from the courtroom and pushed about by the KGB, were reported in the world press and radio. It became obvious during these few days how much ordinary Lithuanians respected Sakharov: an unknown woman came up to him outside the courtroom and presented him with flowers. Sakharov accepted these with gratitude, saying, "the flowers would be more appropriate for my friend Sergei. He struggles and suffers more for your rights."[41]

The editors of the *Lithuanian Chronicle,* in company with many other human rights activists in recent years, have clearly come to see Academician Sakharov as a key spokesman for their cause. His intervention in favour of Plumpa, Jaugelis and their associates in 1974 has already been mentioned.* *Chronicle* No. 15 wrote about him in a tone of outstanding warmth.†[42]

When Sakharov was awarded the Nobel prize, the editors of the *Chronicle* wrote him a letter of enthusiastic congratulations:

> When you, dear Laureate, are despised and slandered by the official press, you will know that thousands of Lithuanians are on your side . . . . Your noble and self-sacrificing example will prompt many to dedicate themselves to the struggle for human rights (Document 96).

The other Russian activist who has become a truly world figure is Alexander Solzhenitsyn. Because he is more "Slavophile" than Sakharov and closer to the position of the Orthodox Church, one might not have expected the relationship between Solzhenitsyn and the non-Slav Lithuanians to be so close, but we have already seen how much he respected their integrity in the camps‡ and they respond to him warmly. When he is attacked, they defend him:

> The Catholics of Lithuania salute and pray for this fine author. Solzhenitsyn's work, *Gulag Archipelago,* reminded many Catholics in Lithuania of the sufferings they or their parents endured in labour camps, prisons and exile. Solzhenitsyn serves as an example to the Catholics of Lithuania of how one should love one's country and the truth and not surrender to violence.[43]

Solzhenitsyn's "Gulag" terminology seems to be widely accepted and used by Lithuanians.[44] The *Gulag Archipelago* is known to circulate widely in *samizdat* within the Soviet Union; it has also been translated into Lithuanian abroad and this version has also probably found its way back to Lithuania by now.

Some sympathy is shown, too, for the Orthodox Church in Russia – formerly seen as a handmaid of the oppressing Tsarist regime, even now in some ways preferentially treated in Lithuania compared with the Catholic Church.

This new attitude is probably also due to reports from Moscow of the activities of reforming Orthodox priests, such as Gleb Yakunin and Dmitri Dudko. In a declaration expressing solidarity with Russian

*See p. 265.   †See p. 313.   ‡See p. 190.

dissidents (Document 97) Lithuanians mention these priests with approval. The authors of the letter to Cardinal Bengsch* nevertheless see clearly that the present policy of the Soviet regime is to "suffocate" the Russian Orthodox Church and they advocate that the Catholics must take measures to avoid the same fate.[45]

Naturally, however, they have a more ready affinity for other Catholics. Lithuanians, if the *Chronicle* is an accurate guide, are not only concerned to strengthen spiritual contact with a wide variety of Catholic circles abroad, but also to defend non-Lithuanian Catholics at home, such as "tens of thousands of Catholic Germans, Poles and other nationalities in Karaganda and other places of the Soviet Union who have no right to build themselves even temporary places of worship".[46] This has led to an especially protective relationship towards the Eastern-rite Catholics, whom the Lithuanians rightly consider to be in an even worse situation than they are: their Church, originally numbering some four million in Ukraine alone, having been abolished by Soviet *diktat* in 1946, its leaders imprisoned and its terrorized laity either denied the opportunity of worship or forced to become Russian Orthodox. After the war every Uniat priest was accused of collaborating with the Germans. If he converted to Orthodoxy, he was not prosecuted. The mandatory sentence, if he did not, was ten years. The authors of the *Chronicle* uphold the moral calibre of these Catholics, who have maintained their Church only by their readiness to develop underground activities and support it with the blood of hundreds of "uncrowned martyrs".[47] More than once the *Chronicle of the Lithuanian Catholic Church* and Lithuanian clergy have called for Ukrainian Catholic priests to be legally allowed to resume their duties.[48]

The Lithuanians thus see Cardinal Slipyj, who suffered sixteen years of Soviet imprisonment for his unbreakable loyalty to the Eastern Rite and finally won exile to Rome as the result of a secret agreement between the Vatican and the Kremlin in 1963, as one of today's great heroes of the faith, particularly now that he is prepared to break his silence in Rome and speak out on behalf of the persecuted Church.[49] The editors of the *Lithuanian Chronicle* have even written a letter to Cardinal Slipyj asking for his help in combating the influence in Rome of officially-favoured priests such as Monsignor Krivaitis and Dr. Butkus, whom they regard with suspicion.[50]

Some Uniats try to come to Lithuania to seek religious opportunities denied them at home. Clearly the KGB is especially on its guard to prevent this from happening. Nevertheless, there are said to be thirty Uniat priests and one bishop in Lithuania. It is often easier for Uniat activity to be organized from Lithuania. For example, in 1973 Fr. Vladimir Prokopiv, a Uniat priest living in Vilnius, where he was working as a labourer, helped Ukrainian Catholics from the city

*See pp. 135-7.

of Lviw to take a petition containing 1,200 signatures to Moscow; the
petition asked for a Catholic church to be opened in Lviw.[51]

The following brief item related in the *Chronicle* appals one by its
violence, but one is also impressed by the dedication of the young
man, who found a vocation to the priesthood at the age of only fifteen
and took a bold and unusual step to do something about it:

> Vitali Otsikevich, a Ukrainian from the Vinnitsa region, came to Vilnius
> three years ago to learn Lithuanian, wishing to prepare himself to enter the
> theological seminary (the Ukrainians have none). He served at Mass in the
> churches of St. Michael and St. Teresa. He was frequently interrogated by
> the KGB. He was invited to work as an agent for them and promised that
> he would then be allowed to enter the seminary without having to do
> military service. He celebrated his eighteenth birthday on 24 March 1975.
> On 14 May he was found dead in his room in Gardino Street with his face
> battered in.[52]

Looking across the Soviet frontier, the Lithuanians see Poland, a
country with whom relations have been variable in the past, but whose
outspoken Cardinal is now taken as a symbol of the determination of
the persecuted church to make her voice heard – as he did at the
Synod of Bishops in Rome in 1974.* The fact that the situation of the
Church is now so much better in Poland than in Lithuania[53] is seen not
as a cause for envy, but as a flag of hope, albeit a distant one, which
offers a breath of optimism for the future, or at least an inspiration for
those at home to preserve their determination to continue fighting for
what they know to be right. There are 12,000 Lithuanians in Poland
(officially only 6,000). The Lithuanian social-cultural association there
has contacts with Lithuanians in the Soviet Union, there are three
Lithuanian parishes and eight primary schools in which the language
of instruction is Lithuanian, and one secondary school.[54]

Cardinal Bengsch and his East German flock offer a similar ray of
hope, less distant since the Cardinal's visit to Lithuania in the summer
of 1975.[55]

After years – or centuries – of disillusion, Lithuanians have come
not to expect too much in terms of help from abroad. The links with
the Lithuanian diaspora exist, but it is obviously not the policy of those
remaining in the country to draw too much attention to them. Apart
from the ever-present need for religious literature, there is nothing in
the *Chronicle* or other recent Lithuanian *samizdat* underlining other
types of material need. However, foreign radio broadcasting in
Lithuanian (by Voice of America, Radio Liberty, Radio Madrid,
Radio Phillippines and Vatican Radio) offers a very special opportunity. The Soviets try to counteract it by selected jamming, but with
no more than partial success. The evidence, not only of the *Chronicle*
(Document 98), but also of Soviet propagandists,[56] confirms the
importance of this one uncensored news source available, if only with
difficulty, to Lithuanians. Like other Soviet citizens,[57] Lithuanians are

*See p. 126.

obviously extremely anxious to express their gratitude for these broadcasts to those who finance and organize them, while offering outspoken advice about improvements they would like to see. Indeed, one of the main aims of the *Lithuanian Chronicle* is to provide such radio stations with reliable information.

Before the *Chronicle of the Lithuanian Catholic Church* made its appearance, in the eyes of the world Lithuania was a minor Soviet republic which had been incorporated into the USSR in 1940, but about which no one knew much. Yet after twenty-four issues have reached the West, with their wealth of detail about religious and national oppression, Lithuania is coming back on the map and showing its individuality to the whole world. The influence of the *Lithuanian Chronicle* has already made itself felt in four areas: Soviet relations with the West, the Vatican's dialogue with the Soviet Government, the human rights movement in the USSR itself and government policy in Lithuania.

It is important for the Soviet Government to preserve its image in the West to achieve concessions in "détente". One such possible concession – recognition by Western countries of the annexation of the Baltic States – was hoped for at Helsinki when the 1975 Agreement was concluded. However, the *Lithuanian Chronicle* has made it clear that a national movement still exists in one Baltic State at least; this makes it embarrassing for western governments to accept Soviet claims to the country. The Lithuanian émigré lobby in the U.S.A. now has current facts to support its opposition to acceptance of Soviet rule in the Baltic States. In October 1975 Radio Liberty opened a Lithuanian broadcasting section and it now also broadcasts in Latvian and Estonian.

The Vatican, too, has come to recognize the force of the Lithuanian Catholic voice: Radio Vatican has publicly quoted the accounts given by the *Chronicle* of the trials of persecuted Catholics. In its talks with the Soviet authorities the Vatican can rely on the obvious strength of Catholicism in Lithuania which the *Chronicle* reveals.

The links established recently between the Lithuanian and Russian *Chronicles* have led to further co-operation between two aspects of the human-rights movements. In December 1976 a Lithuanian group was set up to monitor observance of the Helsinki Agreement in the republic, on the lines of the Moscow-based Helsinki monitoring group.[58] This was announced in Moscow in a report issued jointly with the Moscow Helsinki group. It seems probable that the links between the Moscow and Lithuanian dissidents became much closer during Sakharov's visit to Vilnius; one of the members of the Lithuanian Helsinki monitoring group is Eitanas Finkelsteinas, a Jewish Lithuanian activist in whose flat Sakharov stayed during Kovalyov's trial. The other members are Fr. Karolis Garuckas,* Tomas Venclova, Ona Lukauskaite-Poškiene and Viktoras Petkus. *Chronicle* No. 23

*He has since died on 5 April 1979.

contains a long declaration from Fr. Garuckas to General Secretary
Brezhnev, calling for the observation of the civil rights in the Soviet
Constitution and the Helsinki Agreement.[59]

From December 1976 to May 1977, the Lithuanian Helsinki
Monitoring Group sent a series of documents to the West, most of
them addressed to the Belgrade Commission, detailing various violations of human rights outlined in the Final Act of the Helsinki Agreement: these included the persecution of Baltic dissidents, discrimination against Volga Germans residing in Lithuania, and the
refusal to allow the re-unification of families by permitting Lithuanians
to join their close relatives in the U.S.A. In April 1977 the Lithuanian
Helsinki Group also sent an important statement on the violation of
religious rights in Lithuania to the Belgrade Commission (Document
99). This statement demonstrates the contradiction between Soviet
laws and the Helsinki Agreement, as well as other international agreements ratified by the Soviet Government, by extensively quoting
passages from Soviet law and official publications which discriminate
against religious believers. This state discrimination against religion is
most flagrantly expressed in the laws on "religious cults". The
Lithuanian Helsinki Group called on the Belgrade Commission to
ensure that, "freedom of conscience" was truly implemented and did
not merely remain on paper.[60] In August 1977, the month when this
Helsinki Group document was published in the *Lithuanian Chronicle*
No. 29, two members of the Group – Antanas Terleckas and Viktoras
Petkus – were arrested.[61] Another member, Tomas Venclova, had
been allowed to emigrate earlier that year.

Perhaps the most interesting aspect of the *Lithuanian Chronicle's*
influence has been the way it has affected the behaviour of some
Soviet authorities and officials in Lithuania itself. On 26 August 1975 a
district teachers conference at Šakiai was told by the Vilnius
representative, A. Sinkevičius, how much interest there was in the
West regarding Lithuania:

> I must tell you this, teachers. You must know that every tactless action by a
> teacher when talking to a religious pupil or his parents is published in every
> detail, without exaggeration, giving the school, the time and the names,
> and is circulated by this journal [the *Chronicle*] not only in this country, but
> in the outside world. This journal is translated into English, French,
> Spanish and other languages. And what do foreigners then think of and
> discuss when they're looking for anything to pick on?[62]

When Fr. V. Černiauskas, from Mielagenai, wrote to Brezhnev
protesting against the persecution of religion in Lithuania, he was
summoned by K. Tumenas, the Council for Religious Affairs official,
and taken to task for writing to Moscow. However, Tumenas told Fr.
Černiauskas: "We will never answer you in writing, because if we did,
foreign radio-stations would start broadcasting everything".[63] The
editors of the *Lithuanian Chronicle* claim that publicity is their sole

defence: "If foreign radio stations did not broadcast the *Chronicle of the Lithuanian Catholic Church,* such officials would skin us alive".[64]
The *Lithuanian Chronicle* is no longer an obscure little pamphlet in a little-known country: it has established itself as a voice that speaks for a nation.

DOCUMENTS

90. FIRST RAYS OF DAWN

In November 1975 a new type-written publication, *Aušra* ("Dawn"), began to circulate amongst the people in Lithuania.

The *Chronicle* reproduces the introductory editorial of the publishers of *Aušra* . . . .

After almost a hundred years *Aušra* has re-appeared. It is as though Lithuanian history has repeated itself – Tsarist occupation has given way to the Soviet. A danger to the existence of the Lithuanian nation has again arisen. Spiritual values are particularly at risk: religion, morals, language, literature and the whole of Lithuanian culture . . . . Systematically and surreptitiously Lithuania is being spiritually ruined and physically destroyed. A section of the nation fails to see this misfortune and is not concerned about the impending danger. Sometimes because they lack understanding and sometimes to gain a piece of bread, they collaborate with the nation's oppressors.

Every effort is made nowadays to ensure silence about Lithuania's heroic past. It is not, therefore, surprising that so little space in the curricula of schools is devoted to ancient Lithuanian history, that the publication of historical literature is so niggardly and that the little which does appear is so mercilessly hacked about by the censors, that Lithuanian history books published before the war are so pains-takingly destroyed. An attempt is being made to blacken Lithuania's past by falsifying historical facts.

Not only is silence maintained regarding Lithuania's past, but also regarding the darker side of daily life. We talk of the growing towns, of our pride in health and the expansion of factories, but keep silence on the growing crime rate, camps and epidemics. Very few are sufficiently concerned about the future of Lithuania, and in particular about the values of her spiritual culture. The attention and capabilities of the nation are directed only towards the growth of the materialistic culture – towards factories, plans and sport, whilst the fallow fields of spiritual culture are forsaken. It is not difficult to de-nationalize and destroy a nation which is decadent, which feeds only on material goods and which gives itself up to drunkenness . . . . We must rouse our nation from this spiritual slumber and this is the task which the revived *Aušra* is taking on itself anew.

The programme of *Aušra* remains the same as it was a hundred years ago:

> to show Lithuanians their past, to evaluate the present correctly; and to assist in planning the formation of the future Lithuania.

Aušra has no political objectives to inspire a revolution or to bring about a return of the capitalist system. Its task is to revive the spirit of the Lithuanians even in the most difficult of days, to inspire national consciousness and national morale and to encourage progress in all spheres. The Lithuanian nation will survive if it is more cultured than its oppressors. Ancient history must therefore repeat itself: the Romans conquered the Greeks by force, but the Greeks conquered the Romans in culture.

Aušra will not provoke nationalist intolerance. It regards as its friends people of peace and goodwill in all nations, those who have good intentions towards Lithuania and wish to share cultural values with her.

Ausra trusts that it will be supported by all those who in their hearts love Lithuania, irrespective of their beliefs, party preferences and obligations. Many even of those in high positions continue to love Lithuania at the present time and concern themselves with the country's betterment, as much as they are able.

Aušra does not claim to embrace all of Lithuania's problems. It greets the *Chronicle of the Lithuanian Catholic Church* which is now in its fourth year and will joyfully welcome any new issues.

We trust that the views enunciated by *Aušra* will spread among young people. We would beg them, with a knowledge of Lithuania's past, to learn to love their native land more fully.

The publishers of *Aušra*.[65]

91. LITHUANIANS "EXILED" ON THEIR OWN TERRITORY

1. After the Second World War about 50,000 Lithuanians remained in the western areas of the Belorussian Republic, namely in Apsas, Gervečiai, Rodune, Varanavas and other localities where the Lithuanian-speaking inhabitants constituted a vast majority . . . .

2. The influence of the Catholic Church in these areas has been completely paralyzed through the closure of churches and the arrest

of priests. The Catholic churches are closed in the following localities inhabited by Lithuanians: Brisviatas, Apsas Vydžiai, Pelesa and elsewhere. After the First World War a Lithuanian parish was established in Pelesa (in the Rodune district). Nine large Lithuanian villages belonged to it. A brick church was built by the efforts and money of the Lithuanians. Mass in the Lithuanian language was celebrated here until 1950. In that year the Lithuanian priest, Vienažindis, was arrested and the church was closed, its steeple demolished and the body of the church turned into a warehouse.

The remaining open churches (for example, in Gervečiai, Rodune) are served by old priests, with no one to replace them when they die. When a priest dies, the local authorities refuse to accept a replacement and the church is closed . . . .

3. The younger generation is becoming not Belorussian, but Russian. Children whose parents speak Lithuanian or Belorussian at home are gradually adopting the Russian language. Not only the schools but also all the public offices, where only the Russian language is used, aim at this result. Cases have already arisen where a boy or a girl has requested a Catholic priest to hear their confession in Russian.

4. The older generation is beset with apathy, disappointed because their long struggle was barren. They have been deprived of human rights. Their church, where in hours of hardship the Lithuanians could find consolation, has been taken away. They can use their native language only in private life. The Lithuanian in his native land is condemned to national death.

What do these 50,000 Lithuanians we are talking about matter? There are not many of us anyway. The Lithuanian-inhabited areas are today disappearing before our own eyes. If history does not take a different course, all of us, a little over two million in the small area of the Nemunas river basin, will disappear, as happened before our eyes with the Prussian Lithuanians on the other bank of the Nemunas – in Tilže, Ragaine and other districts (about 100,000 Lithuanians lived there before the the Second World War), and also in the Klaipeda region. They were ultimately destroyed not by German terror, but by the Russian "liberators", the marching Red Army, leaving an empty space behind. The struggle of the 50,000 Lithuanians in the Belorussian Republic is a symbol of the struggle for survival of the entire Lithuanian nation.

The evil man rejoices when his deeds remain secret. The lie wishes to hide itself from public exposure by operating as truth. When the big fish, the "fraternal" nation, wants to swallow the small fish, this is referred to publicly as the "friendship of nations".

We do not wish to die surrounded by silence and treachery. We are struggling for a life worthy of human beings. We cry: Help us![66]

92. CHURCH AND NATION, 1974

Juozas Šileikis stated that his children read both religious and atheist books and found the truth for themselves. For this reason the atheists were unable to deprive them of their faith.

"Why do you so blindly believe in God?" they asked their host.

"Atheists are truly blind in their nonbelief. Many of them have never read the catechism, yet they insist that there is no God."

"Why do you oppose the party line and why don't you allow your children to join the Komsomol?"

"It doesn't necessarily give a good example. Bring together all the ruffians in the school, bring them into the Komsomol and re-educate them as good people. Then I will be able to entrust you with the education of my children."

"How do you come to have such strong convictions?" they asked Šileikis.

"Because of my religion. Also, Lithuania has been traversed time and time again by many invaders and if Lithuanians were as susceptible to influence as down blown by the wind, it is doubtful whether in our day they would be speaking Lithuanian. For this reason we must hold on to the heritage of our forefathers."[67]

93. THE CASE OF MINDAUGAS TAMONIS

Tamonis, Mindaugas (born 28 August 1940 in Vilnius) – chemical engineering technologist, technical sciences candidate (1968). Graduated from Kaunas Polytechnic Institute in 1962, worked as an engineer at the Daugeliai (Šiauliai District) Construction Materials Combine until 1963. Scientific consultant at the Building and Architectural Institute 1966-9. Head of the Chemical Laboratory department of the Monument Conservation Institute from 1969. Has published scientific articles on cement and concrete hardening.

(*Concise Lithuanian Soviet Encyclopaedia,* Volume 3, p. 560).

The Lithuanian *Chronicle* has written about the refusal of Tamonis to restore the Soviet Army Monument at Kryžkalnis and his detention in the psychiatric hospital of Naujoji Vilnija. After three months of forced treatment Tamonis returned, broken in health. He was no longer able to take part in the creative work of the Institute.

On 25 June Tamonis sent a long letter to the Central Committee of the CPSU showing the illusory confidence of a young scientist, who grew up under Soviet rule in the goodwill of the party leaders.

At the beginning of his letter the author points out that falsehood, which is supported by government representatives themselves, has spread over the whole country. The Soviet Government has no right to require its citizens to behave honestly and conscientiously, because it is compromised by its own actions. The blood of millions innocently murdered is on its conscience . . . . The time has come to bring about a "humanist revolution' which, according to Tamonis could be done by the 25th Party Congress [1976].

Tamonis outlines the fundamental purposes and methods of this "revolution" in seven sections. He proposes an end to the errors committed during the periods of the "personality cult" [Stalin] and "subjectivism' [Khrushchev], and that the graves of Stalin's victims should be honoured.

Speaking of religion, Tamonis proposes that discrimination against believers be ended:

> . . . The Christian faith is based on the same scientific and philosophical foundations as other religions. Since this faith, and the art which has been and is still being created in its spirit, satisfies the spiritual and cultural needs of believers, it is essential to do away with all limitations which prevent Christians and other believers from living a fulfilled life and from feeling themselves to be members of the community with full rights. They want not only to work together with others, but to enjoy equal rights. There must be free religious education, religious and cultural publications, free opportunity to debate, lecture and produce radio and television programmes . . .
>
> . . . Attention should be paid to the fact that there are no antagonistic contradictions between religion and socialism. On the contrary, religion helps socialism – it raises the morale of the faithful, ennobles them, improves their spirits, encourages them to work well and to serve high ideals conscientiously. Religion and socialism are not antagonistic as social systems. They both have the aims of spiritual freedom and high-minded humanism.

At the end of his letter Tamonis condemns Communists who oppose progress. They are accused because discontent is growing among the people and no prospects can be seen of an improvement of the situation in the country. Such Communists, according to Tamonis, "are the real counter-revoluntionaries".

In conclusion, he proposes an end to the cult of the Party and expresses the hope that the individual will become important to Communist party members:

> Only for this it is worth struggling . . . The only door to the future is a clear conscience, true justice and sincere unhypocritical love of mankind.

After sending this letter, Tamonis was again forcibly detained in a psychiatric hospital. Two days later (29 June) his mother died. Only as a result of great efforts was he allowed out for two hours to take leave of his dead mother. On 25 July Tamonis was released from hospital on condition that he would continue to come for three weeks to have injections of Moditen.

Being prevented from expressing himself creatively, and being isolated at his place of work, Tamonis fell victim to deep depression, which was made worse by the behaviour of his relatives. Because his father had been a member of the Lithuanian Activist Front (LAF) in 1941, the KGB exploited this fact for blackmail. KGB agents tried to influence him through his relatives. News spread among the people of Vilnius that the KGB was making efforts to destroy him by driving him to suicide.

On 5 November 1975, Tamonis was found on the railway line between Vilnius and Pavilnys, having died beneath the wheels of a train.

Every sacrifice, no matter of what kind, is a spark added to the altar-fire of freedom and justice. In Lithuania there have always been people who are not deterred by the darkness of mental hospitals and the cold of Russian camps. They are sustained by their concept of a Christian existence and a Lithuanian outlook on life – the conditions for an inevitable spiritual revolution. Perhaps it will happen after we have gone, but it will come – and even by a modest contribution to world spiritual revival we will honour the memory of those people who perished, burning with a boundless love for the world and its creatures and for our nation.

Mindaugas Tamonis is no more. One more sacrifice added to those thousands who froze in wagons, were shot, drowned in the Neris or burned themselves to death. He was not shot, not made to rot in prison, he was not even summoned for interrogation. He was being healed. Moditen-B is a medicine – if you give it to someone who is ill. Given to a healthy person it is an instrument of death. It kills secretly and silently until a person is left with only a body.

He left us, misunderstood by his near ones, taunted by the doubters, slandered and murdered by foreigners . . . . And we? We forsook him and fled because he was walking in the shadow of death.

. . . . And the Lord then took mercy on him and summoned him to Himself . . . .[68]

94. APPEAL TO THE WORLD, 1975

The *Chronicle of the Lithuanian Catholic Church* has received a letter from readers, in which the thoughts reflect the mood of Lithuanian Catholics and express their wishes. The *Chronicle* fully agrees with the sentiments of this letter.

"Recently we heard of the arrest of Sergei Kovalyov, doctor of biological sciences, because of his connection with the *Lithuanian Chronicle*. We Catholics of Lithuania pray to the Lord for this scientist's physical and spiritual health. Nowadays the world is vitally in need of love. Jesus Christ said, 'Greater love hath no man than this, that a man lay down his life for his friends' (John 15:1). We believe that the sacrifice made by Kovalyov and others will not be in vain.

"We bow our heads before Academician Andrei Sakharov, that fighter for human rights in the USSR and, in his person, before all Russian intellectuals of good will. By their courage and sacrifice they have made us, the Catholics of Lithuania, look on the Russian nation in a new way. Their sacrifice is necessary to all persecuted people; it is necessary to the Catholics of Lithuania.

"We sincerely thank the great Russian writer Alexander Solzhenitsyn for his warm words to Lithuanians and his defence of Lithuania's cause. Thousands of Lithuanians, especially former citizens of the 'Gulag Archipelago', pray to the Almighty to bless him.

"We are grateful to the Bishops of Australia, the Australian opposition parties and the Canadian Government for their defence of Lithuania's case. Alas, we cannot thank the Governments of Australia and New Zealand for their recognition of the occupation of the Baltic States. May God grant that they never come to know the 'liberating' hand of Mao.

"As we followed by radio the events at the Synod of Bishops in Rome, we rejoiced at the fact that some Fathers of the Synod – Cardinal Josif Slipyji, Cardinal Stefan Wyszynski, Cardinal Bengsch and others – so courageously defended the persecuted Catholics of Eastern Europe. In the best possible way they also represented us, the believers of the Lithuanian Catholic Church.

"We Catholics of Lithuania thoroughly admire the hunger-strike of Vaclovas Sevrukas and Simas Kudirka – by this means they wished to attract the world's attention to the difficult position of Lithuania's Catholics.

"We thank the editors of the journal *Kontinent** for their warm words to the Lithuanian people and for their invitation to work together with them. We feel that, at present, Lithuanian interests can best be represented by the intellectual forces of our brothers abroad.

"We are grateful to those who have made it possible for Radio Liberty to broadcast to Lithuania and we should like its programmes to devote some space to the history of Lithuania and its cultural treasures; they should report the fight for human rights in the Soviet Union and in Lithuania.

"We follow the Lithuanian-language radio broadcasts from the Vatican, Rome and Madrid and we thank their organizers, especially for publicizing the problems of Catholic Lithuania.

*A Russian journal produced in Paris.

"The Soviet authorities, with the help of the KGB and the Penal Code, is trying to destroy not only the *Chronicle of the Lithuanian Catholic Church,* but also the Catholic Church herself. However, we Catholics of Lithuania are resolved, with the help of the Lord, to intensify the struggle for our rights. We should still like to believe that the Soviet authorities will come to understand their great mistake in upholding the atheist minority and ranging the Catholic masses against themselves.

"We, the Catholics of Lithuania, ask our brothers outside our country's borders and all our friends throughout the world to inform their governments and a wide section of public opinion about the infringement of human rights in Lithuania. Your energies and sacrifice, brothers and friends of Lithuania, are vitally necessary to us at the present time."[69]

95.   THE TRIAL OF SERGEI KOVALYOV, 1975

The preparatory examination and trial of Sergei Kovalyov took place in Vilnius and not in Moscow, despite the fact that he was being charged under Paragraph 70 of the Penal Code of the Russian Republic. It is clear that the Government wanted the fewest possible witnesses.

Kovalyov is a well-known defender of human rights and a brave fighter on behalf of persecuted Soviet citizens, including Lithuanian Catholics. Lithuanians, particularly believers, could not remain indifferent to this shameful court hearing in which a person defending basic human rights – freedom of word, press and conscience – was being condemned. They remember the words of the Gospel: "I was naked and you clothed me, I was sick and you visited me. I was in prison and you came to me." From various places in Lithuania, therefore, people came to the trial in question, wishing to see with their own eyes those who had dared to stand up to "the powerful of this world" and to defend the persecuted. Having learned of the forthcoming trial, believers prayed fervently to the Lord to grant strength to their benefactor.

The Supreme Court also prepared carefully for this trial, as did the KGB. It was clear that Kovalyov's relatives and friends would come to Vilnius for this trial and that its proceedings would inevitably re-echo throughout the world. The lot of the judge in such a trial is not an enviable one. On the one hand, whatever happens, the defendant must be found guilty. On the other hand, the judge must give the appearance of being objective: he has to adhere to the procedures laid down and grant the defendant all his rights envisaged by the law. But can one compromise with the KGB, which for years on end has kept Kovalyov in prison for interrogation? All the Supreme Court judges, therefore, to the extent that they were able, fought shy of this trial. After prolonged arguments this shameful mission was entrusted to the Supreme Court's party organization secretary, Ignotas.

As early as two to three weeks before the trial, some of the Vilnius dissidents* were summoned to the military headquarters or police station, where security men awaited them. The KGB, by persuasion or threats, pressed them to promise that they would not go to the forthcoming trial . . . .

On the morning of 9 December a number of known dissidents and relatives of Kovalyov arrived by train from Moscow: his wife, son and brother; Academician Sakharov; Turchin, the head of Amnesty International's Moscow group; Armenian academician Orlov the physicist, Yury Orlov a member of the Armenian Academy, and his wife; Litvinov and his wife, and others. Having received special permission, the correspondent of the Canadian newspaper, *Toronto Star,* M. Levi, also came with his wife – a total of about twenty people. However, a few others failed to leave Moscow.

KGB men detained T. Velikanova, T. Khodorovich and M. Landa, as these women were on the way to the Belorussia Station. Each was held for a few hours on ridiculous charges which were later not even mentioned; then, after a warning not to try to leave, they released them after the train for Vilnius had departed . . . .

The Vilnius dissidents did not succeed in meeting the Muscovites on arrival. A. Terleckas, V. Petkus and V. Smolkinas of Vilnius had barely shown themselves on the platform when they were arrested by KGB men and taken to the security offices one after the other. In this way, the flowers intended for Kovalyov's wife and for Academician Sakharov faded in the dustbins of the KGB.

. . . .

Since the Vilnius men did not hide their reason for coming to the station, the KGB reprimanded each of them for bad behaviour and threatened to deal severely with them and even to put them on trial if they should attempt to enter the court. Colonels Kruglov, Baltinas and Česnavicius pointed out that Academician Sakharov was mentally ill and that other Moscow dissidents were immoral people. They claimed that the dissidents of Lithuania were not known abroad and that in the event of their arrest the world would remain silent. They threatened that a place was already reserved for Terleckas in a psychiatric hospital and that Petkus would follow him there. They asked them whether they wanted to emigrate to the West.

On being taken to KGB headquarters, Smolkinas of Vilnius immediately wrote a complaint to the procurator that unknown people had forcibly pushed him into a Volga car and driven him to the

*This term originated in the West, but is now increasingly used in the Soviet Union itself.

KGB headquarters without producing any authority from the procurator . . . .

After lunch on the same day all three of the Vilnius men were released, one after another. The time of their release coincided with the conclusion of the court session. In this way the KGB demonstrated their scorn for human rights even before the court hearing began, and showed that the laws defending the freedom of the individual did not apply to them.

Since no one met the dissidents arriving from Moscow, Academician Sakharov and his son-in-law, Yankelevich, were invited by Finkelsteinas, who had travelled with them on the same train, to the latter's apartment. Finkelsteinas, a Vilnius man returning from Moscow, is a Gorky University graduate who has for five years been demanding permission to leave for Israel. Academician Sakharov stayed in his apartment during his visit. Other new arrivals from Moscow went off to stay with people in Vilnius whose addresses were known to them in advance.

The situation for those trying to get into the courtroom was hopeless. Security men stood at all the entrances and allowed no one in apart from officials . . . . Neither was the correspondent from Canada, Mr. Levi, allowed into the courtroom. He argued unsuccessfully that Soviet correspondents could be present at court cases in Canada and that there had been an agreement in Helsinki about unrestricted journalism.

One unidentified woman brought some concealed flowers into the vestibule, unwrapped them and gave them to the Nobel Peace Prize winner, Academician Sakharov, who accepted them with gratitude, saying: "The flowers would be more appropriate for my friend Sergei. He struggles and suffers more for your rights." The woman left, visibly moved, and all those present remembered the kind glance of the Laureate and the flowers presented by a Lithuanian woman pressed to his chest – which he later gave to Kovalyov's wife . . . .

On the first day of the trial only Kovalyov's brother was allowed to enter. The trial continued for four days. Academician Sakharov and other dissidents came to the courthouse each day, but they were not allowed to enter the courtroom. As from the second day of the trial, an effort was made to keep away from the courthouse all Lithuanians suspected of wishing to go inside; those who did manage to do so were chased out . . . .

Virgilijus Jaugelis tried to enter the courtroom, but one of the security men on duty approached him and told him to leave. Jaugelis continued to stand by the door of the courtroom. He was then taken away for "insults and disobedience to a policeman" and was punished with fifteen days detention. During the interrogation one of the policemen struck Jaugelis across the throat with his fist a number of times and the detainee was hardly able to speak as a consequence. Jaugelis then wrote a complaint to the procurator. The commission wrote out an official document stating that no marks from blows were found, only that he was speaking softly. After a few days Jaugelis was released on account of his health . . . .

It had been announced that the verdict would be made public at 2 p.m. on 13 December. In fact, they began to read it out at 1.30 p.m. and witnesses arriving late were not allowed into the room. The dissidents waited in the entrance-hall of the courthouse. Academician Sakharov expressed his anger at such a harsh sentence to the Canadian journalist. The "public" which had been allowed in with special permits came out, surrounded the dissidents and began to mock and insult them. One of them, the "poet" Keidošius, made a special effort. The KGB men, Colonel Kruglov and others, also joined in. The Lithuanian dissidents protested at the fact that the verdict had been reached in the name of the Lithuanian nation.

Keidošius and the KGB men shouted that only they represented the Lithuanian nation. Academician Sakharov burst from the courthouse and ran towards the black maria standing in the road. He began to beat on it with his fists, saying: "Bravo, Seryozha!" . . . .

On 14 December Kovalyov's wife was allowed to see him. She told him of the flowers received and the good words about him from people of Vilnius. He seemed well and in good spirits. The sentence had not depressed him. He was only sorry that for some years he would not be able to help in the struggle for human rights.

This was the atmosphere in which the "open" trial of Kovalyov took place.

Kovalyov's sacrifice has been of great service to Lithuania. The trial hearing and the persecution have shown that the KGB's actions can bring the Lithuanian and Russian nations together. Lithuanian Catholics are grateful to Kovalyov for his pure humanitarian heart and pray to the Almighty that he be granted endurance, health and manifold blessings.

The sacrifices of the Russian dissidents have helped Lithuanians to look at the Russian nation with new eyes. We will greet the Russian scientist Kovalyov on his return from prison as our own brother and best friend.[70]

96.   LITHUANIANS SALUTE SAKHAROV

To: Academician Andrei Dmitrievich Sakharov

Dear Laureate:

On 9 October we heard the exceptionally happy news that you have been awarded the Nobel Peace Prize.

All people of goodwill in Lithuania sincerely rejoice in this high estimate of your courageous struggle for truth, liberty and human dignity and in the fact that your generous heart, which has also embraced the sorrows of persecuted Lithuanians, has not remained unrecognized.

When you, dear Laureate, are despised and slandered by the official press, you will know that thousands of Lithuanians are on your side. Your noble and self-sacrificing example will prompt many to dedicate themselves to the struggle for human rights, on the observation of which a genuine peace depends.

Dear Laureate, we believe that Providence has chosen you, as it has the writer Solzhenitsyn, as an instrument in leading mankind to a brighter future.[71]

97.　WE EXPRESS OUR SOLIDARITY WITH THE RUSSIAN DISSIDENTS (1975)

[original title]

Listening to radio programmes from abroad, we pay particular attention when the announcer says 'Moscow'. We know it not so much from geography books and tourist trips, but because of its notorious prisons and the *Chronicle of Current Events*. We know about the group of Moscow intellectuals who struggle heroically for the rights and freedoms of the people, including those of believers. They do a great deal of good for all those who are persecuted, irrespective of national, racial or religious differences.

The achievements and activities of these dedicated people are, therefore, as well understood and closely cherished as our own by Catholics and Lithuanians of good will . . . . In December 1975 the Supreme Court of the Lithuanian Republic sentenced the Russian scientist Sergei Kovalyov to seven years imprisonment because he had fought against the infringement of human rights in the Soviet Union. Kovalyov also defended the rights of Lithuanian Catholics and his sentence has clearly revealed the true face of Soviet justice.

The Orthodox priest, Gleb Yakunin, was recently forbidden to carry out his priestly duties . . . . Yakunin dared to speak the truth publicly about the cares, agonies and persecutions of the Russian Orthodox Church . . . . May this fine example set by an Orthodox priest also instruct some Lithuanian priests who attempt to serve both God and the atheists.

Another Orthodox priest, Dmitri Dudko, has also worked for many years in Moscow. This young* and zealous priest searched for a way of transmitting the eternal truths to the men of today, and after a

*Dudko was in fact 53 years old in 1975. Obviously this fact was not known to the writer.

number of years of pastoral work he reached the conclusion that discussions in question and answer form would be the most appropriate. In 1974 his church could not accommodate all the would-be listeners. Believers and non-believers, Orthodox, Catholics and even Jews — they all came.

This did not please the atheists and on the instructions of the Patriarch Fr. Dudko was transferred eighty kilometres out of Moscow. Even here, however, the atheist-inspired church council cancelled his contract in December 1975 and Fr. Dudko was again deprived of his duties.

We Catholics of Lithuania express our solidarity with the imprisoned scientist, Sergei Kovalyov, and with the Orthodox priests, Yakunin and Dudko. We invite all Lithuanians, wherever they may be, and all people of good will actively to defend the Russian dissidents and particularly to concern themselves with the release of that noble friend of Lithuanians, Sergei Kovalyov.

Catholics of Lithuania.[72]

98. BROADCASTS TO LITHUANIA

We Lithuanians thank God and all people of good will for the Lithuanian radio programmes transmitted by western radio stations. We would like to submit a few comments.

The Rome radio programme is good. There could be slightly less news about Italy. It is a great pity that the Rome programme is transmitted in the morning, as very few can listen at that time. If it were possible, we would be very glad if these programmes could be transferred to the evening: for example, before or after the Vatican Radio transmission.

We listen with pleasure to Vatican Radio. The announcers are good. Our atheists would be very glad if Vatican Radio confined itself to extracts from the catechism and did not touch upon concrete problems of Lithuanian life. We are grateful that Vatican Radio has its finger on the pulse of Lithuanian religious life. We would like more on the subject of the defence of Christ's teaching. Particular attention should be paid to the Saturday programme, which should be aimed not only at Catholics but at Lithuanians in general. Talks about the Sacraments and other religious matters would be better given on other days. We would like to hear a good ten-minute sermon on the Saturday programme. The essays of Fr. R. Krasauskas on great Lithuanian personalities are popular. The devotional exercise sermons of T. A. Luima were not popular. We listen gladly to programmes on the Lithuanian Church and Lithuanian history in general. Programmes of dry theological content are to be avoided. More material for the young is desirable.

Of late it has been difficult to hear Madrid Radio. The programme is rather weak. Exaggeration in analyses of Lithuanian religious life is sometimes felt. We would like the announcer to be changed if this is possible – or we ask that at least he be provided with an assistant.

The Voice of America is very unpopular. All Lithuanians are tired of American economics. If the Voice of America wants to become very popular it should dwell more on Lithuanian history, its cultural values, the needs of the faithful.

Radio Liberty is very popular. The programmes are good and so are the speakers. Recently there has been much jamming. Nothing can be heard in the evenings. We would like programmes on the russification of Lithuania, the cultural values of Lithuania's past, items from Lithuanian history and similar themes.[73]

99. STATEMENT FROM THE LITHUANIAN HELSINKI GROUP SUBMITTED TO THE BELGRADE COMMISSION

[This lengthy document summarizes much of what is in this book. Here are a few short extracts.]

Since the Second Vatican Council almost all believers in the world practise religious rites in their own language, but the Lithuanians use Latin because they have no facilities for the printing of missals and other essential books. The possibility of making liturgical vessels and church organs remains a dream for Lithuanians . . . .

The majority of Lithuanian Catholics, particularly intellectuals such as school teachers, are absolutely barred from participating in worship, because they would be dismissed from work in consequence . . . .

We therefore address ourselves to the Belgrade Comission appointed to monitor the observance of the international agreement on basic human rights and freedom signed in Helsinki in 1975 and request them to assist us, so that the international obligations which have been undertaken do not remain merely on paper, but are implemented concretely, in order that:

1). The term "freedom of conscience" should be understood and interpreted in the way other peoples of the world do.

2). People should have freedom of anti-religious propaganda, but also of religious propaganda.

3). Believers should also be given freedom to assemble, hold meetings and should enjoy freedom of press and of speech.

4). Those paragraphs of the law on education which restrict freedom of religion and conscience should be abrogated.

5). All those who have taken part in activities to ensure that human rights and basic freedoms be respected and protected everywhere should be released from prisons and camps (N. Sadunaite, P. Plumpa, P. Petronis, Š. Žukauskas, J. Gražys and others).

Fr. Karolis Garuckas,
Eitanas Finkelsteinas,
Ona Lukauskaite-Poškiene,
Viktoras Petkus,
Tomas Venclova.

Vilnius,
10 April 1977.[74]

NOTES TO CHAPTER XII

1. *Russkaya Mysl,* Paris, 27 January 1977, p. 5.
2. *CLCC* 7, pp. 27-8 (E), pp. 12-13 (L). For the whole story of Kalanta, partly as told by an eyewitness, see *The Violations of Human Rights in Soviet Occupied Lithuania,* pp. 17-24.
3. *CLCC* 17, p. 39; *Aušra* 2, pp. 15-16 (MS).
4. *CLCC* 10, pp. 18-26 (E), pp. 9-14 (L).
5. *CLCC* 17, pp. 21-5.
6. *CLCC* 20, pp. 14-22.
7. *CLCC* 8, p. 27 (E), p. 15 (L).
8. *CLCC* 17, pp. 29-30.
9. *Ibid.,* p. 39.
10. *CLCC* 24, p. 36.
11. *CLCC* 6, p. 27 (E), p. 11 (L).
12. *CLCC* 14, p. 22 (E), p. 17 (L).
13. *CLCC* 17, p. 42.
14. *Ibid.,* p. 39.
15. *Loc. cit.*
16. *CLCC* 6, p. 27 (E), p. 11 (L).
17. *CLCC* 12, p. 29 (E), p. 26 (L).
18. *CLCC* 16, pp. 18-19.
19. *CLCC* 17, p. 42.
20. *Ibid.,* p. 41.
21. *CLCC* 6, p. 26 (E), p. 11 (L).
22. *Partiinaya Zhizn,* Moscow, May 1970, p. 58.
23. *CLCC* 17, p. 41.
24. *Tiesa,* 27 March 1973, quoted in *CLCC* 6, p. 28 (E), pp. 11-12 (L).
25. *CLCC* 10, pp. 18-26 (E), pp. 9-14 (L).

26. *CLCC* 2, p. 5 (E), p. 4 (L); cf. *CLCC* 3, p. 13; *CLCC* 7, p. 12 (E), pp. 6-7 (L).
27. *CLCC* 17, pp. 37-8.
28. *CLCC* 20, pp. 23-4.
29. *CLCC* 17, p. 23.
30. *CLCC* 14, p. 19 (E), pp. 14-15 (L).
31. *Elta*, N.Y., January 1975, pp. 5-7; December 1974, p. 10.
32. *CLCC* 20, pp. 14-22.
33. *CLCC* 20, p. 34.
34. *CLCC* 4, p. 34 (E), p. 19 (L).
35. Ed. Peter Reddaway, *Uncensored Russia*, London 1972.
36. *Ibid.*, p. 333.
37. *CLCC* 15, pp. 6-7.
38. Ed. Valeri Chalidze, *Delo Kovalyova* ("The Case of Kovalyov"), Khronika Press, New York, 1976.
39. *Ibid.*, pp. 6-7.
40. *CLCC* 20, pp. 22-3.
41. *CLCC* 21, p. 276.
42. *CLCC* 15, pp. 6-7; *CLCC* 21, pp. 276-284.
43. *CLCC* 9, p. 15 (E), p. 7 (L).
44. *CLCC* 17, p. 34; 19, p. 3.
45. *CLCC* 19, p. 8.
46. *Ibid.*, p. 9.
47. *CLCC* 12, p. 7 (E), p. 3 (L).
48. *CLCC* 1, p. 23; *CLCC* 12, p. 11 (E), p. 7 (L).
49. *CLCC* 14, p. 37 (E), p. 31 (L); cf. *CLCC* 15, p. 2, quoted on p. 126.
50. *CLCC* 23, pp. 2-6 (MS).
51. *CLCC* 9, p. 29 (E), p.16 (L).
52. *CLCC* 17, p. 25.
53. *CLCC* 3, p. 13; *CLCC* 7, p. 14 (E), p. 8 (L).
54. *Aušra* 6, in *Eiropos Lietuvis*, 27 September 1977.
55. *CLCC* 15, p. 2; *CLCC* 19, p. 2. See also p. 135-6.
56. *CLCC* 20, p. 34.
57. *RCL* 4-5, 1975, pp. 46-8.
58. Reuter's Report (unpublished), 1 December 1976, Moscow.
59. *CLCC* 23, pp. 18-24.
60. *CLCC* 29, p. 18.
61. *Ibid.*, p. 31.
62. *CLCC* 20, p. 34.
63. *CLCC* 21, pp. 287-8.
64. *CLCC* 21, p. 327.
65. *CLCC* 20, pp. 13-14.
66. *Violations of Human Rights in Soviet Occupied Lithuania*, pp. 29-33.
67. *CLCC* 9, pp. 31-2 (E), pp. 17-18 (L).
68. *CLCC* 20, pp. 2-8.
69. *CLCC* 15, pp. 2-3.
70. *CLCC* 21, pp. 271-84.
71. *CLCC* 19, p. 11.
72. *Aušra* 2, pp. 56-7 (MS).
73. *CLCC* 16, pp. 49a-49b. (This quotation is from a supplement to *CLCC* 16, which is included in only some of the extant original copies).
74. *CLCC* 29, pp. 13-18.

XIII

CONCLUSION

ALTHOUGH this book has concentrated on the affairs of a tiny nation, tucked away in a corner of Europe difficult of access because of political barriers, speaking an ancient language known to scarcely anyone not born into a Lithuanian family, it is about people who have a message for the world. More, they are upholding principles of personal liberty, freedom of conscience and of speech which are not only utterly valid in themselves, but should also be dear to the 'liberal' human-rights conscience of the democratic nations. The fact that their case is not better known is a comment on the selectivity of that conscience.

Clearly, then, this book implies principles lying just below the surface which are broader than the simple issue of religious liberty, the main theme. The Soviet Union, with its russianizing tendencies and determination to impose a set political pattern on the most diversified group of nations and minorities, is the last great colonial empire of the world. Though the predominant (but by no means the only) skin-colour of the empire is white, it will ultimately be seen that there is even a concealed racial element here, which must eventually be one day exposed to the gaze of the world.

By and large, the debate on all these principles, as they affect the Soviet Union, has not begun even within the Catholic Church, where one would have expected their formulation to have been so clear and decisive. The Lithuanians, in addressing so much of what they have written implicitly or explicitly to the Vatican, clearly expected that this would have occurred.

Given the active Lithuanian community in Rome, the Vatican must have been informed, but any reaction has been a secret one, so cloaked by diplomatic considerations of so-called "Ostpolitik" that not even the mass of Lithuanian Christians themselves are aware of it. Even when Cardinal Bengsch from East Germany visited Lithuania, there were voices heard saying that he was insufficiently informed. Fortunately, however, Vatican Radio has kept up its broadcasts in Lithuanian, thus encouraging its listeners, so the picture is not so one-sided as it might otherwise have seemed.

In the West, even some moderate people who do not criticize the Vatican in general for wishing to put its relations with the Communist Governments on a reasonable footing where negotiation takes precedence over condemnation, are puzzled that there is not at the same time more open moral support for the persecuted. After all, one does not have to conceal one's principles in order to have dialogue (rather the contrary, surely?) and it would seem possible to put the Lithuanian case – and, even more importantly, that of the totally-suppressed Eastern-rite Ukrainian Church – properly on to the international agenda without risking closed doors, walk-outs or, worse, a new wave of anti-religious persecution in Eastern Europe. Non-Catholic organizations, especially the World Council of Churches, need be even less inhibited from giving a lead by diplomatic considerations.

In the late 1940s and early 1950s (not to mention the period twenty years before the rise of Stalin) people were informed, there were Masses on behalf of the persecuted and, even if practical results were only rarely achieved, those who suffered gained immense spiritual support to help them bear their sufferings. It is not easy to determine why these concerns gradually faded during the next quarter of a century, but latterly there have been some signs that they have begun to be discussed again. Perhaps this book may play a part in crystallizing them and imprinting them on the mind not only of Christian people, but of all those who care passionately for the liberty of the individual.

The astonishing election of Cardinal Wojtyla as Pope John Paul II in 1978 makes it certain that much more will happen faster than could possibly have been envisaged.

Beyond being informed and praying, there are growing possibilities of being practically involved, at local level, in working for the Lithuanians and for many other deprived people in the Soviet Union and Eastern Europe. Nijole Sadunaite had no less than three hundred letters from British Christians sent to her in prison. Although they were all stopped, the authorities told her about it, and this in itself inspired her to keep going. Bishop Sladkevičius has recently been permitted to celebrate Mass in a town for the first time and it is unlikely this would have happened without the popular support that there has already been for him in the West.

But the question at the end is not only what we can do for them: it is what they can do for us. Such reasoned and calm, yet utterly determined, defence of the faith when confronted by years of provocation is an example to the whole world, an inspiration which must leave its mark on the religious history of the twentieth century. With the faith being questioned everywhere and many people frenetically seeking to defend it by reinterpreting it into every conceivable modern form, it may be a salutary lesson to see that in its traditional expression it can not only survive in the face of persecution, but even attract the young in growing numbers and teach them eternal values which they avidly absorb, finding in them the only possible antidote to a state-regulated atheism which they reject. In the "Land of Crosses", they prefer to raise another memorial on the hill.

INDEX OF PERSONS

INDEX OF PLACES & COUNTRIES

INDEX OF SELECTED SUBJECTS